THE SOUND O

THE SOUND O

Louis Chude-Sokei

THE SOUND OF CULTURE

DIASPORA AND

BLACK TECHNOPOETICS

Wesleyan University Press   Middletown, Connecticut

Wesleyan University Press
Middletown CT 06459
www.wesleyan.edu/wespress
© 2016 Louis Chude-Sokei
All rights reserved
Manufactured in the United States of America
Designed by Mindy Basinger Hill
Typeset in Calluna Pro

Library of Congress Cataloging-in-Publication Data

Chude-Sokei, Louis Onuorah, 1967–
The sound of culture: diaspora and black technopoetics /
Louis Chude-Sokei.
     pages   cm
Includes bibliographical references and index.
ISBN 978-0-8195-7576-0 (cloth: alk. paper) —
ISBN 978-0-8195-7577-7 (pbk.: alk. paper) —
ISBN 978-0-8195-7578-4 (ebook)
1. Literature—Black authors—History and criticism.
2. Literature and technology. 3. Music and literature.
4. African diaspora in literature. 5. Race in literature. I. Title.
PN841.C47 2015
809'.8896—dc23   2015015502

5 4 3 2 1

FOR TESHOME H. GABRIEL (1939–2010),

without whom I would have believed

all of them instead of all of me.

CONTENTS

Acknowledgments ix

Introduction 1

ONE Modernism's Black Mechanics 21

    Of Minstrels and Machines: Tales of the Racial Uncanny 27

    Karel Čapek's Black Myth 50

    Prognosticating Echoes: Race, Sound, and Naturalizing Technology 68

TWO Humanizing the Machine 78

    Masters, Slaves, and Machines: Race and Victorian Science Fiction 79

    Melville's Man-Machine 91

    Erewhon: Lost Races and Mechanical Souls 100

THREE Creolization and Technopoetics 128

    Sexing Robots, Creolizing Technology 130

    Cyberpunk's Dubwise Ontology 148

    The Music of Living Machinescapes: Creolization and Artificial Intelligence 165

FOUR A Caribbean Pre-Posthumanism 179

    Echolocating Surrealism 182

    Sylvia Wynter's Naked Declivity 198

    Caliban's Uncanny Valley 214

Appendix: A Playlist 225

Notes 227

Bibliography 247

Index 257

ACKNOWLEDGMENTS

Though the writing of this book was brief, its gestation reaches back two decades. In that time the following has been crucial to either its development or my ability to sustain commitment to the work and the profession.

My elders: Teshome Gabriel, without whom I would have left academe before officially beginning; Robert Hill, for his insistence that theorizing + historical archive = relevance; Carolyn Cooper, for her steadfast belief, grounded advocacy, and inspired specificity; Nathaniel Mackey, for providing a model of creative and productive iconoclasm in these hyperconformist times; and filmmaker Henry Martin, whose guidance through the world of sound, culture, image, and idea was all the authenticity needed.

My peers: Michael Veal, for links, expansion, and encouragement; Brent Clough for affirmation and kinship; Dennis Howard and Sonjah Stanley Niaah, for letting me know that Yard was listening; and Klive Walker, for dubwise reasoning at a crucial moment.

My crew: DJ T-bird (Anthony Reid/Baker), for technical knowledge but also evidence that joy trumps attitude every time; Alex Painter, for the generosity and humility that comes from real talent; Ellen Koehlings and Pete Lilly of the mighty *Riddim Magazine,* for support, belief, and the genuine love that a shared enthusiasm makes possible; and to what was the Ebony Tower Sound System, for opening a door to sound experience.

My publisher: Wesleyan, for allowing this book to be what it is; and especially to the editor, Parker Smathers, for patience and insight.

And always to Onyi and Ada, with whom all things are possible and for whom all things are done.

THE SOUND OF CULTURE

INTRODUCTION

A book with such eclectic concerns that brings together disparate disciplines and multiple realms of knowledge is best begun before the beginning, which is to say, with the title itself. *The Sound of Culture: Diaspora and Black Technopoetics* is about the paralleled histories and cultural relationships between race and technology. It argues that how we have come to know and understand technology has been long intertwined in how we have deployed and made sense of race, particularly in the case of blacks and Africans in a world made by slavery and colonialism. The language of one is consistently dependent on or infected with thinking about the other. Though those paralleled legacies are arguably fundamental to the cultural and epistemological worlds we currently inhabit, it is only quite recently that they have become identifiable as a mutually productive dyad in scholarly conversations and cultural representations. Work that explores this dyad, however, tends to be more imaginative and conceptual than historical. This book provides both context and history for how ideas about race and technology manifested in some of the literature, thought, and popular culture of the late nineteenth and the twentieth centuries and how and why race continues to be present in contemporary investigations into technology's possibilities. It also provides critical contexts and histories of how blacks have responded to those intertwined legacies, as well as generated modes and methods of engaging them.

Coming from a perspective that is less grounded in science and technology studies than in the cultural and literary phenomena of the "black" world (quotation marks soon to be explained), what instigates the bringing together of discourses of race and technology are two beliefs and assumptions. First, the primary cultural responses to technological change and to the growing sense that social and historical change was being increasingly generated and motivated by nonhuman processes was expressed in literature that would not be called science fiction until the twentieth century, despite having its roots in the nineteenth. This is obvious enough. What is less so is that this literature, before it was named, was simultaneously engaged with a growing sense that race would provide the template for how the West frames its relationship with those nonhuman technological transformations. Being that two of the most pressing concerns in the nineteenth-century transatlantic world were industrialization and slavery, it should be no surprise that each would allude to or depend on the other in the cultural responses of the time.

Too much of today's thinking about race and science fiction or, more specifically, blacks and technology is rooted in twentieth-century or contemporary narratives as if they were recent phenomena. This makes sense since it is true that in the worlds of music and science fiction issues of race have moved ever closer to the center of cultural and critical awareness. Central to this book's argument is the fact that race was central to how industrialization was conceived or made sense of during the nineteenth century in England and America, as evident in its proto–science fiction as it would be in cultural responses to jazz in the early twentieth century. Today's focus on race and technology, minorities and science fiction or digital media, can therefore benefit from the far longer tradition of such inquiries, narratives, and responses that this book excavates, as technologies based on robotics or cybernetics—for example, there is a reason why terms like *master* and *slave* are still at work in basic engineering colloquialisms. There is also a reason why science fiction is now seen as amenable to black, minority, and non-Western criticism and engagement. The reason is simply that technology has always been racialized or been articulated in relationship to race.

This historical context is particularly necessary today, given the energy surrounding the discourses of Afro-futurism; the increasing popularity and influence of black writers like Samuel R. Delany, Octavia Butler, Nalo Hopkinson; and a broader racial turn in technology and science fiction criticism as evidenced in the work of John Rieder, De Witt Douglas Kilgore, Isiah Lavender, Thomas Foster, Alondra Nelson, Kodwo Eshun, Alexander Weheliye, Ytasha Womack, and so many others. What's really interesting is that it's taken so long for many to realize it, when science fiction has always been open about its dependence on race, difference, and power and when robotics and cybernetics were explicitly conversant with racial metaphors and analogies. These earlier nineteenth-century traditions of thought and narrative need to be reopened and connected to this rich new world of critical reflection and cultural production. That is one of the primary goals of the first half of this book. Another goal is to insert machines into the very processes of not just cultural formation and social and economic change—something at work in contemporary criticism—but racial formation as well. Because if race, gender, and class have become established parallels as we explore and contemplate how difference and otherness operate in Western culture, and if also *animality* has become a necessary participant in such thinking, technology functions in this lengthy if not eternal set of conversations in quite similar ways.

Recall Jean-Paul Sartre's introduction to Frantz Fanon's *The Wretched of the Earth*: "the only way the European could make himself man was by fabricating slaves and monsters."[1] Blacks have clearly functioned as both. But so have machines, particularly when anthropomorphized, embodied, and subject to questions about their abilities to think and their possession of souls and feared for their potential independence. As analyzed and argued in the pages ahead, they become explicit and inexplicit ciphers for ambivalences and anxieties about both race *and* technology. This is even more the case when they become framed as quite monstrous threats to sovereign notions of "man" or "the human." Machines have served that function for quite a long time, which is why it is necessary to apply the critical resources of the contemporary world of scholarship on race to that history.

Instead of merely assuming those metaphoric coincidences between race and technology and extrapolating from them extant racial histories and political configurations, this book provides historical details and contexts for how those metaphors have been deliberately made to coincide, even to the point of having been so naturalized as to be invisible. It is no accident, for example, that robots function like slaves in much science fiction—robot *means* slave, or forced labor. Karel Čapek, the writer who generated that neologism, drew from stories about segregation and lynching in his work. Though others have noted that this "strained parallel" is due to the "anthropomorphic convention" of seeing machines as slaves—and that slaves are as likely to revolt as they are to provide free labor—it has not always been acknowledged how intimate this convention has been with actual racial slavery or in a literature like science fiction that was produced alongside slavery, colonialism, and racial segregation.[2]

Because many contemporary questions of technological anthropomorphism and embodiment are due largely to gender analyses, this forces any rethinking about race, the body, and technology to operate simultaneously through the lens of sexuality. Donna Haraway is clearly the most notable thinker here, but in her wake such critiques have been legion. This simultaneity isn't difficult because almost all the primary texts analyzed in this book find themselves weaving through, juggling, or juxtaposing race and machine embodiment with such questions. As a number of contemporary critics would assert, the very notion of *embodiment* brings to the fore issues of sex, just as we know that conversations about race and racialization—the processes by which racial meanings are made—inevitably hinge on sexuality. In fact, the very notion of technology has often been framed in terms of race. The use of race in many representations of machines in science fiction and in, say, electronic music, is why it has been troubling for many to note the paucity of explicit discussions about race not only in histories of technology but also in cybertheory and what has been called posthumanism. Though it is not true that these latter intellectual formations completely ignore or have no place for race in them—just as it is not true that science fiction has ever been without an awareness of race—they are dependent on previous conceptual traditions or cultural strategies involving race. For example, the now passé image of the cyborg central to Haraway's thinking has always been assumed to be a racialized being, but its very imagining depends on ways of conceiving humanity present in Caribbean and Latin American notions of creolization, and that has yet to take center stage.

Again, science fiction's uncanny ability to echo or parallel racial experiences is no accident, nor is it an insight novel to the contemporary movement or critical tendency called Afro-futurism. It's no accident that questions of whether or not slaves had souls and could think, had intelligence, or were mere mimics continue to be guiding questions in how technology has been framed, from eighteenth-century automata to artificial intelligence and Japanese robotics. The fact of machines as ciphers or co-discursive presences with racial concerns is as true for P. T. Barnum, who came to fame passing a black slave woman as a machine, as it is for Karel Čapek who would turn to black America to give emotional and political charge to his robots and their bloody revolution; it is as true for Samuel Butler, the first to explicitly racialize machines, as it is for Herman Melville, who depends on equivalences between blacks and machines to criticize both slavery and industrialization. It is as true for Jean Toomer, experimental modernist of the Harlem Renaissance who uses robots in the wake of Čapek, as it is for Donna Haraway; and it is as much on the mind of Isaac Asimov, whose canonical Three Laws of Robotics, as we will see, were in part generated in response to a history of racial coding in science fiction. The race/technology dyad is even on the mind of Norbert Wiener, originator of cybernetics, though that has never been discussed in or around cybertheory.

Science fiction novelist William Gibson, who famously coined the term *cyberspace,* has the relationship between race and technology—and reggae too—on his mind, just as do Caribbean thinkers like Aimé Césaire, George Lamming, and Sylvia Wynter. For readers unfamiliar with these Caribbean critics, much of this book will serve as an introduction, just as those who are familiar with Caribbean thought and culture will be introduced to the unexpectedly related work of a novelist like Gibson and thinkers like Haraway, cyberneticians like Ron Eglash and Norbert Wiener, and writers from the Victorian era. These Caribbean and many other black critics receive extended treatment in the pages ahead, particularly in the second half of the book. For those readers indifferent to or for whatever reasons disinclined toward this work's theoretical bent, these sections will be the most challenging. Yet they matter because few would imagine that black cultural criticism and Caribbean thought could offer insights into technoculture, science fiction, and the history of technology or that race is implicated in those histories and traditions. This unique treatment of these thinkers is secondary to a broader reading of the historical and cultural context that allowed those equivalences between blacks and machines to be sensible in the first place.

The second belief and assumption that grounds this book—in other words, that it takes for granted—is a particular understanding of black music. Now it must be emphasized that this is not a work of musicology or ethnomusicology or even primarily about music, just as it is not a history of science fiction. This is a work of literary and cross-cultural criticism that aspires to cultural and intellectual history. What makes it structurally and philosophically possible from a perspective routed in and through the African diaspora is the awareness that black music—from jazz to reggae, hip-hop to electronic dance music—has always been the primary space of direct black interaction with technology and informatics. Music has been the primary zone where blacks have directly functioned as innovators in technology's usage. This isn't to ignore the quite legitimate history of black inventors, inventions, and feats of engineering, both formal and informal that the black diaspora has produced. It is to identify a space where black inventiveness has rarely or successfully been questioned. This space, however, has suffered by largely being described as or thought of as primarily performative, expressive, rhythmic, lyrical, or just musical. As such, to focus on this as a space of sound and sound production is to reorient our listening not only toward the means of aural production but also toward how blacks directly engage information and technology through sound.

That zone of sound has been unique, considering that much of our understanding of the blacks/technology dyad assumes that the former is opposed to the latter or allowed so little access to the latter that the relationship is either rare or adversarial, as in the well-known folktale of John Henry. Black technological innovation in music has functioned in the shadow of what some might still call a "digital divide," which though specifying digital technology has come to stand in for technological access in general and race as a primary source of socioeconomic and technical alienation. As critic Alondra Nelson put it, this metaphor of a "digital divide" is one that features "the ostensible oppositionality of race (primitive past) and technology (modern future)." This metaphor maintains an "underlying assumption . . . that people of color, and African Americans in particular, cannot keep pace with our high-tech society."[3] This alleged opposition holds this book together—particularly the primitive/civilized, black/technology, African/modern binaries. Funny thing about these notions of race or blacks as having been victims of a digital divide is that in the very period that term gained such currency as to have become cliché, blacks in the Caribbean, America, and Europe were busy generating the most sophisticated electronic music and technology-obsessed music subcultures in history. From Kingston, Jamaica, to Detroit, Michigan; from Martinique to Bristol, England, and Capetown, South Africa, this is also the era where black electronic music redefined sound and hearing across the globe. It was arguably the birth of contemporary black "vernacular cybernetics," to use Ron Eglash's words.[4] In this period also West Africans—particularly Nigerians—had erected the largest culture of Internet crime ever known, effectively colonizing what noted Nigerian computer engineer Philip Emeagwali often refers to as the "eighth continent."[5]

Facts like this are what have inspired this book and fueled its research, but again it must be stressed that this not a book about music. Music is a thread linking the various texts and contexts, secondary only to science fiction, which itself is subordinate to the mutually constitutive dyad of race and technology. These facts should make clear why the radical interdisciplinarity of the book is necessary and also why it is one of the work's greatest challenges to readers unfamiliar with the different sources brought to bear on the topic.

The Sound of Culture actually began life in a series of essays written and published between 1994 and 2000 and has continued with another more recent suite of essays. These essays are mentioned here because a few of them have had an impact in various spheres of inquiry as well as cultural production and actually parallel more well-known interrogations of race and technology. It was in these essays where the argument for black sound as a site of technological engagement and an immersion in informatics from analog to digital was argued. These essays were "Post-Nationalist Geographies: Rasta, Ragga and Reinventing

Africa," "The Sound of Culture: Dread Discourse and Jamaican Sound Systems," and "Dr. Satan's Echo Chamber: Reggae, Technology and the Diaspora Process."[6] They were immediately followed by "But I Did Not Shoot the Deputy: Dubbing the Yankee Frontier," and then more recently, "Invisible Missive Magnetic Juju: On African Cyber-Crime" and "When Echoes Return: Roots, Diaspora and Possible Africas."[7] They began an interdisciplinary excavation of a long tradition of black encounters with technology that can be mined to generate correctives to faulty notions of black access, but also to supplement broader understandings of race, technology, and visions of the possible.

As Eglash puts it—and it is no accident that he would hear this so acutely in reggae music—"rap and reggae artists have created a technology for signal processing that would indeed meet the specificities of current cybernetics engineering."[8] It is likely that much of the intimacy between blacks and technology has not been explored due to the all-too-easy assumption that, again, blacks are either in an adversarial relationship to technology or fundamentally opposed to it due to lack of access or differential conceptual and political priorities. None of these arguments need be true. History suggests that they are not.

So music is what provides the "sound" part of the title, more specifically, the sound cultures of Jamaica for whom music or song or lyric is secondary to a larger cultural complex called *a sound*. In Jamaica *a sound* is a common name for those great and enduring cultural institutions began in the late 1950s, called *sound systems*. These collectives (producers, DJs, engineers, selectors, speaker-box carriers, singers, and players of instruments; and now lawyers, media reps, web designers, and so much more) are the foundation of reggae music and its global industry. They have been at the center of every major cultural transformation since decolonization and have participated in not just a few political transformations as well. As a product also of Caribbean migration, that social, cultural, and economic structure helped produce hip-hop in America and any number of genres and subcultures in Europe, the United Kingdom, and even Japan. The noble story of the sound system is far too much to even discuss here. What matters here is that *a sound* in Jamaica foregrounds technology and specific cultural interactions with it; Jamaicans have also produced music that foregrounds technology and specific racial interactions. And this has been influential beyond music. The impact of this culture of technology has been such that Caribbean music and culture have surprisingly been appropriated by certain subgenres of science fiction and are present in Afro-futurism—yet another reason to root this analysis in Caribbean sound culture.

Those early essays that provided this book's genesis were focused primarily on Jamaican sounds as an "alternate public sphere" from which to generate ideas about sound, race, culture, and dispersal.[9] The argument was made that black sound has been a space that also generates modes of critical reflection. This project takes that much further, because alongside the development of Caribbean sound and sound culture there has been a tradition of engaging sound, culture, and technology in the literature and criticism of the African diaspora, particularly in the Caribbean, where important thinkers like Édouard Glissant, Sylvia Wynter, Edward Kamau Brathwaite, Wilson Harris, George Lamming, and Carolyn Cooper have produced remarkable insights on these topics.

Armed with this tradition, this book will go as far as to suggest that the most necessary theorizing and politicizing of artificial life and computer intelligence can and has come from the black diaspora itself as a product of its extensive thinking about the African slave as an automaton, a creature either less than or other to life. Sound makes this all possible when music in these texts is heard more broadly as technological engagement and as the nexus where race becomes a crucial element in that engagement. In other words, music in the texts chosen for this analysis function less as music per se and more as signs of technological reproduction in which blacks function with some degree of primacy. As will be seen, most of the conversations about music in the works discussed are primarily about the means of technological reproduction and the relationship of race or blacks to them. To focus on music rather than sound is to invite considerations this book isn't primarily interested in, such as lyrical meaning, rhythmic analysis, specific musical history, or musicology. This more general use of *sound* is instead part of this book's desire to participate in a number of cultural, intellectual, and artistic conversations—science fiction, Afro-futurism, cybertheory, posthumanism, and postcolonial thought—but to do so through Caribbean and African American literary and cultural criticism as well as studies in the diaspora. But it also intends to nudge against the broader world of sound studies and hopefully generate some insights of use to that even-larger world of technology studies.

Though the habit of most scholars and listeners may have been to focus on black music's qualities of rhythm, lyrical content, melody, performance, and historical context, what has been primarily occurring is direct participation with machines and information technology through sound and sound production (and, of course, now video and Internet as well as software design and engineering). This is not simply a product of digital or postdigital black music and a contemporary world where the technological aspects of music are inescapable. It's also not a product of a contemporary world where our listening practices feature a foregrounding of technology and an increasing masking of the systems and techniques of production (it is now hard to even speak of forces or systems or even process, given the seeming dominance of immediacy and the still hard to shake fantasy of pure, context-free information). To focus on sound is to emphasize its medium, indeed, media.

These interactions with sound, race, and technology—or sound as the primary nexus of race and technology—can and will be traced back to the jazz age and the assumptions around jazz as a product of racist and nationalist notions of black primitivism and simultaneously of new technologies of *massification.* Jazz may not have been an electronic music, but it was certainly assumed an industrial one alongside the blues, which was also making that epic journey from the deep agrarian South into the North and even deeper into electricity. It is that relationship between jazz and "the machine" that will be discussed, because coded in representations of jazz sound are notions of race and Africa. These interactions will also be discussed in the context of that hermetic sound world of Jamaican dub, a music that has found itself as influential to modern electronic music and production as to specific subgenres of science fiction. As will be shown, its presence in cyberpunk literature said far more about machine/human relationships than it did about lyrics, melody, or rhythm. *The Sound of Culture* therefore takes from black music the foregrounding of technology as a springboard to analyze a history of race and machines in literature, criticism, and cultural politics and also in science and technology.

Which brings us to the next important—and arguably most contentious—word in this book's title, "Diaspora." Even though primary texts range from Victorian proto–science fiction to American modernism, and from science fiction to cyberpunk, much of the critical apprehension of the texts is generated from a black diaspora framework. This is not to suggest that the scholarship on, say, Victorian literature or cybertheory is without its necessary supports; it's to say that a part of the methodology here is to extend and supplement this material with quite legitimate critical works that have rarely if ever been used this way (for example, using Caribbean thought to engage American minstrelsy and artificial intelligence; emergent black technology criticism to think about Victorian proto–science fiction and cybernetics; or dub music and creolization to rethink cyberpunk and posthumanism). This technique is intended as an interruption to two main factors: first, the weakness of technology studies to engage thinking about race and racism; and, second, the tacit racial and cultural exceptionalism often generated by Western blacks. After all, too much work that takes "diaspora" as its topic or its limit ultimately falls back on the primary political and cultural assumptions or political preferences of the black West.

One of the greatest myths of the black diaspora—in music, literature, theory, or otherwise—is that common historical experiences and shared cultural or musical influences translate as shared ideological concerns, similar aesthetic motivations, or even shared visions of the past and future. Due to this the black diaspora is all too often imagined as a mere extension of the trials and tribulations, goals and aspirations, of Western blacks or, to be fair, of specific, vanguardist black cultural groups. *Diaspora* easily and often fancifully functions as a lazy metonym for continuity or an excuse to read the world through an African American, subcultural Caribbean or elite black lens. The "black" (hence the quotations) diaspora functions as an assumed sphere of either racial solidarity or accessible social or cultural meanings that can be easily deployed against, say, the privileged black/white binary that defines and delimits black first-world thinking. This privileging occurs despite the fact that the issues and goals, interests, and possibilities found in the black world are far too many, far too complex, far too divergent to even speak of as composing a cultural or political singularity. In this book the diaspora keeps alive these rivaling claims and intentions. It is aware of multiple blacknesses and glories in the impossibility of their resolution, yet is aware of their tendencies to reduce, interpellate, and *impel,* often in the name of solidarity. This is of particular significance in any cultural discussion of race and technology because it has bearing on how the past and the future of black peoples are imagined and which blacks are doing the imagining.

The commitment to the diaspora as a space of black-on-black contestation and differentiation might not be as explicit in the final title term, "Black Technopoetics." There "blackness" might seem deceptively stable, but given the growth of similar neologisms over the past generation as an interest in blacks and technology has grown, it is important to sound a difference. The intention here is not to join those neologisms, which all too often deploy blackness as a knowable force or object or assume it as innately radical. For example, we have had sonic Afro-modernity, or black sonic fiction, and its parent black Atlantic (or Afro-diasporic) futurism.[10] Most recently, we've had black "stereo-modernism" added to the mix, notable for being one of the few such terms that engages Africans from the continent and their own responses to music, diaspora, and technology.[11] There are in fact others, many linked by their insistence on reducing black technological usage—or sound—to political solidarity, if not aesthetic commonality, including those who would see in Afro-futurism a necessarily liberationist ideology or radical movement. Helpful—inspiring, even—as these may be, they do not problematize their prefix enough to address a world where black narratives of technology or expressions of sound operate in vastly divergent ways. Black communities, for example, may not fetishize race or racism either at all or in ways symmetrical with each other, and the blackness sounded in one arena need not be symmetrical to that echoed in another. If, however, there are symmetries made audible outside of a shared dependence on race, then social applications and political manifestations are often deeply differentiated, if not contradictory. Also, those black uses of technology for radical purposes are no more legitimate than those that enable far more prosaic, or even non- or antiradical ones.

Blackness is a far more humble affair in this project. It makes no attempt to systematize or synchronize or argue for some continuity in the various black cultural uses of technology. "Black technopoetics" simply identifies the consistent fact of engagements with technology that are themselves framed in terms of or by blacks. Clearly, there are shared needs and practices for racial resistance at work due to the raw fact of the political realities of blacks in the diaspora, but there is simply no need to impose on them a singular agenda beyond the fact that technology is a zone of racial engagement that operates in tandem with the historical fact that technology itself has carried racial meanings in advance of that engagement. Nor is there a need here to use technology merely to fetishize racial particularity.

"Technopoetics" is a loose and far from canonical term for those engagements with technology as they manifest in the realm of literary, philosophical, musical, or broader cultural realms. To specify a *black* technopoetics, again, is simply to highlight the self-conscious interactions of black thinkers, writers, and sound producers with technology, where a more general racial technopoetics might be at work with white writers who depend on race in their expression of a technological vision, such as, for the purposes of this book, Herman Melville, Isaac Asimov, Tanith Lee, William Gibson, and Donna Haraway. As a more general term it has been in use in modernist literary criticism for some time, which is the source of this appropriation. In modernist studies "technopoetics" emerges from an awareness that though we know that machines have altered our means of perceiving, we still "have a large accounting of what machines are and how they work and even how we think about them, but we have only a very small accounting of how we think them and to what extent such thinking appears in nontechnological things we do."[12] Nontechnological "things" include writing or poetry or (some time ago, maybe) music.

We know that modernists like William Carlos Williams called a poem a machine, and W. B. Yeats would evoke the parallel between poetry and mechanics in "Sailing to Byzantium."[13] We're also familiar with Swiss modernist architect Le Corbusier's oft-quoted definition of a house as a machine for living in. But we know also that a great deal of Euro-American modernism, from poetry to painting, music to fiction, dance to film and architecture all reacted to or attempted to appropriate the new means of production and reproduction and express them in cultural terms. It was in this period that many innovators discovered that "the form of the literary text could be modernized by consciously borrowing from the methods of science and media-technology."[14] More than a few modernist and avant-garde movements deployed metaphors and similes drawn from either new technological forms or a general sense of new social and cultural modes of organization due to industrialization, mass culture, and what was evolving into mass media. A brief list of such movements would be a veritable cavalcade of isms—vorticism, futurism, surrealism, machinism.

The use of technological metaphors—man as machine, the universe as a mechanism, and so on—can of course be traced back to the secularization of the universe at work in Renaissance humanism, the Copernican revolution, and eventually the triumph of Newtonian mechanics. And as Richard Menke reminds us in *Telegraphic Realism: Victorian Fiction and Other Information Systems,* the radical cultural impact of technology was a very Victorian concern: "in the age of the Penny Post and the electric telegraph" it is true that "imaginative writing responds in crucial and defining ways to the nineteenth century's new media and the ideas they encouraged about information, communication and language."[15]

But perhaps nothing has been as influential to the use of technopoetics as the still-controversial Italian futurism. Its importance is worthy of note if only for being the first futurism, without which Afro-futurism, astrofuturism, queer futurism, Chicana-futurism, Kongo-futurism, and others would suffer for want of a suffix. Futurist founder Filippo Tommaso Marinetti makes clear in his "Technical Manifesto of Futurist Literature" of 1912 that a modern technopoetics depends explicitly on a radical use of analogies to foment synthesis between the realm of the technical and the organic in a world where technology has removed conventional borders between those realms: "Just as aerial speed has multiplied our knowledge of the world, the perception of analogy becomes ever more natural for man."

He provides more detail:

> Up to now writers have been restricted to immediate analogies. For instance, they have compared an animal to a man or to another animal, which is almost the same as a kind of photography. (They have compared, for example, a fox terrier to a very small thoroughbred. Others, more advanced, might compare that same trembling fox terrier to a little Morse Code Machine.)[16]

It is due to this use of analogy that Marinetti is credited as "the first artist to create a sort of technopoetics," in which an avant-garde explicitly emerges "out of science and especially out of media-technology."[17] As we will see, this conscious deployment of analogy to force new relationships will be central to the surrealist methodology of French negritude as manifested in the black, antiracist technopoetics of the Caribbean's Aimé Césaire and Édouard Glissant. But for Marinetti and the futurists, analogy—their "synthetic lyricism"—made possible the vision of a world made by both machines and men, an essentially cyborg reality where these two elements cross-breed with each other without, as they often claimed, the weakening presence of women, history, and memory.[18]

Marinetti is wrong, though, in assuming this a particularly modern or modernist conceit. Yes, it might have been systematized by the different movements, especially the ones inspired by futurism; but this was only a formal acknowledgment of the general tendency to deploy what can also be called "associative metaphors" in the case of surrealism.[19] Such "involuntary associations," as Guyanese writer-theorist Wilson Harris would call them, were already present in the lexicon of associations for blacks as liminal, not-quite human beings in the age of racial slavery.[20] They were or were like animals; they were or were like machines; and so they could be and were many things and were figured as such. It is that metaphoric flexibility—or hyperproductive lack as Sylvia Wynter might put it—that makes possible the long tradition of using blacks to either represent technology or metaphorically oppose it; to use blacks as ciphers for machines or to use machines in ways that depend on earlier representations of blacks, even in futurism itself. As Marinetti put it, "analogy is nothing more than the deep love that assembles distant, seemingly diverse and hostile things."[21]

To provide another panorama of the text to come, where a technopoetics operates as described earlier, a black technopoetics can be found at work in, say, Sylvia Wynter's suggestion of artificial intelligence in her affection for Shakespeare's Caliban; it is evident also in the production of black music in the ghettos of West Kingston, Jamaica, and in creole theorist Édouard Glissant's ambivalent feelings toward his computer. One finds it at work in Aimé Césaire's manifestos that celebrate the ability to assemble "diverse and hostile things" like the organic and the machinic as a revolutionary act of black poetics, and in the thought of black queer science fiction author and theorist, Samuel R. Delany, whose visions of the future radically depart from conventional or nationalist racial expectations, particularly those of Afro-futurism.

Despite the interest here in futurism, science fiction, and cyberculture and a commitment to issues of race and colonialism, it's important to distinguish this project from the newly established and incredibly exciting tendency called Afro-futurism. As is now well known, Afro-futurism can be traced to Mark Dery's coining of the term and naming of the context in a 1994 special issue of the *South Atlantic Quarterly* called "Flame Wars: The Discourse of Cyberculture"; Kodwo Eshun's imaginative 1998 text *More Brilliant Than the Sun: Adventures in Sonic Fiction;* John Corbett's essay "Brothers from Another Planet" in his 1994 *Extended Play: Sounding Off from John Cage to Dr. Funkenstein;* and filmmaker John Akomfrah's 1996 film *The Last Angel of History.* Of course, the tendency seemed to become a movement with the 2002 special issue of the journal *Social Text,* devoted to Afro-futurism, edited by Alondra Nelson. All these remarkable works parallel or were contemporary with the production of those essays that made this book possible. These correspondences are welcome and fortuitous. They actually make one feel much less alone and more empowered to make a contribution. Therefore, a good deal of this book is framed as a tacit conversation with Afro-futurism because, due to the excitement and necessity of its presence that movement/critical tendency has had ascribed to it insights and concerns that precede or may be even critical of it. Afro-futurism will be engaged here from a perspective that is as committed to problematizing the "Afro" as it is with providing the historical ground and alternate philosophical models for visions of the possible that depend on race and technology.

This conversation—also with African American criticism, literature, technology, science fiction, and studies in the diaspora—is intended to generate an expansion of precepts, a challenge to assumptions and a clarification of expectations, particularly around the question of racial particularism and the often-dominant concerns of first-world blacks. It is meant also to help supplement the long-standing commitment in black thinking to remapping the past with an injunction to not just imagine futures but make sure that those futures not be colonized by the geographic or ideological limitations of the present—even if those limitations frame themselves through a politics of resistance.

And now, a brief outline of the book itself:

The first chapter may be titled "Modernism's Black Mechanics," but it begins just before the middle of the nineteenth century. Modernism is framed through the story of Joice Heth, a black slave woman whose display brought fame to the notorious P. T. Barnum. Barnum arguably helped create the modern circus and museum, also a modern media based on deception and possibility, which used race and technology to make those elements work. The "humbug" (or "hustle") of Joice Heth occurred at the very moment when a new form of masking erupted as a national, then global, phenomenon: blackface minstrelsy. Further laying the ground for modernism, technological transformation ran afoot as what was called "automata" began to evolve into new forms of technologies—most accessibly with the advent of the phonograph and, most important for twentieth-century metaphor, with the creation of the figure of the robot.

Because of its ubiquity and influence in the years between Heth and a full-fledged modernism and its impact on the early recording industry, blackface is the link between centuries and the primary manifestation of a racial version of what is known as the *uncanny*—that unsettling sense of familiarity and difference as when we encounter dolls, masks, anthropomorphized machines, and, as will be argued here, blacks in a time when their humanity continued to be in question. This chapter focuses on the uncanny as a theoretical lynchpin, as identified initially by Sigmund Freud, but then as a mode of humor by Henri Bergson. Blackface as a popular symbol of a racial uncanny can be considered as a complex coding for American responses to industrialization in the years before and immediately following slavery's end. A discussion of modernism in the nineteenth century is necessary because so much of what we now attribute to the twentieth century in terms of responses to technology and conversations about race and machines can actually be traced to this period. It is the same period where science fiction began its evolution into a specific genre, only to be named and codified in the early twentieth century.

The meanings of the black slave and the meanings of technology are juxtaposed throughout this chapter as way of making sense of that racial uncanny. In fact, much of science fiction's journey to cultural significance has much to do with how it explicitly and implicitly codifies racial and cultural anxieties in this long fin de siècle. Again, the story of Barnum and Heth is not the primary topic of this chapter. The story is a framing device. In it are all the elements that are pursued in its three chapters: the tension between race and technology as a manifestation of the relationship between Africa and its enslaved peoples to a white, colonial modernity; blackface as a ubiquitous mediator between the agrarian past and an urban, technological future; jazz as a sign and sound of Africa and "the machine"; and, more broadly, the way these oppositions between blacks and technology manifested in a range of modernist texts, most notably the plays *R.U.R.* by Karel Čapek and "Man's Home Companion," by Jean Toomer.

As Nicholas Daly put it, "Modernism is not the literature of technology, but one in a longer series of literatures of technology.... The literature of the Victorian period, from the 'industrial novels' of the 1840s and 1850s to the late Victorian fantasies of Wells and Stoker, continued to offer narratives of human-machine encounters."[22] Because of this fact, interest in the nineteenth century becomes stronger and more detailed in the next chapter, "Humanizing the Machine." This chapter is framed by the seemingly innocuous fact that in contemporary engineering, the relationships between whites and blacks during slavery still govern metaphors deployed for technical interactions. Those metaphors or analogies would be deeply considered by Norbert Wiener, father of cybernetics, for whom metaphors of racial slavery and machine/human relations had material repercussions worth theorizing in order to avoid.

How these metaphors came to be present in technological language is the plot, one that one hopes will keep the conversation contemporary and relevant to non-Victorianists and those more familiar with, say, Caribbean and Black diaspora thought or Afro-futurism. In advance of Čapek's robots and their deliberately uncanny relationship to blacks, Samuel Butler's *Erewhon; or, Over the Range* was the first text to explicitly racialize machines and begin the long-standing science fiction trope of robot revolution, where machines revolt and destroy human beings. That trope was intimate with racial fears and colonial tensions in the period when Europe began to suffer from what can be called "late imperial anxieties."

Even Herman Melville would exploit similar anxieties and technological devices in his work, condemning both slavery and rampant industrialization. His lesser-known story "The Bell-Tower" (1856) necessitates a shift to the United States, where Mary Shelley's *Frankenstein* is appropriated to advance a dual-pronged critique of race and industrialization. It is in this same period that specific genres would appear that capitalize on such fears and anxieties. Butler's was one such text, and so was Edward Bulwer-Lytton's *The Coming Race* and the incredibly popular and influential work of H. Rider Haggard. These works had a significant effect on the genre of science fiction. For example, take the highly popular writer Edgar Rice Burroughs, known now primarily for his *Tarzan of the Apes* (1912). Burroughs borrowed from that late imperial milieu in England to help generate a science fiction and fantasy in the United States that was explicitly in conversation with the racial politics of an emergent American empire. Most important in his work are the cultural politics of primitivism that would also undergird the modernism of jazz and the Harlem Renaissance.

Where the first two chapters are focused on the very many ways blacks and technology operated as a fundamental set of conceptual or metaphoric oppositions, the third chapter, "Creolization and Technopoetics" takes as its primary concern rampant notions of techorganic blending and the human/machine interface in the contemporary world. Such hybridity is at work in both the literature and film genres called "cyberpunk" and cybertheory in general, especially in the wake of Donna Haraway's seminal and ubiquitous essay "A Cyborg Manifesto." So much has already been said about these two quite influential moments and traditions, even now as they have metastasized and become fully incorporated into the scholarly world, technology, and popular culture. What wasn't given enough attention was the fact that their use of race borrowed a great deal from the imperial anxieties of Victorian popular fiction in their representation of the late imperial angst of what was once called a postmodern condition.

Race was a presence in cyberpunk and cybertheory. How could it not since they were guided by the sense that "the problems of natural/artificial dualisms encountered by cyborgs are similar to those which plague activists and theorists in the long historical battles against racism"?[23] It's possible that in their use of race, blending, and a postimperial America, cybertheory and cyberpunk had more to do with the emergence of Afro-futurism than faulty notions of science fiction as a "racist" genre or one that allegedly ignores race. The fact that notions of hybridity and blending between human and machine are actually dependent on earlier ideas about miscegenation between human (white) and animals/machines (blacks) has yet to be competently analyzed. When gestures toward race and miscegenation have been made, they haven't drawn from the Caribbean or Latin America, where blending, hybridity, and catalysis have been primary theoretical models for generations. This chapter does precisely that. It uses Caribbean traditions of creolization to make sense of cyberpunk, cybertheory, and what might still be called posthumanism.

Using creolization in this way might prove itself as not that unusual. So much cyberpunk depended on specific references to Caribbean blacks and to the music and process that is dub. Caribbean peoples and philosophical processes being so fore-grounded in cyberpunk authorizes an investigation into how dub generates both a poetics of blending and a politics of race in cyberculture that depends on sound. Having described creolization as Caribbean, it is necessary to provide a history of how it has come to function in the Caribbean as well as becoming seen as exceptional by many in North America. The need to present a history of creolization is also shared by the final chapter, "A Caribbean Pre-Posthumanism." This section provides a genealogy of creolization as a tradition of thinking about technology going back to decolonization in the Caribbean, the French surrealist-inspired movement of negritude, and the broader climate of primitivism in the early to mid-twentieth century (again, the space where science fiction and fantasy became world-shaping forces and where jazz and calypso music became the aural signifiers of complex racial and cultural processes). The goal in this chapter is not only to present a view of race and technology that can challenge and supplement standard histories of technology and racial formation but also to expand Afro-futurism and limit some of its assumptions. The previous chapter's focus on blending and hybridity will here be sharpened by detailing the work of the very Caribbean critics that shape much of the text: Édouard Glissant, Wilson Harris, and Sylvia Wynter.

Though a critical presence in the first section of the book in the discussion of minstrelsy, Wynter's analyses of the modern construction of "the human" is identified in this chapter for its relationship to technology as productive of both the human and those things necessarily in opposition to it—blacks, natives, and, eventually, machines. Although probably more unfamiliar than some of the others, her work is currently becoming more central to the scholarly world. In fact, a handful of books have recently appeared that bring Wynter's thinking to the fore, and a few more are scheduled to soon appear. To focus on her work is to participate in a real groundswell of interest in this Caribbean thinker.[24] Focusing on her "pre-posthumanism," alongside the creole thinking of Glissant and Harris, one hopes will inspire a rebooting of posthumanism and cybertheory and add to the great energy at work in the wake of Afro-futurism. As said earlier, for those for whom Wynter and these other thinkers are unfamiliar the book should serve as an introduction, yet for those who are aware of their work what will be presented here expands their value and that of a diasporic, cultural, and cross-cultural criticism.

But the true inspiration for this work comes, appropriately, from a source in sound. Guyanese-British producer the Mad Professor's 1985 dub album, *A Caribbean Taste of Technology,* has been in mind from the very beginning as a template for a new way of thinking about technology and race and using the one to transform the other. Along with Jah Shaka, the Mad Professor was seminal in keeping Jamaican dub alive in the wake of the dancehall/ragga explosion of the 1990s and in the face of what seemed the demise of a roots reggae that had come to be aesthetically defined largely by Rastafarianism and a rhetoric of racial authenticity that continues to be difficult to shake. Due to the sounds that shared a commitment to this Caribbeanized use of technology, dub would mutate and infect many strains of British dance and popular music. This parallels what Jamaican immigrant DJ Kool Herc would do in early 1970s in New York City, catalyzing what would become hip-hop from the techniques and obsessions of Jamaican sound culture.

Individual tracks from *A Caribbean Taste of Technology* have kept alive the sense that this particular cultural space and its dispersal has been generating something like a tradition of ideas about machines and technology that have already given much to the world of sound production and black technological agency, like "Buccaneer's Cove" and its evocation of historical and digital piracy, "The Heart of the Jungle," an almost pro forma allusion to the primitivism that undergirds his quite radical technological vision. A track that in some versions is called "Obeah Power" reminds us not only that science is a metaphor for the occult in the Caribbean but that technology in the late nineteenth and early twentieth centuries had yet to shake its association with spirits, séances, and the echoic voices of the dead. There are also "Civil Unrest" and "Hurricane Gloria," references to so much of the political and social life in that region; "Uncle Sam's Backyard" and the strong awareness of the global-economic positioning of the Caribbean; and "1011 Digital," emphasizing an embrace of digital space as accessible for blacks in the wake of King Jammy's "Sleng Teng" *riddim* (or rhythm track), which made digital production standard in the Caribbean. This riddim would appear at the moment of hip-hop's popular emergence and Detroit techno's machine catalysis of disco.

What holds all these conceits together on the album is a slippery titled track, the one that fluctuates with "Obeah Power" on different pressings, as is typical of dub. One wonders if the fluctuation is due to the deeply conflicted feelings many Caribbean people, particularly the Rastafari, have toward traditional magical systems (or "negromancy," as it's been derisively called). This version is called "Dream Power," rich with echo and digital glossolalia and glistening with the smooth surfaces that the Mad Professor developed as a pioneer of the British subgenre of reggae called Lovers Rock. "Dream Power" is an essentially imaginative power, yet it is necessarily practical in that it must be realized to be heard, shared, or read. As such, it is as much a description of what engenders diaspora as it is of what sounds the past and echoes the future.

ONE

MODERNISM'S
BLACK MECHANICS

On or about December 1835, American popular culture could be said to have begun. Though it may seem obvious that this is merely a restating of Virginia Woolf's famous declaration in her 1923 essay, "Mr. Bennett and Mrs. Brown," which addressed the change in sensibilities that signal the formal birth of what we call literary or cultural modernism, it comes from Victorian scholar Judith Wilt's paraphrasing of Woolf. Wilt's well-known essay begins, "In or around December, 1897 . . . Victorian Gothic changed—into Victorian Science Fiction."[1]

Wilt's exploration of the birth of science fiction "in the light of imperial anxieties" is largely rooted in questions of genre.[2] The interest here is in exploring how those anxieties as specifically racial were shaped in American popular culture within that space between the formal birth of science fiction—Victorian or otherwise—and the period still called modernism. Unlike Wilt, however, the concern here isn't science fiction per se but its participation in broader conversations and tensions around race and technology as they produce literary and cultural modernism as well as phenomena that function beyond them. This modernism is one in which American popular culture emerges as a world-shaping phenomenon due to those anxieties associated with slavery, colonialism, and industrialism. Though characteristic of the Victorian era, in the twentieth century these anxieties became the primary tensions of race and technology at the core of an American imperial epoch.

This appropriately mythical timeframe ends with 1923, not with Woolf's essay but because it is the much less mythical date of the introduction of the word *robot* into the English language. The term was coined for use in Karel Čapek's *R.U.R.* (*Rossum's Universal Robots*) but derived from the Czech word *robota*, meaning serf, if not slave labor. Much more will be made of this remarkable play, particularly since its anthropomorphizing of late nineteenth- and early twentieth-century anxieties about technology became superimposed on extant anxieties about race and empire in that long fin de siècle.

The year 1835 is when the notorious P. T. Barnum "bought" or acquired the rights to display the slave woman Joice Heth, so-called mammy to George Washington, allegedly 161 years old, from an itinerant showman named R. W. Lindsay. To say that American popular culture began at this moment may be an intentional overstatement, but it is shared by those aware of the uncanny intersections at work in the relationship between Barnum and the woman he called Aunt Joice. As James W. Cook puts it, "if we were to pick a single moment to mark the birthdate of modern American popular culture, this just might be the one: on that fateful afternoon in July 1835, when an aspiring impresario from Bethel, Connecticut took off his grocer's apron and began to think seriously about how to market Joice Heth as a popular curiosity in New York City."[3]

Barnum describes his first viewing of her thusly:

> Joice Heth was certainly a remarkable curiosity, and she looked as if she might have been far older than her age as advertised. She was apparently in good health and spirits, but from age or disease, or both, was unable to change her position; she could move one arm at will, but her lower limbs could not be straightened; her left arm lay across her breast and she could not remove it; the fingers of her left hand were drawn down so as nearly to close it, and were fixed; the nails on that hand were almost four inches long and extended above her wrist; the nails on her large toes had grown to the thickness of a quarter of an inch; her head was covered with a thick bush of grey hair; but she was toothless and totally blind and her eyes had sunk so deeply in the sockets as to have disappeared all together.[4]

Called everything from an "Egyptian mummy" to a "living skeleton," from "venerable nigger" to "The Greatest Natural and National Curiosity in the World," Joice Heth was brought from Africa as a child.[5] It is generally accepted that Barnum built his entire career on her display. He admits as much: it was the "accident" of Joice Heth that "seemed almost to compel my agency," and it was she who "first brought me forward as a showman."[6] She was his introduction into an American public life that he irrevocably changed and a media culture that some argue—including him—he essentially invented.

But where Cook identifies the meeting of Heth and Barnum in July 1835 as that origin moment (or perhaps the meeting of Barnum and Lindsay, Heth being mere property and whose complicity or participation remains enshrouded in fable and confusion), it should be pushed four months further to Boston, Massachusetts. There she was first displayed alongside perhaps the most well-known machine of the age of both wonder and of reason. It should be pushed to the December meeting between Joice Heth a human reduced to an object and the infamous chess-playing machine, "The Turk," an object raised to the querulous status of human. This machine has such a long and complex history of display and literary and cultural reaction that the attempt to account for it here would be both unsatisfying and impossible. Reactions range from Descartes to Edgar Allan Poe to Benjamin Franklin to Walter Benjamin, who would begin his "Theses on History" with reference to it.

Wolfgang von Kempelen constructed the Turk in 1769 for the entertainment of Empress Maria Theresa of Austria. For years it stunned, terrified, and entertained Europe with its eerie mimicry of human beings, playing a game already established as a visible display of reason. This "thinking machine" was eventually acquired almost a century later by Johann Nepomuk Maelzel, purveyor of dioramas, court mechanic of the Hapsburgs, and close friend of Ludwig van Beethoven.[7] Barnum writes that the pairing of Joice Heth and the Turk was in Boston, where they were on display in contiguous rooms. It was also in Boston where Barnum would first meet Maelzel, who would inspire him and through whom he would be instrumental in reinvigorating a tradition of automata that had long fascinated and flummoxed Europe.

Maelzel would will his collection of automata to Barnum, who he considered his American protégé. But despite his passion for automata and the fact that mechanical oddities would become as much a part of his repertoire as were monstrosities, Barnum ultimately "led the way for human oddities to replace mechanical curiosities in the public imagination."[8] This was, after all, a mere three years after Thomas D. Rice's staggeringly successful performance of "Jim Crow" in New York, and Barnum quickly began using blackface performers in his shows alongside the display of automata, "exotic" peoples and "freaks."

What makes the meeting of black slave woman and machine a necessary starting point for this book was what happened next, something that hasn't been covered by the well-documented history of freakery, ethnographic display, and the birth of both the museum and the carnival and circus complex. Though Barnum is notoriously unreliable, it is best to have him tell the story, despite the narrative slight of hand at work in that relentless presentation of innocence, characteristic of all his autobiographies:

When the audience began to decrease in numbers, a short communication appeared in one of the newspapers, signed "A Visitor," in which the writer claimed to have made an important discovery. He stated that Joice Heth, as at present exhibited, was a humbug, whereas, if the simple truth was told in regard to the exhibition, it was really vastly curious and interesting. "The fact is," said the communication, "Joice Heth is not a human being. What purports to be a remarkably old woman is simply a curiously constructed automaton, made up of whalebone, India-rubber, and numberless springs ingeniously put together, and made to move at the slightest touch, according to the will of the operator. The exhibitor is a ventriloquist, and all the conversations apparently held with the ancient lady are purely imaginary, so far as she is concerned, for the answers and incidents purporting to be given and related by her are merely the ventriloquial voice of the exhibitor.[9]

Keep in mind the stress on the "ventriloquial," the suggestion that she was merely a black mask for white voice. There is little doubt that Barnum himself or his associate Levi Lyman was in fact "A Visitor." There is also little doubt that the very idea to suggest to the public that Joice Heth was a machine came from Maelzel himself. Maelzel did have a long history of passing a machine for human, particularly that impersonation of a machine by someone clothed in the skin and turbaned costume of Orientalist fantasy (a "Turk").

Barnum continues,

Maelzel's ingenious mechanism somewhat prepared the way for this announcement, and hundreds who had not visited Joice Heth were now anxious to see the curious automaton; while many who had seen her were equally desirous of a second look, in order to determine whether or not they had been deceived. The consequence was, our audiences again largely increased.[10]

The presence of the Turk clearly had some impact on conditioning the public to imagine Joice Heth as a construct of the age of industry, an American version of automata but masked in the dark flesh and withered femininity of a far more intimate, local, and familiar racial stereotype. That was not enough to guarantee the success of the hoax. The Turk was eventually revealed to have functioned by a steady sequence of diminutive chess prodigies hiding behind the machine-mask. It played chess but was a manmade artifact, carved largely of wood. Most notably, *it did not speak,* and the phonograph and the spectacle of recorded speech was still decades away (though it is true that Von Kempelen is also famous for having begun work on one of the earliest voice synthesizers in 1769).

So the question is this: why were P. T. Barnum and the early market for freakery and human oddities able to so easily sustain this particular humbug? Why was it credible and indeed logical? And what would be the repercussions of this masquerade in which race, Africa, sexuality, minstrelsy, technology, and artificial intelligence all came together in one performance?

This chapter is an attempt to answer these questions by situating them as primary concerns of American modernism and the popular culture it would produce in the twentieth century. The goal is to make sense of how sense was made of Joice Heth in that period and how echoes from those meanings continue to structure both racial thinking and technological advancement. This requires a perspective informed by at least two seemingly dissimilar critical trajectories: those focused on race and colonialism and those invested in histories of technology. What is most exciting about these trajectories is not just that they are only rarely considered in collusion and so can give rise to new ways of thinking about race, history, and technology. It is the fact of rich and surprising moments, where each has always made productive incursions on the other.

And so we proceed in three parts: first, an extended discussion of minstrelsy as a broad-based, transnational, cultural phenomenon deeply implicated in ideas about technology. Though rooted in plantation slavery, by the period known as cultural modernism the form became a way for whites and Europeans to deal with the loss of nature and their own dehumanizing by the forces of industry by projecting all manner of primitive meanings and desires onto the blackface mask and the black body it connoted. Joice Heth may not have been a minstrel but was marketed much like one—a black body through which a white voice spoke—and helped give rise to the presence of minstrels in the Barnum shows, but her presence as possible machine, or passing for one, is crucial to how minstrelsy would function as a form whose pleasure derived primarily from its relationship to an increasingly technological environment.

The primary conceptual parallels in this chapter are therefore those between primitive blacks and nature, black music (particularly jazz) and technology, and the Freudian uncanny as both sign of racial terror as well as of humor. Caribbean thinkers have been very notable in this intellectual realm, with the plantation and black folk culture being rich with the kind of metaphoric meanings necessary for a black technopoetics. Therefore, Sylvia Wynter, George Lamming,

Antonio Benítez-Rojo, and even Aimé Césaire feature in the discussion of blackface's relationship with industrialization.

The second part of the chapter follows blacks and the minstrel mask into early twentieth-century American robotics, as the blacks/technology dyad becomes, for example, literalized by the Westinghouse corporation in the wake of Karel Čapek's monumental play *R.U.R.* due to its success at blending racial terror with histories of labor and modern anxieties about technological replacement. Reading Čapek in this context proves just how embedded the term *robot* was in race but also how implicit and explicit are histories and narratives of technology embedded with those of racism. It is that intimacy between those histories and narratives that would allow black modernist Jean Toomer to suggest them in his well-known 1923 work, *Cane,* as well as much lesser experiments in drama.

The chapter concludes by isolating the actual role of early black music in these conversations about race, technology, and the modern. In each section black music is the central presence in the conversations and assumptions around race and technology, particularly through minstrelsy, radical modernism, popular culture, and what eventually became science fiction. The focus here is on black music as a mechanized form, as mediated by machines like the phonograph in the wake of automata. By returning to the work of Joel Chandler Harris and his "Uncle Remus" for an early vernacular take on race and the machine, the function of "the Negro" in this period will be argued to operate not just as "nature" but also as a sonic and symbolic force necessary for the naturalizing of technology. This is of great importance for modernism but also for how race endures in subsequent conversations about human replication or simulation. Such conversations range here from the Freudian uncanny to Japanese roboticist Masahiro Mori's notion of an "uncanny valley," which concludes this book as its arguments about race, technology, and creolization are brought to bear on the contemporary world of artificial intelligence.

But to begin, we explore the curious story of the minstrel and the machine. We may start with the era of modernism, where that relationship is first notably articulated in the European avant-garde and in American popular culture, but it returns us to Barnum's time and a Victorian world on the cusp of the kinds of transformations that would necessitate the bringing together of those two figures.

OF MINSTRELS AND MACHINES:
TALES OF THE RACIAL UNCANNY

Were we to trace Euro-American modernism back toward some elementary set of concerns, influences, and obsessions, we could isolate two primary clusters of meaning among the intersecting many at work within the shock of America's relentless global expansion. This expansion was generated far more by cultural and technological influence than by techniques and axioms of territorial domination, and these two clusters keep focus on domestic racial subjugation and colonial domination alongside the "soft power" of what was once called "cultural imperialism." The first cluster is the so-called machine aesthetic. Produced by and through the West's difficult and ambivalent responses to industrialization, it would find its political and social fulfillment in an America that announces its global presence through the language of inevitability, the language of the *new*.

In America technology was celebrated as being central to its democracy, but also as a natural sign of it, despite its initially disorienting and continually irruptive presence in a nineteenth century where as a defining issue it was arguably second in importance and controversy only to slavery. As Leo Marx insisted in *The Machine in the Garden,* "There is a special affinity between the machine and the new Republic."[11] Even now in the wake of industrialization, most will still take this technoexceptionalism for granted. This ideological claim is framed as an almost spiritual if not divine fact. Yet this "special affinity" is nothing without the nation's "peculiar institution."

In one of the few works to include a historical foundation to the ideas being explored here, historian Daniel R. Headrick provides necessary parameters: "Among the many important events of the nineteenth century, two were of momentous consequence for the entire world. One was the progress and power of industrial technology; the other was the domination and exploitation of Africa and much of Asia by Europeans. Historians have carefully described and analyzed these two phenomena, but separately, as though they had little bearing on each other."[12] America's global expansion would be fueled both by ideologies of racial dominance *and* of technological advancement. Each would buttress the other, a fact central to literary and cultural production and the politics of race as a parallel effect—an echo—of technology. America's exceptional relationship to technology has been described as an "Imperial Mechanics," which "refers to the interrelationship between imaginaries of empire and conceptions of machine-civilization." Leo Marx's "special affinity" was nothing less than "the machine as the dominant representation of U.S. superiority and supremacy in the Western Hemisphere."[13]

Yet despite the "triumph" of industrialization and the fetishizing of technology in the United States—not to mention what Ricardo D. Salvatore describes as "the shift from Manifest Destiny in the mid-nineteenth century to Benevolent Informal Empire (Good Neighbor Policy) in the fourth decade of the twentieth century"—the dominance over the landscape and the erasure of the frontier would only strengthen the nostalgia for nature that, as Leo Marx famously identified, continues to define an American political and literary sensibility.[14] Utterly absent from Marx's otherwise magisterial work is the issue of slavery that is much more implicated in both the pastoralizing and technologizing of the American literary and cultural landscape than he would allow. The African slave's function within those very notions of nature and nostalgia is much more central than Marx would have it. Race is a primary factor not only in nineteenth-century industrialization but also in the process of modernization and the cultural experience of modernism through its assumed special intimacy with nature. The slave's "innate" participation in notions of barbarism, *animality,* and primitivism was due to its African origin; it therefore consistently functioned as a contrast for notions of "the modern." The presence of the machine in the garden is most certainly mediated by that of the slave on the plantation. The violence of the latter becomes an absolutely necessary questioning of the very possibility of an American pastoralism.

The second cluster of interest is, therefore, the cultural legacies of West Africa. They will be here called, as they were by many Euro-American moderns and black nationalists alike, the "African aesthetic," despite being a category with such a gloriously troubled history that one can use it only as a sign of still troubling conflicts embedded behind and among multiple masks. This African aesthetic was so capaciously imagined that it would cover everything from jazz to calypso, minstrelsy to the literature and art of the Harlem Renaissance, and ran the gamut of the European avant-garde, from, say, the so-called Negro Poems of dadaist Richard Huelsenbeck (random cacophonic noise meant as resistance to the hegemony of logic and bourgeois sense and sensibilities) to the affectionate racist primitivism of the poet Vachel Lindsay. For many in this cultural climate, Africa began to represent both what "we" had lost and what "we" could or should be. The European avant-garde is significant not only in their shameless embrace of this aesthetic but in making clear either that there was no temporal contradiction between primitive and modern or that the secret of the modern was to incorporate both without contradiction: "The excitement of modern and technological innovations enticed some members of the avant-garde, and they cultivated a lifestyle that embraced both an idealized primitive past and a modernist '*esprit nouveau*' future." In Paris, in particular, "this 'African aesthetic' was a state-supported style."[15] The strong connection between this style and lifestyle with technology was manifested in a European or American sense of *cultural lack* in relationship to technology and a general alienation from the imperatives of industrialization, a lack that would motivate primitivism, even among black moderns.[16]

Also notable about the European avant-garde was that they mediated Africa through African American and to a lesser extent Afro-Caribbean cultures in a way that many blacks wouldn't do. There was still a strong legacy of shame as well as a strong sense of cultural superiority in relationship to Africa and its peoples among diaspora blacks in this historical period. But then there was the Marcus Garvey movement and the work of W. E. B. DuBois and others committed to affirming Africa's cultural and historical centrality to the modern world. These emergences would only feed and were fed by the fetishes of the avant-garde. Together they nourished the tendency to read Africa as an omnivorous sign for a diaspora of interlinked black differences and aesthetic positions vis-à-vis the West—hence, an African aesthetic. This aesthetic describes a tendency and a sensibility rooted less in any quantifiable or provable historical authenticity despite the dependence on anthropology and ethnography that characterized so many of the modern movements that would draw from it. Instead the African aesthetic functioned—functions—as the flexible rationale for relationships between and among blacks and their varied cultural products during and after slavery.

It has been well documented how modernist movements from cubism, surrealism, dadaism, and futurism to primitivism, negritude, Pan-Africanism, and the Harlem Renaissance depended on some invention of Africa or some construction of an African aesthetic to either highlight a contrast with or to enable a critique of a Western culture also of their devising. Take as a brief but important example, Italian futurist Filippo Tommaso Marinetti, whose provocative novel from 1909, *Mafarka the Futurist,* was subtitled *An African Novel.* Not only was the novel set in Africa, but its main protagonist and characters are African, specifically Arab and sub-Saharan. Most analyses focus primarily on its notable misogyny and its obsession with technology, violence, and the inhuman without seeming to realize that all those issues depend as much on race as they do on the notorious technofetishism of the futurist movement. Noting the work's dependence on race, technology, and an African aesthetic is necessary primarily because it was the product of the first futurism and was openly engaged with the Italian attempt at empire. Also, any book formally tried for obscenity is eternally important.

In advance of *Mafarka the Futurist,* in the "Founding and Manifesto of Futurism" race, Africa, and colonialism are given an intimate yet unpleasant vision of origins when Marinetti recalls "the blessed black breast of my Sudanese nurse."[17] Mafarka creates his own son without the aid of a woman (the novel's misogyny is both well known and in-your-face, as was Marinetti's). His son is a bird-shaped yet invisible machine called Gazourmah, who eventually causes the collapse of the world after challenging the sun. Importantly, this blending of race and technology also depends on sound. Mafarka dies in a gorgeous haze of what Marinetti calls "total music." This is all in keeping with Marinetti's view of jazz music and dance as both new and in opposition to the European classicism his movement despised: "We Futurists prefer [dancer] Loie Fuller and the 'cakewalk' of the Negroes."[18] This in no way meant that Marinetti wasn't a complete racist; it's just the case that black music—not black people per se—as a product of the machinic now had much more to offer his radical modernism than anything rooted in tradition, history, and the hierarchies of value his movement sought to destroy.

In *Mafarka* and the work of Marinetti and the futurists the "cyborg" is arguably first theorized, though without the countercultural valences that made that figure so attractive to Donna Haraway. In the 1910 "Extended Man and the Kingdom of the Machine," Marinetti dreams of the day

> when it will be possible for man to externalize his will so that, like a huge invisible arm, it can extend beyond him, then his Dream and Desire, which today are merely idle words, will rule supreme over conquered Space and Time.
>
> This nonhuman, mechanical species, built for constant speed, will quite naturally be cruel, omniscient, and warlike....
>
> Even now we can predict the development of the external protrusion of the sternum, resembling a prow, which will have great significance, given that man, in the future, will become an increasingly better aviator.[19]

Marinetti's vision closely suits the actual etymology of the neologism *cyborg* in his reference to a ship's prow and to a mechanical exoskeleton that enables humans to become better aviators. Neuroscientist Manfred Clynes blended organism with cybernetics to coin the term, and it comes directly from the Greek word *kybernetes,* or steersman. That this vision of a supplemented male, a blending of human and machine, would be preceded by its representation in *Mafarka the Futurist,* a book for which Africa is a metonym for a world and its apocalyptic becoming, is simply stunning. Colonial Africa, robots, music, war, misogyny, and a strange anxiety of maternal influence: it would be challenging to find a stronger recipe for modernism. In anticipation of arguments ahead concerning race and science fiction is the description of Mafarka as an "anti-feminist imperialist with designs to conquer the sun and to engineer the prototype of a perfected, mechanized race."[20]

Because the Negro in all these dialectical manipulations of modernism inexorably represented nature, the primitive, *and* the pretechnological—and because Africa was both the Negro's point of origin and irreducible essence—*Mafarka the Futurist* was prophetic but also in keeping with a premodernist set of concerns. These constructs, after all, ultimately manifested a set of relationships between Africa and its dialectical other: technology, industry, or a civilization that had already been describing itself in such terms, certainly since Thomas Carlyle. In his work on jazz in the machine age Joel Dinerstein accurately characterizes the scene in modernist America: "To engage machine aesthetics, Americans of all ethnicities appropriated a West African derived cultural aesthetic." In his rather optimistic hearing, African American cultural practices actually helped America integrate itself into the new tempo and sensibilities of a machine age: African Americans "stylized machine rhythms and aesthetics through inquiry, experiment and social experience" and essentially "assimilated" or "colonized" or "integrated" the machine on behalf of the broader culture.[21] More will soon be said of this analysis, but it is correct insofar as the relationship between blacks and machines already allowed for a working sensibility by the time of Italian futurism. Marinetti could then fuse Africa and the machine in a narrative that celebrates colonialism and violence—born out of his and his nation's emergence as a colonial power in North Africa and in Turkey—because by then each opposition could feed and propel each other in sensible ways.

Africa, after all, was seen also by the colonial imagination as a source of economic regeneration, just as jazz and calypso once they hit the streets and the cabarets of America and Europe and were appreciated as forces of cultural and sexual regeneration. As with Marinetti, Africa was "a regenerating land . . . consecrated as a mythological territory where the metamorphosis of man and his environment unfolds in the institution of a new era."[22] Another way of putting it is that Africa and its people functioned in this climate of psychic, social, and economic alienation to render machines less alienating, close to the natural. Technology is naturalized through race and made intimate, but also inevitable.

So it suffices to say that from the sun setting of rule Britannia to the pallid emergence of an American century, all these patently modern tendencies, movements, and transformations figured the Negro and Africa in *some* relationship to "the new." As such, blacks were linked to technology and new techniques, which also established links between race and that other significant twentieth-century sign of otherness, the machine. As a metaphor, the machine connoted depersonalization, monotony, regimentation, and a submission to abstract forces of power regulated either by obscure elites or, as Thomas Carlyle suggested, by the nonhuman process itself. Again, by Marinetti's time, such a daring combination of race and technology could make sense. In America both these categories would share the cultural spotlight during the period between the display of Joice Heth and the first use of the word *robot*. The interbreeding and interdependence of their uncanny anxieties would require strategic moments where the two blend and pass for each other rather than function as the antinomies that they did and often do represent. In these moments of masquerade all that was relatable to Africa would share and exchange space with all that was imaginable through the metaphor of the machine and the social and historical forms that quickly came to be described thusly.

To speak of masquerade, race and Africa in this period of American popular culture is to speak of minstrelsy. Blacks were represented overwhelmingly by references to and the tropes, images, and sounds of blackface. New forms of music were advertised and marketed through such images, black performers both willingly and unwillingly performed in blackface or in modes that drew from minstrelsy, and the very power dynamics that shaped the form would haunt the work of writers and artists who struggled to break away from its grinning clutches. In analyzing Africa and the machine and historicizing their fundamentally modern influence on each other, what we will then find in the nineteenth century are two of the twentieth century's most distinct products facing and doubling each other: the minstrel and the robot.

Again, in the years beyond this designated period the various figurations of the Negro and estimations of its cultural impact generally employed Africa in complex yet often-contradictory ways. Marinetti's was only one of many, which isn't to suggest that only white Europeans and Americans would deploy Africa promiscuously. Africa could safely signify everything from an abyssal or timeless anteriority to the recolonization of the West by a suppressed primitivity or of the superego by the id. It could also be the presence or return of a nonrational instinct in the midst of a materially powerful but internally decaying cogito. It could be the dangerous threat of atavism lurking beneath the slick processes of a democracy forced to contend with the new type of humanity represented by blacks after slavery. These uses of Africa were made affectively accessible through the presence of jazz, primitivist literature and art, banana-skirted dance spectacles, or the complex legacies of blackface, particularly after it became technologized in sound by "coon songs" in film and in advertising. They would also be both strengthened and contested by the various claims on Africa and its legacy deployed by black cultural and political movements operating both within and against the interests of Euro-American modernism.

This ambivalent fascination with colonial Africa, African America, and the Caribbean was most certainly the case during the interwar period, a moment characterized by a crisis of faith in technology inspired by the trauma of World War I. It was this crisis and the anxieties that it generated that would enable the rise of a widespread cultural tendency that can be described by the seemingly oxymoronic term, *primitivist modernism*.[23] It was a period where for many people black culture—then as now a lazy generalization—was the ultimate sign of being modern, urban, and indeed urbane.[24] Something about that oxymoron, perhaps due to its own energy of contradiction and possibility, made sense and style at that time. More important, the various movements and cultural tendencies of modernism would deploy the tensions generated by the juxtaposition of these two clusters of influence. They did so to explore and exploit the anxieties that they depended on. For example, as a symbol of the natural and the pretechnological, the African aesthetic and the Negro who represented it was either untouched by or opposed to the industrial technology that had brashly come to define newness in America, the newness that made American modernity exceptional; or the Negro pioneered a quite novel set of sensibilities in which tradition and the modern, the organic, and the technological were made to somehow jive or swing.

The Negro's supposedly innate ability to swing and jive was obviously an aspect of the furor and conversation surrounding the music and dance spectacles of 1920s America. Though we may now remember that music and those spectacles as rooted in black vernacular culture, they were initially seen and heard as machine-age spectacles, as elaborate rituals of the submission of art to the logic of the machine. The massive wall of pistons that was a brass-led big band, the inhuman machinic accuracy of jazz choreography, the volume that generated a wall of sound generations before such a production technique would be named—all held together by blacks dressed in styles so exaggeratedly crisp and attitudes so confident that they seemed to mock if not erase the past; it was all quite irresistible. Dinerstein describes the big band as "a grassroots vernacular music created by socially mobile ethnic groups that had integrated European-derived chords and harmonies with Afrodiasporic rhythms and performative approaches: European hardware, African American software."[25] Pioneer of modern architecture Le Corbusier would have concurred, "the Negroes of the USA have breathed into jazz the song, the rhythm and the sound of machines."[26] In his 1937 essay, "Mechanical Spirit and US *Négres*," Le Corbusier argues for the parallel between the "African Aesthetic" and the "Machine Aesthetic." For him they were mediated by jazz sound, which had "touched America because it is the melody of the soul joined to the rhythm of the mechanical. . . . It is the American music, propelled by the *Négres,* and which contains the past and the present, Africa with premachinist Europe and contemporary America." It was in short, "the old rhythmic instinct of the virgin forest" learning "its lesson from the machine."[27]

As Jeremy Lane points out in *Jazz and Machine-Age Imperialism,* "there was no shortage of attempts to interpret jazz as representing some kind of techno-primitive hybrid among early French commentators on the music."[28] Though Dinerstein is often similarly utopian in his celebration of the healing properties of African American culture when topically applied to white malaise—"big band swing *made sense* of factory noise, and the lindy hop gave the opportunity to *get with* the noise"—Jazz was seen and heard as something else too.[29] For many conservative critics it was the sound of whites submitting to the depersonalized rhythms of industry. H. L. Mencken heard it as the "sound of riveting, for example." Noted twenties-era antijazz crusader Daniel Gregory Mason claimed that jazz was "so perfectly adapted to robots that the one could be deduced from the other. Jazz is thus the exact musical reflection of modern capitalistic industrialism," hence the German critic Theodor Adorno's notorious description of jazz as a form of fascism, one could say in blackface if one dared anger a vociferous few.[30]

As often noted, Adorno's reading was based on a mishearing of jazz through the lens of the quickly more popular and adulterated "big band" sound, and his was largely a criticism of technology and its impact on popular artistic forms and on notions of individuality. Jazz's roots in improvisation and American racial politics were either lost to him of flatly rejected due to the sound's overall position in capitalist production. Jazz was merely the illusion of individuality against the overall standardization of the means of production. But with great respect for and fear of both sides of the "Adorno versus jazz" argument, it cannot be engaged here. The fact that jazz for him was intimate with industrialization and a product of technologization is quite enough, as is the fact that for many critics in America, it was the sound of a corrupting black influence at the dawn of the first century of freedom. These arguments were soon to be replicated at the dawn of a postmodernism signaled by the emergence of a new, even more technologized and even more corrupting musical form: rock and roll.

These observations about primitivist modernism can, however, be traced back before the jazz age, the Harlem Renaissance, surrealism, dadaism, and futurism to the birth of plantation minstrelsy. They should be traced thusly given minstrelsy's impact on film, music, dance, and visual art and on even the politics of early twentieth-century black assertion.[31] A long-lived and still mutating form, blackface survived slavery, the plantation, and the transition of blacks from inhuman other to embattled human being. By virtue of its popularity in wildly different contexts, it translated nineteenth-century American plantation culture into modern forms that would disperse throughout the cabarets, sound recordings, literary texts, and images that fed cultural modernism.

Although an admittedly simplistic binary, these clusters of influence and anxiety did bring together two specific ways of reading and experiencing the cultural influence of Africa and the machine in that long American fin de siècle. Minstrelsy would benefit from these. On the one hand, there was an old Romantic fear of a dehumanizing, depersonalizing technology and its concurrent loss of nature. Though an evenly distributed fear as significant to northern transcendentalism as it would be for, say, a southern plantation owner, it was felt most potently in the South due to its connection to a specific and increasingly threatened socioeconomic way of life. On the other hand, there was a much more specific and explicitly American fear: that of an increasingly humanized—which is to say liberated—African American social, cultural, and political presence. It was an overwhelming fear of a black subjectivity that had previously been demarcated by law and by science as inhuman or subhuman, reasonless, and most certainly soulless. In the South this too was uniquely felt and uniquely feared.

The nineteenth century was when contemporary meanings of technology would begin to congeal, just as would the current meanings of race and culture.[32] The very notion of the machine or even industry would evolve from merely material descriptions, tools, and objects into signs and metaphors of abstract social and historical processes. These metaphors would also begin to function as markers of specifically Western forms of power and descriptions of social and political systems and, as Locke would have it, of a deterministic social order. This would be the case just as the category of race would itself evolve beyond raw physical or biological data to provide abstract historical and cultural formulations confirming non-Western and specifically African inferiority. These terms—race, technology, culture, and the machine—would be given transformative impetus by the fresh legacies of Darwinian evolution amid the industrial revolutions in colonial England and in an American slave economy buttressed by it.

This economic and cultural system of slavery is of great significance because it was the source of what would become blackface minstrelsy and the complex and variegated world of American racial stereotypes and the popular culture that would be based on them. Far in advance of modernism, the jazz age, and a formalized primitivism, the plantation sealed the relationship between blacks and machines and expressed it in performance through blackface minstrelsy. It is this context that gives credence to critic Thomas Foster's insight that African American culture "might be understood as prefiguring the concerns of virtual systems theory" by reframing the issues of "cyborg embodiment and cyberspace in terms of the racial problematics of passing, assimilation, and blackface minstrelsy."[33]

Artist-critic Beth Coleman would put it more figuratively, yet more bluntly: "Slavery had been a preview to what it's like to be a machine. And that subjection to the inhuman became a national obsession."[34] Jazz was a national obsession and then an international one. Blackface would too become internationalized as both a visual sign of that sound, particularly how it was marketed on sheet music and phonograph and gramophone covers and with the importance of coon songs in general for the foundation of a black and American popular music and industry. Eventually blackface became a sign of technology itself as the black voice however performed—and by whomever—became key to how an American empire is heard.

Coleman also writes, "in the fantasy of the Industrial Revolution and the destiny of the twentieth century all are subjected to mechanization (rendered object or fetish)."[35] As a system, the plantation was a significant precursor to the regimentations and formal, time-driven depersonalizations known as Fordism and Taylorism. It is this insight that motivated Caribbean thinkers like the venerable C. L. R. James to stress the plantation as a "dominant industrial structure" and to argue that it was on the plantation that slaves became disciplined into distinctly modern subjects in advance of formal freedom.[36] In the appendix to the *Black Jacobins* he writes, "Wherever the sugar plantation and slavery existed, they imposed a pattern. It is an original pattern, not European, not African, not a part of the American main, not native in any conceivable sense of that word, but West Indian, *sui generis,* with no parallel anywhere else."[37]

There are claims that it was the racism of official Marxism that inspired the rejection of this argument about the plantation as "a quintessentially modern institution of capitalist exploitation," one emphasized by James's student Eric Williams in his influential *Capitalism and Slavery* (1944).[38] The suggestion here is that any primary claim on "the modern" even in terms of exploitation was threatening to a white radical status quo. Corollary to this are the insights of anthropologists Sidney W. Mintz and Richard Price, who caution against seeing the plantation and slavery as being such an overwhelming space of power; after all, "slavery, as the basic social institution in Afro-America influenced the free as much as it did the unfree."[39] Due to this reciprocity "the conception of slaves as mindless automatons, simultaneously trained to deny their own humanity, while being called upon continuously to respond in human ways to the demands the system made upon them, is exposed in all its mythical character."[40] Perhaps this is what C. L. R James means when he argues that because the plantation was a "modern system," slaves "from the very start lived a life that was in its essence a modern life," modern in the sense of regimented but characterized by psychic, social, and structural contradiction: ghosts in the machine.[41] In a similar and helpful way, critic Bill Brown has argued, "The relations of the slave system were soon to become the paradigm for making sense of technological culture."[42]

The description of the slave ship as a machine (and a factory) is also important here as a precursor to the disciplinary, identity-producing machine of the plantation.[43] After all, "one machine served another." A West Indian planter once described the former in 1773 as "a well-constructed machine, compounded of various wheels, turning different ways, and yet all contributing to the great end proposed."[44] The image is a literal version of the kind of machinic assemblages at work in the thinking of French philosophers Gilles Deleuze and Félix Guattari, but here fueled by black bodies. These thinkers have had no small influence on

Caribbean thinkers like Édouard Glissant and Antonio Benítez Rojo. The latter's "plantation machine" is one "whose flux, whose noise, whose presence covers the map of world history's contingencies, through the great changes in economic discourse to the vast collisions of races and cultures that humankind has seen."[45]

Benítez Rojo's use of the plantation as machine is initially in the spirit of James and Williams, as a more concrete metaphor of social, cultural, and technological processes. It quickly expands to describe not just specific Caribbean plantation and postplantation societies, peoples, and economies. It then becomes metaphoric of all other possible metaphors—of nature, the archipelago, technology, commerce, and varieties of thought. There is "the judicial machine, the political machine, the ideological machine, the economic machine, the educational machine, the military machine, the family machine, and even the revolutionary machine." There are even "machines of machines," at which point the metaphor becomes unhelpful in that it is even more promiscuous than "Africa."[46]

This same technologizing of the pastoral through the plantation system in America and the Caribbean is what also motivates Sylvia Wynter. For her the plantation is not a perverse pastoral environment but a "social machine" in which "the Negro then becomes the *symbolic object of this lack which is designated as the lack of the human.*" She does this in a 1979 essay called "Sambos and Minstrels" that, unbeknownst to most of its readers, attempts not only to shift the conversation of blackface from America to the Caribbean, but also to reroute thinking about technology. Wynter refuses the logic of naturalization that in and after slavery worked so hard to render the plantation the organic and natural home of the *darky* while simultaneously denying that patrimony by way of its innate Africanness. For her the plantation is instead a *machine* that "colonized, above all, Desire."[47] A complex social machine, it allowed desire to "work 'freely,'" a process which suggests that instead of erasing black subjectivity (that which was already being erased by slavery), a new kind of black *non-African* subjectivity was being produced on the plantation on the eve of slavery's demise and which would be an antecedent echo of modernism. This essentially *modern* subjectivity, as James insisted, may have been produced in the name of an industrial notion of freedom, but it would limit the meaning of the word in advance of its formal achievement.

Wynter's description of the Negro-in-the-machine importantly evokes Aimé Césaire's famed *Discourse on Colonialism,* in which he describes the machinery of colonialism's process of "thingification," in which the "indigenous" becomes transformed into an "instrument of production."[48] It also evokes founder of cybernetics Norbert Wiener's notion that *"what is used as an element in a machine, is in fact an element in the machine."*[49] But the Sambo stereo/archetype simultaneously drew its charge and value from the suggestion that Negroes were actually outside the machine, the antithesis of production and the lacuna of an industrial temporality. In other words, they were other to a regimented notion of time. In this guise, they were not only lazy but also immune to the work ethic, a position dialectically necessary in the construction of a certain kind of technological whiteness: "Central to the bourgeois ideology is the idea of the atomistic individual as a responsible agent. By constructing Sambo as the negation of responsibility, the slave master legitimated his own role as the responsible agent acting on behalf of the irresponsible minstrel."[50]

Wynter acknowledges that Sambo is merely the double in a pair of stereotypes including Nat, the rebellious figure drawn from Nat Turner. Despite the obsession with racial resistance that delimits much scholarly conversation and inquiry, Wynter finds in Sambo a far more intriguing set of possibilities that do not need liberation or rebellion to give that figure value (especially since the line between revolution and collaboration is often hard to parse in a form like blackface or any mode of performance, even academic). As she understands, the comic is far more complex than the melodrama of formal refusal.

In the relationship between white master and black childlike mimic, the primary terms may have been racial, but the overwhelming context was a struggle with nature. This nature was capricious, the wilderness of both the unconscious and an American landscape seen as yearning for domestication. The plantation, after all, was a significant part of the process of geographically domesticating the nation. Yet for whites during the early years of industrialization in America and in advance of jazz, that comic figure of the minstrel offered the spectacle of escape from what was beginning to seem an all-encompassing deindividuating system. This system not only erased nature but robbed whites of their own sense of agency and power in an increasingly regimented socioeconomic order: after all, to domesticate nature is to become domesticated by it, to render the landscape livable is to render it intolerable to the imagination. It is no exaggeration to suggest that it is fear of this order that has fueled generations of science fiction narratives in which whites fear their own mechanization and dehumanization in a world where what Aristotle in *The Politics* described as animated tools gain consciousness and seek revenge.

This rapidly changing agrarian landscape featured a dramatically shifting industrial economy and the threatened transformation of slaves into citizens—

animals into humans—that fuels the *theft* side of the dialectic in Eric Lott's foundational work on blackface minstrelsy, *Love and Theft*. To play or enjoy blackface masquerade was also to resist the new industrial regime, its responsibilities, and its clockwork temporality. In Wynter's words, blackface offered southern whites "the barest minimum of an affective and emotional life . . . to be sustained in the wilderness of technological rationalization."[51] In advance of the phonograph, the Sambo mask was an escape from mechanization through the pleasures of an always flexible and always performative African aesthetic. This aesthetic was the chthonic doorway into a raw, primitive, and hypersexual nature. As such it was distinct from whiteness and the West as possible, despite being an indigenous product of modernity and a necessary presence within it.

This use of minstrelsy to construct a debased yet popular culture that enables and maintains a white sense of humanity in that wilderness of industrial modernity goes much further than spectacle and pleasure and play. It is through the minstrel stereotype and blackface mask that the white colonial, racist "self, to constitute itself as human in the normative conception, must then conceptualize the possibility of lack, the lack of the intellectual faculties, of being the non-human, of being Sambo."[52] Wynter reminds us that during slavery, blacks were not only poised between the categories of human and animal. The Negro was also poised between rational agent and soulless machine, between mindless brute and what Caribbean literary great George Lamming once described as "man-shaped ploughs."[53] Or to use another reference from Norbert Wiener, slaves may not have been "machines of metal" but had long been in the logic of chattel slavery, "machines of flesh and blood."[54]

Lamming's description of a machine/instrument analogous with a slave is worth fully noting as yet another foundational set of insights on race and technology coming from the Caribbean. Lamming anticipates cybertheory in *The Pleasures of Exile* by imagining the changing roles of black machines in the plantation system. He describes the evolution of consciousness, intelligence, and agency in said tool (which historically shouldn't be so unique given that this great work was published in 1960 and the ideas of media theorist Marshall McLuhan and Norbert Wiener were, as they say, in the air). The black machine becomes a rebellious tool: "There is a change in the relation between this plough and one free hand. . . . No one can explain the terror of those hands as they withdraw from the plough." Ultimately, "some new sense of language is required to bear witness to the miracle of the plough which now talks."[55]

As with cybertheory the focus in Lamming is not on static, fixed bodies and identities, roles, and social structures; it is on transformation, one that given his dependence on C. L. R James's work (particularly the *Black Jacobins*) is of revolutionary consequence for even what that ploughs think of themselves: "It is a transformation of such dimensions which the owners must have anticipated; but the property could never be encouraged to think of itself as a source of possibility. Every method was therefore employed to separate the slave from a logic of a spirit which might soon declare his future on the side of freedom."[56]

In light of Césaire, Benítez Rojo, Lamming, and James, Wynter's description of the experience of blackface performance as an experience of the "possibility of lack" emphasizes that the plantation Negro was neither human nor animal but something or somewhere else. Wynter's possibility of lack was experienced through Sambo not as a complete being but neither as an inanimate object. Instead "he" was a figure of pure, unadulterated liminality—a creature of the in-between and the incommensurably beyond. He was pure ambiguity, therefore almost infinite possibility. This isn't merely literary deconstruction; as Donna Haraway would say, it is "liminal transformation."[57] Much like Haraway's cyborg figure, Wynter argues that Sambo is a less a sign of racial binaries than of "the scapegoat-carrier of all alternative potentialities that are repressed in the system. Sambo becomes the representation of all desire that flows outside the dominant order."[58]

Because Sambo was a kinetic figure, a performed being whose mask was relentlessly in motion, because the Negro was *not* inert and recognized as central to labor and the economy, this liminality could incorporate the *idea* of machinic production. Indeed it did. Machines, after all, were also *others*. They bore some uncanny relationship to the very slaves that they would eventually replace.

Before the twentieth century and in the period under consideration, the idea of machinic production had already been anthropomorphized. By the age of industry it had been embodied as perhaps a way of containing the anxieties and contradictions of a social world no longer under divine or even human control. Machinic production and reproduction had been visualized and culturally registered by automata, those figures of artificial life that were also popular spectacles in sideshows and carnivals alongside the display of Africans or other natives and which featured all manner of blackface coonery. Though dating back centuries, these machines—many of which were fraudulent, featuring bodies buried behind or below the machine mask, like the Turk—were resurgent in nineteenth-century America due in no small part to the efforts of "America's greatest showman" P. T. Barnum.

In the antebellum period the relationship between blacks and machines were so established that there were a great many "automaton 'Negroes'" produced in America, which were on display in the same spaces where oddities, curios, freaks, Negroes, and minstrels were often featured: "Black people and apes were fitting forms for automata since they both posed—in different degrees—questions for white audiences about bodies that resembled dominant conceptions of 'the human' but that may or may not have lacked fully human powers of intentionality or rational agency. Black automata, additionally, repeated at the level of amusement slavery's system of bodily domination."[59] Blackface automata, a minstrel machine, had become so common as to be mass-produced: "Banjo-playing black minstrels, whose images were freely plagiarized by the automaton houses, responded by stylizing their movements into machinic jerkiness and wearing expressions of fixed exuberance on their faces."[60]

In the spirit of providing a nonbinary view of this history of minstrels and machines, it is worth mentioning the work of African American entrepreneur John W. Cooper, who entered into this market around the same time Marinetti was birthing Gazourmah. Though there is very little known about him, the fact of his race slightly reverses or supplements this conventional power dynamic of human/machine as a statement of dominance/submission and the anxieties of reversal. Cooper would do so with his own fabrication and display of black machines sometime around 1909. His black minstrel automata shows lasted at least ten years and were good enough to earn him the title "The Black Napoleon of Ventriloquism."[61]

Taking seriously just how the "discourse of technology was and still is imbricated within discourses of race, civil rights and slavery," literary critic Michael Chaney points out how "proslavery ideology conceptualizes so-called inferior races as functional commodities dehumanized to the status of mere tools."[62] Benjamin Reiss would concur: "in their natural state [blacks] were like beasts; but in a perfect state of slavery, they could become, if guided by a master's rational will, something like machines or prosthetic devices."[63] But though he is three or four generations late in locating this intersection of race and technology "alongside the Civil Rights and feminist movements" and the concurrent discourses of McLuhanesque cybernation (it is in fact a Victorian conceit), Chaney is right to argue that "slavocratic society may also reflect a commonplace recourse in prescience literature, which assuaged patriarchal anxieties regarding a technological revolution that was then unfolding," one which presaged "the new age in technology in terms of a return to the age of slavery."[64]

This latter point should be challenged and clarified. The "return" in question here is more accurately a white fear of their own transformation into slaves by machines, *not* a return to the age defined by American's peculiar institution in which blacks were slaves. What Chaney describes is instead more a fear of *reversal,* of a sudden loss of power, than a return to an antebellum status quo. This fear of reversal will attend each technological change and ultimately make it racial since it is almost always articulated in the language of black slavery—from automata to cybernetics. As a Victorian conceit these anxieties are most prominent in a spate of popular fictions that will lead the way to the formal development of science fiction in America. These are the texts Judith Wilt has in mind and which are the subject of the next chapter.

Because Donna Haraway's still influential "ironic political myth" of the cyborg emerges from and depends on the primary transgression between the categories of human and animal, Chaney is on point to make the claim that *that* myth is perhaps doubly political or triply ironic in that it is ultimately rooted in "the category disputations over the black body in America, between what constituted human and animal," and so Haraway has provided, in essence "a theoretical abstraction of African-American slave subjectivity" through the lens of gender and technology.[65]

True, but P. T. Barnum got there first.

To theorize the fluctuating relationship between human and animal, blacks and whites as they relate or react to industrialization, Sylvia Wynter arguably got there first. Even if she didn't, it's useful to say she did because, as critic Alexander Weheliye writes, "These discussions, which in critical discourses in the humanities and social sciences have relied heavily on the concepts of the cyborg and the posthuman, largely do not take into account race as a constitutive category in thinking about the parameters of humanity." Wynter's work provides a "conceptual precipice from and through with to imagine new styles of humanity," much in line with cyborg and posthumanist thought.[66]

Though cyborg discourse and posthumanism are the primary concerns for a later chapter, Sambo can here help make full sense of the cyborg as both a new style of humanity and a raced being. This latter point may have been taken for granted in cybertheory and posthumanist criticism, but its history has almost never been explored. Sambo is a figure also of labor and pleasure going back to the craze for automata and then with the craze for jazz as a product of what automata would evolve into: the phonograph. In much the same way, that now slightly dated symbol of the cyborg is necessary to make sense of Sambo as a product of technology. Both figures depend on automata, on what Freud will famously name "the uncanny" and then on what would be called in 1923, "robot." Because everything Sambo is or is not, the robot is and is not. They bear the same uncanny relationship to the human—which is to say, to the white.

Sambo is an exemplary carnivalesque figure of a "lack" necessarily opposed to white Europeans. In Wynter's thinking, Sambo is comparable to medieval jesters and clowns, figures of that which is opposite to "man" but also opposite to reason, rationality, and restraint. With the expansion of the industrial age, however, such a "figure of Chaos" like the minstrel "would no longer function as the Icon of a Defect of Natural Reason, since with the rise of purely middle class culture, the Defect or Lack-state of the Fullness of being was now to be that of the Lack of a mode of human being, the Indo-European, now made isomorphic with Being human itself." In her description of the birth of the Renaissance or the shift into modernity, these "figures of Chaos" or types of performance blurred, mocked, and questioned the notion of reason by being that which was not reasonable, was in fact clownish, irrational, libidinous, and childish. They represented "entropic chaos to the order of the dominant model of Being" that then served "to refigure the aesthetic order, expanding the limits of the boundary-maintaining system of the We."[67]

In expanding what Europeans thought of themselves, these figures express what Sue Zemka describes as "the loss of certainty that attends an expanding category of "humanness . . . unhinged from the conceptual, social, cultural, and physical markers that formerly maintained a balance between its universality and its exclusiveness."[68] This is Wynter's "chaos." Like the minstrels, anthropomorphized machines are also a threatening supplement to "system of the We." They provide the image of a hyperrational inhumanity and the spectacle of a humanness gone beyond the bounds of whiteness or of a European sense of themselves as universal. As will be argued, this is the primary insight and fear at work in narratives ranging from Samuel Butler's *Erewhon* to Čapek's *R.U.R.*

The secularization of knowledge during the Renaissance made those "figures of chaos" less central, due in part to the kind of maritime exploration that was also central to this period and which brought into the evolving European schema other forms of life that served that purpose, particularly indigenous peoples in the Americas and then soon after, black slaves from Africa. Like the clowns and rogues and fools that preceded them—and the blackface minstrels that would hearken back to that past—the purpose of these new forms or classes of life was not simply slave labor. It was also epistemological. It enforced the notion of reason by way of the spectacle of its lack, which is to say it enshrined the notion of the human in whites by denying it in blacks. But that unreason and nature would first inhere in the native Indios and then be shifted onto Africans is a crucial point:

> The internment of the New World peoples would be followed by that of the African lineage groups, homogenized under the commercial trade name of "Negro." This objectification of the human was justified at first in religious terms as divinely caused by the Curse placed on Ham. Soon the shift would be made to the humanist concept of Natural Causality, of a by/nature determined difference of reason, in which the African mode of cultural reason was seen as a non-reason; and his internment in the plantation system as slave labor, as being carried out for the purpose of rationalizing him/her as an inferior mode of being in need of rational human baptism.[69]

Rationalization and baptism emphasize the question of soul at work in the relationship of human to its various others, either black or metallic. It is a question still alive in contemporary robotics and artificial intelligence, just as it has animated generations of science fiction. In Wynter's thinking, these categories of otherness on the margin of the human are certainly not equivalent, but they have exchange value. They are used to balance and orient the center through the process of rationalization. Critic Clevis Headley writes, "Wynter frames otherness in terms of what is the other of man."[70] But though he, like most of Wynter's readers, sees these oppositions in exclusively racial terms, her vision of otherness is so radical as to invite or demand far more than mere flesh.

As Barnum knew or suspected, both slave and automata could conceivably function as each other symbolically because they did exactly that historically. It is precisely these relentless slippages between Negro, animal, and machine, inhuman, nonhuman, and subhuman that makes the Freudian uncanny necessary as a conceptual element in the coming together of minstrel and machine. Wynter's critique of the human frames these parallels within a Caribbean context of race and performance, but also in terms of the comic. That is why Sambo can be deployed without the excessive trauma that the figure is made to evoke in a North America where minstrelsy's possibilities still remain stigmatized. Wynter's thinking also precedes and completes Haraway's by questioning the human to detail its limits and to explore the very possibility of entry into it by those subjects previously named antithetical to the category. As demonstrated in her discussion of Sambo, that category too is dependent on the uncanny.

The uncanny entails that which is dreadful, fearful, and terrifying but also which is simultaneously familiar, long known, and intimate. It produces intellectual uncertainty and epistemic ambivalence precisely because it pollutes self with other, binding the former to the latter despite repressing the latter as an irreconcilable otherness. As Eric Lott tells us, the uncanny is also a source of humor: "Clowning is an uncanny kind of activity, scariest when it is most cheerful, unsettling to an audience even as it unmasks the pretentious ringmaster. Blackface performers, often inspiring a certain terror as well as great affection, relied precisely on this doubleness."[71] In Freud the uncanny signifies the presence of a double, albeit one "concealed and kept out of sight." It includes "the impression made by wax-work figures, artificial dolls and automatons" and that "intellectual uncertainty whether an object is alive or not, and when an inanimate object becomes too much like an animate one."[72] That stress on automatons as well as artificial dolls reminds us that the uncanny was also dependent on technological innovation.[73]

For Henri Bergson, working in the considerable wake of Freud's essay, these figures of artificial or synthetic life would be examples of a comic sensibility precisely due to being uncanny semblances of humanity through automation: "This is no longer life, it is automatism established in life and imitating it. It belongs to the comic." Bergson's *Laughter: An Essay on the Meaning of the Comic* demonstrates just how imbricated the discourse of uncanny doubles and machines were with the anxieties of race. It updates and completes the Freudian uncanny by way of its own uneasy relationship to minstrels and machines:

> We begin, then, to become imitable only when we cease to be ourselves. I mean our gestures can only be imitated in their mechanical uniformity, and therefore exactly in what is alien to our living personality. To imitate any one is to bring out the element of automatism he has allowed to creep into his person. And as this is the very essence of the ludicrous, it is no wonder that imitation gives rise to laughter.[74]

This is what Wynter argues as the psycho-affective disequilibrium healed by Sambo, by his kinetic mask and racial masquerade; this is a more sanguine reading of Dinerstein's sense that blacks assimilated technology on behalf of the wider nation. It is also classic performance theory, classic parody, and, of course, classic minstrelsy and carnival.

As we will see, Bergson's analysis is also a product of a long and familiar history of romantic racism, where the other is prized for its ability to heal the imbalances of the white or Western self—particularly in the context of alienating new technologies. These insights will ultimately express how from analog to digital the black other is almost always implicated in or conscripted by a white need to make sense of new relationships to new technologies as they "creep into his person." These technologies accomplish this fearsome invasion of the self initially by way of imitation—by mimicking and therefore drawing attention to the "element of automatism" that is already there but masked as nature.

Modernism being the focus here, it's necessary to distinguish this use of automatism from that which was central to the creative methodology of French surrealism. What that movement called "psychic automatism" was primarily a method of directly accessing internal thoughts, images, and ideas and expressing them without the mediation of reason, convention, or standard creative procedures. It may have sounded like a technological metaphor or process—as in André Breton's description of it as a "true photography of thought."[75] But it was in fact a response to a by then familiar anxiety: a fear of losing agency, which "can be traced back to the later nineteenth century, when electrical technologies began to link bodies and machines in continuous circuits of activity."[76]

Narratives that emerge from this fear of losing agency have been described in terms not uncongenial to Wilt: as "melodramas of uncertain agency" that emerge when "the machinelikeness of persons and the personation of machines" generate mixed but intense responses.[77] For the surrealists, that anxiety required them to chart a way around the systems of power and control that had already rendered the modern European psyche subject to logic and conventional morality. It had, in their view, become like that of a machine and lost its spontaneity (this would also be why they celebrated the Negro as an example of direct access to the id, the subconscious, and the ancestral). Needless to say, surrealist automatism was deeply committed to Freud.

Bergson's is a well-known and influential essay. It is remarkable that so few have ever noted the racial politics or racist technopoetics of his theory of the comic. Bergson in effect describes blackface minstrelsy as a cure for the modern, essentially white disease of automatism. This is evident when he asks, in a much more problematic way than with Freud's talk of androids,

> And why does one laugh at a negro? The question would appear to be an embarrassing one, for it has been asked by successive psychologists . . . and all have

given different replies. And yet I rather fancy the correct answer was suggested to me one day in the street by an ordinary cabby, who applied the expression "unwashed" to the negro fare he was driving. Unwashed! Does not this mean that a black face, in our imagination, is one daubed over with ink or soot? . . . And so we see that the notion of disguise has passed on something of its comic quality to instances in which there is actually no disguise, though there might be.[78]

The most obvious aspect of this passage is, of course, its not-so-subtle dependence on blackface minstrelsy in a description of a "real" Negro, a black person so overdetermined in "*our* imagination" that she or he irrevocably partakes of that comic tradition even without the mask. Bergson goes so far as to leave us with the dangling possibility that even when there is no "ink or soot" (or burnt cork), the mask's traces exist in perpetuity, epistemologically "unwashed." The memory of the mask contaminates the experience of flesh, and the presence of organic flesh merely articulates a previous strategy of masquerade. Less obvious is the fact that by this 1911 essay, the very notion of automatism as a Western problem had already become so racialized that the Negro was merely one of the list of doubles for white subjectivity and the human, as enumerated by both Freud and Bergson. As such, Sambo functioned alongside other "figures of chaos" that generated that fear of losing agency. Far in advance of the cyborgs of Haraway and Chaney, the linkage of Negro, dolls and automata, and blackface and machine already operated with an unquestioned logic, each as a mask of the other.

To clarify the previous point, Bergson's various references to "our living personality" or "our imagination" clearly does not include the Negro as a subject. In the essay, the Negro is more closely related to androids than to even an "ordinary cabby." The Negro is a mere doppelganger for "our living personality," being a sign not of life nor of the category of "human" but a double for it—innately comic and irrevocably in disguise. After all, it is not the Negro who is prone to or victim of automatism, nor does the Negro benefit from the experience of uncanny doubling; he merely comments on it all, brings "our" attention to it, and thereby allows "us" to laugh at and transcend it. In this reading, the Negro does not share in the full experience of the uncanny or the comic quite simply because he—or "it"—is so deeply linked to its primary cause or source.

Bergson's conclusion seals the link between blackface and automata, contextualizing that most fully realized historical expression of a racial uncanny, which was the meeting of America's greatest showman and a female African slave in 1835:

> Let us then return, for the last time, to our central image: something mechanical encrusted on something living. Here, the living being under discussion was a human being, a person. A mechanical arrangement, on the other hand, is a thing. What, therefore, incited laughter was the momentary transformation of a person into a thing.... WE LAUGH EVERY TIME A PERSON GIVES US THE IMPRESSION OF BEING A THING.[79]

Of course, the opposite corollary is also true and even more significant for American slavery *and* blackface minstrelsy: "we" fear and dread the moment whenever a *thing* gives us the impression of being a person. In a "slavocratic" racial economy, this slippage occurs just when a designated thing dares assert itself as a person through the mimicry of human codes, suggesting the capacity for reason and literacy and thereby making a claim on kinship. This moment of slippage, as we saw in Lamming's discussion of the plough that can speak is what gender theorist Judith Butler has described as a category crisis.

It is evident and traceable in performance but the uncanny must be located in much stronger material circumstances. As it characterizes the relationship between white and black, human and inhuman other, the uncanny must be rooted in something more historically concrete than the mere dis-ease in sensibility described by both Freud and Bergson. Bill Brown is to be commended for identifying it as a product of the "contradictory legal status of the American slave—both human and thing." Considering the history of American law and its ambivalence to the category status and substantive quality of the black slave, Brown is absolutely correct to attribute a specifically "American uncanny" to U.S. law through which "the slave becomes the source of uncanny anxiety."[80]

It is the complex ambivalence in both U.S. law and in colonial racism itself—this kinship/alienation dialectic, this animal/human/machine problematic—that is of greatest consequence in the partial definition of a racial uncanny (since the uncanny can only be partially defined, being a fragmentary sense of completion in relation to a plenitude that is relentlessly suggested but always refused on the basis of race or a machine's lack of life or soul). This philosophically partial yet legally institutionalized definition enables Wynter to posit a diasporic Sambo as the ultimate product and sign of "category crisis": "It is in the sense that we should view the Sambo stereotype as the scapegoat-carrier of all alternative potentialities that are repressed in the system. Sambo becomes the representation of all desire that flows outside the normal order."[81] Through the Sambo figure and its logic and legacy of primitivism, through its doubling for and mimicking of the white rational subject, all forms of otherness—like machines—too have an echo and eventually, a (black) voice and face. Recall that what links the uncanny other to the fragile self is not just the former's vague anthropomorphism but its penchant for mimicry.

Recall also that from automata to a "mimetically capacious machine" like the phonograph, machines were widely feared for possibly possessing reason and thought and becoming terrible replacements for humans.[82] It is through those machines—particularly the phonograph—that the sound of black voices, for example, made such a cultural impact that they began a history in which race or its aural signifiers functioned as a mask for the socioeconomic regime that the machine itself actually stands for, much in the way that Sambo spoke racism and white anxieties through a black mouth. Many people first encountered the phonograph in those very sideshows and spaces of freakery where both automata and Negroes were displayed or performed. It too was a curiosity, a threatening vision (or sound) of the supplantation of human (white) being.

The uncanny is therefore the space of epistemological uncertainty and cultural anxiety where the minstrel meets the machine, but also a space of wonder and pleasure: "When the machine takes on the status of performer, it undergoes a transition from the functional to the marvelous."[83] A figure of transformation, Wynter's Sambo should be read against the "imperial mechanics" of an emergent global empire that depended as much on technological advancement *and* popular culture as it did on biological racial categories: "For a deep chord has been struck here by early twentieth-century advertising and popular culture, substantiating the primitivism that Charles Darwin connected to miming prowess."[84]

As the missing link between animal and human, Sambo was the link to that other threat to white centrality that was also the figure of a complex desire for cultural power and that also operated through mimicry: the robot. As a generalized sensibility, the uncanny contains them both and makes necessary the two most well-known responses to anxiety and uncertainty: laughter and terror.

KAREL ČAPEK'S BLACK MYTH

None of these associations between machines and minstrels should be seen as exclusively rooted in the racial anxieties and technological naïveté of the nineteenth century, nor are they product of the postfuturist obsession with machines that would characterize the "scientifiction" of early 1920s America. The connection between Africans and robots was by the 1930s so normalized as to become a material sign of industrial control over multiple histories of labor: "In the early twentieth century, there is a reaction in the realms of technology away from the automaton as rarefied ornament, a movement to stop it merely performing and send it to work. This is where the robot makes its appearance."[85] The year 1930, for example, is when Westinghouse designed and manufactured its own minstrel machine, Mr. Rastus Robot, the Mechanical Negro (also called the "Mechanical Slave"). As reported in *The New York Times,* this machine could "sweep the floor, switch lights on and off, rise, sit down and talk," all at his master's request.[86] Here is one description of "this talented performer":

> During the electrical and radio exhibitions of the past season, the increasing perfection of those mechanical servants, now popularly called "robots," has been the most spectacular feature. One of the finest yet produced, for human appearance and versatility, is "Rastus." . . . He has the powers of speech, of using his hands, of rising and sitting—although, to date, the complicated maneuvers of walking seem to have been a little too much for biped automatons. . . . Within its figure is a miniature talking-movie equipment; that is to say, a 16mm. projector, containing film with appropriate speeches in sequence on the sound track. This is operated at the proper time, and gives Rastus a very copious vocabulary—in a rich, baritone voice.[87]

The focus on his voice, a *black* voice, was quite typical of early sound-recording culture. There was a general belief that black voices had a tonality better represented by the new medium.[88] Rastus actually had a vocabulary of six words and wore the stereotypical overalls of the southern black worker, complete with colored bandana around his neck. His skin being made of rubber brings to mind the "India-rubber" that Joice Heth was reputedly made of.

More important than his uncanny semblance of a southern black man is the fact that he was called *Rastus.* There may be no more common name in the lexicon of American minstrelsy. It ranges from the character Brer Rastus in Joel Chandler Harris's infamous Uncle Remus cycle to almost every other advertising product in the early twentieth century that used blackface or black stereotypes to sell everything from coon songs, popular fiction, and radio programs to the original Cream of Wheat. Rastus became so common that it became a pejorative term for African Americans. Along with Katrina Van Televox, the robot housemaid, and other domestic and domesticated machines, Westinghouse used these robots ostensibly to advertise itself and its products as it had been doing since 1927. Due to a shared minstrel nomenclature Rastus evokes the Harvard computing machine constructed in 1944, called of all things, "Bessie"—one of the most common names in the lexicon of black female stereotypes. Described as "not the brightest of her breed," we are told that she is "dim-witted and slow," in comparison to her children and grandchildren, but that she is a breeder, "a progenetrix." It's difficult not to hear old stereotypes of black women's sexuality as terrifyingly rampant and prolific. Apparently the men who designed her tried "to deny that they are creating their own intellectual competitors."[89]

Joel Dinerstein suggests, "as with blackface minstrelsy, white men could only express their desire for machine aesthetics by putting a mask—a black face—on it."[90] Helpful insight, but it doesn't acknowledge that the desire for a literary or cultural aesthetics of the machine is shot through by the uncanny, which is to say it is also a product of tremendous fear and generates as much a need to perform as to contain. What was actually being advertised with these machines was control over those anxieties of supplantation and of losing agency that had beset Americans in the wake of the nineteenth century. Those anxieties were manifested in beings "now popularly called 'robots'" in the wake of Czech writer Karel Čapek's *R.U.R. (Rossum's Universal Robots)*. This *other* uncanny other would have been named automata by Freud and Bergson and P. T. Barnum. Čapek's play premiered in New York in 1922. By the 1923 English publication of *R.U.R.,* the word *robot* rapidly supplanted the much more common terms *automata, automaton,* or even the surprisingly ancient term *android.*

The figure of the robot doubled and threatened the definition of whites as exclusively rational while promising a future of leisure similar to that of southern slave owners. *R.U.R.,* after all, was about a robot revolution in which the machines not only rise up against their human masters and slaughter them but also evolve "souls" of their own. Certainly by the 1927 release of Fritz Lang's film *Metropolis*—a film influenced by Čapek's play—a robot could be seen as a replacement for humans, but also something threatening in that it could easily *pass for* humans. In fact, due to its explicitly feminine and blatantly sexualized manner, it could also be uncannily seductive, as is the case in *Metropolis.* After all, the uncanny other is both known and unknown. It signifies knowledge but also the unruly energies of difference that empower the need to formalize, categorize, and control it—often by controlling its representation, replication, and reproduction, as seen in Westinghouse's robots, which are necessarily black, slaves, minstrels, females, and maids.

This brings us to the first words seen on the stage of *R.U.R.:* "'CHEAP LABOR. ROSSUM'S ROBOTS.' 'ROBOTS FOR THE TROPICS. 150 DOLLARS EACH.' 'EVERYONE SHOULD BUY HIS OWN ROBOT.' 'DO YOU WANT TO CHEAPEN YOUR OUTPUT? ORDER ROSSUM'S ROBOTS.'"[91] Labor is stressed, but race is arguably present before the play itself begins, though masked by machines that are named slaves—or forced labor—in their original language. To render a robot in familiar stereotypes and historical meanings was to domesticate it; to mask it in racial terms or meanings rendered anxieties palatable. This then returns us to Freud. Due to its roots in infantile psychology, the double is directly connected to male castration anxiety: "male patients declare that they feel there is something uncanny about the female genital organs."[92] *Metropolis,* for example, evokes race and gender anxieties simultaneously in its use of the robot, setting out for industrial modernism what Nicholas Roeg's *Blade Runner* will set out for cybernetic postmodernism. Andreas Huyssen points out that by the time of the film "woman, nature, machine had become a mesh of significations which all had one thing in common: otherness; by their very existence they raised fears and threatened male authority and control."[93]

Lang's "machine vamp," as Huyssen calls her, is not only a product of early twentieth-century apprehensions about technology and industrial capitalism. There is also the castration anxiety that emerges due to an increasingly liberated female sexuality. The film dramatizes how the changing social roles of women and their increasing access to technology threaten male authority and control. If you recall, the mad scientist Rotwang's plan is to create a race of "machine men" to replace the drone-like white male workers. This plan to use soulless automatons necessitates the insertion of race into a narrative that then corresponds with white working class *male* fears of African American workers in industrial production, which is why the robot represents both racial and sexual difference. It begins by looking physically different—like a machine, its wires and circuits exposed, its art deco textures signifying a pristine inaccessibility, a coldness, stiffness, and severity that is stereotypically white. At the insistence of the Master of Metropolis, Rotwang transforms the robot into the likeness of the pious Maria, smoothing out its extreme physical otherness, mimicking the norm that is the white woman's body. Initially under the control of the white elite, the robot *passes* for human, for a woman.

Then things change. Something takes over. In moments of mad abandon, the robot begins to dance, wildly sexual, seductive, and erotic, mimicking the explosive movements of Josephine Baker or that set of projections of black women's sexuality called the flapper. Lang would have had access to such representations throughout Germany's Weimar Republic, where jazz music and dance performances were popular (it's worth pointing out that *vamp* is both a vernacular term for seductress as well as a musical motif common in jazz.) Lang's vision was inspired also by his visit to New York City in 1924. But the seemingly out-of-control machine with increasingly sexual expressions and gestures leads the workers to riot. They destroy the machines that had enslaved them and the city of Metropolis itself. In America, these anxieties of race and sex and technology represented in the film could hardly have gone unnoticed, particularly in a period where black culture and political expression ranged from the musical to the riotous, the openly antagonistic to the conceptually persuasive. If they did go unnoticed it was due to the great success of so masking race by technology that the latter managed to usurp the arguably much more threatening former.

Before discussing Čapek's representation of a robotic future and its dependence on machines as possible analogs for blacks, it is important to acknowledge that the very question of the Negro's modernity—well, its moder*nism*—had already been rendered an open question in minstrelsy itself. As such, minstrelsy was complex enough to make the fabrications of Westinghouse seem palatable or enabled them to use a comfortable set of racial meanings to lessen the fear of new, uncanny technologies. As before, that question of the Negro's temporality hinged on the representation of Africa. Questions about the Africanness of the Negro vis-à-vis its American modernity were embedded in its fundamental narrative tensions, which depended on a rural/urban split. Most minstrel shows featured two distinct types of Negro, suggesting how blackface performance was divided as to whether or not the Negro was the rural or African past or the urban modern. In this dialectic, Sambo was simply the rustic plantation dweller inseparable from the symbolic economy of slavery; his bookend, Zip Coon, was linked directly to (and often known as) Jim Crow. Where the former represented nostalgia for the plantation and a ludic rejection or a biological failure of the work ethic, the latter was its double, the slick urban dandy introduced into minstrelsy by George Washington Dixon in the 1820s. Zip Coon was notoriously "uppity" and mocked for his aspirations; he did not know his place despite the fact that he was probably the earliest representation of a black hyperconsumer in American history (not to mention being the forerunner of all forms of contemporary post–hip-hop pimpish masquerade): "He was northern, urban, a freedman, and a sartorially splendid dandy."[94]

Zip Coon in fact *dared* to be placeless, divorcing himself from the economy of the plantation machine while claiming both the North and the freedom of migration (after all, for blacks to move in a context of such racial violence was threatening and so required a significant amount of courage). In shifting places like the itinerate and often flashy bluesmen and blueswomen soon would, he suggested that space should be or could be shared with urban, modern whites while reminding them that the plantation, Africa, and even Sambo were irrevocably in the past. Zip Coon was thus a self-conscious and self-fashioned product of the coming machine age and of a changed, migratory sensibility. Of course, in performance, the gravity of his threat made him much more vulnerable to jokes about lynching and much more threatening to those blacks uneasy with the threats to the status quo represented by his masquerade. Zip Coon achieved all this while the much more organic Sambo basked in the safety of a pretechnological and nondemocratic stupor, a stupor understood as being due to his fundamentally "*African* nature."

For Eric Lott the two types of Negroes in classic minstrel theatre represented a geographic "sectional break," attendant with all the political, social, and ideological distinctions that would build up to the Civil War. Insofar as the South was linked to the past and the North the utopian site of postemancipatory dreams, the split was an equally temporal affair.[95] As evident in the terms used to describe and refer to antebellum blacks and then to minstrelsy, the question of the Negro's temporality, of which century he belonged in, was framed also in global terms, rendering Lott's "sectional break" transnational. The assumptions of the time were such that race, culture, and origins were seen as innately bound. Therefore, this African nature was rendered as a loose, self-governing network of meanings and uses (an aesthetic) alongside the belief that minstrelsy was indeed an autochthonous form. Blacks, for example, would be simultaneously contained by the relentless descriptions of minstrelsy as "African," "Ethiopian," "Egyptian," "Dahomean," or similar designations as seen in the very way Joice Heth would be advertised, even in advance of the blackface era. These were not random or throwaway terms. Even when deployed in descriptions of whites in blackface, the terms detailed a relationship to or a governing body of ideas about the African continent, emphasizing its pretechnological lack of history and its people who—unlike, say, those in India and China—had not proven themselves worthy by the civilizational indices of literacy and technological sophistication.

Particularly relevant in the lexicon of a then nascent advertising and racialized media spectacle, minstrels and minstrelsy were continuously advertised by terms of inflated patrimony such as also "Congo," "Senegambian," or even "Abyssinian." Eric Lott points out that this "national cultural form" was presented and considered as the "Æthiopian drama" while simultaneously acknowledged as "the lowest description of American farce . . . not without originality, considerable invention, and a rich vein of burlesque humor."[96] Certainly the terms were deployed mock-heroically—the use of something high sounding and noble to describe the base and the comical. There is a trace of that in the need to call Rastus Robot, *Mr.* Rastus Robot. It's a curious deflection when such a potent and patently American folk form consistently draws attention to itself by way of signifiers of the African continent. It is most certainly a technique of managing a racial uncanny rooted in a space external to the United States. It was meant to remind audiences and performers that the Negro was not truly a native, not indigenous despite being bound to the spatial and social regimes of the plantation. The terms made it clear also that the Negro *and* the continental African were unfit for modernity and for the responsibilities of full citizenship due to that biocultural link to a place of unquestioned savagery and darkness. And they were deployed aggressively, relentlessly *Africanizing* the African American's primitive and premodern "nature" precisely when debates about black humanity and modernity were gaining ground in politics. Arguably, this racist use of Africa was at the root of the still much-ignored anti-Africanism in much late nineteenth-century and early twentieth-century African American culture and politics. For whites to so Africanize black Americans could only inspire some blacks to publicly reject those origins in favor of an exaggerated American patriotism. This black hostility and disdain toward the African continent would later be transformed—though never fully reversed—by various Africa-centered movements, from Ethiopianism to Pan-Africanism to New Negroism.

One acknowledges the omnipresence of Africa in the representations of minstrel masquerade and therefore in (or against) the robot. But Wynter's imaginative theorizing strays a bit too far out of the realm of historical accuracy when she argues that "the American Minstrel show is a direct development out of the popular folk cultures of Africa, with possibly, as the Jonkunnu plays show, contributions from the parallel folk cultures of precapitalist Europe."[97] That it is "direct" is of course debatable. But in light of her reference to "Jonkunnu," a Caribbean folk festival of subversive masking and ludic play also rooted in slave culture, it is clear that in her view, blackface functions much more broadly within ritual forms of the carnivalesque in and beyond the African diaspora than simply within the binary racial dramas of nineteenth- and twentieth-century America. Unlike others for whom "Sambo was a peculiarly American institution," her strategy is ultimately to dislodge blackface from functioning as the almost exclusive sign of American racial trauma that so many desire for it to be.[98] She is not as general, however, as Caribbean thinker Orlando Patterson, for whom Sambo is "an ideological imperative of all systems of slavery, from the most primitive to the most advanced."[99] Wynter insists blackface be seen in a longer continuum of African expressive play anterior to an ever-privileged American racial trauma. She attempts to emphasize what Mikko Tuhkanen argued so well about minstrelsy: that it is an already "hybrid," creolized, and therefore "diversionary" cultural form.[100]

Historians and scholars point out that "early minstrels . . . had understood slave music not as African but as close to nature. Correspondingly, they perceived slaves as part of nature—part of the nature of the South."[101] But the attempt in minstrelsy to render the plantation as the home of the darky and the organic site of his nature was in no way an attempt to de-Africanize black slaves. That would be ultimately to claim them as belonging to the same historical continuum as their white masters or to suggest that they had a prior, more authentic claim on the United States. Since Africa and the nature of African Americans were ultimately homologous in a time when race and culture were synonymous, these mock-heroic descriptions—again, Abyssinian, Senegambian, or Ethiopian—drew from a debased Africa to mock-authorize an emergent American form that wore the mask of its Negro presence while speaking white anxieties about a changing landscape in a vernacular appropriated from blacks. In such an intricate dance of belonging and disavowal, America and Africa were surely what allowed the form to be claimed by whites without attributing to blacks credit as its creators or its inspiration.

Yet despite affirmations of pride and racial newness, black moderns were as ambivalent about Africa as they were about Sambo. For writers like Langston Hughes, Claude McKay, and even Alain Locke and W. E. B. DuBois, Africa was a point of orientation in the face of what archprimitivist Claude McKay would describe as "the ever tightening mechanical organization of modern life" in which blacks were now "milling through the civilized machine."[102] Even black modernist Jean Toomer would respond to the "civilized machine" through seemingly direct appropriations from Čapek's myth of robot revolt. For these moderns, this was a civilization that still bore strong doubts about their humanity and still depended on Sambo despite the fact that many whites were turning to a symbolic Africa out of a fear of losing theirs. Ironically, what whites feared in this transition was the loss of a humanity that they had long denied to actual slaves and blacks themselves. Wynter argues that Sambo was the denial of that humanity rendered as masked spectacle. He was also the sign of affective life for those threatened by the spiritual and emotional death of industrialism and modernization that would so feed modernist literary and cultural expression. He was the necessary other of the robot, the ultimate sign of disaffected life, pure labor, and the dehumanization brought about by those same forces that made him necessary.

For blacks in the midst of what Claude McKay described as "a world-conquering and leveling machine civilization," Sambo flickered in and out of the various movements, tendencies, and cultural explosions called modernism as the link between "the African aesthetic" and "the machine" and between a slave past, an industrial present, and a unpredictably mediated technological future.[103] In such a future blacks were as likely to end up as images on the covers of commodities, as recorded sounds echoing through the lips of whites, as strange fruit dangling from southern trees, or even as products of Westinghouse. So even though parodic, imprecise, and dense with racist, romantic, and fuzzy nationalist intent, the presence and legacy of blackface minstrelsy did help popularize and domesticate a flexibly defined African aesthetic as a counterpoint to the "machine aesthetic" in the wider climate of early twentieth-century American modernism. This occurred in the wake of the fateful meeting of "America's greatest showman" and the African female slave, Joice Heth.

As is well known, the success of displaying Joice Heth as both decaying African animal and then as the epitome of mechanical engineering set Barnum on a career that profited greatly by the display of automata, freaks, what Leonard Cassuto specifies as "racial freaks"—natives from Africa and the South Sea Islands—*and* minstrels (though he soon came to regret his association with "nigger singers," even as they became the most popular part of his repertoire).[104] In this commercial and spectacular relationship the blending of the African aesthetic and the machine aesthetic was already on the way to being naturalized in the American imagination with the logic of one being buttressed by the historical and cultural associations of the other. This uncanny relationship and history is at the core of American mass media and popular culture. It is, after all, a popular culture that functions largely by way of naturalizing artifice in the language of the inevitable, the language of nature, and, all too often, the language of race. The suggestion of one aesthetic *as* the other was not just credible but necessary to a form of commodification rooted in slavery and in racial travesty.

We should add to the mix of images, ideas, and intentions that structure the African aesthetic the growing fetish for African masks that conditioned much of the modernist impulse due to their impact on artists ranging from German expressionists to Henri Matisse, Pablo Picasso, and Amedeo Modigliani. Not only were West African sculpture and black new-world sound and dance important to modernism, but also the masks themselves were products of both colonialism (which brought them to the West) and anticolonialism (which made them popular).

But look closely. The blackface mask is ineluctably linked to West African masks—exaggerated lips and eyes, the color and texture of the cheeks, the way they function as references for unknown or unknowable black multitudes. Each is a visual cue for—or perhaps an echo of—the other. It's not too much to suggest that the face of the robot Maria in *Metropolis* bears some uncanny resemblance to them as well. After all, if the minstrel was the spectacle of blacks as inferior, soulless, and subrational, then the robot is the spectacle of that other that is still soulless, yet hyperrational and possibly superior. Both figures of chaos, they are also imitations of life.

Even more uncanny: the year after *R.U.R.* premiered in the United States, Harlem modernist Jean Toomer would give the strange title "Rhobert" to a short story appearing in his famed collection, *Cane*. Poetically and historically rooted in the antebellum South, *Cane* is set in a place where "the Dixie Pike has grown from a goat path in Africa" and where the children of slaves who carry "race memories of king and caravan,/High-priests, an ostrich, and a juju-man,/Go singing through the footpaths of the swamp." In the story the titular character has lost track of this Africa. The story is no work of science fiction but instead is Toomer's criticism of a soulless northern black bourgeoisie adrift from its organic cultural roots. If not criticism then elegy, since Rhobert is mourned for, sung to, and watched sinking, as much burdened by race as by embourgeoisement, which is to say, freedom.

Toomer describes him in the following way: "Rhobert wears a house, like a monstrous diver's helmet, on his head. . . . Rods of the house like antennae of a dead thing, stuffed, prop up in the air." Imagine the metallic head, with antennae, a lifeless thing but moving despite its lack of soul: "Like most men who wear monstrous helmets, the pressure it exerts is enough to convince him of its practical infinity." We are told, "The dead house is stuffed. The stuffing is alive."[105] Is it too much also to hear the echo of Čapek here: Rhobert, Robot, *Mr. Robot?*

Toomer further describes this creature's world: "Life is a murky, wiggling, microscopic water that compresses him."[106] This particular description of life is fascinating because though we think of Čapek's robots as the mechanical beings that have been imprinted in popular culture since *Metropolis,* the robots in *R.U.R.* are generated by a murky, wiggling protoplasm found in the ocean. They behave like living matter but are not living matter and so it is easy for old Rossum to synthesize them and build bodies for them. Rossum's robots are biological machines, though produced far in advance of the notion of genetic engineering; it's important that they are mass-produced in a factory, a process that spoke very much to the era's understanding of power and a technology that fed fears of disempowerment.

If convincing, this would be the earliest appropriation of Čapek's vision by an African American writer. Granted, "Rhobert" does not give us enough to make full claims on Toomer's technopoetics. But it wasn't just that singular story that brings Toomer into the conceptual orbit of science fiction. We know in the wake of his deep and extended study with philosopher-mystic Georges I. Gurdjieff, Toomer's less-known work took on a quite science fictional cast. Influenced by Gurdjieff's work such as the mammoth early 1920s work *Beelzebub's Tales,* as well as Gurdjieff's notion that most modern people were automatons, divorced from their true spiritual life, Toomer produced work that used imaginary technological and prosthetic devices to emphasize just how far modern man had strayed from an enlightened spiritual path.[107] Race, in fact for Toomer, was a sign of that straying.

If not convincing in "Rhobert," then Toomer's interest in technology, robots, and science fiction can be found more obviously in his little-known notes for an even lesser-known and almost never formally discussed play, *Man's Home Companion.* Written in 1933, two years before he distanced himself from Gurdjieff—and two years after George Schuyler's explicitly science fictional Harlem classic, *Black No More*—he subtitled the play "an a-drama in one scene." In classic speculative fiction style it was set in "any workday of the week any week of any future year, or, perhaps this year."[108] This is a world where it takes only two hours by "airship" to get from New York to Chicago and where, apparently, women work and men crave their wives' attention. It is the gender reversal that stands out in the play since race is never mentioned; yet what makes race crucial to the play is both Toomer's desire to decentralize it and his commitment to emphasizing sexual difference and cultural alienation in technological terms.

The characters include a maid who is a "technochaser" named Argive and whose description is almost as long as the play itself. It seems clear that Toomer wrote the play primarily so that he could present this creature to the world. Argive "is a greatly improved and subtilized bi-sexual robot, able both to speak and to respond to the spoken word." In this drama she merely "assume[s] a female role," suggesting that the machine is not only bisexual but is capable of performing for both genders. He emphasizes, "She is not an ordinary cumbrous over-complicated robot resembling a clodhopper suit of mail," as was common in the wake of *Metropolis.* Instead, "she is slim, transparent, but ten times as strong as steel—a dazzling spectacle, wonderfully and, somehow, sinisterly fashioned."[109]

Toomer's description goes far beyond anthropomorphism and sexualization, so far that it begins to explicitly seem a modernist abstract, precisely what he concludes. The language is that of a technofetishist, or someone for whom science fiction or technology offers a poetic and imaginative freedom that race perhaps does not:

> Her head is elongated, that is, somewhat oval egg-shaped. It is entirely without sutures and has only three apertures: one, a lip-like opening inlaid with a bright brassy metal which serves as a mouth; and two others, gill-like openings, two slits on each side of the head. Underneath one of these is concealed the ingenious mechanism for recording and registering sounds, including the sounds of the human voice. Under the other is the mechanism for doing the same thing as regards radio-transmitted power and control. She has no neck at all. Her elongated burnished head rests on bearings directly connected with the body. Her chest is narrow, and also elongated. But instead of tapering down, as the ideal human figure does, it sort of streamlines out into what we humans beings would call a jolly round belly. In this belly are the main words, delicate and ingenious beyond words. Her limbs are elongated and slim, amazingly beautiful forms reminiscent of those aimed for by sculptors of the abstract who desire to model perfect prototypes of fishes, birds, and so on.[110]

It is fascinating that Toomer would so insist that she is like a human being in the play—sexually and in assumed female form—yet provide us with such details that suggest an image that's almost impossible to visualize. What grounds the machine in anthropomorphism is its social role, its gendered position as "maid." Like Westinghouse's Katrina Van Televox, she wears the necessary apron and perfectly acts the part of a stereotypical housewife, which we soon learn the "real" wife is not (Argive consistently throws the husband sympathetic or pitying glances and it is suggested that the "problem" is his wife's complex and demanding work schedule and the main character's emasculation by a highly developed technological world).

Toomer spends a great deal of time detailing how Argive works, focusing on her body and "the ingenious mechanism for recording and registering sounds, including the sounds of the human voice," all operated by "radio transmitted power and control."[111] This should remind us of how important the phonograph was as a new machine specifically for the transmission of voices; as such it maintained the legacy of automata but for a mass audience. It should also remind us that where race and technology appear together, sound is often never too far away. Though sexually available for both the husband and the wife, it is the husband who makes use of Argive, a sign of the great alienation between this hypermodern couple, who have literally forgotten physical intimacy. Argive is the one he calls darling and with whom he spends his lonely nights dancing and listening to jazz (of course). Sadly, there is no image of sexual or romantic interaction in the play or in the notes, though it is suggested. To see the author of *Cane* attempt *that* in 1933 would have been worth the cost of production.

There is another machine character in the play, an "aniphograph" of the main character's wife, Lucille. An aniphograph is an "animated photograph" or "talking picture" that operates by voice control: "In reality it is one of the most amazing of modern inventions. . . . To make it respond, all one has to do is call the person's name while at the same time syringing it with a highly concentrated plasmic fluid." This replicant of Lucille looks "wistfully" at the husband and Argive dancing, wishing she had been made "full length." Apparently this double for Lucille "is an excellent companion of one's lonely hours" since the real Lucille is so busy with "the board's auxiliary meets," preventing people from installing "showerbaths in our airships," and fending off corporate competition.[112]

The Čapek influence is there, as it is in Westinghouse's robots. By 1933 it would have been unlikely that Toomer would have explicitly racialized his robots or his characters since by then the politics of identity and the process of racializing were anathema to him. But robots allowed him to express spiritual emptiness, sexual dysfunction, and the anxieties of gender role reversal in this play, where it's possible that in "Rhobert" he could get at the fear of cultural loss in the process of rapid urbanization in the wake of the Great Migration. After *R.U.R.* the robot as an embodiment of long-standing anxieties and fears was open enough a symbol to have contemporary anxieties and fears accrue to it. This use of the robot in Toomer is akin to Wynter's description of the minstrel's "alternative potentialities" that enable Sambo to capture or represent other othernesses.

If indeed Toomer could be inspired by the Czech writer, it could also be because Čapek's robots—again, *robota,* serf, menial, slave—were in explicit conversation with American race politics though it's almost difficult to find critics who seem aware of it. Most focus primarily on the robots as signs of labor or as "expressionist symbols of the danger that modern man may be dehumanized by the very world of technological civilization which he has created."[113] The focus on *R.U.R.* as being primarily about "man" and "machine" and the struggle between them has allowed the false universalism of both categories to limit the play to what it communicates about technology and the increasing "loss" of humanity that was a cliché of this period, as it was in the nineteenth century and as it still is today.

Since *R.U.R.* has as its precedent not only Mary Shelley's *Frankenstein; or, The Modern Prometheus* (1818) but also Samuel Butler's *Erewhon; or, Over the Range* (1872)—both narratives in which machines turn against their creators—it makes good sense that critics and audiences could frame it only in what was by then a tradition of how embodied technology was represented, as antagonistic. But Čapek was more than a little aware of American race relations. He alluded to them in this and other works. Take, for example, the 1936 *War with the Newts,* another apocalyptic fantasy, which bears remarkable similarity in theme and concerns to *R.U.R.* When published in the United States the following year, this novel almost had the impact of *R.U.R.*[114] In it humans are faced with a new form of life, in this case a "race" of highly intelligent salamanders discovered off the coast of Indonesia. These beings are initially exploited and enslaved by humankind but eventually—like the robots in *R.U.R.*—adapt, evolve, and rebel. And win.

The novel is a clear satire of the emerging racial theories of Nazism as well as a mockery of colonialism, but much of the Newts' movement through human society explicitly parallels how blacks were making their way through the United States at that time. For example, the novel begins with the arguments of viciously racist characters in advance of the discovery of the Newts. We are then told by the threatened white captain of the multiracial crew, "the prestige of the white race was at stake." After discovering the Newts and their various uses as free labor, there develops a trade in them that in the novel is clearly meant to echo the transatlantic slave trade. Once it's realized that Newts are intelligent and can speak, they become fashionable, like Joice Heth and other human oddities put on display, and then like blacks during the jazz age in New York stage revues. In parts of the Midwest they face strong, deeply moralistic sentiments. Organizations spring up to contain the spread of Newt-mania. When there are anti-Newt demonstrations, surrogate violence ensues as "negroes were partly hanged and partly burned to death."[115]

Lynching is very much on Čapek's mind in *War with the Newts.* In fact, the lynching of blacks and the lynching of Newts takes on a familiar social and indeed sexual shape. More than anything else it is that act of violence that makes it abundantly clear how closely Čapek intends for us to read the Newts as or in relationship to blacks. The following passage is worth noting in full because it is so clear and rich that it needs very little critical embellishment:

> (While on this point it might be mentioned that, especially in America, from time to time accounts appeared in the papers of girls who had been violated by Newts while bathing. As a result cases became more frequent in the United States in which Newts were hunted down and lynched, chiefly burnt at the stake. In vain the scientists protested against these actions by the mob, pointing out that because of their anatomical structure a crime like that on the part of the Salamanders was physically impossible; many of the girls swore on oath that they had been molested by the Newts, and therefore for every decent American the matter was perfectly clear. Later on public burning of the Newts was restricted, at least in so much that it was only allowed on Saturdays and under the supervision of the fire brigade. At that time also the movement against lynching the Newts originated, at the head of which stood the Negro, Rev. Robert J. Washington, which was supported by hundreds of thousands of members, almost all of whom of course without exception were Negroes. The American Press began to assert that this movement was political and subversive; and as a consequence attacks on Negro-quarters broke out, and many Negroes were burnt for praying in the churches for their brother Newts. Indignation against the Negroes reached its climax when from the burning of a Negro church in Gordonville (L.) the whole town caught fire.)[116]

Not only are Newts and blacks symbolically linked; they become political allies in a common in/sub-humanity.

In keeping with his satirical bent, Čapek tells us at the end of this passage, "this only has indirect reference to the history of the Newts," which in its intentionally deflective way merely emphasizes the centrality of blacks to the story. That history is also one where there is much discussion about how to define the Newts as a race, the rights of the Newts, how they should be treated, what legal status they have, how they should be paid, where they should live, and whether or not they could assimilate. Can they be baptized? Do they have souls? What is the nature of their sexuality? Is their power as producers or as consumers? Then the Newts become radicalized, and there are socialist Newts, capitalist Newts, accommodationist Newts, old-school Newts, and new-school Newts. And when the Newts recolonize Africa and rename it "Lemuria," they chant like any good Garveyite would, "Lemuria for the Lemurians" instead of the Pan-Africanist, "Africa for the Africans."[117] Čapek's "indirect reference" now seems viciously glib.

References to race and to African Americans are far less indirect in *R.U.R.,* and so the intention here is not to limit its reading to a racial one but to bring out the racial resonances that, though taken for granted, are in fact built into the play. The very reason the main human character, Helena Glory, goes to the island where the robots are manufactured is for abolitionist purposes—she does, after all, call them her "brothers," encourages them to stand up to their oppression, and insists that as a member of the Humanity League, she is here to "liberate" them. Though blacks are never mentioned openly as they are in *War with the Newts,* the robots are likened initially to Native Americans. In the universe of the play, Helena represents that growing number of people who insist that robots be dealt with "like human beings" (23). It's not fully clear how much Čapek expects us to laugh at this stereotype of the white progressive who seems to socially define themselves by their commitment to the pain of minorities. She passionately argues that they should receive wages and be allowed to vote and seems to feel the injustice of their oppression far more than they do. The robots are initially bemused by her description of their condition, as she initially can barely tell the difference between robots and humans on the island. This will turn out to be an important point in the first act, because in the final act we are introduced to her robotic double after she has been killed along with almost everyone else.

The real drama between Helena as the self-appointed voice of the voiceless and the staff of the company R.U.R. has a good deal to do with the issue of souls. It frames the play. That it does causes one to wonder why. Where exactly could Čapek have gotten the idea that the issue of souls would be necessary in the representation of a servile caste that are uncanny and teeter on the edge of humanity? The answer to this has to do with the logic of servitude and the history it finds inescapable. Strother Purdy puts it this way in his essay, "Technopoetics: Seeing What Literature Has to Do with the Machine":

> But we may doubt that servants could have faded from view and then disappeared altogether without the concomitant emergence of the machine, even though the fading started before laborsaving devices entered the home. What seems to have been more important was the *fantasy* of the utterly discreet, silent, dependable servant that was stimulated by the emergence of the machine, as it had been earlier by the institution of slavery in its most bizarre and inhumane forms.[118]

Robots, we are told early on in the play, "are not people. Mechanically they are more perfect than we are, they have an enormously developed intelligence, but they have no soul" (12). Helena isn't the first to try to locate their souls. The island factory entertains a great many "preachers and prophets," "Missionaries, anarchists, Salvation Army," and all kinds of religious sects interested in saving or discerning the souls of the robots, to no avail: "You can say whatever you like to them. You can read the Bible, recite logarithms, whatever you please. You can even preach to them about human rights" (22). Her response to these points is sentimental, suggesting that "love" is what they need. And in one profound moment she asks if since the robots have no souls do they have "no love, no desire to resist?" (24).

"Resistance" stands out in her attempt to locate or define soul. Dr. Helman, R.U.R.'s psychologist in chief tells her that robots might not love, but as to the desire to resist there are curious moments when robots seem to act irrationally. These are moments when they

> seem to go off their heads. Something like epilepsy, you know. We call it Robot's cramp. They'll suddenly sling down everything they're holding, stand still, gnash their teeth—and then they have to go into the stamping-mill. It's evidently some breakdown in the mechanism. (24)

One robot describes it as a glitch, an error in the works that should be removed. Helena perceptively and prophetically proclaims, "no, no that's the soul" defined as "a sign of revolt" (25). Eventually Helena realizes that robots are not like humans at all and so her work with the League of Humanity is meaningless.

But the glitch begins to spread. Unbeknownst to their human masters the robots have another agenda, masked by their soullessness but made inevitable by their growing sense of superiority. One says to her, "One Robot can replace two and a half workmen. The human machine, Miss Glory, was terribly imperfect. It had to be removed sooner or later" (23). At this stage in the play such a statement is not as sinister as it will be when the robot revolution turns to a massacre of the human race (and one finds it hard to accept that African American satirist George Schuyler wasn't paying close attention in advance of his *Black Empire*, which was serialized between 1936 and 1938 and featured blacks turning machines—including robots—against whites).

Soon robots form their own organizations and political movement, and the company R.U.R. attempts to manufacture "National Robots" as a strategy akin to the Tower of Babel. The general manager explains, "each factory will produce Robots of a different color, a different language. They'll be complete foreigners to each other. They'll never be able to understand each other. Then we'll egg them on a little in the same direction, do you see? The result will be that for ages to come one Robot will hate any other Robot of a different factory mark." In other words, they plan to induce racism and xenophobia in robots, as a product of divide and conquer. The psychologist in chief adds, "by Jove, we'll make Negro Robots and Swedish Robots and Italian Robots and Chinese Robots" (61). By this point in the play it becomes clear that robots are a mask also for blacks, operating much like Wynter's Sambo—a scapegoat for alternatives and anxieties.

The robots strike before the humans can act. At the cusp of genocide they declare, "The power of man has fallen. By gaining possession of the factory we have become masters of everything. The period of mankind has passed away. A new world has arisen. The rule of the Robots" (96). Most fascinating about their rise to power is how so much of their rationale is based on how they have come to define humanity. For them the human cannot be defined by its alleged soul but by something far more clearly defined and observable: its ruthless desire for power. In their own thinking they have *become* human by virtue of having seized power from human beings and having exterminated them. The last human being, the last man, says near the end of the play, "nothing is more strange to man than his own image" (105). But the robots have the last word, silently, in that the "Robotess" Helena falls in love with a robot and they set about to repopulate the earth. A new Adam and Eve, they "belong to one another," and equality is achieved in the absence of human beings (114).

The last words of the play are the first words: the last man reads from the book of Genesis, the story of creation now rendered uncanny. Critics tend to read this ending as confirming how "biomechanical beings become humanized through their development of independent self-consciousness" or "how life, by its own mystique, will continue to assert itself in spite of all man's attempts to regiment it."[119] These readings are too sentimental for a play as violent as this, where it seems the case that equality or "soul" is possible only when one race has been exterminated. After this play, hearing these biblical words featuring the injunction to be fruitful and multiply, to hold sway over the living creatures of the earth, and to replenish the earth and subdue it, all that stands out are its expressions of power: *subdue, hold sway.*

That focus on power as perhaps the true soul of humanity is whittled down from generality when we consider how hard Čapek worked to identify whites, colonialism, and fascism as particular segments of the human race that during his time were viciously whittling down the human race into *races.* Robots are clearly a figure of that partitioning, and as such they are necessary parallels to the other other of "man"—blacks. Čapek ventriloquized racial politics through them, an act of minstrelsy, if you will. It was an act that depended on the fact that fears of machine uprisings would function as the dominant metaphor. It makes sense that it would. By the play's premiere in 1922, actual racial violence and black uprisings were still echoing in the United States. *R.U.R.* appeared in the wake of what James Weldon Johnson famously named "Red Summer" in 1919, that wave of race riots that swept across parts of the United States after World War I. In many cases this violence had much to do with whites fearing themselves replaced by black workers in northern industries, certainly in Chicago, where the play opened in 1923. There was also the more recent memory of the bloody Tulsa race riots of 1921. That critics at the time or since have spent so much energy focused on the man-versus-machine angle suggests a need to deflect from the great fear of a metaphor's material implications.

PROGNOSTICATING ECHOES: RACE, SOUND, AND NATURALIZING TECHNOLOGY

In his near-classic *The Recording Angel,* Evan Eisenberg points out that the actual legacy of automata in the twentieth century was machines like the phonograph or gramophone. Since so many automata were used as music boxes and existed for entertainment purposes and for refined contemplation in a European context, it is no surprise that they would evolve as they did in America. This emphasizes something more interesting than their pedigree: that in the years between Joice Heth and *R.U.R.,* ventriloquism and masquerade become increasingly properties of technology. "Mimetically capacious machines" were beginning to define the difference between centuries and, in the United States, the difference between cultural powers and relations between social groups.

Robots are another product of automata:

> The phonograph is admirable when accurate and laughable when inaccurate. The robot, which we had imagined as a refined automaton, a statue that returned embraces, has turned out to be no such thing. In fact, the romance was over the minute Karel Čapek, smack in the industrial heart of the Habsburg empire, coined the word "robot" from the Russian root for "work." The robot was the image of alienated labour, what men would become after a few years on the assembly line. It was the pipe dream of the master, the nightmare of the slave. Then it began to haunt the master (make your tools too sharp and they may turn on you) and secretly comfort the slave, who might soon have his own slave.[120]

Eisenberg is generally very aware of the relationships between African Americans and the history of sound recording, yet he maintains the common reading of Čapek's robots as merely representing "alienated labor" or as figures of class struggle. But in a country still reeling from racial violence and where, unlike Europe, radical political assertion—of the kind that Čapek was also alluding to—was strongly linked to racial politics, the play's vision of an extremely violent robot war depended on much more immediate concerns. Then of course there is Čapek himself, consistently deploying race alongside all those meanings that made the play as rich a work of literature as it would be an influential work of science fiction, which was only a few years from being formally named. Yet in the final two sentences of Eisenberg's passage the racial meanings intrude too far to be ignored. The slave haunting the master, turning on the master, becoming a master, and the master becoming a slave—clearly a great fear of proletarian revolt in the wake of the Bolshevik Revolution. And these meanings are present in *R.U.R.* just as they are in *Metropolis*.

In the nineteenth century such an expectation was so strong in the American South that it became a crucial set of narrative tropes: the black rapist, the brutish automaton that sets fire to the plantation, racial revenge as the first gesture of freedom. Those two sentences prefigure the next chapter of this book, which charts in advance of Čapek the notion that machines and humans need be figured in a master/slave dialectic. In this tradition the necessary conclusion to that dialectic is not synthesis—as will be the case in cybertheory or "cyborg feminism," topics of an even later chapter—but violence and supplantation.

Čapek was not the first to narrate the relationship between human beings and machines in racial terms, but his vision has proven to be the most influential.

Interestingly, for Eisenberg the difference between phonograph and robot is arguably based on "soul" or something very like it:

> Why is it worse to be a robot than an automaton, worse to imagine oneself a phonograph than a music box? The eighteenth-century music box, like the eighteenth-century man, was endowed by its creator with a character. The phonograph, like the mass man, has no character to speak of, or sing from. It has no music of its own. It only reacts to the data fed it.[121]

It's an odd question. Eisenberg doesn't ask which machine one prefers over the other, but insists one imagine what it would like to *be* one or the other. The difference here is "character," something apparently had by automata, whereas robots and phonographs merely react, or possibly just mimic. Phonographs function within a commercial enterprise and are products of popular culture. They are here described the way mass culture was almost always described in the twentieth century—soulless, artificial, reactive. Despite his significant popular culture nous, Eisenberg's argument is essentially split between high culture and low culture, meaning that what gives automata "character" is its role within an elite socioeconomic (almost aristocratic) realm. At least it knew its master. This was only true up until, at least, Johann Maelzel and Barnum, when automata became *massified* and put on public display. They were accessible to all and could be placed adjacent to Joice Heth, for example, as was the Turk.

The idea that the slave will have his own slave—its own machine that can be used against the master—is intriguing, as is the idea that the machine secretly comforts the slave. It suggests that it would be valuable to explore early interactions between slaves or ex-slaves and machines, particularly those that suggest the kind of intimacy that generates meanings. These interactions would be comparable to notable critic Henry Louis Gates's "trope of the talking book," which he famously described in *The Signifying Monkey* (1988), as a crucial moment of black literary origins in a context where literature was the primary technology validating the human. In Gates, scenes where slaves discover or witness the seemingly magical power of literacy and its attendant capacity to transform are at the roots of an African American literary and political tradition. For slaves the very act of reading was a mode of resistance to the notion that they could not read; their engagement with the Bible was a mode of resistance to the notion that they had no souls; and the fact that books provided both comfort and modes of rebellion against the master requires little argument.

The supplementary figure offered here, then, is the "trope of the talking machine." "Talking machine" was what phonographs and gramophones were colloquially called in the early days of their display and eventual commodification. This trope marks a necessary early stage in a history of black technopoetics, where technology emerges as a primary mediator between the inhuman and the human and does so through race and sound. These descriptions of a first black encounter with a new technology stand as important stagings of the interaction of race and technology, as was the display of Joice Heth, whose ability to speak was the primary source of wonderment. They occur before and at the cusp of an early recording industry that would partly establish itself with coon or "Negro" songs by white singers until the first African American hit, "The Whistling Coon," by ex-slave George W. Johnson in 1891. Johnson was the first African American to make records, and he recorded this song thousands of times before it was possible to mass duplicate master recordings. This trope would be a crucial first step in answering Paul Gilroy's call for "A comprehensive history of that special period in which phonographic technology first made black music into a planetary force."[122]

It should be no surprise then to discover this trope of the talking machine in one of the most important and controversial "black" literary works of the nineteenth century. There is a brief discussion of that new, strange and alien machine "The Phonograph" in *Uncle Remus: His Songs and Sayings* by Joel Chandler Harris (1880). The machine isn't present in the conversation and is something closer to rumor; but the conversation it generates—indeed, a discourse, or the ground zero of one—is both productive and predictive:

> 'Unc Remus," asked a tall, awkward-looking negro, who was one of a crowd surrounding the old man, "wat's dish 'ere w'at dey calls de fonygraf—dish yer inst'ument w'at kin holler 'roun' like little chillun in de back yard?"[123]

The discussion is framed exclusively within an African American, plantation context with different types of blacks, ranging from the "tall, awkward-looking negro" to "younger negroes" to "one of the practical negroes" and becomes a reflection on a new technology as it is first made sense of within a vernacular culture.[124] One hesitates to say a "black" vernacular culture, however. Harris's "Uncle Remus" tales remain controversial for their depiction of the docile rural darky whose dialect stories of wisdom and instruction, while charming in their day, became uncomfortable for black moderns desperate to redefine themselves according to their own largely urban and Africa-centered self-images. Like Rastus and Bessie, Uncle Remus became a term of insult, much like Uncle Tom. But where Rastus Robot and Bessie the computer were being deployed as comforting images of the past used to mediate the cold threat of a new technology, Uncle Remus was just that: a romanticized past quickly losing ground to a nation beginning to make absolute claims on technological newness itself.

Chandler Harris's association with minstrelsy isn't simply due to his representation of blacks or his exaggeration and celebration of a black dialect common on the minstrel stage and eventually omnipresent in recorded "coon songs." It is due also to his work featuring a ventriloquizing of blacks. One could say he was a coon singer of a sort: a white man who wrote as a black man who spoke in a dialect that was quickly becoming a significant political problem. Despite this, black moderns highly rated Harris for his archiving of folktales and folk idioms that were disappearing in the face of the rapid urbanization of African American culture. James Weldon Johnson, for example, assessed the Uncle Remus stories as crucial to the creation and emergence of a national poetics. In his introduction to his important *Book of American Negro Poetry* (1922), he wrote, because it was rooted in African American culture, this national poetics was particular, "due to a remarkable racial gift of adaptability; it is more than adaptability, it is a transfusive quality."[125]

Race as both adaptable and transfusive—protean not essentialist—again brings to mind Wynter's argument that Sambo was an important scapegoat for alternative potentialities for all differences and antagonisms at work within a given social, cultural, or philosophical system. Blackface was mutable, mobile, as were its sound and interpretations. It was always able to represent many contexts and types of intentions, including those were seemingly opposed, like love and theft, or assumed contradictory, like Africa and technology.

It was clear to Johnson that the particularities of African American culture could be traced back to Africa, an argument much more controversial than it would be generations later. Tellingly, Johnson also links Harris and Uncle Remus to the sounds of African American popular music made globally "all conquering" by performances, talent, drive, and racial pride, but technically by phonography.[126] It's not unusual, then, that the "tall, awkward-looking negro" would personify the machine as something able to "holler," a living thing or a creature that shouts. The property of phonography to replicate the human voice is central to how and why anthropomorphizing machines became inevitable. These machines spoke, so they were like people, but not quite. In the early days of recording technology, people's responses to these machines were generally with less wonder than absolute terror. They were encountering the human voice disembodied, the human itself disembodied, and the spectacle—both aural and visual—of speech rendered no longer exclusively human. The Turk, for example, had a voice box that allowed it not only to speak, but in French, a language then associated with such cultural sophistication that it could only have generated greater insecurity. If you recall, Joice Heth's own voice was argued to be in fact the voice of a white man behind her machine mask.

Uncle Remus admits to not yet having seen a phonograph. He's certainly heard much talk of them. He "kinder geddered in dat it wuz one er deze 'ere w'atzisnames w'at you hollers inter one year an' it comes out er de udder." He says later,

> All you gotter do is ter holler at de box, an' dar's yo' remarks. Dey goes in, an' dar dey er token and dar dey hangs on twel you shakes de box, an' den dey draps out des ez fresh ex deze yer fishes w'at you git fum Savannah, an' you ain't got time fer ter look at dere gills, nudder.

Again, speech is emphasized, sound as doubled, ventriloquial, *dubbed.* But it is also reciprocal, indeed with a note of resistance, which as Čapek's Helena defined, is one of the defining qualities of "soul": "Hit's one er deze yer kinder w'azisnames w'at sasses back w'en you hollers at it."[127] Slight though it is, there is a sense here that the machine "sasses you back," which suggests volition, individuality, and a quality of refusal. Such a hearing of the phonograph is a key step toward personification, then anthropomorphizing and then *robota.* But because Uncle Remus is generally being represented in this vignette as folksy and simple and rural, this response to technology comes off as naive and backward, quaint.

Good old Uncle Remus does say something fascinating, though, considering the impact the talking machine will have on the United States and on African American and black diaspora cultures. One could consider it prophetic:

> Hit's mighty funny unter me how dese folks kin go an' prognosticate der eckoes inter one er deze yer l'on boxes, an' dar hit'll stay on wel de man comes 'long an' tu'ns de handle an' let's de fuss come pilin' out.[128]

To prognosticate is to prophesy, and echoes are important sonic qualities and symbolic figurations of space, time, and, of course, replication, doubling (aka *dubbing*). Echoes are also signs of the past, in that they represent a sound or a signal that has already been deployed and is in decay. There is a creative tension here between that which foretells and that which has been told. A much later discussion on dub music as the most explicit space of black technopoetics in sound will depend on this hearing of black uses of technology and the technique of echo. But echoes here should be read as Jacques Attali would read them, as "premonitory," when he argues that "the noises of a society are in advance of its material conflicts." For Attali, recorded sound and music "makes audible the new world that will gradually become visible."[129] Eisenberg also suggests this and echoes the "all conquering" triumphalism of Weldon Johnson when he writes, "On records the black musician was no longer a minstrel with shining eyeballs, but simply a musician. . . . If invisibility betokened the fallen estate of the black man, it was also his main chance to conquer. And that is just how the black sensibility did—to a degree—conquer America."[130]

Uncle Remus's sense of the machine as generating or performing reciprocity as well as future possibilities; his prediction that blacks would engage recorded material as their primary interaction with informatics and technologies of reproduction; and Čapek's idea that robots will inevitably develop souls since "soul" is something quite other to what we humans might think it is—this is all premonitory. After all, who would have thought at the turn of the century that race, sound, technology, and culture would take the shape it has?

There is one more minstrel/machine connection of note, one more example of the trope of the talking machine and of echoic prognostication necessary to complete this chapter. This occurs after Joice Heth, just under a decade after George W. Johnson's "Whistling Coon." Johnson's song would, of course, anticipate a future in which hit songs performed by blacks would no longer be a novelty as his was, and by 1936, when blues legend Robert Johnson recorded his classic "Phonograph Blues," black relationships with the talking machine were common and intimate enough for him to explicitly sexualize.

But this version of the trope of the talking machine anticipates the relationship that the United States established between race and machines for the rest of the twentieth century. In 1901 the minstrel performer Bert Williams began what would be the first significant recording career of a black artist in the United States. George W. Johnson may have had two or three "hits" (vaguely stated, given how many of them were just versions of "The Whistling Coon"), but Bert Williams would be the first that could be described as being as much a recording star as a stage performer. In 1906, five years after his first encounter with the talking machine, Williams signed a lucrative exclusive contract with Columbia Records. Up until the commercial boom of race records in the 1920s, he was one of the only black performers whose voice was readily available as a recording. One source claims that at his peak in the talking-machine business Bert Williams was making $100,000 a year, an astronomical amount for that period.[131]

Williams was apparently very aware of the importance of the new technology and committed himself to the phonograph as a new site of dialect performance:

> Williams was more absorbed in the sound of his own performance. It was hard to tell anything from the poor quality of the recording techniques, which could only reproduce a shouted roar, but he had practiced his songs and worked on his dialect so conscientiously that he wanted the records played over and over, comparing how he had always though he sounded to the strained music coming from the cylinder machine. At that time theatrical stars refused to make records, contemptuous of the poor quality of the sound reproduction and afraid that people who owned their records would tire of their acts. But despite the apparent disadvantages of the new recording process, when Williams was invited to come back to the Victor studio in another month, he agreed. He was to sing into recording mechanisms for the rest of his life.

It's a remarkable image to conjure, the great black blackface performer hearing his voice repeated back to him, over and over, studying his voice mask and perfecting it finally from a distance. His care and attention clearly paid off. An advertisement in New York's *Age* shows just how popular he and, more important, his recorded voice were:

> Bert Williams, Caruso, Tetrazzini
> and other world famous artists can be heard
> in your own home
> by getting a
> TONE-A-PHONE
> The latest and cheapest high-class phonograph made.
> $10.00
> Guaranteed to equal any $25.00 machine
> Will Play All Disc Records.[132]

An early Victor catalogue attests to the significance and success of Williams and his partner, George Walker, as early artists of sound and as incentives to a new market for these technological commodities:

> The most popular songs of the day are the "Ragtime" or "Coon Songs." The greatest recommendation a song of this kind can have is that it is sung by Williams and Walker, the "Two Real Coons." . . . Although Williams and Walker have been

engaged to make records exclusively for us at the highest price ever paid in the history of the Talking Machine business, and although their records are the finest thing ever produced, being absolutely the real thing, we add them to our regular record list with no advance in price.[133]

Note the stress on the authenticity of the black voice—performed by minstrels no less, or rather *black* blackface minstrels in a metasignifying of irreducible realness. The power of this machine to introduce many whites to the sound of black voices, to the intimacy of spoken word or songs across social and legal gulfs, cannot be underestimated. Soul is also the sound of a common humanity. But the stress on realness is remarkable because this hyperbolic claim on the black voice is used to naturalize the talking machine in a way that Dinerstein would likely agree.

But naturalizing comes at a cost. As with Rastus Robot, the idea that this intimacy between blacks and technology is innately celebratory or even conceptually unique is challenged by science fiction, popular culture, and conceptions of labor, where it is far more complex, often sinister. Remember, these machines were terrifying for the early consumer. Sound recording had yet to strip itself of associations with the occult and the sheer size and alienness of these technologies took years to domesticate. Race and sound played a significant part in that domestication. After all, if it speaks a black, vernacular voice, how alien can this machine be? If it speaks as a beloved darky minstrel, how cold and threatening could it be? If it speaks in warm familiar tones of the Negro stereotype *as finally perfected by Negroes themselves,* how artificial can it be?

The minstrel voice is here exploited as a sign of intimacy with the alien other, a sound used to mask the uncanny. In this case the analog warmth of Sambo is used to domesticate a new technology—one *other* makes *another* other familiar—familiar enough to sell. Where Čapek used machines to express deeply troubling racial concerns, here blacks are used to placate deep anxieties about technology to market machines and sustain a racist status quo through technology. The minstrel figure here mediates between two of the twentieth century's great others: the machine and the African American in the first century of freedom. The quest to domesticate one requires the evocation of the other. Here is intimacy without compromise, engagement without danger. The listener is guaranteed power over the machine, as it now operates within a stable racial and mimetic hierarchy.

This should sound eminently familiar. It will, hopefully, evoke a continuum that will by the end of this book look like a tradition, as this particular iteration of the "trope of the talking machine" was prognosticated by the strange case of a wizened black slave woman passing for or being passed as a machine. Because she was a slave—a mere thirty years before full legal emancipation into the "human"—she was actually being passed as a machinic simulacra of something other than a human being, something already passing for something else and could therefore be used to pass for *anything* as long as it existed on the far edges of the human. In her mask an old social and economic system passed as new and a new technological system of culture and power masqueraded as organic. With Joice Heth, dumbstruck audiences partook of the glory of a new commodity masquerading as an old one and witnessed an old performance of nature naturalizing and therefore legitimizing one that had already changed.

TWO

HUMANIZING THE MACHINE

Race and technology came together in the Victorian era, as Europeans were forced to make sense of the implications of colonial expansion and the repercussions of industrial power. One of the more important methods of this sense making emerged in that moment of transformation that Judith Wilt acknowledges at the beginning of this book's first chapter: from Victorian gothic to science fiction.

To contextualize the turn to Victorian fiction, it is best to first contemporize this material, certainly for readers for whom Victorian literature or early science fiction are as far afield from, say, Caribbean thought or even black music. To do this it is worth noting just how naturalized has been the racializing of technological relationships in contemporary thinking about technology. For example, the terms *master* and *slave* are still common in engineering colloquialisms and are neither incidental nor accidental. Such contemporary usage is rooted in the racial politics of the Victorian era and its proto–science fictions and in the manifestation of cultural and social anxieties endemic to that era of formal colonism. That late Victorian texts—for example, Samuel Butler's *Erewhon* or Edward Bulwer-Lytton's *The Coming Race* (both from 1871)—are important progenitors of science fiction is rarely debated, but their dependence on race, racism, and colonialism and their fear of reprisal, revolution, and racial retribution has never really been fully explored. That dependence is important to understanding the enduring racial subtext of the genre. It is also why it has become easy to use terms like *master* and *slave* to describe basic technological relationships and why an awareness of these racial parallels have been common for scientists like Norbert Wiener, father of cybernetics.

The second section follows this train of argument from colonial England to slave-era America, where the work of Herman Melville directly borrows from the shared root of both Butler and Bulwer-Lytton: Mary Shelley's *Frankenstein.* He does that to offer a dual-pronged critique of both slavery and industrialization through the trope made famous by Butler in *Erewhon,* that of the machine turning against its master. But it is in the lengthy final section where a close reading of Bulwer-Lytton's and Butler's texts reveal in detail how race, racialization, slavery, colonialism, and technology become a part of the DNA of science fiction from its genesis.

MASTERS, SLAVES, AND MACHINES: RACE AND VICTORIAN SCIENCE FICTION

African American mathematician and cyberneticist Ron Eglash once asked a set of questions that one would have expected of either a literary critic or historian of science or science fiction. One would also have expected his questions from that very rich contemporary tradition of inquiry into the birth of race as object of scientific knowledge and the entrenchment of racism as one of its primary social and judicial products. That the questions remain open rather than fully answered is no doubt due to conceptual and intuitive gulfs still existing among science, science fiction, race, and technology. We begin with them for two reasons: first, they show just how central the race/technology parallel has been to Western culture; and second, to answer those questions in any satisfactory way requires some attention to late nineteenth-century proto–science fiction, which is where that very parallel becomes central to the genre. It is in that genre that the parallel will be naturalized to the point of becoming colloquial.

In two brief essays Eglash explores the common use of that no more Hegelian cliché of "master-slave" in common technical and "patent descriptions which specify a control relation between two devices."[1] A simple example of this usage can be drawn from the world of consumer electronics, where a powered speaker is usually described as the "master" and secondary speakers that draw power from it are called "slaves." Industrial clocks also operate that way, as do many linked computers. One essay is titled "Broken Metaphor: The Master-Slave Analogy in Technical Literature" and the other, "History of the Phrase 'Master-Slave' in Engineering Terminology." In them he asks, "Why did the metaphor only emerge long after the literal practice had disappeared from the U.S. and Europe?"[2] Those still unfamiliar with this analogy may immediately recall a similar if not more common one: male/female hardware mating interfaces (or plugs), which should remind us yet again how intimate racial and sexual dynamics are, even at the level of seemingly inconsequential metaphors and especially in the context of technology.

To rephrase Eglash's question, why does the master/slave dialectic survive in scientific vernacular as a statement of technological relationships when the social experience that grounded the metaphor no longer obtains? Eglash states that this particular use of master and slave did not have any immediate racial overtones in Hegel, despite its function in a worldview fully known to be racist. However, as Susan Buck-Morss and others since C. L. R. James have pointed out, due to the scale and impact of the French Revolution we should assume if not accept that race in some way infected all aspects and angles of Enlightenment thought, especially when it came to the issue of freedom. And it is a quite serious postslavery material concern that prompts Eglash's seemingly minor question: in 2003 Los Angeles County received a discrimination complaint by an employee who found the phrase so difficult to use that the county agreed that it should no longer be used in official documents due to the "cultural diversity and sensitivity" of the city.[3]

Questions about masters, slaves, and machines help in translating the story of Joice Heth and P. T. Barnum and of race and technology into a foundation story not only of modernism but also of a far broader and infinitely more complex modernity structured by the dual anxieties of slavery and industrialization. It's a modernity shaped by systems of human unfreedom, like colonialism, and those of seemingly infinite potential and relentless dynamic expansion, again, like colonialism. As in the previous chapter, the concern is to argue for how those anxieties buttress, pollute, and reproduce each other. The goal here is to trace those relationships in some of the literatures of both England and the United States in those years leading up to and immediately beyond the fateful meeting of the showman and the slave who as a figure "connected the age of Newton to the age of railroads."[4] Joice Heth also represents a connection between the age of chattel slavery and empire to contemporary cyborg theories that though they became increasingly concerned with issues of race, gender, and technosocial embodiment still have yet to acknowledge their indebtedness to this period. In ignoring the shared and competitive anxieties of nineteenth-century Europe and America, these traditions of thinking have dangerously neglected writers and thinkers who were as engaged with race and technology then as we are today; writers like Samuel Butler, Edward Bulwer-Lytton, and Herman Melville.

That "master-slave" itself didn't "become a common part of the engineer's lexicon until after WWII," forces Eglash, author of the quite remarkable *African Fractals: Modern Computing and Indigenous Design,* to query, "Just how was it that a morally criminal social practice became the metaphor of choice for a ubiquitous phenomenon in engineering?"[5] Why would such an "ethically suspect" analogy give rise to a now unquestioned "technosocial metaphor"?[6] These questions become even more intriguing when, according to his research, there was no indication that engineers who began using it from the turn of the previous century held a positive view of slavery. Eglash claims that if they thought much of race relations at all they were more likely to disapprove of it. He finds no evidence that the analogy was present before the Civil War or during the institutionalization of chattel slavery in the South, where one would have imagined that it had greater purchase, but he agrees that though "it is almost certain that there was no conscious intention to echo pre–Civil War discourse on runaway slaves . . . that still leaves the possibility of a metaphor operating at a subconscious level."[7] Yes, and since the end of formal slavery would only signal the beginnings of new forms of racism—especially of the "subconscious" variety—and the flourishing of a scientific racism that wore social Darwinism as its mask, it is hard to imagine why the continuing value or charge of the analogy should be surprising.

The analogy was first used in 1904 in Cape Town, South Africa, of all places, but that was sixty years after slavery had been outlawed there. The city is also known as the home port of the Royal Navy's West Africa Squadron, famous for freeing captive slaves from passing ships. Because of the indifferent or actively nonracist political views of the engineers and scientists that helped institutionalize the metaphor, Eglash surmises that it likely functioned in progressive if not antiracist terms. Its value was not as a nostalgic validation of slavery but to signify "a machine that operates in the way that people should not."[8] Though a counterintuitive stretch on his part, for such a morally negative metaphor to become habitual even in the supposedly "objective" or "values-free" fields of science requires a far more complex history of the process by which it becomes comfortable or credible. After all, Cape Town in the early twentieth century was reeling from the effects of the Second Boer War (1899–1902), despite the noble efforts of the West Africa Squadron. These effects quickly manifested in an increase in racial prejudice that would lead to ever more legal methods of social control that culminated in the formation of apartheid. It becomes less easy, then, to accept the suggestion that the master/slave analogy was initially used as a critique of slavery in this climate because that racial climate was fast becoming one of state-sponsored violence and institutionalized bondage.

Eglash's questions are vital because they are ultimately about the intensity of a metaphor in its ability to codify historical relationships. They are about the sedimented racism of seemingly lifeless objects, which because they are arranged in relationships with one another, cannot escape certain "grammars" of dominance fundamental, in this case, to Western culture in an era defined by colonialism, slavery, and industrialization. As argued, it is that fact of dominance that enables the dominated and exploited—blacks and nature—to be changed and exchanged within the logic of a notion of white power that depends on its own metaphoric equivalence with technology. To recall one of Michael Adas's strongest points in *Machines as the Measure of Man,* that equation was in fact a secondary effect of technology itself. The raw fact of technology provided enough rationale for cultural supremacy in advance of the need for biological racial categories. In other words, technology acted as racial evidence and was taken and insisted as objective proof of cultural superiority: "few disputed that machines were the most reliable measure of humankind." This leads Adas to go so far as to argue that "racism should be viewed as a subordinate rather than the dominant theme in European intellectual discourse on non-Western peoples." Though one is hesitant to fully endorse this due to an awareness of how racism and the process of racialization did and does infect notions of technology, Adas's desire to reject or criticize the "racist reductionism" in the criticism of our time is most welcome.[9]

Eglash is correct to conclude that despite the lack of direct racist evidence in this etymology of master/slave in scientific vernacular, its "social resonance ... is as much about the wage slave of the 20th century as it is about enslaved Africans of the 19th."[10] It is that "social resonance" that calls for a broader history of this analogy, both its linguistic vehicle and the historical relationships that provide its tenor, especially since Eglash is indebted to the work of Norbert Wiener, the mathematician father of cybernetics, which he described as "the science of control and communication in the animal and the machine."[11] Wiener is worth a brief discussion not only for his impact on cybernetics, cyborg theories, and *African Fractals,* but also due to his interest in race and his dependence on those earlier technological anxieties that would manifest in, say, engineering colloquialisms. It is more than likely Wiener's sensitivity to race that informs Eglash's very interest in how machine/human relationships become framed in racial terms. For example, in terms reminiscent of the futurist Filippo Tommaso Marinetti, Wiener once defined his new field as depending primarily on "*analogies* between living organisms and machines."[12] This is simply to emphasize that cybernetics is both science and a technopoetics; analogies but also material relationships: as Wiener defines cybernetics, it is the "general study of communication and the related study of *control* in both machines and in living beings."[13] That analogy is itself a technology of control was clearly not lost on Marinetti two generations before.

N. Katherine Hayles points out that "In first-wave cybernetics, questions of boundary formation were crucial to its constructions of subjectivity."[14] This matters because Wiener was very clear on the material bases of the master/slave, race/technology analogies in his *The Human Use of Human Beings* (1950). The very title of Wiener's book so suggests slavery—humans *using* other human beings—and the book so often refers to it that it is quite stunning that Afro-futurism or various cyborg or posthumanist theories have yet to take on its assumptions or engage cybernetics from its roots in these explicit racial analogies and material relationships. Especially since, as Hayles points out, subjectivity was an early if not primary concern for Wiener and will manifest in his continual wrestling with ethical issues like that of racism. This absence of engagement operates despite the fact that Afro-futurist Kodwo Eshun eloquently described Wiener's book as W. E. B. DuBois's *The Souls of Black Folk* "updated for the Analog age."[15]

Beyond the metaphoric, there are real-world racial parallels in Wiener's work. Cybernetics as a science of communication and control was explicitly considered in terms of American racial politics, in terms of mastery and slavery. Wiener writes,

> Most of us in the United States prefer to live in a moderately loose social community, in which the blocks to communication among individuals and classes are not too great. I will not say that this ideal of communication is attained in the United States. Until white supremacy ceases to belong to the creed of a large part of the country it will be an ideal from which we fall short. Yet even this modified formless democracy is too anarchic for many of those who make efficiency their first ideal. These worshipers of efficiency would like to have each man move in a social orbit meted out to him from his childhood, and perform a function to which he is bound as the serf was bound to the clod.[16]

The rhetoric is of course familiar: modern life makes us all robots, an insight that precedes the word *robota* and is in fact Victorian in the wake of Thomas Carlyle. Yet note how that insight had become an Americanized cliché by the time of Wiener's technological revolution. White supremacy and race so easily gives way to a more general sense of social bondage as "each man" is reduced to medieval servitude by those "worshippers of efficiency" that function as industrial timekeepers, clocks, essentially. This type of control is industrial, modeled on the form of the assembly line, what Wiener likens to fascism:

> The businessman who separates himself from his employees by a shield of yes-men, or the head of a big laboratory who assigns each subordinate a particular problem, and begrudges him the privilege of thinking for himself so that he can move beyond his immediate problem and perceive its general relevance, show that the democracy to which they pay their respects is not really the order in which they would prefer to live. The regularly ordered state of pre-assigned functions toward which they gravitate is suggestive of the Leibnitzian automata and does not suggest the irreversible movement into a contingent future which is the true condition of human life.[17]

This passage is useful also in its dependence on older reactions to technology and its transformation of social life into something that could be or was represented by machines. But note how focused on power Wiener is and the relationship between the social world of industrial capitalism and its impact on "the true condition of human life." Now, to be far more specific about the place of race in cybernetics, Wiener writes, "Let us remember that the automatic machine, whatever we think of any feelings it may have or may not have, is the precise economic equivalent of slave labor."[18] It certainly is economic, but also metaphoric. Eshun puts it in more mythic—hence, creatively imprecise—terms, echoing a number of contemporary critics in and around Afro-futurism: "Like the robot . . . the slave was actually manufactured to fulfill a function: as a servomechanism, as a transport system, as furniture, as 3/5 of the human, as a fractional subject."[19]

Not only had the analogy of slave/machine become naturalized by the time of Wiener's work, so was the very question of affect, of whether the machine "may have or may not have feelings." In 1950 he would conclude his presentation to the American Academy of Arts and Sciences thusly: "Whether we say that these machines think or do not think, or even whether we say that they live or do not live is a quibble over words which are adequately defined for the normal everyday contingencies of life, but are not adequately defined for the greater problems which these new machines present."[20] These may seem odd equivocations in their suggestion that a machine *could* have feelings or could have life, but given the analogies deployed by Wiener and the tradition of science fiction he is more than marginally aware of, they reflect a growing concern for the ethics of a technological notion of otherness that can be traced back to the historical ground of the analogy itself: slavery.

Wiener would make this point clearer in "Some Moral and Technical Consequences of Automation." As he puts it, "the problem," of the use of "learning machines"—machines that can learn to read, play chess, evaluate complex situations, and function in warfare—"is a moral problem . . . very close to one of the great problems of slavery." Why is this a moral issue, if the machine is merely a machine, unless, of course, one believes that machines are capable of being much more than they are. In the section subtitled "Man and Slave," Wiener continues only to culminate in a reference to Samuel Butler, who will eventually become our focus:

> Let us grant that slavery is bad because it is cruel. It is, however, self-contradictory, and for a reason which is quite different. We wish a slave to be intelligent, to be able to assist us in the carrying out of our tasks. However, we also wish him to be subservient. Complete subservience and complete intelligence do not go together. . . . Similarly, if the machines become more and more efficient and operate at a higher and higher psychological level, the catastrophe foreseen by Butler of the dominance of the machine comes nearer and nearer.[21]

What this tells us is that the notion of a potentially sentient, cognizant, and affective machine draws attention to how cybernetics emerges out of an awareness of those questions of a black slave's humanity central to late nineteenth-century culture, knowledge, and politics in England and America. As Eglash puts it in another helpful essay, cybernetics as a "science of computation and control systems is merely a thin disguise for methods of social domination and control."[22] Wiener's words should serve to remind us that cybernetics was no "thin disguise" but was in fact quite cognizant of the social history behind its metaphors and analogies in a way that cybertheory hasn't always been.

Were Eglash to have been a historian of science fiction, he would most likely have acknowledged that engineers and scientists have long been great readers of that genre in which that "morally negative analogy" had been naturalized as a staple of human relationships with technology. To broaden the context of the master/slave analogy, then, is to move out of the realm of technohistory and science into the realm of literary history. It is to bring the history of race to bear on science fiction in the attempt at getting at how science itself functioned as subject to both. After all, that analogy had been present in the genres and tendencies that would coalesce into science fiction in between late

Victorianism and modernism, certainly by its first usage in Cape Town and in advance of cybernetics.

What will be argued here is that these genres operated with a remarkable political flexibility in that they were able to use one side of the analogy (machines) for the other (race) and therefore answer Eglash's questions as to how and why technology became racialized and then naturalized. The argument will also engage Aaron Worth's identification of "an important yet underexplored topic in Victorian studies," which is the function of "technologies in serving as prostheses of thought during the period."[23] In this period those meaning-making prostheses operated through familiar grammars of dominance that structured the master/slave analogy in technical language and would become the primary topoi of fin de siècle popular fiction on both sides of the Atlantic.

John Rieder has stated that "the complex mixture of ideas about competition, adaptation, race, and destiny that was in part generated by evolutionary theory, and was in part an attempt to come to grips with—or to negate—its implications, forms a major part of the thematic material of early science fiction."[24] That these ideas were generated largely in the wake of slavery and were in tandem with formal colonialism gives historical grounding to proto–Afrofuturist Greg Tate's influential comment that "being black in America is a science fiction experience."[25] Of course, one would want to expand this shared experience and its sensibilities beyond the borders of the United States: "Science fiction comes into visibility first in those countries most heavily involved in imperialist projects—France and England—and then gains popularity in the United States, Germany, and Russia as those countries also enter into more and more serious imperial competition."[26]

This coming to grips with or negating the implications of cultural dominance or regression in the genre as it begins to coalesce and emerge, usually manifests in narratives of or arguments about rampant immigration or race mixing. Or they were nightmare fantasies of racial revenge or natural or global calamity that achieved widespread popularity before H. G. Wells, whose work is well known for capturing a "Britain sprawling toward its imperial climax" complete with the "anxieties of decline," all before the formal birth (or naming) of science fiction.[27] One could throw a wide and helpfully imprecise net to capture a broad sense of the manifold expressions of these themes in the literature and popular culture of the time. It would include works ranging from any number of English gothic novels operating with the conventional "return of the repressed" mechanism, to more overt American texts like Thomas Dixon's *The Clansman* (1905), which would of course become notorious as the film *Birth of a Nation* (1915) by D. W. Griffith. This latter text should be remembered as a major attempt to technologize a modern form of black visual representation before the first "talkie," *The Jazz Singer,* with its minstrel apparatus that became dependent on innovations in sound technology. And in keeping with the previous chapter's concern with modernism, for good measure one could mention German historian Oswald Spengler's 1918 *Decline of the West* and American fanatic Lothrop Stoddard's 1922 *The Rising Tide of Color against White World-Supremacy.* None of these are science fiction, but they share a historical ambience—that "return of the repressed" cliché for one thing and, for another, that sense of the world gone mad in the wake of slavery's end, black cultural renaissance, and the increase in agitation against lynching and for greater participation in democracy.

With formal colonialism also on less secure footing, the works Rieder alludes to are indeed narratives of imminent racial and cultural catastrophe. Many arrive before the transformation into the so-called new imperialism of the 1880s that would see Europe focus more on cultural and economic control rather than on conquest and that would initiate the infamous "scramble for Africa." In England this literary self-fetishizing of decline would manifest in a spate of proto–science fictions that featured a "sensationalist cashing in on the genre's images of destruction and downfall" and an almost willy-nilly manufacturing of categories of otherness—like monsters, aliens, and machines—to represent and contain an increasing multitude of fears in the midst of a panoply of transformations.[28] In these fictions, Patrick Brantlinger has written, "the outward movement of imperialist adventure is reversed," and the positivist European subject suddenly victim to doubts, disease, madness, and death and reflecting an increasing suspicion that the empire was, if not materially in decay, becoming enough of a strain to affect the dark continents of European subjectivity.[29]

Given the overwhelmingly racist notion of cultural expansion that undergirded the popular fictions of imperialism, it is no accident or surprise that those narratives of decay and decline would also operate in racial terms. Though such fictions began earlier in the nineteenth century than acknowledged in the previous quoted passage, the most conspicuous and historically significant of these "regression fantasies" in England would include familiar texts like H. Rider Haggard's very influential *She* (1886–87), Robert Louis Stevenson's *Dr. Jekyll and Mr. Hyde* (1886), or H. G. Wells's *War of the Worlds* (1898), though the modernist capstone of this tendency toward self-fetishizing of decline as historical justice or racial revenge would eventually be *Heart of Darkness* (1901) by Joseph Conrad.[30] These anxieties of decline are, of course, also rooted in Darwinism, as those who had defined themselves as "the fittest" begin to question both the will and the moral rectitude of that self-definition. The economic viability and material bases of it also become less grounded in inevitability:

> The point to be emphasized here is not Darwin's own treatment of race per se but to note how it accords and sustains the overwhelming centrality of the racial issue in late nineteenth-century Europe. The sense of lesser breeds threatening a pure race, of Western civilization possibly facing spiritual decline as a result of racial mixture, and of the empire and civilization vanishing in the face of barbaric forces (admittedly, now both inner and outer) hangs palpably in the European air.[31]

Bruce Mazlish's implication here is that these anxieties are dependent on Charles Darwin's belief that evolution as a process is indifferent to "better" species or those ostensibly or self-marked as "superior." Roger Luckhurst complements this insight with another side of this fantasia: "Darwin's comforting promise that evolution was directed towards ever-increasing perfection was qualified later in the century by the observation that organisms could just as easily regress down as progress up the evolutionary ladder."[32]

Borrowing primarily from the important work of John Rieder, Patrick Brantlinger, and Roger Luckhurst, the particularities of this "European air" are linked in this analysis to a colonial context where abolitionism, mutinies, and the morally negative impact of slavery and empire begin to intrude on English fictions. This ranges from colonial adventure narratives to satiric utopias and "invasion scare" stories, which flourished in the decades straddling the nineteenth and twentieth centuries. All these nascent genres depend "on the anxieties consequent on the imperialist enterprise: the expected counter-attack, the dreaded regression, the threatening future, the unhuman."[33] Or, as Brantlinger defines the "Imperial Gothic," its three principal themes are "individual regression or going native; an invasion of civilization by the forces of barbarism or demonism; and the diminution of opportunities for adventure and heroism in the modern world."[34] Though the cult of degeneration was never as strong in the United States as it was in England, one could hardly find a better encapsulating of the primary themes of Stoddard, Dixon, and Griffith in the United States a generation or so later. In fact, they are also the primary themes of influential

American pulp/science fiction writers such as Edgar Rice Burroughs and Robert E. Howard.

Again, such concerns precede the late Victorian fictions focused on by Judith Wilt, in the previous chapter, and Brantlinger. When we go back a bit further to, say, Samuel Butler's *Erewhon* and its once rumored doppelganger, *The Coming Race,* by Edward Bulwer-Lytton (1871), the second of Brantlinger's themes would have to be either modified or appended. These are texts in which white civilization is faced with the discovery of vastly superior *other* races and civilizations whose potential to destroy or supersede Europe is rooted largely in the power and advancement of their "unhuman" and potentially sentient machines. They feature technologies so beyond human comprehension that they might as well be supernatural. Through narratives that reverse the racial and cultural status quo, these writers and others explored precisely what the early twentieth-century American race fanatics would fear, given their turn to a social Darwinism: that *other* races could or would or perhaps even should come to power. Though speaking of a contemporary context of digital technology and modern computing, Eglash grasps the semiparanoid tenor of these late nineteenth- and early twentieth-century fictions when he suggests a compensatory motive: "By referring to a master/slave relations in devices, professionals may reassure themselves that they will remain masters of machines."[35] This is arguably another reason the master/slave analogy took: it offered an enduring and nostalgic fantasy of racial control—in science no less—while the realities of power were becoming increasingly difficult to determine.

However, one needn't trace a genealogy of the "master/slave" so quickly over to a late imperial England (or pre-apartheid South Africa) and its fears of losing racial control and cultural centrality. Before discussing that context it's important to acknowledge its American resonance in slavery and in literature. The analogy had already been grounded in America far in advance of the 1923 translation of Čapek's *R.U.R.,* which Eglash rightly identifies as crucial to the general definition of "an autonomous device that obeyed its master."[36] He goes on to say that Čapek's fantasy is successful because it "ameliorates a tension between a desire for more autonomous machines"—progress—"and a desire to retain human mastery."[37] For white readers that tension operates in the language of early science fiction as a method of ameliorating the tension between more autonomous and indeed politically volatile blacks and a desire to retain mastery through whiteness *as metaphorically represented by technology.* "Regression fantasies" of the "Imperial Gothic" were most certainly shared in a country where formal slavery was still in place despite its anticolonial, revolutionary past, because "mastery" was increasingly questioned by abolitionism, slave escapes, and sporadic violence.

The obvious parallel between the Negro as a "device" and the machine as potentially "autonomous" can be traced back to American expressions of anxieties that weren't predicated on an explicit interest in slavery or race relations. It can also be found in those that seemingly evade it. The former would conspicuously include Henry Adams. As Leo Marx—who will less conspicuously represent the latter—tells us, Adams was perhaps more terrified of the implications of technology than Thomas Carlyle or a great many Victorians, from Charles Dickens to Samuel Butler. To clarify how those tensions or anxieties were, as Leo Marx argues, structuring for the evolution of American writing and thought, he quotes an 1862 letter from Adams to his brother Charles:

> Man has mounted science and is now run away with. I firmly believe that before many centuries more, science with be the master of man. The engines he will have invented will be beyond his strength to control. Some day science may have the existence of mankind in its power, and the human race commit suicide by blowing up the world.[38]

To the contemporary reader these words are so common as to be cliché. Even the most hardened viewer of B movie science fiction would find them trite, as would those for whom each development of technology brings with it the same redundant backlog of cultural fears and predictable responses. Without its necessary historical context one would probably place such a quote at the birth of the atomic age or after the devastation of Hiroshima and Nagasaki, when the possibility of "blowing up the world" becomes so terrifying a reality that it comes to dominate pulp science fictions and political conversations. Adams, like the English Victorians, was the product of a world where slavery and colonialism were concerns as powerful as a seemingly rampant industrialism, which threatened an America once prized as its alternative. Those issues were also the source of apocalyptic terror. At the start of the Civil War they were so threatening as to generate this hyperbolic image of planetary destruction far in advance of the actual technological capacity to do so. It is therefore legitimate to suggest that in Adams's language the master/slave, race/technology parallels partake of a shared social resonance, one strong enough to generate that level of hyperbole. Not impossible: Adams in his own words felt the dynamo as "a moral force, much as the early Christians felt the Cross."[39]

It's worth pointing out that for Adams, "mankind" and the "human race" are far more proscriptive than they might sound. He means, of course, whites, since the letter was written a year before the Emancipation Proclamation was ratified and three years before the end of Civil War. Blacks were not yet quite yet human, technically speaking, and were still in that liminal space between beast of burden, preindustrial machine, and possible citizen. Evident here is the fear that machines, essentially, would win the great evolutionary battle for supremacy. Because that battle is rooted in a vision of all-or-nothing civilizational otherness, it can be imagined and described only in racial terms.

The fear is most manifest in Adams's terror of the "dynamo," which can be traced back to Samuel Butler's *Erewhon* and "Darwin among the Machines," the section that was published nine years earlier in the wake of his first reading of *The Origin of the Species.* The "nightmare vision of race suicide" that Marx identifies in this passage is therefore far more in keeping with the apocalyptic colonial and racial comeuppance at work in the "Imperial Gothic" quasi genre. It is a particular deployment of the "return of the repressed" that H. G. Wells borrowed from the "Imperial Gothic" and bequeathed to a century of pulp exploitations.

MELVILLE'S MAN-MACHINE

In *The Machine in the Garden,* Leo Marx famously renders that tension between Adams's "dynamo" and the American pastoral ideal, a "great issue of our culture," one "waged endlessly in American writing ever since." That such a "great issue" and an "ancient war" endlessly waged could almost ignore slavery has got to be one of the most flabbergasting aporias of its time. Slavery comes to the fore of Marx's study only when he discusses ancient Greek slavery. He goes as far as to quote Carlyle's "force did for them, what machinery does for us" but immediately detours to a discussion of wage laborers in Britain rather than black slaves at home.[40] To use another word for *aporia,* it is certainly one of the most significant *evasions.* But it is his focus on that tension between the machine and the garden—technology and nature—that makes Leo Marx such an important resource. The racial politics of machines and nature had become naturalized into a kind of institutional common sense by the time of the work of Scottish astronomer Sir David Gill, whom Eglash claims was the first to use the term *master-slave* in 1904 to describe his sidereal clock designed for use at the observatory in South Africa. Eglash writes that the fight against the analogy was a "losing battle" because from then on the term "slave clock became increasingly common" and from there gave rise to its usage in circuitry, hydraulic cylinders, and, of course, digital computing.[41]

The master/slave, race/technology parallel isn't noticed in Marx because its naturalization was already so complete that the famed author of *The Machine in the Garden* could write so eloquently about Jeffersonian democracy and the impact of technology, for example, with little consideration of an American pastoral that was as dependent on the plantation system as it was on its own industrial anxieties. Jefferson's *Notes on Virginia* is a key text for Leo Marx; however, in it Jefferson famously prophesies that one of the repercussions of slavery would be imminent "convulsions," such as race war or the extinction of one race by another. So if "the machine" threatens "the garden," or "the garden" eventually pastoralizes the machine by "superimposing order, peace, and harmony upon our modern chaos" as it does in Marx's analysis, he is more right than he realizes when he perhaps too vaguely concludes his magisterial work with the proclamation that "the machine's sudden entrance into the garden presents a problem that ultimately belongs not to art but to politics."[42]

Henry Adams may have missed it, and Leo Marx may have evaded it. But no greater chronicler of nineteenth-century American anxieties than Herman Melville would technologize the master/slave analogy directly and attempt to render it racially intelligible. That a significant portion of America's experimentation in industry and technology was happening in New England places him very much in the midst of that chaos of terror and possibility. This historical context is well known and is expressed powerfully and allegorically in his magnum opus, *Moby-Dick,* hence Marx's attention to this work at the end of *The Machine in the Garden.* Granted, "race and slavery are not the major themes in *Moby-Dick*.... They form a discontinuously surfacing but always present undercurrent in the human relations represented in the novel."[43] But the reading of *Moby-Dick* as participating in racial coding has in fact become standard, certainly since Toni Morrison's famous interrogation of Melville in her 1988 "Unspeakable Things Unspoken: The Afro-American Presence in American Literature." Sadly, despite her highly influential analysis, her description of the "Africanist" presence as the "ghost in the machine" isn't particularly attuned to the full resonance of that productive technological cliché.[44]

Melville actually introduced an explicitly racial technopoetics in his work. It isn't done in *Moby-Dick,* which he wrote five years after, but in a story published decades before *Huckleberry Finn.* It is remarkable that this story isn't mentioned in *The Machine in the Garden* or in Morrison's essay. Well known to Melvillians, the short story is "The Bell-Tower" and was published in *The Piazza Tales* in 1856. Set in a more than slightly gothic European setting, for some time it has been read as an allegory of mid-nineteenth-century America in the wake of commercial locomotives, the sewing machine, mass production of various tools and items, and the emergence of a new class of industrial patrons.[45] Here the ghost in the machine is the explicit specter of slavery in the midst of technological change. Melville would even write in *Harper's Magazine* the same year that "machinery strikes strange dread into the human heart, as some living, panting Behemoth might."[46] To speak of industrialization in America was for him to simultaneously speak of the spectacle of black freedom in the context of racial revenge and white liberal fears of a justified revolution that was often narrated in sexualized terms. After all, it's not too far to suggest that machines are here analogized with the "panting" black male in late nineteenth- and early twentieth-century narratives for whom the first task of freedom was raping white women.[47]

"The Bell-Tower" is also an interesting supplement to Eglash because among other things it is about clocks, which, as Leo Marx reminds us, were the "favorite 'machine' of the Enlightenment" due to their linking of "the industrial apparatus with consciousness." Of course, that status as favorite machine came with a great fear of its implications. It subordinated "humans" to "an impersonal and seemingly autonomous system."[48] Michael Adas also references the "profound reorientation of time perception" that clocks would have on European subjectivity. He will go so far as to argue that the newly mechanized view of space and time had far more to do with how Africans were seen and judged than would increasingly biological notions of race.[49] In other words, a privileged relationship to a newly technologized sense of space and time was, in Adas's view, more determinative of cultural supremacy than the crude rhetoric or emergent science of skin.

In keeping with this horological history, "The Bell-Tower" makes clear its focus on time and technological mastery by a tale in which the "great mechanician," Bannadonna, is ultimately killed by his own automaton. Or, in Melville's own final words, it's a story in which a "blind slave obeyed its blinder lord; but, in obedience, slew him. So the creator was killed by the creature."[50] More important than Melville's use of time to signify how, as Leo Marx puts it, "the laboring man becomes a machine" is this fact of the "slave" killing its creator. That's certainly most important to Melville. And his death occurs accidentally: the machine isn't seeking revenge. It isn't even aware of its actions. The morality of the act is of a quality beyond human. But Melville doesn't render the meaning of the killing politically ambiguous, given how he frames the story and describes its characters. What makes the fairly conventional and predictable moral of the story resonant is the fact that Melville leads us through characteristically dense thickets of metaphor to get to that predictable conclusion. In those thickets he establishes strong and elaborate historical parallels between automata, industrialization, and slavery. Through them he charts the emergence of an America whose rise to global power would depend on its mastery of both machines and the domestication of their reproductive processes and the rise of what C. L. R James would identify in his legendary 1953 work on Melville, *Mariners, Renegades and Castaways,* as the modern totalitarian "type." For James, Ahab is an example of this type, whom Leo Marx would describe as "the perverted, monomaniac incarnation of the Age of Machinery."[51] James, however, in the work he began before *Mariners*—the brilliantly unfinished *American Civilization* (1950)—upsets the binary reading of Ahab as technology and the whale as an intransigent or perhaps resistant "nature." He sees in the whale "not a mere fish" but "the conquest of the air, the mastery of atomic energy" because in his time "the contact with Nature is so much more mechanized, complicated and scientific."[52] In other words, for James the whale is technology and its implications and Ahab its authoritarian product.

Leo Marx does discuss the moment in *Moby-Dick* where Captain Ahab jokingly orders an automaton from his blacksmith, Prometheus. For James this is a tellingly casual indictment of an imminent confluence of technology and power, not only for its time but also for a world shaped by the anxieties of a postwar fascism, where race and technology had rendered Melville's "ambiguity." As James writes of the automaton, "it is precisely this that is the aim of every totalitarian dictator—hundreds of millions of inhumanly strong, capable, technically efficient men with no heart to feel, without aspirations, except what their masters tell them."[53] Though slightly less monomaniacal and dictatorial than Ahab, Bannadonna is also a "totalitarian type," cut from the same cloth. Melville describes him as someone who "in firm resolve, no man in Europe at that period went beyond" and whose hubristic pride compared to those who fashioned the Tower of Babel.[54]

Melville establishes his belabored metaphoric and allegorical parallels to present in capsule form the interlinking of two of his great political and literary concerns. The story is "not only a rejection of technological progress but also a fearful response to that other contemporary phenomenon—the institution of Negro slavery."⁵⁵ To link those concerns at a time when they perhaps weren't so easily imagined as complementary, Melville presents his automaton and its creator thusly:

> He still bent his efforts upon the locomotive figure for the belfry, but only as a partial type of an ulterior creature, a sort of elephantine helot, adapted to further, in a degree scarcely to be imagined, the universal conveniences and glories of humanity; supplying nothing less than a supplement to the Six Days' Work; stocking the earth with a new serf, more useful than the ox, swifter than the dolphin, stronger than the lion, more cunning than the ape, for industry an ant, more fiery than serpents, and yet, in patience, another ass. All excellences of all God-made creatures, which served man, were here to receive advancement, and then to be combined in one. Talus was to have been the all-accomplished helot's name. Talus, iron slave to Bannadonna, and, through him, to man.⁵⁶

Melville's description of the automaton is without explicit racial elements. But in the story his specific interest in race is mediated by a longer historical interest in technology, free labor, and creation and production. For example, by naming the "iron slave" Talus, he traces it back to the legend of Talos, the giant bronze man of Greek mythology with lead for blood. Created by the gods to protect the island of Crete, histories of automata are incomplete without this reference.

But in this description of automata Melville gives us a parody of not only Greek and Christian creation myths but also the hubristic replacement of divine creation for a mechanized, secular vision of production. We are told, for example, that for Bannadonna "machinery" was "miracle," "Prometheus, the heroic name for machinist," and "man, the true God." He gives us also a vision of industrialism's gendered relationship to metaphors of labor or reproduction in which a masculinized system of creation suffers from a terrible case of womb envy. It is envy so terrible that the entire system of productivity, novelty, and power is rooted in a sexualized form of socioeconomic *ressentiment.* In the already well-worn language of a late nineteenth- and early twentieth-century expansionist mythos as well as mid-twentieth-century "mad scientist" cliché's, Bannadonna's goal is also "to solve nature, to steal into her, to intrigue beyond her, to procure someone else to bind her to his hand . . . to rival her, outstrip her, and rule her."⁵⁷ This is narrated alongside the desire to use technology to create a "serf" and a "helot," new subjects of domination that signify a long history of exploitation while existing in the story ultimately to negate the very process of their own creation (to kill their masters).

Melville's sexualizing of the industrial process is not unfamiliar in the need to see machines as an "other" within a grammar of dominance that fluctuates between gender and race. These differences alternately threaten or question a default self-identification of culture or civilization as male, white, and technologically driven. As John Rieder puts it in the context of the nineteenth century (and as the work of Haraway and so many others have embellished for the twentieth and twenty-first):

> Both gender and racial identity turn on the crucial pivot that articulates biological determination and cultural construction. Both involve the expression of identity in anatomy, on the one hand, and the performance of identity according to culturally and historically variable scripts, on the other. Race, like gender, poses the dual questions of the boundary that separates nature from artifice and the limits of human control over one's place and destiny in the world.[58]

In this regard, the "The Bell-Tower" is merely a continuation of another semi-famous minor story of Melville's. Published the same year, though not in *The Piazza Tales*, it's titled "The Tartarus of Maids." This story features a coherent if not systematic use of "sexual symbols to display the peculiar perversion and sterility of the factory system." It also depends on race, slavery, and the colonial exotic to make that sexualized point:

> Machinery—that vaunted slave of humanity—here stood menially served by human beings, who served mutely and cringingly as the slave serves the Sultan. The girls did not so much seem accessory wheels to the general machinery as mere cogs to the wheels.[59]

The relationship between servitude, racism, and power is of course explored more famously in the story "Benito Cereno," also in *The Piazza Tales*, a tale also known for its use of blackface minstrelsy. But race and the exotic play such a part in this story, not simply because of the use of the words *slave* and *sultan*, but in how they are intertwined. The parallel between machine and Negro is made clear by the description of technology as being generally like a slave. Women are now serving this slave much in the way that blacks serve the sultan. Women are supplementary "cogs" to the machine, not so much as accessories but secondary functions. Melville is much less vague in "The Bell-Tower." He makes the relationship between blacks and machines clear by way of the story's epigram, an enigmatic piece of poetry that introduces his cautionary fable and arguably defines it: "Like negroes, these powers own man sullenly; mindful of their higher master; while serving, plot revenge."[60]

Melville's story was published just three years before John Brown's raid on Harpers Ferry but the very same year Brown began his violent campaign to end slavery in the South. Also, the memory and cultural impact of the 1831 slave revolt led by Nat Turner was still strong in abolitionist circles. This is a period in which the myth of the black rapist as a necessary product of abolitionism had become standard in those years before the Civil War. It's fascinating to read the chain of power at work in this epigram. Machines are here likened to blacks that in this case are the true powers that own man—meaning whites, the only humans in this vision of creation. Yet black slaves serve a higher master, no doubt a divinity that guarantees them moral supremacy due to their victimization and inevitable retribution as they serve and plot sullenly and righteously.

There are other links between machines and black slaves in the story, which only explicitly mentions blacks or American slavery in those detached but insistent words. These links are admittedly small but seem much less so in the wake of that ponderous epigram. For example, when Bannadonna refers to his creation by name—a creature that has "no personality" despite having "intelligent features" and who was resolved to have not only "the power of locomotion" but also "the appearance, at least, of intelligence and will"—he equivocates, hesitates, corrects himself, and calls the creature "it" instead. And when the "iron slave" kills Bannadonna, there is a glimpse of its "manacled arms."[61] When facing a group of visiting magistrates, the creature is so uncanny to them that Bannadonna feels the need to assure them that the creature has no soul, an argument that was familiar enough during chattel slavery for it to be exploited here.[62] The ultimate point of these parallels and linkages between a history of automata and industrialism, chattel slavery, and creation is that despite the accidental nature of Bannadonna's death, there is some historical comeuppance at work. The violence is framed as retributive even though the "metallic stranger" is incapable of rancor or motive.[63]

It should be obvious to any serious reader that there is another significant antecedent to Melville's "The Bell-Tower" and its representation of automata, hubris, and faux-divine creation gone haywire. That is Mary Shelley's *Frankenstein; or, The Modern Prometheus* (1818). As Leo Marx points out, Frankenstein's monster was merely behind what became a more widespread set of tropes and clichés that would generate in America the "widespread and largely impotent anxiety generated by mechanization."[64] In other words, it is also significant to the history of the master/slave analogy. It is because of Shelley's creation that it would be possible to code "morally criminal" social and historical relationships like chattel slavery into the vernacular language of technology as an effect of those literatures that coalesced into science fiction at the height of cultural modernism.

For the sake of historical accuracy it should be emphasized that the racializing of automata occurred in the wake of this significant antecedent and its attention to labor and class, not the other way around. But it is also true, as many have pointed out, that Shelley's creation, like much of the writing and thought produced in its time, was influenced by multiple accounts of slavery in the transatlantic world, particularly in the wake of the Haitian Revolution.[65] Slavery was accompanied by slave uprisings and abolitionism, and Shelley herself was an abolitionist who went so far as to boycott sugar due to its connection to the slave trade.[66]

In Elizabeth Young's *Black Frankenstein: The Making of an American Metaphor,* it is the racializing of this figure of labor and class that "stands at the convergence of an Anglo-American equation between slavery and monstrosity, an American narrative about the founding of the white nation in filial revolt, and a consequent American tension between this founding narrative and the equally foundational presence of slavery." Would that she had explicitly added technology to her analysis of race, monstrosity, otherness, and American foundationalism, because it is quite obviously key to the very reading of what she calls an "American Prometheus: Victor Frankenstein as slave-owner." She does point out that Melville's "mechanical focus is consistent with popular versions" of Shelley's story just as "The Bell-Tower" is crucial in the translation of a romantic critique of reason and science within "the orbit of abolitionism."[67] Key to Melville's awareness of this antecedent is in his use of the name "Prometheus" in "The Bell-Tower," which Young calls an "adaptation" of *Frankenstein: The Modern Prometheus.* It most certainly is an adaptation. We know that Melville got a copy in London and also that there are a great many allusions to race and slavery in *Frankenstein.*[68]

In Young's reading, Melville's use of Shelley "indicts the slave-owner," whereas an ex-slave writer like Frederick Douglass ("echoed" also in the work of David Walker in his militant *Appeal to the Coloured Citizens of the World* of 1829 and resonating particularly in the era of Nat Turner) would use this racialized automaton "as an oppositional symbol of the African American slave, the American nation, and the conflicted relationship between them." In this Americanization the Frankenstein myth builds on the "uneven" but extant antiracist and anticolonial sympathies at work in Shelley's novel, which place the creature "within the slaveowning and colonial enterprises" and is critical of them but unable to transcend them, as most notably argued by Gayatri Spivak. Young makes clear that Douglass and Walker more than likely did not read Shelley's novel, but she argues for a "complex 'echolalia' between them," in which the popularization of the Frankenstein myth had already been so adaptable that its racialization was inevitable once it hit the United States.[69]

The Frankenstein myth and monster, the very racializing of automata that Young charts across a range of American cultural phenomena, had actually been constructed and deployed in Victorian England in far more explicit ways. The particular use of Shelley's mythic creation in mind here may have been published afterward, but "The Bell-Tower" is and has been one of *Frankenstein*'s most notable echoes. Also, it made a far greater impact and has had a far greater influence than Melville's work, because it is where machines are directly racialized for the first time and where the analogy between slaves and machines is employed to suggest an imminent and primary threat to white civilization.

The author in question here is Samuel Butler, and the book is *Erewhon; or, Over the Range,* called by some "the second great satire of the nineteenth century" after Jonathan Swift's *Gulliver's Travels*.[70] It is a work that has canonical status among science fiction writers due to "The Book of the Machines," which "originates the conceit by which machines develop intelligent capacities and enslave mankind."[71] Neither Butler nor *Erewhon* are mentioned in any of the frankly quite wonderful works on race and technology that has emerged in the wake of Donna Haraway's "A Cyborg Manifesto." John Rieder briefly mentions Samuel Butler in *Colonialism and the Emergence of Science Fiction.* He rates "The Book of the Machines" for its "attempt to parody Darwin by substituting machines for organisms" as an early attempt to "subvert profoundly the distinction between the natural and the artificial."[72] Surprisingly, its focus on race and slavery isn't discussed.

References to Butler and *Erewhon* are more common in histories of artificial intelligence and research outside the realm of literary criticism and cultural or critical race theory. Written as both a riposte to and a serious consideration of the implications of Darwin, Samuel Butler's machine creations needn't have been African or African American or even black to evoke the double anxieties of race and industrialism. It's unlikely that Butler was even thinking about slavery or the fate of the British Empire at all. His critiques were much more broadly civilizational and mobilized primarily against the values and standards of metropolitan British Victorian culture. Yet due to Butler's immediate colonial experience and the rich currents of religious and scientific conversation of which he was a part, race inevitably found its way into his vision of cultural decline, produced by and deployed against the political, philosophical and popular rhetoric of technological advancement. Race infected that vision so much that it could no longer be contained or controlled by analogy, at least not those of labor and class, as in *Frankenstein* or "The Bell-Tower."

In *Erewhon,* specifically in "The Book of Machines," the need to contain or repress the inhuman other produced by Europeans manifests in what Henry Adams's would see as a potentially retributive vision of race suicide. The fear of former slaves melds with the fear of machines in ways that establish the contours of the racial uncanny as a permanent feature of the response to technological change. More than any other text, *Erewhon* provides us with the origins of, if not the answers to, Eglash's questions.

EREWHON: LOST RACES AND MECHANICAL SOULS

In keeping with Judith Wilt's myth of generic beginnings as Victorian gothic changes into science fiction in "or around December, 1897," here is canonical science fiction historian Darko Suvin's origin moment: "If ever there was in the history of a literary genre one day when it can be said to have begun, it is May Day 1871 for U.K. SF." Though one hesitates in accepting any such declaration of generic origins, particularly with a genre such as science fiction, which was and is fed by so many streams, this date matters to this analysis because of the texts Suvin insists are at the genre's "May Day"—Bulwer-Lytton's *The Coming Race* and Samuel Butler's *Erewhon.* Suvin's origin date is more than twenty years before Wilt's periodization, and so it is the stretch of time in between them that is important. Appropriately, the date is rooted also in an increasing sense of cultural and economic anxiety:

> The reasons for this date of birth are complex, but there is no doubt that the immediate stimuli were the Franco-Prussian War and the Paris Commune of 1871, and in a more diffuse way the political regroupings in the U.K. attendant upon the 1867 suffrage reform. But . . . deeper reasons must be sought in a crisis of confidence in societal values and stability.[73]

For Suvin, the reasons behind the birth of this genre are not so much colonial or racial, despite his acknowledgement of a cultural crisis of confidence and a great concern about the very status of England in the comity of nations. His focus is on "the ideologies of various social groups in contemporary Britain, as they were trying to come to grips with and work upon the largely new historical force-field taking shape in their lived experience."[74] But those ideologies are easily drawn into conversation with race and colonialism since this was a period where "ideas of social emancipation were consonant in some quarters with ideas of national threat for the British," given the presence of race and empire in so many of the books emerging in this period.[75] Also, it is now over twenty years since Suvin's *Victorian Science Fiction in the UK* (1983), a work that continues to be controversial and problematic. The "stimuli" he stresses are now rarely discussed without reference to the kind of global shifts in power, culture, race, sex, and empire that are at the center of this analysis, even within continental Europe.

That day in question is when Samuel Butler, a returning colonial from the settler colony of New Zealand, delivered the manuscript of *Erewhon; or, Over the Range* to his publishers in London. What makes this day so significant for Suvin is because it was also the day that two other texts appeared. George Tomkyns Chesney's *The Battle of Dorking: Reminiscences of a Volunteer* was published, a now barely remembered but important precursor to the work of H. G. Wells and the first of that subgenre of Victorian pulp writing, called either "invasion scare" or "future war" fictions, that lasted until around World War I. These are narratives in which England or Europe is attacked and invaded by unspecified or alien forces. The stories are as much focused on the terrors of externality and a sudden victimization as they are on critiquing the current state of internal structures of culture, class, power, or national unity and their impact on the possibility of resistance. That they also exploit the reality or terror of decline is an obvious factor. The "alternate history" subgenre of science fiction can be traced back to Chesney's novel.

Chesney was deeply involved in exploiting that late imperial zeitgeist in popular fiction and the increasing loss of confidence in empire that fed the heightened sense of external and internal threats. Patrick Brantlinger points out that the shift in the Victorian intelligentsia from a more blindly positive view of empire to one more ambivalent, if not negative, had a series of quite material sources: for example, the Morant Bay Rebellion in 1865 (known in England as the Jamaica Rebellion or the Governor Eyre Controversy), an almost continuous set of "troubles" in Ireland, and the Indian Mutiny or Rebellion of 1857, also known as India's first war of independence.[76] This latter event is exploited in Chesney's novel of 1876, titled *The Dilemma,* which narrates its romantic melodrama against the quite sensationalized backdrop of the Indian Rebellion.

The Dilemma reminds us that the anxieties behind these various historicizing gestures—alternate or imaginative—were no mere paranoia. They exploit the presence of slave revolts, abolitionism, and the turn to resistant violence in the struggle against slavery in the United States. "Darwin among the Machines," for example, was produced in historical and geographic proximity to the New Zealand (or Waikato) Wars that took place from 1845 to 1872 between British-backed settler colonists and the indigenous Maori, who provided armed resistance to the encroachment on traditional lands. Butler's very arrival coincided with the Invasion of Waikato that in 1863 brought more British troops to New Zealand than anywhere in the world. It is therefore necessary to read in *Erewhon*'s vision of utopia and its English self-critique quite material fears of European destabilization much in the way white anxieties of black freedom would manifest in the literatures and cultural phenomena of late nineteenth-century America.[77]

The third text in this triumvirate of generic self-recognition published also on that fateful day in 1871 is Edward Bulwer-Lytton's *The Coming Race,* a book so similar to Butler's that it was often assumed to be the work of the same author. Many in fact assumed *Erewhon* was its sequel. This confusion frustrated Butler, even though both authors published their respective visions of utopia anonymously and despite the fact that Bulwer-Lytton's text was so successful that it inflated Butler's sales—at least until Butler was announced the author.[78] Bulwer-Lytton, after all, had the greater literary reputation. As a best-selling author, in his time he was second only to Charles Dickens. Mary Shelley thought him a "magnificent writer" capable of being "the first author of the age" years before *The Coming Race* was published.[79] His politics were also significant. Bulwer-Lytton was secretary for the colonies in 1858 and had an aggressively expansionist imperial agenda.[80] History, however, has been on the side of Butler because Bulwer-Lytton's novel would eventually be remembered due to Butler's mentioning of it in his preface to the second edition of *Erewhon*.[81]

Because the similarities between these two books are so telling, they are both necessary to understand how race and machines first came together in English literature in the years following P. T. Barnum and Joice Heth and in the wake of *Frankenstein,* particularly through the trope of the "lost race," one of the most enduring and prolific fantasy and science fiction tropes of all time. John Rieder describes this motif as one "where a traveler or group of travelers encounters a previously isolated race or civilization in an exotic, nearly inaccessible setting." He historicizes it thusly: "From around 1870 to World War I, there were two major strains of the lost-race motif. One, drawing largely on utopian and satiric traditions, ran from Samuel Butler's *Erewhon* (published in 1872) to Charlotte

Perkins Gilman's *Herland* in 1915. The other, more commercially successful and numerically predominant strain of lost-race fiction ran from H. Rider Haggard's attempt to out-do Robert Louis Stevenson's adventure fiction in *King Solomon's Mines* (1885), to Arthur Conan Doyle's attempt to out-Haggard Haggard in *The Lost World* in 1912."[82]

Bulwer-Lytton's novel features the discovery of a superior and technologically advanced subterranean lost race in England who pose a threat to an "inferior" Britain. It concludes not only with the terror of racial submission to "our inevitable destroyers" but the attendant fears of miscegenation.[83] Butler's novel features the discovery of a superior and technologically advanced lost race in colonial New Zealand who so feared the imminent power and superiority of a race of their own creation—machines—that they outlawed them after a cataclysmic war between political parties on the side of or against machines. Bulwer-Lytton's novel features the standard optic of classic utopian fiction as the white hero is introduced to a strange new world with values, mores, and opinions meant primarily to mark a parodic contrast to the standards of Victorian England. So does Butler's.

Most important, the two novels have in common a dual politics of race. On the one hand we have the lost race encountered by the narrator-hero and on the other we have the presence of another servile and emergent group—machines. So much science fiction is indebted to the complex space in between these two books and their intertwined legacies. But how both writers arrive at their representation of extreme otherness in the broader attempt to critique their own societies is immensely valuable. In fact, how they titillate their readers with the spectacle of submission to an other, of an imminent political reversal, and a strongly moral sense of historical comeuppance is what makes Suvin's origin date historically more resonant (but not necessarily more accurate) than Wilt's. But because it occurs earlier, Suvin's date shows just how rich was this literary seam in the years until H. G. Wells, who generally gets solitary credit for mining it with his classic *War of the Worlds* in 1898.

Since race is tertiary to Suvin and secondary to Wilt and hasn't featured much in the criticism of mid and late Victorian proto–science fiction—even Brantlinger and Rieder spend little time detailing how racism works in the histories and texts they bring to bear or engage in much critical work on race— we can reframe the conversation about cultural anxieties and representation, technology, and genre. We should reframe them in a context engaged in race as well as in rethinking that long period sketched by these and other critics.

Because despite the fact of the telling generic classification of lost race, not much thought or research has been spent exploring the genre's actual racial politics. Even Rieder's treatment of it is primarily about its fetish for maps and cartography. Little thought has been given to the quite curious fact that *race itself* would be so prominent in the stories that the fact of *multiple races* would become structural to the genre, particularly in America since the lost-race motif eagerly crossed the Atlantic early in the twentieth century, helping to establish American science and fantasy fictions in an era of segregation, primitivism, and racial violence. The genre's very fetishizing of race and its overwhelming obsession with ethnic, social, and cultural differences reflects and refracts its historical period. It was a period, after all, defined by slavery, colonialism, segregation, evolution, and various modes of racial thinking, from the quasi-scientific—as in the legitimizing of ethnography—to the nationalistic.

Though quite varied in intent and application, the lost-race genre was essentially based on the discovery or revelation of peoples who have been forgotten or thought to be extinct or who have never been known to history. Again, the genre operates in "a fictional community whose history develops in radical isolation from the author's known world" and "can be used to show us a cognitively strange new relationship in sociopolitics . . . in technology . . . in biology . . . or in other matters."[84] Cross-cultural comparison is the point here, racial and ethnic comparisons as well as the drawing out of sexual and sociopolitical differences in Conan Doyle, Butler, Bulwer-Lytton, Haggard, and eventually in America with Robert E. Howard and Edgar Rice Burroughs, who explicitly depend on those earlier British writers. Lost-race narratives were also intimate with and authorized by what would be eventually called anthropology. For example, they focused on the discovery of various tribes and cultures and civilizations that immediately functioned in the ethnographic imagination of American and European imperial expansion, due to the genre of colonial travel writing and narratives of exploration that were immensely popular in the nineteenth century.

In lost-race books, however, race functions in most cases to narrate cultural and political decline or cultural opposition in explicitly racial terms in that period where biological notions of race were beginning to ossify in the scientific literature and in the politics of empire and slavery. As is clear in both Butler and Bulwer-Lytton, these races were either primitive or more sophisticated, but if they were the latter they had long past their prime as civilizations—race being of course a metonym for culture. As such, they presented the spectacle of what was facing or could face the West at the dawn of a new century (or what faced England with the prospect of an American century driven by its rapidly growing technological power, something very much at work in *The Coming Race*).

In American pulp fictions the terror of specifically black difference and the spectacle of black autonomy are so terrifying as to demand white male dominance and mastery in ways perhaps more intense than in Butler, Bulwer-Lytton, or Haggard. Such assertions of power are always set against a kaleidoscope of lost or ancient or hidden peoples, tribes, and races, almost all structured according to a hierarchy and a racial status quo eerily in line with that of the author's time. For example, the subgenre arguably reached its apogee with Edgar Rice Burroughs, famous creator of "Tarzan of the Apes" and "John Carter of Mars." Both characters first appeared in serial form in 1912, with the former appearing in a novel in 1914 and the latter in 1917. More than anyone else Burroughs shows the zeal with which a racist pulp readership took to the notion of lost races and exotic peoples. The fairly obvious racial politics of the Tarzan series have long been controversial, but the "Barsoom" (or Mars) series feature a fervent race consciousness that makes the Tarzan series seem tame. With its always detailed array of red, yellow, green, black, and, of course, white Martians, the races projected in outer space far outnumber those found deep in the heart of his fantasy Africa:

> He set his novels in impossible or improbably places, identified with ultra-exotic locales, whether Mars or Venus or the depths of darkest Africa, the kinds of unexplored spaces where the creative imagination may roam at will without fear of contradiction by verisimilitude-bound critics. Who was to say, in 1912, that there was no life on Mars, the setting for his first published (and immediately successful) novel, and who was to deny in the age of Kipling and H. Rider Haggard that a white infant could be raised up to be a king among anthropoid apes and discover lost cities in the African jungle?"[85]

Burroughs would even invent a race of "synthetic men" of Mars in 1940, just when the rainbow had been exhausted. Burroughs is the most important link between the "Imperial Gothic" and an America where the genre of science fiction would ultimately be named: "Not only did Burroughs acknowledge the primacy of the western scene even while bidding it farewell, but he projected the American imperial (and protective) zeal into outer space, making of Mars what Theodore Roosevelt had made of the western hemisphere, a ward of the United States."[86]

Perhaps the only American writer who would come close to Burroughs's focus on races—lost or invented ones—is Robert E. Howard, most famous for "Conan the Barbarian." Despite having a limited interest in the wider racial politics of primitivism and the genre, Howard strove to "reinvent Burroughsian futuristic primitivism," as Roger Luckhurst aptly describes.[87] Not only did Howard invent a timeless icon that would outdo Tarzan's primitivism and savagery, but he would practically invent the Sword and Sorcery subgenre. Though his oeuvre ranged wider than even Burroughs's, his entire Hyborian mythos was set within a lost continent littered with ancient civilizations and lost races. It could be no accident that his lost continent was curiously identical to maps of the African continent. There are kingdoms of Asgard and Zingara, Iranistan and Ophir, Kushites and peoples of the Empire of Zembabwei, to name just a few. Howard worked hard to cram into the continent of Africa every race, culture, history, and civilization known to modern times and more than a handful of those that range from myths and legends to those on the border of fiction and the occult.

In addition to the legitimate cross-cultural curiosity that had driven expansionist narratives from the era of explorers such as Richard Burton and John Speke, another motive behind lost-race books is made much clearer in these American texts that worked to present the spectacle of racial differences and cultural differentiations in a world after slavery yet still defined by colonization. In both Burroughs's and Howard's work there is a tremendous enthusiasm for the license to generate new cross-cultural comparisons in the name of race. These fictions function as a kind of pulp ethnography driven by the old imperial gaze but tempered by the knowledge that the gaze was now limited, questioned and so increasingly imaginative. In Burroughs, for example, even in *Tarzan,* there is a far greater sense of wonder at racial and cultural differences than there was in the era of British colonial adventure narratives. This is clear in the absolute glee in his relentlessly naming, describing, and "discovering" new races, civilizations, and peoples. Just in this series there are more distinct African tribes than can be listed here: different tribes of apes; people from Opar, the lost colony of Atlantis, or from the lost city of Xuja; the lost races of Ho-don and Waz-don in the prehistoric lost valley of Pal-ul-don; the lost empires of Minunia; the people of the world of Pellucidar, deep in the earth's core in flagrant homage to *The Coming Race;* the lost cities of Ivory and Gold; or Athair, the lost city of diamonds. This list can continue even without Burroughs's commitment to detailing the stereotypical national differences between the French, English, Germans, and Americans.

In the wake of these writers, lost-race narratives gave way to the various sub-

and microgenres of science fiction—and its obsession with aliens—and fantasy. This is certainly the case by the mid-twentieth-century work of J. R. R. Tolkien, who popularized the use of race to structure difference and cultural typologies in his fiction. The blurring of morality and species in his fiction (and the South African context of his work) has long led to charges of racism, despite his own very clear antiracism and his very strong hostility to Adolf Hitler and Nazi race science and their actual interest in his work.[88] But it is that rampant fetishizing of difference that drives those charges that have attended his legacy from its inception to the most recent film adaptations—that and his overdependence on race to describe cultural and civilizational differences, particularly while making clear his deep hostility to industrialization, demonized in his work as a dark force that poses lighter races against darker and sometimes hybrid, magically constructed ones.

Suvin's vague description of "other matters" in lost-race texts may actually include representations of alternative social organizations *as* racial formations, as is typical in both utopian fictions as well as colonial travel narratives. Race, however, is at the far extreme of Suvin's concerns, but he does point out "as a historical genre, the lost-race tale uses instead (and on the contrary) uncouth combinations of tribal, slave-owning, and feudal societies, usually with a beautiful princess and wicked high priest in trio with the virtuous white explorer-protagonist. This nostalgia of primitivism has been highly influential in the historical development of SF."[89] Of course, none of this is unfamiliar in the Tolkien mythos. It is no surprise that Tolkien read *Erewhon* and subscribed wholeheartedly to its anxieties about industrialization.[90]

The Coming Race incorporates so many nineteenth- and early twentieth-century notions of race or human difference, from phrenology to craniometry to skin color typology and all that would coalesce into eugenics, that it boggles the mind that this text and other lost-race texts haven't been explored in the context of race and slavery. Suvin argues that what made Bulwer-Lytton stand out from his peers in the emergent genre of Victorian science fiction was in fact "his remarkable anticipatory intuition of the shifts in his readers' ideological nuances and preoccupations."[91] This intuition of his readers' profound racial anxieties is evident in a letter Bulwer-Lytton wrote to his publisher:

> The only important point is to keep in view the Darwinian proposition that a coming race is destined to supplant our races, that such a race would be very

gradually formed, and be indeed a new species developing itself out of our old one, that this process would be invisible to our eyes, and therefore in some region unknown to us. And that in the course of the development, the coming race will have acquired some peculiarities so distinct from our ways, that it could not be fused with us, and certain destructive powers which our science could not enable us to attain to, or cope with.[92]

This letter merely summarizes the conclusion of the novel, where our narrator reflects back on the world he has escaped, but knowing that in fact it is a world to come:

Only, the more I think of a people calmly developing, in regions excluded from our sight and deemed uninhabitable by our sages, powers surpassing our most disciplined modes of force and virtues to which our life, social and political, becomes antagonistic in proportion as our civilisation advances,—the more devoutly I pray that ages may yet elapse before there emerge into sunlight our inevitable destroyers.[93]

It is a particularly late Victorian and early modernist conceit to find at the end of one's explorations the source of one's own extinction. It's a positively Conradian sense of negation: "the nightmare of being swallowed by the world's dark places has as its obverse side the solipsistic fantasy of swallowing the whole world."[94] Recall Henry Adams's hyperbolic apocalypse. Think also of H. G. Wells's *War of the Worlds*, that famously dark satiric reversal of the colonial enterprise. The focus in the latter passage on "a people" who will inevitably become resistant as a colonial civilization spreads, on a different "race" able to actually defeat and replace Europe, is also not far from Melville's conclusion in "The Bell-Tower."

That racial supplantation and civilizational reversal are inevitable in *The Coming Race* is linked to them being destined by evolution in Bulwer-Lytton's letter to his publisher. Science then became the materializing of morality. The idea that "the coming race" would be so distinct that there would be no possibility of fusion must be isolated because it is this sense of radical opposition and species distinction within the category of human—an ultimately racial one—that is recontextualized as forms of blending by cyberpunk literature, cybertheory, and Caribbean creolization.

But as with all such talk of new species emerging out of old ones, racial replacement and the anxieties of mixture and decline, it is unsurprisingly narrated through miscegenation. This is at work in *The Coming Race* between the white hero who naturally submits to his obvious superiors and the dominant female of the lost race, the Vril-ya, reminding us that with pulp social, racial, or cultural reversals almost always hinge on sexual ones. Note this early description of the peoples our narrator discovers under the earth. Sitting around him with "the gravity and quietude of Orientals," they have "sphinx-like faces, with the deep dark eyes and red man's colour; above all, the same type of race—race akin to man's, but infinitely stronger of form and grander of aspect, and inspiring the same unutterable feeling of dread."[95] One could easily supplant "dread" for the uncanny but nevertheless see in this a world of fin de siècle racial and cultural differentiations alongside the reversal of the extant colonial status quo. The white hero after all is not just subject to their gaze; he is to them a combination of curio and pet.

The closest thing to dramatic tension in the novel—beyond that relentless and overblown feeling of dread and anxiety as the gothic mutates into science fiction—is when our hero from the inferior white race is chosen by the female of the race, Gy-ei, as the women are called. This union encounters a society that does *not* allow miscegenation for fear that it will weaken the Vril-ya. This racism occurs despite us learning in the novel that the Vril-ya and humans (whites) are descended from the same Aryan stock and despite the novel's fairly heavy-handed comparison of these race and sex laws to those regarding blacks in America.[96] Our hero is forced to escape back to the surface to save his life, though he makes it clear that it is only a reprieve, given the inevitability of the emergence of the race that is coming.

Much of the relationship between our narrator and the in/super-human woman in the text, however, is hardly romantic or even sexual. It is described through fear and anxiety since the choice-less and weak white male hero (whose lack of name renders him even more vulnerable and open to the surrogacy of the audience) faces a race whose children are powerful enough to wipe out entire human populations. His very presence in the subterranean world is meant to provide white readers with a sense of historical reversal and a political submission spiked with a frisson of the sexual, and so when he escapes with the help of the Vril-ya woman Zee, the reader is far from heartbroken.

This shift in the popular literature from narratives of racial superiority to those of doubt, regression, and cultural backsliding would have precisely the aforementioned sexual repercussions: "After the mid-Victorian years the British found it increasingly difficult to think of themselves as inevitably progressive; they began worrying instead about the degeneration of their institutions, their culture, their racial 'stock.'"[97] This shift is clear in the work of one writer who spans both of these tendencies and was the most popular and influential writer of this period: H. Rider Haggard, who Suvin rightly describes as the "codifier" of the lost-race genre and who makes the work of Edgar Rice Burroughs possible.[98] Bulwer-Lytton was a major influence on Haggard, the latter having first read *The Coming Race* in, of all places, colonial Africa.[99]

As is well known, Haggard's use of the lost-race trope in *She* and in *King Solomon's Mines* was grounded in the European disbelief that the great city of Zimbabwe, discovered in 1871, could have been built by Africans and so had to be the product of a lost race of some European or lighter extraction.[100] Much of the lost races of the Tarzan series maintains that suspicion. *She* is also set in an underground world, as is, by the way, Jules Verne's *Journey to the Center of the Earth*, translated also in 1871 and, along with *Erewhon* and *The Coming Race,* a part of a number of "hollow earth" fictions inspired by fanciful but erroneous ideas present in early nineteenth-century geology (the most notable culprit of the hollow-earth theory being the American John Cleves Symmes Jr.). As mentioned before, Burroughs would exploit the hollow-earth setting in 1929 with *Tarzan at the Earth's Core.* That text was only a crossover novel to tie in the character Tarzan with an entire series of seven novels set in Pellucidar, the lost interior world beneath the earth's crust, which he published from 1914 to the one published posthumously in 1962.

But there is a crucial difference between Haggard's two most influential works that speaks to changes in the language of empire as it comes to bear on the genre that will be exploited past its sell-by date in Burroughs. There is a clear and profound difference, for example, between the hypermasculine colonialist jingoism of *King Solomon's Mines* and the sexual and political insecurities of *She*. *King Solomon's Mines* may have promised an earlier imperial vision of adolescent male fantasy, conquest, and a world of natives split between the inhuman and the noble. *She*, however, was the "Imperial Gothic" by rote, featuring "the expected counter-attack, the dreaded regression, the threatening future, the unhuman," with a soupçon of concern and anxiety for the "New Woman" of late Victorian feminism (it's worth remembering the titular character's full, official honorific is *She-Who-Must-Be-Obeyed*).

In *She* the titular character makes plans to travel to London to claim the throne from Queen Victoria and conquer the British *and then* all other empires. This plan to colonize Britain is made even clearer as a subplot in the sequel published almost twenty years later, *Ayesha: The Return of She* (1905). This is the novel where we are first famously told something that we now easily associate with either Benedict Arnold in the context of nationalism or Salman Rushdie in the context of postcolonial exile: "My Empire is of the imagination."

Haggard would emphasize the magical, whereas Bulwer-Lytton would the technological and in fact subordinate the former to the latter—hence the presence of Vril in *The Coming Race,* which powers everything from flying vehicles to all manner of technology and which became so influential in British popular culture that the word is at the source of a still common meat-extract energy drink called Bovril (the word being a combination of Bovine and Vril). Vril also became central to an entire underground of pre-Nazi race pseudoscience rumored to have had some impact on the Third Reich. This racist impact was only after Helena Blavatsky and the theosophist movement—also influences on Jean Toomer—claimed Vril as a real spiritual force. From them it would disseminate in the subterranean world of occultism and those committed to ancient lost races and civilizations like Atlantis. Crucial here is the belief that Vril was a technological power, or at least a source of energy, as is the case in *The Coming Race.*

This brings us to another reason *The Coming Race* was so easily confused for *Erewhon:* the presence of automata, or anthropomorphized machines. Though not central to the narrative, and deliberately taken for granted as secondary presences, automata in Bulwer-Lytton are domestic slaves. David Seed points out that though automata had been produced and manufactured since the previous century, it was in the nineteenth century that they began to be seen less as distractions, curios, and display items than as laborsaving devices. In *The Coming Race* there "is no suggestion of the opposition between humans and machines that was emerging in nineteenth-century science fiction and that was to become a major theme in the genre." Seed does acknowledge that they do function in Bulwer-Lytton as an "underclass."[101]

This idea of there being as yet no opposition between humans and machines should be kept in mind, alongside Bulwer-Lytton's notion that the "coming race" would be one with no possibility of "fusion" between them and humans. We are, after all, talking about metonyms for race and class in the years just after slavery, when sexual and social oppositions were described as natural, not political. But most tellingly common in Seed's otherwise helpful introduction to Bulwer-Lytton's novel is its discussion of race, automata, and "racial displacement" without reference to the racial politics of the late nineteenth century. He discusses Melville's "The Bell-Tower" as a "parable of automation taking over the role of a human workforce," yet there is no reference to Melville's antislavery themes and that very explicit poetic epigram.[102]

Just as Melville would evoke "soul" to describe automata, so would Bulwer-Lytton far in advance of W. E. B. DuBois and Karel Čapek. Seed is right to have pointed out that in Bulwer-Lytton the relationship between automata and the Vril-ya is nonproblematic; however, in the description of new machines we find ourselves eavesdropping on an old conversation emerging from, as Norbert Wiener would have it, new analogical relationships. Bulwer-Lytton writes,

> If a heap of metal be not capable of originating a thought of its own, yet through its internal susceptibility to movement, it obtains the power to receive the thought of the intellectual agent at work on it; and which, when conveyed with a sufficient force of the vril power, is as much compelled to obey as if it were displaced by a visible bodily force. It is animated for the time being by the soul thus infused into it, so that one may almost say that it lives and it reasons. Without this we could not make our automata supply the place of servants.[103]

The parallels between industrial age queries about automata and contemporary questions of artificial intelligence are so clear in this passage that one wonders why so many tend to root these concerns in that mid-twentieth-century generation of Wiener, Marshall McLuhan, and eventually science fiction's new wave or in the generation of cyberpunk. The racial parallels are even stronger, here and in "The Book of the Machines." Because what stands out are the parallels between that interrogation of whether machines can think and operate independently and those questions that asked whether the black slave was "capable of originating a thought of its own" or was simply "compelled to obey" or if Africans had the capacity to "reason" or were even in possession of souls.

As with *R.U.R.*, soul, reason, volition, and agency bring us finally to *Erewhon*. The connections and ideas latent in the "Imperial Gothic" and displayed in Bulwer-Lytton's *The Coming Race* become clearer there. They are in fact theorized by Butler, having developed them over his time in New Zealand as a sheep farmer, casual racist, and middling-to-fervent settler colonist. James Smithies provides a context for how "Darwin among the Machines" establishes the geographic and intellectual assumptions behind what would become *Erewhon*:

Consequently, perhaps, "Darwin Among the Machines" is rich with a sense of wonder at the "evolution" of machinery; just as the giant New Zealand moa had come and gone, perhaps, so too might mankind be superseded by machines. . . . Articulated in Butler's writing by way of a meditation upon machine culture, the topic prefigured New Zealanders' fascination with eugenics in the 1920s. . . . Viewed in this context, Butler's dawning machine philosophy suggests a creative interpenetration between the familiar tropes of Victorian racialism and colonial futurism.[104]

That colonial racialism and futurism are interlinked as early as this is a point necessary as much to contemporary cyber and postcyber theory as to Afrofuturism; that a machine philosophy emerged in the midst of antipodean colonialism is a necessary corrective to the explicit focus on machine aesthetics usually located in European and American modernism. As absurd as it might have seemed upon publication, where it was dismissed as a satire, a joke, or an attack on evolution, "it was reflective of a sometimes playful, sometimes deep-seated concern throughout Victorian society about the rational implications of Darwin's theory when expressed in the context of the machine-age."[105] Upon reading it, Charles Darwin was surprised by the fact that it was written in a colony due to his assumption that in such a place only "material interests" would have mattered to its author.[106] However, as Haggard, Burroughs, and many others would emphasize, colonies were as much spaces of imaginative projection as they were of material exploitation.

It cannot be stressed enough that Butler's vision of utopia and the impact of technology was produced "in a nascent colonial society where pastoralism undoubtedly reigned, but where modernity was impacting with obvious and increasing force," one in which open warfare between settlers and indigenous Maori was occurring. It was a troubled utopia. Race and technology met there in violently nonmetaphoric ways: "few places in the world could have offered a more stark reminder of the complex relationships between nature and technology" than colonial New Zealand.[107] The only comparable place one could imagine at that time, as Leo Marx would surely agree, would have been the Deep South or the Western frontier of the United States. All these spaces were in part product of that "utopian myth of idyllic expansion" underwritten by the material and technological facts of colonial domination.[108]

In the colony Butler "found a dominant ironic metaphor for his satire on Victorian English values, and so created an imagined world where churches are banks, invalids are criminals, and universities teach unreason. Reversal, absorbed into his imagination as he looked back on his New Zealand years, is the essential strategy of *Erewhon.*"[109] Reversal is clearly at work in the novel, but also historical retribution, which is something easy to mistake for justice. So where the quasi-nuclear and fully mechanized utopia in *The Coming Race* had stabilized any potential social or sexual tensions by way of an omnipotent Vril power, Butler presents a nontechnological society five hundred years after a traumatic uprising that occurred due to fears of an imminent machine intelligence and artificial life. In this utopia machines have been left present only as a testament to the Erewhonians' ideological commitment to highly developed academic philosophies of "Inconsistency" and "Evasion." Butler's satire of the British intellectual world he had left behind is comparable to Jonathan Swift's. In the wake of that uprising technology is branded a disease, and disease is treated as crime just as the sick are punished and imprisoned. It is telling that Butler calls the uprising a "Civil war" one year into the American conflict. He also names it a "revolution," and it caused the deaths of approximately one half of the population.

Upon arrival, our ethnocentric narrator assumes immediately that they are a backward people, seeing them much as Butler himself saw the Maori. James Smithies writes,

> Butler's attempts to describe the antipodean Other . . . and his subsequent engagement with evolutionary and machine theory were always informed by a broader imperial discourse to which he had easy access. The "explorer," "scientist," "colonist," "tourist" and "financial speculator" tropes were all in widespread use, and there is every reason to assume that Butler's stay in the antipodes brought these to the surface. Add to this the discursive framework provided by philosophical materialism and the global excitement offered by the industrial revolution, and the creative context behind *Erewhon; or, Over the Range* becomes clear.[110]

The tropes that Butler draws from, by the way, are also central to colonial adventure fiction and the fantasies of colonization and exploration that grew out of them and mutated into science fiction. After all, the figures of the explorer, scientist, colonist, and tourist are present in most of those narratives, ranging from Haggard's work to Arthur Conan Doyle's Haggardian colonial adventure, *The Lost World* (1912). These figures are present even in African American novelist Pauline Hopkins's 1903 *Of One Blood,* where the lost-race myth was used to advance an African American exceptionalism that lent credence to the ethnocentric notion that continental Africans couldn't function in modernity without elite black American guidance. In its description of the superior science fictional machines of this lost race of blacks she also manages to support the faulty notion that cultural and racial value could be or should be evaluated through technological indices.[111]

Another important genre at work in Butler's "staging of an alien cultural encounter" that is as crucial to the legacy of colonialism as it is to science fiction is ethnography, which in the case of *Erewhon* becomes explicitly a "mock-ethnography."[112] But our narrator realizes that the Erewhonian lack of technology is in fact a choice, a quite powerful statement in the context of a Victorian industrialism developing so fast that it no longer seemed possible to be reigned in by human intentions or state-sponsored economic or social initiatives. Indeed, it began to take on a life and historical force of its own, hence the need to personify or humanize it as a way of containing it at least symbolically:

> What was the meaning of that room full of old machinery which I had just seen, and of the displeasure with which the magistrate had regarded my watch? The people had very little machinery now.... They were about as far advanced as Europeans of the twelfth or thirteenth century; certainly not more so. And yet they must have had at one time the fullest knowledge of our own most recent inventions. How could it have happened that having been once so far in advance they were now as much behind us? It was evident that it was not from ignorance. They knew my watch as a watch when they saw it; and the care with which the broken machines were preserved and ticketed, proved that they had not lost the recollection of their former civilization. (53)

The impact of his watch—again, what Leo Marx called the favorite machine of the Enlightenment—should bring to mind the previous conversation about Melville's "The Bell-Tower" and Ron Eglash's focus on clocks as that which generated the master/slave dialectic in technical language.

Our narrator's immediate judgment of Erewhonians recalls Michael Adas's argument that more so than race, comparative technological development functioned as the primary barometer for hierarchizing cultural differences in the nineteenth century. This moment in the novel confirms that the use of technological comparisons cross-culturally was a process in which technology was itself raced, as was the lack thereof. For our narrator to discover that this "lost" people have abjured what his own race has only begun to fetishize signifies a level of development he isn't able to process. In other words, they have successfully rejected and abandoned technology, that being a sign of their evolutionary sophistication. It is perhaps the most significant critique of technology in the novel. The fact that modern Erewhonians now looked at machines "with the feelings of an English antiquarian concerning Druidical monuments or flint arrow heads" is a powerful narrative statement of civilizational relativism and what can be called a temporal humility lacking in the accelerating technopolitics of the time (142). Still, the overall sense of Erewhonian culture presented by Butler is of fear, racism, resentment, paranoia, and colonial power. At the end of the novel our narrator imagines he could return to enslave its natives. He even contemplates doing so under the guise of converting them to Christianity, using their advanced future against them as if it were a primitive past.

The civil war in Butler's utopia is between two political parties, the machinists and the antimachinists, spurred by the writing of "The Book of the Machines" by a scholar at the height of Erewhon's industrial age. In "The Book of the Machines," the mysterious author doesn't argue but in fact *proves* that "machines were ultimately destined to supplant the race of man, and to become instinct with a vitality as different from, and superior to, that of animals, as animal to vegetable life" (63). This use of the "book within a book" trope is not unusual in fantasy or lost-race texts as a way of playing with the issue of authenticity or narrative truth. The discovery of a lost diary, for example—Burroughs uses it in *Tarzan of the Apes,* but by then it was a canonical gesture—keeps possibility and that old imperial urge alive. This framing device also hearkens back to the narratives of colonial exploration that would give rise to this genre and that would have an influence on what would become ethnography and anthropology. In a time where European exploration had yet to reach that point of geographic and cultural satiety infamously lamented by Marlowe in *Heart of Darkness,* and when there was still a sense of worlds yet to conquer, narratives such as these could still operate with the logic of infinite possibility, hence the need to pretend at truth even in what was acknowledged as wildly fictional. What Laura Chrisman says of Haggard's vision should be said of all these texts, from Conrad to Rice Burroughs: not only do they blend scientific rationalism with capitalist global expansion, they do so through the old rhetoric of "wonder," which manages to combine "terrestrial realism and an extra-terrestrial marvellousness."[113]

Another common presence in such texts alongside the "book within a book" or "story within a story" trope—used also by Joseph Conrad—is the use of a magical grimoire or ancient manuscript that provides the key to the narrative's true origins. This book operates as a framing device for a culture still on the edge of that age of wonder and expansion. Haggard would use this trope so much that one wouldn't be faulted for thinking that he invented it. H. P. Lovecraft—mentor to Robert E. Howard—would also depend so much on it that many might attribute it to him (the *Necronomicon* by the "mad Arab" Abdul Alhazred for example). For Butler, this trope was a way of masquerading ideas he knew to be controversial in the form of a dialogue. It also added to the layers of anonymity that surrounded *Erewhon,* initially to his detriment in that it caused readers to easily mistake him for Bulwer-Lytton.

Beginning with an affirmation of Darwinian historical scope unique for its immediate focus on the "potentiality of consciousness" instead of biology, "The Book of the Machines" presents what must be one of the most potent statements of relativism in a time when relativistic thinking was heretical and absurd (143). It denies evolution as a strictly human process and links it to something so indifferently macrohistorical that it is mere prejudice to limit it to human beings. In this granting of consciousness to machines, what Leo Marx called "race suicide" in his discussion of Henry Adams, becomes inevitable. It is inevitable because it is a product of having proffered the category of race unto machines to balance that sense of imminent extinction already at work in the zeitgeist:

> There is no security"—to quote his own words—"against the ultimate development of mechanical consciousness, in the fact of machines possessing little consciousness now. A mollusk has not much consciousness. Reflect upon the extraordinary advance which machines have made during the last few hundred years, and note how slowly the animal and vegetable kingdoms are advancing. The more highly organized machines are creatures not so much of yesterday, as of the last five minutes, so to speak, in comparison with past time. Assume for the sake of argument that conscious beings have existed for some twenty million years: see what strides machines have made in the last thousand! May not the world last twenty million years longer? If so, what will they not in the end become? Is it not safer to nip the mischief in the bud and to forbid them further progress? (144)

Much could be said here about how this antedates the work of Marshall McLuhan and Norbert Wiener, as well as the work of contemporary thinkers like Ray Kurzweil and Hans Moravec. Butler describes the "self regulating and self-adjusting contrivances which are now incorporated with the vapour-engine" that prove that "unless man can be awakened to a sense of his situation," all that is left is the manifesting "of the doom which he is preparing for himself" (160). This attributing of consciousness as well as race to inhuman and nonhuman entities is similar to how Caribbean thinkers like Wilson Harris and Édouard Glissant imagine the macrohistorical force of creolization and will be implicated in how Sylvia Wynter historicizes epistemic shifts and theorizes liminality in the context of race and colonialism. It is also very obviously an important antecedent to cybertheory and posthumanism, as made clear in phrases like this: ""After all then it comes to this, that the difference between the life of a man and that of a machine is one rather of degree than of kind, though differences in kind are not wanting" (159).

But even before Butler begins to explicitly use the language of race and biological differences to describe machine culture and reproduction, it is difficult from this vantage point to not think him as aware of his analogies as was Melville. Simply substitute "blacks" or "the Negro" or even "the colonized" for machines and a dimension of meaning opens up that simply cannot be accidental, given his commitment to Darwinian views of race, culture, and historical transformation. For example, his take on technology is clearly product of a sense that there was something deeply wrong with contemporary relations of power and servitude. The Luddism in passages like the ones previously quoted inspired Norbert Wiener to insist that we not take Butler's vision too seriously because "neither he nor anyone around him could understand the true nature of automata, and his statements are rather incisive figures of speech than scientific remarks."[114]

What Wiener is missing, though, is that Butler's figures of speech are not so much based on technology itself but on how it had emerged as a seemingly independent historical process, as Thomas Carlyle would famously point out. Butler's stress in "The Book of the Machines" is on the process of evolution and how it allows for the assigning of meanings and agency to objects or forms of being that previously were seen as not being capable of consciousness or their own autonomous movement through time. Butler is speaking about power, how it grants meanings and distributes the category of "human" or of "life." He is explaining how it can or will shift and produce unexpected if not earned reversals of these meanings. This is why even though Suvin agrees that *Erewhon* acknowledges Butler's focus on "the discourse of power," this reading disagrees with his notion that the use of conscious machines "is defeated by the overwhelming literalness of the narrative vehicle."[115]

To grant those, as Sylvia Wynter describes, liminal "figures of chaos" like machines (or blacks) the very language of anthropomorphism is to imagine a possible future in which they will be fitter than those that previously dominated them. The very fact that supplantation is a stronger possibility in *Erewhon* than complementarity is sign of a deep quasi-religious dread of the return of the repressed: "may not man himself become a sort of parasite upon the machines? An affectionate machine-tickling aphid?" (148). As figures of speech, these statements elucidate the building blocks of a discourse, one that immediately becomes racial because of the charged elements at play in his historical moment, such as slavery and colonialism. Those elements contributed to the broad sense that there would be immense moral and material repercussions for both of those world historical phenomena.

"The Book of the Machines" goes on to suggest how illogical it would be "to imagine that because the life of machines is a very different one to our own, there is therefore no higher possible development of life than ours; or that because mechanical life is a very different thing from ours, therefore that it is not life at all" (156). This is a dark sense of cultural relativism. But once life is established in or proffered to the animate yet artificial other, the language of race inevitably flows from the evolutionary argument. Extant technologies are argued to be as "to the future as the early Saurians to man," largely due to the rapidity with which they grow, evolve, and transform and regardless of their current innocuousness (146). Even the watch worn by our narrator one day "will remain the only existing type of an extinct race" (147). This reference to earlier stages in the evolution of technology is later contrasted with the mysterious author's own sense of the relativism of geological time and the evolutionary place of humans in it:

> I shrink with as much horror from believing that my race can ever be superseded or surpassed, as I should do from believing that even at the remotest period my ancestors were other than human beings. Could I believe that ten hundred thousand years ago a single one of my ancestors was another kind of being to myself, I should lose all self-respect, and take no further pleasure or interest in life. I have the same feeling with regard to my descendants, and believe it to be one that will be felt so generally that the country will resolve upon putting an immediate stop to all further mechanical progress, and upon destroying all improvements that have been made for the last three hundred years. (162)

Before this official recommendation the author speculates on what he sees as the imminent power of speech and reason in machines and on their capacity not just to adapt, but to actually reproduce themselves. Machines may be thought as servants who "owe their very existence and progress to their power of ministering to human wants, and must therefore both now and ever be man's inferiors." But man as the "ruling spirit" is merely a temporary state of affairs. We then enter into a set of descriptions that do not need embellishment to evoke chattel slavery, because they actually depend on the kind of knowledge that was once deemed scientific in analyses of blacks:

> This is all very well. But the servant glides by imperceptible approaches into the master; and we have come to such a pass that, even now, man must suffer terribly on ceasing to benefit the machines. . . . Man's very soul is due to the machines; it is a machine-made thing: he thinks as he thinks, and feels as he feels, through the work that machines have wrought upon him, and their existence is quite as much a *sine qua non* for his, as his for theirs. This face precludes us from proposing the complete annihilation of machinery, but surely it indicates that we should destroy as many of them as we can possibly dispense with, lest they should tyrannize over us even more completely. (149)

In *Erewhon* soul exists because it is inorganic, a construct, a "machine-made thing." The argument that it is machines that create souls in humans emphasizes the kind of reciprocity at work between beings that share an evolutionary process, which is Butler's point. In this passage "soul" is the product of a distinction between self and other in which "the other" is not human. Because that inhuman other is what generates "soul," that product is hardly a mode of distinguishing between self and other. It is merely *claimed* as the solitary possession of man. It is not an essential or God-given quality. This notion that it is the servant who produces the soul of the master due to the "work" they have "wrought upon" him is a priceless insight and returns us to the Hegelian dialectic. "The Book of the Machines" is a testament to the force and factor of *recognition* in terms of a mutual awareness of the other's self-consciousness and the symbiotic nature of even vertical domination.

But where Hegel saw freedom as that mutual awareness of one another's self-consciousness, Butler sees material reversals and historical justice. Again, the very idea that reversals or reprisals are necessary and inevitable grows out of Darwin: "it is the machines which act upon man and make him man, as much as man who has acted upon and made the machines; but we must choose between the alternative of undergoing much present suffering, or seeing ourselves gradually superseded by our own creatures, till we rank no higher in comparison with them, than the beasts of the field with ourselves" (160). Servitude, in this view, is both camouflage and adaptation. It is a form of masquerade as well as a biding of time: "This is the art of the machines—they serve that they may rule. They bear no malice towards man for destroying a whole race of them provided he creates a better instead; on the contrary, they reward him liberally for having hastened their development.... Yet these are the very things we ought to do, and do quickly; for though our rebellion against their infant power will cause infinite suffering, what will not things come to, if that rebellion is delayed?" (150).

A few pages later:

> The very nature of the motive power which works the advancement of the machines precludes the possibility of man's life being rendered miserable as well as enslaved. Slaves are tolerably happy if they have good masters, and the revolution will not occur in our time, nor hardly in ten thousand years, or ten times that.... Our bondage will steal upon us noiselessly and by imperceptible approaches; nor will there ever be such a clashing of desires between man and the machines as well lead to an encounter between them. Among themselves the machines will war eternally, but they will still require man as the being through whose agency the struggle will be principally conducted. In point of fact there is no occasion for anxiety about the future happiness of man so long as he continues to be in any way profitable to the machines; he may become the inferior race, but he will be infinitely better off than he is now. (161)

Note how the language diminishes the novel's focus on technology and begins to highlight human relationships coded in talk of machines. It isn't an exaggeration to see conversations about slavery and race contemporary to Butler. Also present are visions of colonial independence that assumed that natives would war among themselves eternally but would still depend on man, as in European man who, as Wynter emphasizes throughout her work, arrogates to himself sole ownership of the category.

The idea that European man, when made inferior, would be "infinitely better off than he is now" is a curious statement given the heightened adversarial nature of the relationship between man and machine, master and slave, self and other in this rhetoric. According to "The Book of the Machines," the anticipated benevolence of machines can be determined through a comparison with how humans treat animals and how interdependent humans and animals have become:

> In like manner there is reason to hope that the machines will use us kindly, for their existence will be in a great measure dependent upon ours; they will rule us with a rod of iron, but they will not eat us; they will not only require our services

in the reproduction and education of their young, but also in waiting upon them as servants; in gathering food for them, and feeding them; in restoring them to health when they are sick; and in either burying their dead or working up their deceased members into new forms of mechanical existence. (161)

This is explicitly about morality, which is what arguments or conversations about the soul are ultimately skirting or attempting to sketch. But morality isn't an absolute quality and empathy not an innately human characteristic if soul is produced by machines or through our relationship to them. In Butler human and soul are products of reciprocal relationships that instead operate under the cunningly self-serving ideology of "do unto others since one day they will inevitably be in a position to do unto you." One could see this as a quite brutal justification of slavery due to a set of anxieties not uncommon in the transatlantic ethnic imaginary of the time. Genocide becomes valid, not because blacks are inferior but because they are if not potentially superior then still very likely to do to others precisely what has been done to them.

Butler's view of the universe goes back to the birth of modernity and the idea of an entirely secular and therefore mechanistic universe. In this context man is merely a highly sophisticated machine, a few evolutionary steps above a watch. It also simultaneously evokes William Paley's deistic view of "God the Watchmaker" in his 1802 treatise, *Natural Theology; or, Evidences of the Existence and Attributes of the Deity Collected from the Appearances of Nature* that Darwin refutes in *Origin of the Species* but that endures in what is called "intelligent design."

The possession of soul in "The Book of the Machines" is described appropriately as a product of power. Despite being produced reciprocally, soul is inevitably something to be claimed and deployed by that group in power who is then authorized to produce race as that which is *soulless*. Soul here is an after-effect—an echo—of the social struggle over the right and the power to proclaim and describe life and to contain and control the definition of the human. It is that adversarial and resistant conversation about otherness in *Erewhon* that begs to be creolized simply due to its inability to imagine other possible relationships between race and technology, master and slave, self and other. That so much time and effort would be spent on "the expected counter-attack, the dreaded regression, the threatening future, the unhuman" in "Imperial Gothic" or lost-race or invasion-scare narratives shows how difference in them could ultimately be imagined only in oppositional terms.

To clarify: the machine as a *raced being* had to be represented by Butler as absolute in its species difference from whites as blacks were thought to be, or rather claimed by some to be, since it was well known that blacks and whites could and did intermix. The logic of creolization, on the other hand, insists that even under cover of night or the lush privileges of denial, oppositions merge and blend and notions of species difference become revealed as purely political and discursively unsustainable. As the next chapter argues, this too is the logic behind cyberpunk and posthumanism. In fact, Sue Zemka, one of the few critics to be aware of the interplay between colonial knowledge making and technohistory in *Erewhon,* puts it this way,

> Species definition is now conceived in dialectical terms, as an ongoing process of social conflict between groups that exchange the roles of servant and master class. In keeping with this dialectical frame, the dilemma regarding the definition of man is now rendered in the language and imagery of class-based political struggle and upheaval, the conceit being that class tension is here located outside the species, in the schism between humans and their machines.[116]

She may be pointedly aware, for example, of "the trace that English-Maori relations leave on the text," but she misses the function of race as a foundational aspect of the machine/human "schism," especially given *Erewhon*'s explicit use of biological understandings of human differentiation and the broader historical context of late Victorian political anxieties. In the wake of *Frankenstein*—where machines function in part as a metonym for class relationships—race, slavery, and colonial power motivate Butler's anthropomorphizing of technology.

And there is something else that will become more the focus of cyberpunk, cybertheory, and posthumanism: to mobilize class, race, and power in the context of biological notions of differentiation is almost inevitably to deploy or depend on sex. To question man and machine in dialectical terms is to suspend or ignore a crucial aspect of classic dialectics: synthesis, which is to say—materially speaking—sex. The oppositions between white and black, human and machine, in the world and mind of Samuel Butler were in dialectical tension, but given the realities of race and miscegenation during the nineteenth century, sex or something like it was analogically inevitable in "The Book of The Machines."

In "The Book of The Machines" there is an almost pornographic obsession with machine breeding, miniaturization, and the sexuality of automata. Though we do not get an explicit representation of machine/human coupling, we do get extended discussions of reproduction and the relationship of this new other to the embattled white colonial self in sexual terms:

> Surely if a machine is able to reproduce another machine systematically, we may say that it has a reproductive system. . . . And how few of the machines are there which have not been produced systematically by other machines? But it is man that makes them do so. Yes; but is it not insects that make many of the plants reproductive, and would not whole families of plants die out if their fertilization was not effected by a class of agents utterly foreign to themselves? . . . These little creatures are part of our own reproductive system; then why not we part of that of the machines?
>
> But the machines which reproduce machinery do not reproduce machines after their own kind. . . . Here, again, if we turn to nature we shall find abundance of analogies which will teach us that a reproductive system may be in full force without the thing produced being of the same kind as that which produced it. . . . Machines can within certain limits beget machines of any class, no matter how different to themselves. Every class of machines will probably have its special mechanical breeders, and all the higher ones will owe their existence to a large number of parents, and not to two only. (153–54)

Not even *Frankenstein* went this far. Recall in Shelley, that the creature's desire for a mate inspires in his creator a fear of an entire *race* of monsters that would threaten humankind. It is that fear of the automaton's uncontrolled, autonomous sexuality and its own control over its process of reproduction that causes Victor Frankenstein to destroy the monster's mate before completing it. Passages like this have caused many to see "The Book of the Machines" as prophetic in the context not only of cybernetics but also of nanotechnology, which depends on both miniaturization and machinic self-replication. But due to that strictly technological history there has been blindness to its engagement with the language of race and slavery. Along with evolution these are the primary contexts from which Butler could draw analogies of reproduction, dominance, sexual power, and the anxieties of supplantation.

Without the direct context of slavery these missing racial links are still uncanny, if not obvious. They are there in the very attempt to describe fertilization by foreign agents and interdependence without consanguinity and how it is possible to be a part of the reproductive process of this new life form yet distinct enough to imagine it simply a process kept to "their own kind." Passages like this allude to the interruptive power of man over another species' reproduction. This obsession with the language of natural science is linked in the text to the imminent cultural and political dominance of the creatures being so scrutinized and feared. To historically astute readers, this should give the game away, as does the quick move from sexual reproduction to taxonomy:

> Here followed a very long and untranslatable digression about the different races and families of the then existing machines. The writer attempted to support his theory by pointing out the similarities existing between many machines of a widely different character, which served to show descent from a common ancestor. He divided machines into their genera, subgenera, species, varieties, subvarieties, and so forth. He proved the existence of connecting links between machines that seemed to have very little in common, and showed that many more such links had existed, but had now perished. He pointed out tendencies to reversion, and the presence of rudimentary organs which existed in many machines feebly developed and perfectly useless, yet serving to mark descent from an ancestor to whom the function was actually useful (155).

Colonialism and the very biological sciences that fed nineteenth-century racism here generate a transgressive expansion of the definition of the human. Yet the fact that Butler insists on evolutionary biology and race in his representation of machines forces us to contend with technology as a metonym for that which reduces man to those who have souls and those who don't: race.

This passage is just one of many that depends on a description of technology that was not available to Butler from any lexicon of industrialization: miniaturization, self-duplication, and a sophistication that evolves from the machinic into forms such as organs. Though speaking of much later materials and contexts, critic Martin Kevorkian states that "the interface zone with these incipient robo-races may well present new dangers, albeit ones indexed to fears with readily available historical analogs."[117] Sure, Butler was an imaginative writer and the genre of utopian fiction allows such wild invention. But good science fiction borrows from the credible and functions as an extrapolation on materials present in the author's own time and context. And he wasn't *that* good. What *was* available to Butler were "historical analogs" drawn from biological science, slavery, and nineteenth-century race thinking. Also available were the political and social anxieties that motivated the work in the very first place. Further proof of this can be found in those long extended sections where "The Book of the Machines" not only explores evolving techniques of machinic reproduction utterly without precedence or corollary in his time but relays in quite staggering detail the possibilities of selective breeding.

Ironically, as a staunch Darwinian, Butler had to have believed in the anthropological theory of monogenesis—that all humans descended from a common ancestor—since he projects it onto machines. But there would have been some anxiety in maintaining that belief while drawing such strong equivalence between machines and blacks. After all, if blacks were human after all, then that would then suggest they and whites also shared an ancestor. Machines as a metaphor of absolute difference served to keep the bloodlines separate. Still, a sentence like this would have to have sent some small shudders through both writer and contemporary readers: "These little creatures are part of our own reproductive system; then why not we part of that of the machines?" (153).

Rather than see *Erewhon* in sexual or racial terms, Sue Zemka sees the turn to machines in the language of nineteenth-century biological science as a product of a radical shift to materialism. For her it is a satire of the shift to materialism that inevitable reduces biology to the machinic. In this shift, man begins to lose centrality as the locus of knowledge, power, and history. She describes it as "the loss of certainty that attends an expanding category of humanness, a humanness unhinged from the conceptual, social, cultural, and physical markers that formerly maintained a balance between its universality and its exclusiveness." That exclusiveness was profoundly racial and clearly gendered. In her reading, the rising waves of mechanization are less a metonym for the "rising tide of color" but for the inevitable defetishization of man:

> *Erewhon* pronounces—however prematurely—the death of the humanist subject that animates the utopian myth of idyllic expansion and its imperialist subtext. In the aftermath of the Erewhonian critique of humanism, the credibility of Western cultural and ethical knowledge's lies in partial waste. They begin to be supplanted in the novel by a thoroughgoing scientific materialism, a materialism that denies any quantitative difference between the biological mechanisms of living systems and the cognitive and cultural activities of human beings.

Zemka identifies "the multiple, mobile, and contested boundaries that *Erewhon* erects in and around the category of man."[118] But the text's quite detailed and exhaustive conversation about those boundaries contest man through machines and by likening machines to slaves, Africans, and colonial others. Materialism, though, manages to obscure too much. That privileging of the critique of man only manages to supplant and mask the racial politics of that critique. This is troubling considering how clear Butler is about race in "The Book of The Machines." To suggest that the supplantation at work in Butler's thinking is explicitly focused on technology misses the fact that technology is a metonym for race in *Erewhon,* and the human is a metonym for white Europeans. This point is important to repeat because of the very fact that *Erewhon*'s dependence on race and slavery has been easily missed. This neglect is in large part due to the inability of readers of its prophetic take on technology to see how it models the future through the full range of anxieties of its political present.

THREE
CREOLIZATION AND TECHNOPOETICS

More important than juggling forms of difference against a backdrop of evolution, colonialism, industrialism, and utopian fiction, *Erewhon* establishes important conceptual and historical relationships between race, technology, and artificial intelligence in advance of Karel Čapek's *R.U.R.* This is also in advance of a modernism where, as argued before, those relationships had become so naturalized as to be invisible, though audible in the sound world of the jazz age and perceptible in the basic fabric of the genre that would be named "scientifiction" by Hugo Gernsback two years after the premiere of Čapek's play. This genre, as Samuel R. Delany has pointed out, is as much a mode of reading as a way of writing, as much a way of making texts make sense as a method of exploring new codes and contextual relationships.[1] One is reminded here also of Wilson Harris's notion that "the true capacity of marginal and disadvantaged cultures resides in their genius to tilt the field of civilization so that one may visualize boundaries of persuasion in new and unsuspected lights to release a different apprehension of reality, the language of reality, a different *reading* of texts of reality."[2]

Delany and Harris are two thinkers who have never before been yoked together—the former an African American science fiction novelist, theorist, and provocateur and the other a Guyanese novelist, poet, and quite idiosyncratic philosopher. Yet bringing them and the distinct traditions they represent together will be par for the course in the rest of this book. It is in the spirit of both authors, for example, that one can read the turn to machines in *Erewhon* and Melville's "The Bell-Tower" as a reimagining of the relationship between colonial or slave-owning whites and their subhumanized and objectified others in the context of an imminent freedom. In these texts such a reimagining is accomplished by mediating that relationship through another crucial other—technology, another soulless "thing" that was hardly inert and was also a source of cultural transformation and moral and social anxiety.

These nineteenth-century works employ metaphors that seemed fantastical only because the absurd social realities on which those relationships were based had been so normalized. Machines in these texts operate as a metonym for blacks, just as during slavery blacks were metonyms for labor, technology, and—as this chapter emphasizes—all that occupies the liminal space among primary conceptual categories such as human, animal, and machine. If humans could be rendered sub- or inhuman, then machines by that same logic could be rendered sentient, human, *raced*. If (black) humans could be bought and sold, then machines could conceivably be agents of their own evolution and liberation as well as of human (white) subjugation. The latter possibility would borrow from explicit and latent anxieties about the former, and the former would help give rise to the language on which the latter would depend.

The three sections of this chapter move forward from the nineteenth century by way of the historical reality and critical paradigm of hybridity. They explore how various notions of techorganic blending in the wake of cybernetics, Donna Haraway's "cyborg feminism," and the science fiction genres of cyberpunk engaged and depended on traditions of racial thinking to produce new ideas about the relationship between bodies and machines. This engagement and dependence will be particularly manifest in the image of the cyborg but also will be revealed to be intimate with Caribbean traditions of creolization; after all, if blacks were or were like machines, then the cyborg—the mixture of human and technology—could hardly escape racialization. This should not be as unusual as it sounds since with cyborg feminism and cyberpunk came more conversation about race or about the racial construction of the human than ever before in or around the genre of science fiction. The chapter initially focuses on how techorganic mixing functions as a metaphor for colonial race mixing but then isolates how a shared interest in hybridity becomes characteristic of both late twentieth-century science fiction, music, and postcolonial thought.

To make this book's arguments about race and technology work and to establish creolization as a necessary paradigm, it is necessary to provide a history of creolization itself as a Caribbean intellectual tradition. Its relationship to alternate traditions of racial thinking, specifically from World War I, is also essential, given that it is posed here as a critical alternative or productive supplement to posthumanism and Afro-futurism. The goal here, as with the pairing of Delany and Harris, is to bring science fiction, cybertheory, and Afro-futurism into a shared conversational space with black diasporic thought through the work of Caribbean thinkers like Édouard Glissant, who is also essential to this chapter.

Detailing the historical and conceptual relationships between Caribbean creolization and science fiction is featured in the second part of the chapter, and the latter can be read in the context of the former, but then the section turns to the presence of blacks in contemporary science fiction, particularly in the wake of that genre called "cyberpunk." For example, that Jamaican dub music and Rastafarians and their symbols were such a part of that literature and its filmic representations was much more than either accident or mere exoticism. The presence of Caribbean music and culture in cyberpunk was produced by an appreciation of the creole and technological properties of Jamaican sound, even though the attendant intellectual tradition of creolization was likely missed by William Gibson, Jeff Noon, and others. Through the history of race in cyberpunk and a reading of Gibson's canonical 1984 novel *Neuromancer*, it is argued that it is in dub music that the Caribbean and contemporary science fiction merge. This mixture provides a perfect entry point for creolization to infect not just science fiction but also posthumanism and Afro-futurism.

Of course, to speak of cyberpunk, *Neuromancer*, or posthumanism for that matter is to speak of artificial intelligence. After detailing the place and use of technology in the work of Wilson Harris and Édouard Glissant—which occurs largely in their conversations about sound—and the ways their modes of creolization depend on both music and science fiction, the final section concludes with a discussion of artificial intelligence in Glissant's highly influential *The Poetics of Relation* (1997). Artificial intelligence is argued to be a logical extension of creolization as a black posthuman technopoetics, particularly in the work of Wilson Harris and Édouard Glissant and certainly in the work of Sylvia Wynter, whose challenging and often opaque ideas occupy the book's final chapter.

SEXING ROBOTS, CREOLIZING TECHNOLOGY

In the previous chapters of this book, relationships between blacks and technology are structured as colonial oppositions between whites and machines. This deployment of race operated much in line with nineteenth-century racialist thinking, where the distinctions between an emergent anthropology and an evolving genre were indeed porous. As John Rieder notes, "In the period of science fiction's emergence, this kind of racism extended into scientific discourse with the controversies concerning monogenetic versus polygenetic theories of the origins of the human race, that is, the question of whether white people and nonwhites were really distinct species."[3] But the contemporary context of the genre is much changed in its awareness of new relationships between self and other as mediated by race. African American scholar De Witt Douglas Kilgore argues that "perhaps the greatest challenge or potential of contemporary science fiction is to imagine political/social futures in which race does not simply wither away but is transformed, changing into something different and perhaps unexpected. This would require paying attention to an actual history of race (and racism) in which what constitutes the Other and the Self is always under revision."[4] Kilgore rightly sees this generic potential within a social and cultural context where race can no longer be assumed as static and self and other as discreet.

Yet Kilgore's argument merely brings to mind assumptions that have been at work in Caribbean thinking for at least a century, as does Rieder's point. The relationships of blacks and machines are here analyzed through a lens shaped less by race and species oppositions and more on blending or synthesis. In essence, the Caribbean provides a distinct critical context for *creolizing* these historical processes and theoretical categories. This differential vision of possibility is due to the interaction and transformation of foundational categories such as race, gender, the body, and ultimately the human as primary mechanisms of identifying and revising other and self. Machines must be seen in this context as the ultimate metaphor of the historical contingency of these foundational categories.

This hybridizing gesture bringing race, racism, and racial formation together with machines and technoculture will be familiar to some readers due to those very many science fiction writers who sprung up in the wake of the mid-1980s cyberpunk movement and those also very many critics and artists that emerged in the wake of Donna Haraway's cyborg feminism. Admittedly, this subgenre has lost much of its pull and its bite, and its sobriquet is now one that many of its practitioners abjure. Even Samuel R. Delany has described cyberpunk as "a pervasive misreading of an interim period of urban technoculture."[5] Coming from him, this comment matters since William Gibson in particular has cited Delany's work as a central influence. Yet cyberpunk—even in its more fashionably retro steam-punk variation—continues as a known reference point for its wide spreading of the human/machine interface beyond the sphere of technoculture or critical theory. Because of this familiarity with cyberpunk and cyborg feminism, it's worth first discussing what is less familiar: their relationships to race and collusive interests in the Caribbean.

At the forefront of consideration is precisely what John Rieder proposes in *Colonialism and the Emergence of Science Fiction:* "one of the most striking ways early science fiction handles the discourse of race is in these two repetitive, complementary figures of anatomical distortion, the hybrid and the cyborg."[6] Rieder's point must be thickened, however, since the hybrid figure of the cyborg is merely one of many conceptual hybrids at work in cyberspace and since his justly influential work, despite its topic, isn't primarily interested in the various nonwhite writers, thinkers, or cultural movements at work alongside the very history he helpfully provides. As another critic, David Crane, suggests, the cyborg as a figure of race and racialization is inevitable, given the impact of colonialism on science fiction and of race on machines:

> It should not surprise us . . . that representing the otherness of cyberspace might involve forms of racial and ethnic otherness—especially hybridity, with its negotiation of identity and difference. Nor is it surprising that hybridity would be privileged, celebrated, and even fetishized in the attempts to portray the shifting boundaries of an emerging postcolonial global economic structure, and especially a resistance to that structure. Hybridity figuratively envisions these geopolitical and conceptual transformations, linking them to the technological transformations with which they are implicated. Haraway, in ironically manifesting the cyborg as the potentially revolutionary subject of postmodern technoculture, exemplifies this within the cultural studies Imaginary.[7]

To limit this to institutional knowledge rather than acknowledge its far earlier and wider reach and history would be an act of professional myopia we should always guard against. Haraway's manifestation merely brings to light for the "cultural studies imaginary" what has long been present in science fiction and in technoculture and artificial intelligence, from Samuel Butler to Čapek, Norbert Wiener, Marshall McLuhan, and golden age writers like Isaac Asimov, who would extend the robot/race parallel much further than anyone then or since. Rieder's proposition establishes what has been assumed thus far and what is argued explicitly here in ways he does not: first, that the very history of the genre is in conversation with traditions of racial thinking, from slavery and colonialism; and second, that the history of race mixing and cross-cultural interactions are too at work in the genre as notions of race and gender intersect and evolve against a backdrop of technological transformation.

Though it has been implied thus far, it is worth being clear about the fact that Haraway's blending of woman and machine—the latter's masculinism having long been embedded in the language of industrialization—is a gesture of eroticism. As such it is a profound act of creolization. Sex is, after all, the often-unnamed force behind the coming together of antinomies, particularly heterosexual sex, as Robert Young pointed out in his important work on colonial notions of hybridity.[8] Gender then becomes a way in which those antinomies and bodies themselves are marked and rendered sensible and meaningful. As even Fritz Lang knew as far back as 1927 in *Metropolis,* anthropomorphized machines could not help but partake in our economies of gender, sex, power, and narratives of social transformation. And the fear of the other was merely one part of a desire for that other.

As mentioned in the last chapter, proto–science fiction already hinted at the sexual possibilities between human and other, not only through the requisite miscegenation subplots but also through the very turn to machine sexuality in *Erewhon.* The genre would then imagine far more explicit human/machine sexual interfaces in advance of cyborg feminism and cyberpunk than those imaginable in a nineteenth century so conditioned by absolutist notions of racial differences. But to even imagine such a coming together of oppositions such as human and machine requires a sociohistorical template to frame it. This template is slavery and the various conceptions of blacks as humans or animals or machines. This is why Haraway's work and science fiction from Samuel Butler and Edward Bulwer-Lytton to Herman Melville and H. G. Wells, to cyberpunk and other modes of posthumanism can also be interpreted through resources available to Caribbean and black diasporic thought. In addition to a mutual dependence on race and colonialism and sex and power between and among these traditions, there is also a shared commitment to aesthetic and cultural blendings.

Again, machine/human intimacy as a metonym for cross-racial desire is suggested in *R.U.R.* as well as in *Erewhon,* but it would be made literal in early science fiction stories like Lester del Rey's "Helen O'Loy." Published in 1938 in *Astounding Science Fiction,* the story features a human robot love relationship and marriage. In 1944 C. L. Moore, a woman writer, published "No Woman Born," also in *Astounding Science Fiction.* In it a famous dancer, disfigured by fire, has her mind placed into a golden machine body, which causes her to perform femininity, desire, and humanity. But the text that matters for this discussion is *The Silver Metal Lover* (1981) by Tanith Lee—not a major work, but for some a beloved one. It appears just before Bruce Sterling's early 1980s fanzine *Cheap Truth,* which signaled the emergence of cyberpunk, hence its historical significance. Lee's gesture toward the literal and physical blending of oppositions is surely the missing step in the evolution of cyborg theorizing and is as tellingly dependent on race as are the analogies at the root of cybernetics. It bridges the tradition that sees robots as static, absolute others to cyborgs who represent, as Haraway's and Wiener's works show, a middle space between human and machine, a space that makes intimacy possible, if not inevitable.

The Silver Metal Lover is about a young, wealthy white woman who falls in love with a robot in a world where, like *Erewhon,* machines are becoming so lifelike they present a threat to humans, particularly those of the working and lower classes. They have taken over much of world's employment and, most threateningly, have begun to take over the arts, which in the novel are where humanity or an entity like the soul is manifest. Like *Erewhon* and *R.U.R.* the novel asks the question of whether or not machines have souls and therefore can truly love rather than just perform programmed duties. The machine in question is named "Silver," as in S.I.L.V.E.R. (Silver Ionized Locomotive Verisimulated Electronic Robot). Appropriately, sound is central to his characterization: "he" was constructed for music, song, and general entertainment, including sexual pleasure. Described as having a voice like a "minstrel's but futuristic," and with "savage" rhythms at his disposal, Silver roams the city with his guitar like a wandering bluesman, performing "the human" in a language that can't help but recall race while providing the frisson of interracial sex. "He *was* human," our besotted narrator relentlessly claims, "only his skin gave him away—and the skin might be makeup. He moved like an actor, why not paint himself like one?"[9]

Though never described in explicitly racial terms, the logic of historical associations coded within the genre makes it difficult to see the story as simply about human and machine love. Silver is bought and sold and exchanged throughout the book and considered property. He is shown to develop a soul by the novel's end, though by then the sexual and romantic relationship is well documented and traced in a world where such intimacies are socially forbidden. To even engage in them leads to such a severe loss in social standing that the characters end up eking out survival in an urban ghetto. Heightening the novel's melodrama and its dependence on racial sanctimony, the doomed couple lives on "Tolerance Street." In other words, *The Silver Metal Lover* is a fairly standard star-crossed lovers' story blended with a miscegenation story layered on top of a narrative about the anxieties about technology and the eroticization of difference. That they all work so well together in what is essentially a young adult romance is a telling sign of how fully naturalized these distinct themes had already become in the language of the genre—to the point of cliché.

But though *The Silver Metal Lover* makes explicit the techno-eroticism of cybernetics and cybertheory, Lee was unable to think beyond *Romeo and Juliet* despite Silver being aware that being human is merely "Just another kind of machinery. Sometimes less effective. Biologically more attractive."[10] The implications of the collapsing borders between human and machine aren't taken very far. Due to public protest over the increasing verisimilitude of the robots, the relationship is destroyed by the corporation that manufactured Silver.

Haraway's deployment of the cyborg, on the other hand, goes very far indeed, though it strangely depends on an assumed cross-breeding while eradicating the very process by focusing primarily on its product. But it should be familiar as a gesture to those for whom such "border wars," as she puts it, between human and machine evoke race, slavery, territorial domination, rape, and bestiality. Haraway's description of cyborg poetics as deliberately "monstrous and illegitimate" is then to be read much more in the context of race, colonialism, and slavery than originally conceived.[11] Certainly race and gender are on Haraway's mind, hence the great impact her work has had on thinking about race and gender in the context of technology. This is because, as Rieder puts it, "the hybrid-cyborg pair is a hyperbolic extrapolation of racial division" *as well as* sexual difference.[12] Caribbean creolization, however, is not explicitly on her mind. Her assumption of hybridity enables its necessary intrusion here because as such "extrapolations" the "hybrid-cyborg pair" become prime examples of that process Édouard Glissant calls "synthesis-genesis": birth and mixture, mixture *as* birth, authenticity as a product of collision or collusion.[13]

As is very well known, feminists of color inform Haraway's deployment of the cyborg as a primary tool for the critical analysis of identity even though her use of the figure is essentially a white "polymorphous" configuration. But it goes a bit far to suggest that she presents "explicitly a politics of race and technology," as some have done either directly or by implication.[14] Haraway's intent is clearly to enable racial readings of what was already gendered as masculine: technology. Yet there is no attention to miscegenation, for example, which, as Evelynn M. Hammonds points out, has long been the primary "instance of border crossing between the human and the 'other.'"[15] In the history of racial slavery such border crossings were rarely as deliberate on the part of blacks and without the kind of subversive ironies at work in Haraway or much of the cybertheory that came after.

So rather than the border-blurring jouissance of Haraway's admittedly utopian vision of machine and woman coupling and its focus on "pleasure in the confusion of boundaries" and "responsibility in their construction," it is important to remember that race mixing in the cultural politics of the nineteenth and early twentieth century was primarily an act of violence that served as a way of maintaining distinctions between the two "species" involved.[16] This is where pulp texts like the work of Robert E. Howard, Edgar Rice Burroughs, and others become important in the development of American science fiction. In them, the threat of miscegenation is often disguised as species difference and used to titillate as much as to terrify.[17]

"Monstrous and illegitimate" couplings served to formally identify race with culture as an absolutism, despite the fact that blending did threaten notions of absolute difference by virtue what they produced—the creole, the hybrid, the neither/nor rather than the both/and. Racial blending, mixture, or attendant notions of "passing" may have had a way of blurring borders, but they also emphasized originary distinctions, hence the need to police those borders. Widespread anxieties around such couplings—as well as fears of black male sexual potency as well as the rape as revenge motif—reflected not certainty but the embattled nature of a whiteness fearing its own cultural and political decline. The fears of mixing and alleged weakening of blood, exaggerated notions of diseases and the immigrants who supposedly carried them, the fear of being biologically less than or other to a cultural, social, or pigmented standard—these are and were popular responses to creolization. As argued in the previous chapter, in the transatlantic arena anxieties of decline were conceived both in relation to a less secure sense of colonial power in Europe and an American civil war, where slaves began that slow transition from subject to citizen (inhuman to human).

Victorian writers were largely unable to think of racial differences in ways other than absolute, and so anthropomorphized machines bore the brunt of the symbolic labor of race. They could only hint at sex, though in consistently hinting at it they made its fulfillment necessary for subsequent generations of writers. But we can now see through these oppositions in a way Butler could not. Through creolization we can engage them in a more satisfying historical way than even Haraway could. This is because theorists of creolization are focused on those "depths of mutuality" that depend on another Hegelian process:

synthesis, albeit of a kind that would have been perverse to Hegel and violently penalized in nineteenth-century America and the Caribbean because it was explicitly dependent on interracial sex.

To engage posthumanism and the cyborg as a racial figure in cyberpunk, it's important to contextualize the use of creolization in this book. The fact that the Caribbean has been notably committed to terms like *métissage, hybridity,* or *créolité* is a testament to how much of its social and racial relations have been shaped by cross-racial sex as well as the often violent collusion and collision of disparate racial, social, and cultural types. Later the problematic tendency toward reading these terms as specifically Caribbean will be discussed, since the very term *creole* was "a peculiarly American invention . . . rooted in, born and indicative of contact between European and African people and cultures in the Americas" (one hastens to add that the term is also rooted in contact with indigenous peoples as well).[18] But the relationship to these terms and concepts is not the same as in North America, where even today talk of race, culture, and history in the context of a benevolent, productive, or inevitable synthesis is still heretical. Harris's "depths of mutuality" are far less fetishized in American racial thinking than they are in the Caribbean, and so one faces some trepidation in attempting to explore them as a necessary stage in a black technopoetics.

Much of this suspicion of creolization is due to a widespread and historically rooted fear of how cross-cultural interaction has been framed in the United States: against a backdrop of racial violence as well as a mutual desire to consolidate identity or emphasize and exploit its contrasts. This latter is what Harris would call a shared "conquistadorial habit" that makes it difficult to explore those "involuntary associations" between cultures even in wildly unbalanced, unfair, and uneven interactions.[19] To put it frankly, for creolization theorists like Glissant and Harris, racism is simply not enough to forestall either the complexity of cross-cultural exchanges or to render mute modes of critical reflection or imaginative production based on them.

Critic Françoise Lionnet reflects on a similar interpretive conundrum. "My quarrel, then, with terms such as 'assimilation and 'acculturation' when used in the (post) colonial context," she writes in reflecting on the differences between a French Caribbean context of race and the North American, "is a quarrel with history: the terms have acquired a negative connotation because they underscore the relation of subjugation that exists between the colonized culture and the hegemonic system."[20] With the cultural, legal, and numerical superiority of whites in North America, and a cultural and economic system founded on maintaining white privilege, that process of mixture seemed or was largely unidirectional and indeed oppressive, so much so that even its hybrid products and its productive fusions had to be either politically denied or masked by a sometimes strategic authenticity, or "blackness." In fact, North American racial thinking so fetishizes the violence of cross-cultural and cross-racial contact that it's no surprise that there is often little focus on the viability of its products *as being due* to that violence. There is a fear that to do so would be to either ignore the past or, even worse, forgive it. Arguably, this is also because in North America miscegenation is overwhelmingly read and thought in primarily sexual terms rather than through culture and its attendant metaphors, as is present in the Caribbean.[21]

Obviously, the Caribbean also suffered from and was invented by slavery and structured by staggering amounts of racial violence and continuing social inequities; the fact that it shares the context of blood, race, power, rape, and exploitation yet has still generated alternate modes of conceptually framing that history should be enough to give creolization primacy in transnational conversations about race. It is therefore really no surprise that it is in the North American context where creolization has had to sneak in under the cover of a postcolonial focus on hybridity and its simultaneous commitment to non-American racial formations. In many ways it poses a threat to the hegemony of an Anglophone black diaspora predicated on the assumptions generated primarily by American racial thinking.

Much black first-world thought has established notions of resistance that all too often fall in binary terms: primarily black/white. For Wilson Harris this establishes a problem not for actual cross-culturality, or what Glissant would call *créolité,* but for how it is conceived. "The tragedy," Harris writes, "[is] in reinforcing a fixation with protest, a suppression of profoundest creativity to throw bridges across chasms, to open an architecture of space within closed worlds of race and culture." There is no fear of erasure here. There is an almost mystical trust in the complex products of historical inevitability. There is also the understanding in Harris that cultural interaction will *continue both voluntarily and involuntarily;* if not, it freezes, renders absolute, and oppresses even in the name of resistance: "For without complex revisionary bridges . . . conscience is paralyzed by dogma; and freedom, in my view, grows increasingly susceptible to a hidden mafia or ruthless establishment within civilization."[22]

Thinkers like Glissant, and Harris, though quite different from one another, focus less on the binary oppositions between black and white, colony and metropole, master and slave. Harris's work is noted for being so free of "racial exclusiveness" that it features "no 'we' and no 'they'" at all.[23] These thinkers focus instead on the productive though often violent processes of mixture and transformation—not unitary being, as Glissant would have it, or its attendant categories of race or culture. It is that fluidity around race, identity, bodies, origins, and subjectivity that makes creolization sympathetically linked to cybertheory.

One writes now in the hope that Lionnet is correct in suggesting that this Anglophone, North American recalcitrance can open up to "a more cautious understanding of the dialectical and complex phenomena of ethnic interactions that have existed in this country since the beginning of colonial times." As she puts it, "it is not assimilation that appears inevitable when Western technology and education are adopted by the colonized"; instead, it allows "individuals to stand in relation to the past and the present at the same time, to look for creative means of incorporating useful 'Western' tools, techniques or strategies into their own cosmology or *Weltanschauung.*"[24] This is important because, as Wilson Harris points out, though in the colonial context "Creoleness became a form of self-deceptive division," still "it harboured within itself a potential for the renascence of community."[25]

Like Harris and other Caribbeanists and Caribbean peoples making incursions into that deep and privileged North American intimacy between black and white Americans, Lionnet is focused on synthesis. Like many who do, she does so following not Hegel but instead archcreoliste Édouard Glissant. Synthesis differs in Glissant from Hegel—and from Haraway—due to his appreciation of the sexual and miscegenative grounding of the process and his great appreciation for its flawed and violent mechanisms and ongoing legacies of inequality. The intimacy of master and slave in Hegel is not the kind of intimacy that generates the coming togetherness of *créolité.* It is an appreciation of that violent historical process that motivates Glissant's refusal to fetishize or privilege any of its founding elements. For example, there are no static and totalized masters or static and sympathetic slaves in this vision. Such elements exist merely to be transformed in a process that may seem utopian but is, in Glissant's thinking, indifferent.

This is why his notion of synthesis "does not fall into the kind of humanism where idiots get trapped," as he states in *Caribbean Discourse,* a humanism that could wear a white face as easily as a black one.[26] Synthesis here is as threatening to masters as it is to slaves, or to the legacy of mastery as it is to the legacy of resistance. This fear of a particular humanism explains Harris's great fear of the "trickster faces of nature" that "may easily beguile us so that we absolutize" opposing racial or cultural differences as a "consolidating partiality, partial appearance" and transform them "into an absolute frame, an absolute good" on any side of the political spectrum.[27] As an inexorable product of inexorable culture contacts, creolization instead "demonstrates that henceforth it is no longer valid to glorify 'unique' origins that the race safeguards and prolongs." Glissant's reference to "race" and to "unique origins" is applicable to blacks as well as to whites: "no people have been spared the cross-cultural process."[28] In similar terms Wilson Harris describes the need to reject the "sovereign individual as such," an insight and argument that, as will be shown, is utterly at home in cyberpunk and posthumanism.[29]

Glissant goes so far as to controversially though accurately suggest something one could never imagine being suggested by a black first world—particularly African American—thinker. Like Harris he argues that creolization be seen as the metanarrative of slavery and actively be taken up as a realm of possibility: "Western thought, although studying it as a historical phenomenon, persists in remaining silent about the potential of the slave trade for the process of creolization."[30] That slavery could in any way be described as *productive* is of course taboo to contemporary debates and forms of knowledge that are erected on resistance and vindication despite being articulated by those who are as much products of creolization as they are of slavery.

Understandably, many of those forcefully rendered inhuman tend to work hard to recover and reinstitute natality, roots, and origins by a process that Glissant calls "reversion," or "the obsession with a single origin." Not only is this the case in North America, but also in the Caribbean. They may not be willing to "minimize the idea of Genesis," especially in a social, legal, and economic context where their very presence was rendered alien and often persecuted as such. They are likely to reject his dictum that "the abandonment of pure original values allows for an unprecedented potential for contact" since that contact has been primarily figured by a relation of racial terror and dominance. Nevertheless, Glissant describes creolization as a historical inevitability "in a world destined to synthesis and to the 'contact of civilizations.'"[31] It is clearly not just the sometimes ugly and often unequal process by which cultures come into contact, but in fact an indifferent, transhistorical process as industrialization came to be understood by the publication of *Erewhon*.

And it is a process, hence Glissant's insistence that it is "a method and not a state of being"; creolization is no ground of identity because it "can never be accomplished, nor can we go beyond it." This seeming acceptance of the process should not be taken to be blindness to its historical conditions. Glissant is very attuned to the fact that the synthesis of master and slave was a traumatic coming together of the human and the inhuman, of the putatively technological with the supposedly natural. The latter was subject to the former and consistently unequal in relation. That was coming together, however, despite the still ringing echoes of its initial interactions and the still material ramifications of its inequalities are still necessary: "Creolization, one of the ways of forming a complex mix—and not merely a linguistic result—is only exemplified by its processes and certainly not by the 'contents' on which these operate."[32] In this he is closer to the conceits of Samuel Butler than one would previously have thought. Creolization is for Glissant an analog for evolution, or rather a broader evolutionary process without man as its center, a belief Butler shared. Samuel Butler, of course, saw the relationship of human and machine in apocalyptic terms. For him there was no full blending possible, just a reversal of master and slave, which was the dominant narrative in science fiction up past *Erewhon* until perhaps the work of Isaac Asimov.

Again, contemporary conversations about race and technology, humans and machines, are less focused on the apocalyptic oppositions of the Victorian era and the absolutisms of species difference. As Haraway points out, even differences between organic human bodies and machines have become increasingly untenable. The relationship between the two have been framed as having merged in ways that suggest that the history of bodies and the history of machines not only intrude on each other but are in fact mutually constitutive. This is an example of creolization at work. Cyberpunk and cybertheory can therefore be noted for what one could call a *will to inauthenticity,* as human subjectivity becomes less dependent on a sacrosanct body and the attendant tropes of nature and the organic. There is no fear here of erasure, but a faith in hybridity to produce novelty—Glissant's "synthesis-genesis" at work.

Such tropes as the "organic" or "natural" are traditionally attributed to the romantic self and are thusly deployed in cybertheory and artificial intelligence as dated or nostalgic oppositions; as argued before, their racialization is a direct product of slavery and colonialism. Haraway's work stresses that these tropes are also gendered in the way that the romantic self and its technological apparatus have been. Samuel R. Delany's commentary on Haraway's sexual politics is insightful: he describes her work as being primarily in response to feeling that the women's movement had been "too reliant on notions of 'the organic' and 'the natural,' seen in an essential opposition to the technical and the scientific." These notions gave "small heed to the fact that 'the natural' and 'the organic' are empowered by, and indeed only exist as powerful conceptual and explanatory categories because of, modern science and technology."[33]

Haraway's innovation was, of course, to imagine the oppositions blended or to see in blending a politics. It evokes a racial parallel in Kobena Mercer's well-known essay "Black Hair/Style Politics," where he points out the contradictory function of Afro hairstyles or Rastafarian dreadlocks in the black power era as signs of resistance through the claim on the trickster faces of the "natural." As passionate as was the claim on roots, there was a deep contradiction in these affirmations of black nature. These tropes would be dominant in the music of the era, soul, funk, but particularly reggae: "The 'nature' brought into play to signify a desire for liberation and freedom so effectively was also a Western inheritance, sedimented with symbolic meaning and value by traditions of science, philosophy and art."[34] Mercer's point shares the same historical framework as Ron Eglash, who presents a technological context for this debate about race and the natural as it manifests in the lived politics of blacks in the West. It's worth reading them back-to-back:

> In the first years of American cybernetics, analog and digital systems were seen as epistemologically equivalent, both considered capable of complex kinds of representation. . . . But by the early 1960s a political dualism was coupled to this representation dichotomy. The "counterculture" radicals of the cybernetics community—Norbert Wiener, Gregory Bateson, Hazel Henderson, Paul Goodman, Kenneth Boulding, Barry Commoner, Margaret Mead, among others—made the erroneous claim that analog systems were more concrete, more "real" or "natural," and therefore (according to this romantic cybernetics) ethnically superior. In social domains, this converged with Rousseau's legacy of the moral superiority of oral over literate cultures.[35]

Because Rousseau's legacy vastly antedates the cybernetic counterculture it's more likely that it was the impact of the former that shaped the science and metaphors of the latter, so the "conversion" in Eglash's history could do with a stronger sense of causality. This would have occurred much in the way that master/slave as a general cultural set of historical and contemporary social and cultural relationships would help naturalize technological metaphors.

Eglash continues,

For African-Americans this meant a debilitating valorization. They could use this ethical claim to combat some racism, but only in terms of identifying as unconscious, innocent natives in a lost past. Thus African modes of representation in the use of sculpture, movement and rhythm were often abandoned to modernist claims that Africa was the culture of non-representation, the culture of the Real.[36]

As sophisticated a reading this is of the intersections of race and technology in black American life, it maintains a fantasy of racial innocence by suggesting that black notions of nature were dependent on the errors and fallacies of technoculture. Narratives in which blacks were "unconscious, innocent natives in a lost past" have been at work in black thinking since the nineteenth century and are still a cornerstone of much black politics. Ethiopianism, Pan-Africanism, Rastafarianism, negritude, Afrocentrism—these movements and forces didn't require cyberculture radicals to ground their sense of racial authenticity in either natural or analog representation. The specificity of black nostalgia and black primitivism—particularly as it relates to Africa—will be explored later, but that Eglash finds the two poles of black relationships to this analog/digital split to be "reggae versus rap" is telling, given that the former makes the latter possible and that the former's use of the roots/analog equation was upset by the emergence of dub and dancehall.

In Mercer's view, radical race politics has or had the potential for a disrupting of such nationalist articulations of the natural or the organic much in the way Haraway's cyborg gestures suggested. Mercer makes clear that such a disruption works as much against extant traditions of primitivism in the black world as it does against romantic racism. There has also been a common will to inauthenticity in the black diaspora, one as troubling to Afros and dreadlocks as it would have been to Margaret Mead and Norbert Wiener. This is present in Mercer's argument that chemically enhanced black hairstyles were wrongly maligned as apolitical or accomodationist when in fact they were essentially subversive due to their deliberate nonnaturalism. Mercer argues that these artificial hairstyles rejected those other natural styles that ultimately functioned within Western notions of the organic despite being signs of resistance to colonial incorporation or assimilation into a racist society. Mercer ultimately reframes nature or the organic through the lens of the creole, rendering it inauthentic to any given regime based on racial orthodoxy—particularly nationalist ones.

That will to inauthenticity is central to the work of Glissant and Harris also, as a product of their defetishizing of human and racial identity. What cybertheory and creolization share is a foundational dependence on these racialized and sexualized tropes of nature and the organic and a common need to violate their integrity by bringing them together with the inauthentic, for example, with the machine.

But what makes creolization specifically Caribbean? This is as pertinent a question as the question of what it is that makes technology exclusively or exceptionally Western. It is true that now familiar terms such as hybridity, catalysis, *métissage,* and *créolité* as unproblematic spaces of reinvention, resistance, and recombination are all too often used to disavow their first-world resonance and provenance in the wake of postcolonial thought. They are increasingly present as North American or British scholars and critics find ways to use the Caribbean as "raw materials ... for metropolitan consumption," as Mimi Sheller put it in her study of the uses of terms invented by Caribbean theorists, like transculturation, transversality, and, of course, creolization.[37]

Creolization moved from a "politically engaged term used by Caribbean theorists located in the Caribbean in the 1970s, to one used by Caribbean Diaspora theorists located outside of the Caribbean in the 1980s, and finally to non-Caribbean 'global' theorists in the 1990s." Sheller concludes that the "current 'Creolization paradigm'" therefore has "little to contribute to an operative theory of conflict and unequal power relations" in that region.[38] But there is something innate to creolization that does invite its own appropriation. Anything, any body of knowledge or cultural form founded on antifoundationalism will always find itself belonging everywhere or claimed by anyone. This is and has been, for example, the fate and promise of sound, even that which has been as rooted in specific racial experiences as black music.

What really is troubling about the sense of the Caribbean as *ur-creole* space is actually how it allows the Caribbean to function as a site for intellectual projection. For example, North American or British scholars tend to project onto the Caribbean concepts that essentially function as *other* despite or because of their desire to critique (their own) Western domination. So we get the Caribbean as the amorphous, *hyperorganic* "non-West" as well as the primitive, premodern, *u topos,* the ultimate space of blending where "reason" and its linear temporalities inevitably end or go baroque in a temperate climate. This tendency to project is also endemic to black nationalism across the diaspora, where racial romanticizing ranges from the flimsy to the pathological. It is particularly strong among many postcolonial critics who, despite strong critiques of racial nationalism, still manifest romanticist desires for difference coded in cultural if not racial terms. Creolization as a sign of the Caribbean manages to serve those desires.

Astute readers should recognize this now common celebration of the Caribbean as the fallout from the "one size fits all-ism" of postcolonial criticism and some of the cruder examples of American transnational and diaspora studies, where difference is often *undifferentiated* and alterity relentlessly mined as antidote to whatever it is first-world scholars find themselves tired of or mired within. That's why more astute critics are rightly troubled by this tendency for creolization to function as a magic bullet for Western knowledge producers exhausted with and critical of their own intellectual biases.[39] To be fair, it is also a magic bullet for contemporary Caribbean writers and scholars eager to peddle notions of difference in exchange for the comforts of institutionalization.

Creolization often depends on a "linguistic turn," an overdependence on language to either validate or elevate anthropology or to give literature or poetics the scientific heft of anthropology.[40] Thinking based on this overdependence on language isn't always as nuanced as it should be and is actually prone to massive exaggeration and analytic confusion. After all, processes of culture, politics, identity, and power in the Caribbean operate not only in non- or extralinguistic ways but also outside of the concerns and priorities of first-world analysis. Glissant himself is not innocent of this overvaluing of language (though being a writer and poet, one would hardly expect otherwise). This is the case despite his attempts to guide against seeing creolization as "merely a linguistic result."[41] Glissant's dependence on an overstylized and often immaterial poetics is often grounded by a weak attention to history, just as Sylvia Wynter's work has been characterized by a "tentatively constructed and imprecise ideational system."[42]

In the desire to see in the creole the solution to singularity and the monadic—and the antidote to a hypertechnological West—one can trace a genealogy of the Caribbean from Thomas More's *Utopia* to *The Tempest* to the "noble savage." It is a familiar set of gestures, not even alien to contemporary tourism and the romantic racism of a commodified Caribbean escape. In the next chapter these gestures are at the heart of that artistic and political movement from which Caribbean creolization springs: negritude. But these uses ignore the severe limits of the process of creolization and its more problematic function within the Caribbean. A potent example of such limits lies in Jamaica, where the tourism and nationalism borders have arguably been blurred for a long time, largely via reggae. This is an island that often uses creolization and also hybridity as a strategic method of disempowering its black majority to privilege its creole microminority and where the hybrid has been a signifier of not just the elite but the explicitly racist as those in between do their best to remain above blacks socially, economically, and culturally. Another limit is evident in the fact that creolization in no way prevents the Caribbean from producing relentless cultural or religious orthodoxies in reaction to it—the fundamentalist Jamaican Rastafarian movement being just one notable example. Nothing, after all, feeds authenticity more than does the creole, and nothing feeds creolization more than its disavowal.

Having acknowledged these necessary caveats, the Caribbean as the locus for creolization is still a geographic and cultural necessity for this analysis. For one thing, catalysis, hybridity, *métissage,* and *créolité* in language and culture have for some time been acknowledged formally as the dynamic process of Caribbean cultural genesis in advance of postcolonial thought quite simply because, as Édouard Glissant puts it in *Caribbean Discourse,* the Caribbean was founded as "a multiple series of relationships." Multiple open relationships, one hastens to add, without the material means to culturally, politically, or economically sever any or solidify one. Due to this, many Caribbean writers and critics have *actively staked out creolization* as their theoretical turf, as an exceptional space of Caribbean intellectual production alongside its known fundamentalisms and obsessions with particularity. These latter relationships—fundamentalism and particularity—are acknowledged in Glissant despite his reluctance to engage the relentless nationalisms and ethnocentrisms that also describe the Caribbean. Those forces often get lost in his great desire to see the Caribbean as a region on the cusp of abandoning identity or the "intolerable alternative" that is nationalism altogether.[43]

Even with the imprecision and utopianism of much of its arguments, creolization in the Caribbean is an attempt to ground autonomous self-description. Creolization also allows Caribbean critics and writers to operate against, within, and without the dominant racial politics of North America. As an act of intellectual autonomy creolization is at work against what Silvio Torres-Saillant pointedly identifies as that tendency of many contemporary Caribbeanists to "surrender to the epistemological might" of postcolonial theory and neglect the Caribbean's legacy as a "thought-producing region and cradle of indigenous paradigms." For Torres-Saillant, influential Caribbean thinkers have too often been shunted into the postcolonial frame and have become recognized less for their indigenous paradigms and more for their conscription into a "new academic world order" that ultimately shifted its interests away from the Caribbean and into the "broader" context of Western critical studies.[44]

In this postcolonial framing, Glissantian creolization, or Antillanité, needs no grounding in Caribbean centrality. The Caribbean as a whole becomes epiphenomena of a white, black, or brown first world that professes globality merely to emphasize its own parochialism. This is an ongoing problem. Much of this book is an attempt to address it by foregrounding Caribbean thinkers in contexts few would have them traverse. To begin to transform this problem, it must be remembered that creolization does have an alternate genealogy. Not only has it been claimed by scholars, critics, theorists, and writers in and from the Caribbean, creolization has been central to how the Caribbean makes sense of its own popular cultural production. It is there, for example, in both formal and informal understandings of food, culture, history, and, of course, music. It is also foundational to Caribbean civil society, complete with its contradictions but necessary to the enduring struggle to contain racial fragmentation and the cultural particularities that spring from too much obsession with discrete origins.

Creolization has been claimed as an indigenous paradigm as well as a form of intellectual distinctiveness. As Torres-Saillant points out, the pre-postcolonial pedigree of creolization is there in the work of Glissant, Edward Kamau Brathwaite, George Lamming, and Sylvia Wynter. Torres-Saillant traces it back to Aimé Césaire and the group behind the journal *Tropiques* in the early 1940s who were devoted to a kind of syncretism produced by transcending the dialectics of rational thought through a use of language and metaphor they thought revolutionary. This, of course, is the context that generated negritude.

But despite its Caribbean pedigree and those who would render creolization an oxymoronic essentialism in the tropics, it is or has always been a world process, as anthropologist Ulf Hannerz famously pointed out.[45] It is present *in all contexts,* which is what drives the need to suddenly recognize in the Caribbean the fact that "the postmodern 'conditio humana' resembles what has been the 'conditio Caribbeana' since at least the sixteenth century."[46] It is this fact that guides the universalism of Glissant. It also guides the work of Sylvia Wynter, for whom the sixteenth century is perhaps even more crucial than the nineteenth because of it being the ground zero of a particular fiction of science called "the human." And it is this sociocultural hyperawareness of the process of creolization—as product of colonialism *and* the evolution of technology—that makes it necessary to take seriously both externally imposed and internally generated notions of mixture, which cluster around the Caribbean like a squall.

CYBERPUNK'S DUBWISE ONTOLOGY

In his meditation on the "catachrestic nominalism" of the term *cyborg*, Alexander Weheliye writes, "If the coexistence of 'the human' with various 'technological' structures and processes presents one of the central challenges of the contemporary world, then Afro-diasporic subjects and cultures surely form a crucial part of this mix."[47] As argued throughout this book, these subjects have been a crucial part of this mix in every technological transformation since industrialization and in the popular fictions that emerged in relation to those transformations. If technological transformation were to be read through the nexus of sound, race, and technology—as in the context of the jazz age, for example, and the innovations of reggae, hip-hop, and techno—blacks have been direct participants as well as subjects in these transformations. It is because of this nexus of race and technology and the historical intimacy of that parallel that it is not so strange that cyberpunk fiction and film made fairly constant references and recourses to race and black music in their attempts to question or problematize the human.

Race has often been both sub- and metatext of science fiction. As De Witt Douglas Kilgore asserts, "this genre devoted to social extrapolation has race as part of its operating system." Race was far more present or unavoidable in cyberpunk than in much mainstream science fiction after the new wave, which from the 1970s at least marked "an almost joint effort by white writers to bring their genre into dialogue with the civil unrest, political activism, and artistic innovation produced by African Americans in that era."[48] Cyberpunk arguably returns to that movement's countercultural posture and sympathies in that the new wave was explicitly focused on the great social and cultural revolutions of the time, such as those around race, sex, gender, the Cold War, and empire. In work from the 1980s to the present, ranging from William Gibson, Pat Cadigan, and Bruce Sterling to more contemporary writers such as Neil L. Asher, Ian McDonald, George Alec Effinger, the particularly gifted Jack Womack, and so many others, Africa, blacks, or nonwhites have been significant to the narratives, and race has been a topic of varying degrees of importance. This variety is a corrective to the notion that "forecasts of a utopian (to some) race-free future and pronouncements of the dystopian digital divide are the predominant discourses of blackness and technology in the public sphere."[49] Such a statement requires either more clear evidence or a more specific definition of the public sphere. De Witt Douglas Kilgore proves himself to be exceptional as one of the few as rooted in the genre, as he is in black thought when he asserts: "The racial history of science fiction . . . is confined neither to Afro-futurism nor to the production of its black artists; it is also a legacy of its dead (and living) white writers. Following this point does not require that we change our sense of the genre's foundational texts but how we frame and read them."[50] His thinking is also very much in line with the observations of both Samuel R. Delany and Wilson Harris that begin this chapter.

But in looking back at that recent phenomenon of cyberpunk, what stood out and what has had lasting impact was in fact that figure of the cyborg, the part-human, part-machine figure that, though birthed in the fascist fantasies of Italian futurism, reemerged as a complex sign of either humanity's imminent demise or its transformation. As Haraway put it, "Contemporary science fiction is full of cyborgs—creatures simultaneously animal and machine, who populate worlds ambiguously natural and crafted."[51] It takes little effort to read back to Melville, Butler, and Shelley and note the intimacy between the concerns of industrialization, colonialism, and slavery and the contemporary moment explored by Haraway. What makes that earlier period far more resonant is its dependence on the representation of *the Negro* as "simultaneously animal and machine."

In the wake of cybernetics as a science of communication and control, cyborgs would serve among many things as an image of both the possibility of cross-cultural and cross-racial interaction (i.e., they were almost human, like us) as well as its denial due to absolutist notions of racial difference (i.e., they were machines, a different species, not like us at all). The goal of technology became then not to create machines to supplant humans but to use technology to extend human capabilities. This led to a growing sense of intimacy between hardware and the organic and an intensified sense of the uncanny racial histories and politics of that intimacy. Cyberpunk would amplify those associations common in earlier narratives and exaggerate them from the point of view of a new understanding of the porous boundaries between flesh and machine. By way of this radical questioning of the body, cyberpunk would reverse the old question of "what is a machine" by directly questioning what older narratives only hinted at: the role and status of the human.

Precyberpunk writers such as Philip K. Dick and even a golden age writer like

Isaac Asimov had more than a little to do with paralleling the cyborg, robot, replicant, or android with the slave or other subordinated groups. It is present, for example, in Asimov's stories published through the civil rights period and beyond such as "Galley Slave" (1941) or "Segregationist" (1967) or in more contemporary works like *Robots and Empire* (1985). This latter work, as Martin Kevorkian points out, "brings the colonial dimension of roboculture most forcefully to the fore," but "Asimov has consistently developed parallels to the black experience from his earliest robot novels onwards."[52]

Asimov's interest in race goes further than fiction. His famous "Three Laws of Robotics" currently guides the robot industry and artificial-intelligence research. African American science fiction critic Isaiah Lavender makes a strong suggestion that these laws produced a machine that "resonate with the antebellum South's myth of a happy darkie—a primitive childlike worker without a soul, incapable of much thought—cared for by the benevolent and wise master."[53] A powerful resonance, yet these laws were produced as a corrective to the intense fears that such machines presented to the West in the wake of Čapek's *R.U.R.* Asimov was hostile to the dramatization of "the mechanical man that proved a menace, the creature that turned against its creator, the robot that became a threat to humanity."[54] Science fiction grand master Brian Aldiss describes this as even "a boringly predominant feature" of the early American pulps in those years leading up to World War II.[55] Considering that the robot as a figure was rooted in racial anxieties from Butler to Čapek, it was *that* racism Asimov was attempting to correct, or at least engage. To his credit, and as his stories and fiction attest, Asimov does see the overall historical parallels and suggests that the very tradition of science fiction also acknowledged them in advance of his groundbreaking work. This is clear when he states that his work aimed at rejecting the dominant or even obvious notion that robots were "symbols of minority groups . . . not pathetic creatures that were unfairly persecuted so that I could make Aesopic statements about Jews, Blacks or any other mistreated members of society."[56]

In the same period as cyberpunk's ascendance, mainstream American science fiction films—as public a sphere as one can imagine—also deployed race in notable ways. High-profile films like *Johnny Mnemonic*—based on a William Gibson short story—*Hackers, Virtuosity,* and *Strange Days,* all from 1995, for example, employed blacks as signs of technological competency. And their presence was more than decorative in that they functioned centrally for the dramatizing of the cultural experience of new technology and new relationships with machines.

The trope of the black computer genius in films like *Minority Report*—based on the work of Phillip K. Dick—*Terminator 2: Judgment Day, Independence Day,* and others became so common as to be contemporary cliché. For critics like Martin Kevorkian this was less a celebration of black access to technology than a suspicious representation. It did not represent the liberating possibilities of technology or the utopian possibilities of race-less digital space but instead an American ambivalence to race superimposed on its ambivalences about technology and power. Race is, again, deployed as a sign of anxieties about technology. As one critic put it, "Sometimes overtly, sometimes more subtly, the characters' blackness intermediates between the representational conventions of narrative film and the 'new technologies' that those films depict. The one helps make the other visible, so to speak," much like the parallel between minstrel and machine in a much earlier context or the broader representational conventions of race and technology as argued throughout this book.[57]

While there is much to critique in these films, the very fact that race and machines are represented with any degree of intimacy is notable. This was, after all, during the burgeoning digital revolution where a term such as *digital divide* was gaining currency. In these narratives blacks at least are not represented as crudely pretechnological or just simply primitive; nor is their relationship with technology played for laughs or exploited as incongruous. There exists also a notion of technological mastery in these representations or of the possibility of such mastery that works against older representations of blacks and machines. This being the very period where black electronic music began to come of age in Jamaica, America, and Europe, and the work of Samuel R. Delany, Octavia Butler, Steven Barnes, and others began to seep out of the ghetto of science fiction, something commendable is at work in these narratives where blackness *and* technological acumen are suggested.

In keeping with the trajectory narrated from late Victorian proto–science fiction, these contemporary narratives—film as well as cyberpunk literature—operated in the broader context of a then radical vision of postimperial globalization, decentered multinational capital, and Western social and economic decline (or a transformation so fundamental that it can only be narrated as decline). Race was hardly something these writers and filmmakers could ignore. Admittedly, they in many cases focused less on the interests or experiences of the other and more on using the other to signal changes or anxieties in either the primary white narrator or the assumed white consumer of those fictions. But these texts assumed the decline of the sovereignty and sanctity of the human or represented it as an embattled category in the face of increasingly invasive forms of technology and modes of capital.

Cyberpunk's often-gleeful celebration of the dominance and ultimate victory of the machine—or at least that intimate standoff or compromise between flesh and fabrication that is the cyborg—owes a great deal to *Erewhon* and, of course, *Frankenstein*. The same applies to what in the wake of cyberpunk was loosely termed *posthumanism*, a set of highly technologized conversations and intellectual trajectories that depart from the sacrosanct secular vision of the human as established from the European Renaissance. According to Cary Wolfe, posthumanism "names the embodiment and embeddedness of the human being in not just its biological but also its technological world . . . and names a historical moment in which the de-centering of the human by imbrications in technical, medical, informatics and economic networks is increasingly impossible to ignore."[58]

A more slippery beast than even cyberpunk, posthumanism is described thusly by Joel Dinerstein: it is "the synthesis of Western rationalism, Christian disdain for the animal body, and superiority over the Other," which creates a "faith-based narrative whereby scientists eliminate all subjective experience to focus on the dream of a mechanical brain from which they can then upgrade the human race."[59] It is true that this form of techno-utopianism is rooted in a secular religious impulse or often gives way to one. The early twentieth-century American embrace of technology was often framed in religious terms, and it's no secret that the digital revolution was and is similarly framed. But limiting posthumanism to the scientific community and its prejudices allows Dinerstein to make a mistake common to those who see in posthumanism a secular fundamentalism that supplants Christianity's software but maintains its cultural biases. Yes, there is or was that tendency in cyborg theorizing to celebrate or imagine a transcendence of the body through technology, just as it became more likely that technology would transcend hardware. That tendency in no way could be said to have defined cyberpunk, cybernetics, or cybertheory in general, given its obsession with blending and hybridity.

Critics, including Haraway, have politicized the posthuman by refusing to maintain a thinking about technology that exists "in the simulacrum without referentials" and which so fetishizes that "disdain for the body" that is ineluctably connected to a disdain for the racial other *as body*.[60] Posthumanism and its cyborg avatar are for these critics oppositional. "The fact that the cyborg's existence is simultaneously material and political is absolutely crucial to the influence of Haraway's text," which is why "analyses of cyborgian existence have been well adapted to political readings."[61]

N. Katherine Hayles, for example, has been very clear on the "material base of all cyberexperiences" and has argued for radically grounding all cyberculture in material politics. For her, this reading of posthumanism as "escape" is a "pipe dream," which is interesting only if we explore "why it is a compelling imaginary at this cultural moment."[62] The pipe dream part communicates on its own terms; but the second part of Hayles's point can be quickly addressed. The reason the escapist or transcendent aspects of posthumanism have been compelling has been precisely because of the material realities of this cultural moment: immigration, diversity, scarcity, and challenges to white and male power. Like previous science fictions the dream of elsewhere is fed by increasing anxieties about the here and now.

Dinerstein's view of the posthuman is similar to Alexander Weheliye's view of cybertheory as having "little if anything to say about the intricate processes of racial formation, whether U.S.-based or within a more global framework."[63] This is a view that Martin Kevorkian also shares, hence his attempt to bring "race into the discussion of computers and by considering technology as a factor in racial constructions of identity."[64] But it is a mistake to assume that it is in the era of cyborgs that race emerges as a factor in thinking about technology, science fiction, or posthumanism; as seen earlier in this work, race is both explicit and implicit in the genre from its birth. Also, since Norbert Wiener had race very much on his mind, cybertheory has long been imbricated with race. Since black human beings had been "coded as natural machines" to generate wealth and because this socioeconomic framework, along with its violence, would impose a "science fictional existence on African slaves and their descendants, figuring them as cyborgs in a white human world," it's easy to agree with Ben Williams in his insightful essay on Detroit techno that "slavery, the original unit of capitalist labor, is . . . the originary form of the post human."[65]

One begs to differ, again, with Isaiah Lavender, whose important *Race in American Science Fiction* consistently suggests that science fiction has *not* been aware of the embeddedness of race in its use of technology. In a discussion of cyborgs meant to emphasize the genres' alleged blindness to issues of race and difference, Lavender writes, "My own thinking diverges here from that of posthumanist scholars in that I consider these new beings as new races."[66] But this is hardly a divergence. Readers and scholars have long been aware of this because it is precisely the metaphoric as well as explicit meaning behind such figures in science fiction, from Mary Shelley to *Neuromancer,* from *Erewhon* to Philip K. Dick's *Do Androids Dream of Electric Sheep,* from *The Human Use of Human Beings* to *The Silver Metal Lover* to Čapek, who along with Samuel Butler has an earlier claim on what Lavender calls "meta-slavery."

It is also not completely true that science fiction "has mirrored rather than defied racial stereotypes throughout much of its history."[67] This too general statement is akin to that which helped popularize Afro-futurism "to challenge the notion of a future without race."[68] The work of Asimov, Philip K. Dick, Robert Silverberg, Thomas Disch, Maureen McHugh, Ian McDonald, Jack Womack, or any number of writers (even far less progressive writers such as Edgar Rice Burroughs, Robert E. Howard, and the controversial Mike Resnick) suggests otherwise. There is a reason why metaphors of difference, hybridity, and race *work* in talk about cyborgs, robots, and replicants. It is a part of the genre's DNA and operates to engage readers in difference, alterity, and related issues and histories. One sides here with De Witt Douglas Kilgore, who also critiques generalizations about race and science fiction: "a reading of the past half-century of sf indicates that the issues at the heart of our experience of racial politics have also been a signal feature of generic production."[69]

Because machines were always-already racialized in science fiction, perhaps too much was taken for granted, hence the possibility of missing the presence of racial contexts and concerns in cyberpunk or posthumanism. But it is too much to suggest that the posthuman is a necessary "escape from the panhuman," as Dinerstein does, especially since his notion of the "panhuman" is itself described as a product of a "creolized world history."[70] The primary political and conceptual problems lay less in the prefixes *post* and *pan* than in the loaded and limited category of the human itself. Such generalizing is an easy thing to do if one assumes that technology and its meanings and uses are always culturally, racially, or socially one-sided: always necessarily, as he puts it, a "white mythology." This latter assumption is opposed to the ethics of cyberpunk. As a genre or movement, it is known for its fascination with reinvention and the use of technology in ways opposed to its original intentions and by communities unexpected to have access to those technologies, from Japan to Brazil to Africa. In this regard posthumanism is already reflective of a panhuman history because even he shows valuably in *Swinging the Machine* that race has always infected thinking about technology and blacks have already creolized technology. Posthumanism is a dynamic phenomenon since technology is too subject to the process of creolization, to vernacular appropriation in the absence of formal mastery or institutional control.

Though published alongside Dinerstein's essay, David E. Nye provides a more variegated vision of posthumanism when he identifies the use that Caribbean peoples made of the Internet in ways that defy the notion of a "digital divide." Nye points out that Trinidadians did not "embrace a global culture that weakened their sense of identification with their own nation or culture"; instead, "they used the Internet to project pride in their own nation, to broadcast its music, to educate others about their islands, and to sell its products and vacation experiences."[71] This is very much in line with the fact that the computer may have once been seen as the ultimate "harbinger of standardization," but by the 1980s became seen as an "engine of differentiation," indeed, of diversity. To further strengthen the point that this is a confirmation of creolization at work, Nye points out two things. First, Trinidadian Internet use strengthened rather than weakened that element at the core of creolization as an analytic and a world historical process: *language,* particularly the vernacular. Second, the disembodied global experience of the Internet "did not seem to overwhelm but rather to strengthen the local, for example, making it easier for the music of Trinidad and Tobago to reach the rest of the world."[72]

One wonders then how technology in this case could be then understood as a "white mythology." This is especially the case since Dinerstein himself astutely describes creolization as an assault on or a laying bare of the devices of "the Enlightenment ideal of the liberal human subject ('the human')."[73] This gesture against or exposing the human as a fundamentally racial category as well as a gendered one is one of the most important theoretical and conceptual links between posthumanism and Caribbean creolization—that and music, the "distinctively fluid and effective conduit for the kinds of non-hierarchical exchanges that creolization thrives on."[74]

It should therefore be no surprise that it is through music that the Caribbean directly found its way into posthumanism. Not through jazz or even Trinidadian soca, which began to evolve into a digital direction by the mid-1980s, along with other Caribbean music but through a sound at the core of Caribbean technopoetics: Jamaican dub. Dub makes all those turns to digitization in Caribbean sound possible. From William Gibson's definitive cyberpunk novel, *Neuromancer* (1984) to Jeff Noon's *Vurt* (1993) and his truly remarkable *Needle in the Groove* (1999), to more music compilations and recordings that one could possibly list comprehensively (the Macro Dub Infection series from 1995 to 1996 being of particular significance), this music began to be heard as a technological vision of a future far less definable in exclusively white terms than it always had been. A reviewer of Macro Dub Infection shows just how known and naturalized the presence of dub in cyberpunk and cyberculture was by the time of the compilation: "one might hypothesize that entering dub's vertiginous expanses is good training for exploring [Virtual Reality], where depth perception and a mastery of the intricate layers of nested windows will be invaluable. Recent events bear out this cyber-dub connection."[75] He goes on to reference *Neuromancer* as a central text in that cyberdub connection.

The history and influence of dub being so complex and intricate, it would be embarrassing to attempt detailing it here. One is grateful to those that have joined this writer in the quest to rescue dub from its marginal intellectual position in global culture despite its central technological and cultural influence. For the history of science fiction what matters is that it is through dub that the Caribbean became integral to the mythos—or at least soundtrack—of that primary text, *Neuromancer,* which among many other things is famed for popularizing the word *cyberspace* after being coined by the author in an earlier short story. *Neuromancer* is therefore a key text in the already brought together of creolization and technopoetics, the Caribbean and information technology and their attendant tropes and vernacular meanings. It is no overstatement that this novel and others in his "sprawl trilogy" (*Count Zero* and *Mona Lisa Overdrive*) have had more to do with popularizing posthumanism than Haraway's—or Wiener's—entire oeuvre.

Despite anxieties about the total domination of global capital and the vision of a world that is truly omnicolonial, the view of the future in Gibson's works is as creole as one can imagine. Caribbean cultures are important to that view. It is that kind of a vision that would motivate his use of the loa of Haitian voodoo in *Count Zero* as forms of artificial intelligence. Gibson would do so after reading an article in *National Geographic* no less (again, the colonial past in the cybernetic present). Most appealing to Gibson is the notion that voodoo is a hybrid religion and a countercultural belief system that enabled "the kind of multiplicity Gibson achieves when overlaying the language of technology (subprograms) upon the language of religion (loa)." Gibson found "voodoo's notion of god appropriate to a computer society."[76] And as a "street religion," it presented "like cyberspace itself . . . an alternative method of conceptualizing the system."[77] In other words, these Caribbean traditions function for him essentially as analogs for digital recombination, a process that operates also through syncretic, nonlinear, and therefore "magical" processes. Emma Bull would follow in this trajectory in her 1991 novel *Bone Dance.*

Neuromancer also deserves attention for its inclusion of Jamaican Rastafarians into the universe of science fiction. This would be replicated in the cult film *The Adventures of Buckaroo Banzai Across the 8th Dimension,* made the same year, and would give way to the quickly popularized trope of the dreadlocked alien in more than a few films, from John Sayles's classic *The Brother from Another Planet* to the Predator series and the *Star Wars* universe. It's not an exaggeration to say that dreadlocked blacks—particularly men—were a part of the visual lexicon of cyberpunk. The presence of reggae and Dub and Rastafarians in the work of Gibson, Bruce Sterling, Jeff Noon, and others, however, have been contentious in the making sense of representations of posthumanism or any "ambiguously natural" space within which it operates. As one critic would have it, Gibson "twisted the cultural tradition of Rastafari into his postmodern, tech-inclusive milieu" and "disregarded Rastafari's essentialist roots in favor of a cyborg politics, as laid out in Donna Haraway's *Cyborg Manifesto.*" As such the Rastafari in Gibson's novel reveal a "political alternative to the hyperrational, individualistic, parasitic realm that characterizes postindustrial capitalism in the novel because it affirms social commitment and community, intuition, and the body." In choosing them Gibson portrays "potentially empowering modes of identity that may counter the alienation of cyberspace."[78] In other words, the Rastafarians in *Neuromancer* signify a utopian alternative culture but also a hyperorganic opposition, not to whites but to machines and an utterly technologized world and those humans hybridized by machinic incorporation.

To readers attuned to the history of colonial representations of blacks or touristic representations of the Caribbean, this supposedly liberating set of alternatives is, however, troublingly familiar. That blacks still represent the body and the resistance to technology, intuition, and any form of alternative is reminiscent of a romantic racism older than lost-race fictions or *The Tempest.* As Afro-futurist Kali Tal puts it,

> No African Americanist could miss the repetition of the figure of the black technoprimitive in science fiction in general and cyberpunk in particular. From the "Rastas in space" exoticism of *Buckaroo Banzai* and the reggae-flavored data havens of Bruce Sterling's *Islands in the Net,* to the gritty street cred of the characters played by gangsta rapper Ice-T in *Johnny Mnemonic* and *Tank Girl,* the magical

touch of *The Brother from Another Planet,* and the wise guides of *The Matrix,* the sci-fi/cyberpunk trope of blackness as simultaneously a site of wisdom, danger and unimpeachable hipness is baldly apparent to anyone with an eyes to see it.[79]

Technoprimitivism is clearly at work in these narratives and in some critical responses to them, and in the wake of the sensationalized American terror of Jamaican drug posses during the 1980s, which ran alongside the radical transformation of reggae from an analog to a digital form, the hipness factor in this use of Rastafarians and dub was also clear. To their credit, cyberpunk authors were indeed obsessed with urban subcultures of all sorts. Given the punk aspect of their ethos, the turn to reggae, dub, and Rasta was in keeping with some of the British punk movement's affinities for Caribbean migrants and their sound cultures. In fact, the earliest example of an explicit connection between punk, reggae, and posthumanism can be found in the work of the highly influential singer-composer-artist John Foxx. Founder of Scottish post-punk/techno-pop band Ultravox!, his choice to render his 1976 paean to cyborgic incorporation, "I Want to Be a Machine" on a dub rhythm—followed by a reggae song, "Dangerous Rhythm" with its celebration of "surging and merging"—may have seemed incongruous but was in retrospect prophetic. Cyberpunk's dub lineage arguably begins there.[80]

Technoprimitivism, however, makes the notion that these characters represent an empowering alternative to postindustrial capitalism questionable since the exotic or the primitive largely exist as narrative, cultural, or symbolic oppositions to technology rather than humanized alternatives or legitimate spaces for the presumed reader to occupy. There is no sense in *Neuromancer,* for example, that Case, the protagonist, would want to be or become one of the Rastas or that their resistance is anything more than symbolic with a strong dose of quaint. Truthfully, one would be surprised *not* to find some degree of primitivism in the cyberpunk texts Tal discusses. The primitive seems always necessary in narratives that explore what happens when whites reach their social, cultural, or technological borders. The flip side of this, of course, is also true: race often functions as a fiction that enables a hyperorganic humanizing of the white self once it loses its moorings, as was the case of jazz in the early twentieth century. That too is the function of the primitive, to ground the white subject in a new environment. Sound artist–critic David Toop sees the primitivist connection this way: "Urban, rural, tropic, aquatic, lo-tech, mystical. This was the source mix from which William Gibson drew (sentimentally, some critics think) when adding the humanizing element of Rastafari and dub to his *Neuromancer* narrative of tech-Gnosis."[81] "Humanizing," is, of course, another word for naturalizing, and, as we have seen, this has long been a function of race, as a mask for the machine.

Clumsily, though still to its credit, *Neuromancer* deploys "blackness"—from the tribal, scarred African on the first page of the novel all the way to the dreadlocked Zionites and their deep-space cruiser, *Marcus Garvey*—not as an opposition but as a necessary supplement to technology. The Zionites may be primitivized, but they are not luddites or technophobes. They are not like the gypsies in Samuel R. Delany's classic *Nova* (1968), persecuted and marginalized for their refusal to accept cyborg "studding" and technological incorporation. The Zionites employ technology on their own terms and within their own cosmology, something central to dub as a sonic signifier and example of the process of technocreolization. In Antonio Benítez Rojo's words, dub as a product of a specifically "Caribbean machine"—here meaning sound-system culture rather than the heavy Deleuzian metaphors the critic is given to—contributes to a process common in contemporary sound production: "slicing pieces of sound in an unforeseen, improbably and finally impossible way."[82]

Mark Dery describes the Zionites as "romanticized arcadians who are obviously very adroit with jury-rigged technology ... superlunary Romare Beardens—*bricoleurs* whose orbital colony was cobbled together by space junk."[83] The Romare Bearden reference is an attractive one, though it has within it the sense that Caribbean figures of comparison evade the critic. An African American blackness becomes the common ground or representative standard. But few people intimate with either Rastas or Jamaican sound culture and its notorious techno-obsessions or with even Kingston itself could read this without a warm chuckle of local recognition. Along with other nonwhites and despite the hipness factor that is due to the fascination with subcultures endemic to early cyberpunk, the Rastas in Gibson's novel participate in the presentation and construction of a distinct future. Such a future might have seemed alien to white or black American readers at the time of the novel's publication, but it did speak to the long lineage of outer space narratives, images, and references in dub music and reggae culture as well as the shift to digital sound occurring in Jamaica. The shift to an explicit Caribbean cyborg poetics would be made audible a year after *Neuromancer* with the arrival of producer King Jammy's "Sleng Teng," made with a Casio MT-40. This was the first all computerized "riddim," and it revolutionized Jamaican popular music and the global sound culture that it had begun to erect in the years before formal decolonization. In his temporal intimacy with this Caribbean context and these shifts and with what seems an uncanny awareness of them, Gibson's Rastas exist in a future that barely exceeds its present.

Yet there is a question that remains unasked about *Neuromancer*'s racial politics. Why would Gibson chose *these* blacks rather than the far more intimate, far more representationally standard and local African Americans? Why Caribbean blacks instead of the far more technologically savvy, economically empowered, and culturally influential black American social world? If you recall, through the addition of dreadlocks, even the African American rapper-actor Ice-T becomes Caribbeanized in his roles in cyberpunk narratives; not only do we have the mystic Rasta named Virgil at the center of John Sayles's *The Brother from Another Planet* (1984), who leads the dreadlocked alien into a weed-induced nighttime inferno, but the very musical leitmotif that runs throughout this narrative set in an African American–dominated Harlem is based on Trinidadian steel-drum rhythms. Why is the Caribbean, as Kevorkian described, the "preferred cyberpunk flavoring," second only to Tokyo?[84]

Samuel R. Delany, whose creole futures have been threatening to some putative Afro-futurists such as Greg Tate, also doesn't ask this question in an interview with Mark Dery. Delany responds to Gibson's use of Jamaican Rastafarians and dub music uncharacteristically, as if he were a racial nationalist: "You'll forgive me if, as a black reader, I didn't leap up to proclaim this passing presentation of a powerless and wholly nonoppositional set of black dropouts, by a Virginia-born white writer, as the coming of the black millennium in science fiction; but maybe that's just a black thang."[85] One could easily trump these "as a black reader" claims of authoritative thangness by revealing them to be more local than their universal postures suggest. Delany, like Tal, relies on a more generalized critique of racial representation that historically allows African American critics to ignore micropolitical or cross-cultural differences in the services of a first-world racial vanguardism.

Nothing in Delany's or Tal's critiques suggests a knowledge of or interest in the Caribbean or Rastafarianism and how that millennial ideology became intimate with music in Jamaica by the 1960s as well as with the tourist trade in the 1980s. Both of these factors contributed to its hipness as well as its increasing loss of political efficacy. Were the intricacies of Rastafarianism to be engaged by these critics—or *Rasta,* which is colloquially acknowledged to be far less orthodox than, say, Rastafari or Nyabinghi, to respond also to Delany's problem with Gibson's choice of term—Gibson's representation would seem far more potent as a critique than most black readers would like to admit.

Despite the romantic rhetoric of post-Garveyite black nationalism that still enshrouds Rastafarianism, by the mid-1980s a good deal of the movement had been reduced to precisely being a "powerless and wholly nonoppositional set of black dropouts" who existed primarily on the fumes of revolutionary politics and wallowed in a primitivism of their own devising.

This change in Rastafari and its attendant roots reggae in part explains its easy co-optation by the tourist industry as well as the generational shift to a dancehall/ragga poetics and cultural politics in the mid-1980s. Dancehall was a harder sound, less universal, less sentimental, and far less oriented around fantasies of authenticity or Garveyite politics. If anything, dancehall was deliberately antiarcadian and less dependent on the bucolic romanticism of Rastafari. And it did not fear sex. It used digital technology as a prominent sign of its departure from roots and its engagement with, as Gibson would call it, postnational sprawl. Delany may be troubled by Gibson's depiction of the Rastas as beings with "shrunken hearts," with bones brittle with "calcium loss."[86] Yet that is a moving vision of a group so driven by racial and cultural essentialism that their ideology inevitably ossifies and grows brittle. Their hearts are shrunken because they have lost what power they once had: nostalgia will do that—sap the spirit, weaken resolve. They have lost the capacity to function in a world where the natural merely signifies a longing for an ever-mythical wholeness.

Gibson gives us a tragic view of a movement that had become fragile due to its commitment to an authenticity impossible in the universe of *Neuromancer,* or in any other. Race and resistance may give them dignity, but theirs is an authenticity that is nevertheless impossible and key to their representation in the novel. And to Delany's point that the novel does not present the Zionites as having any women is hardly the fault of Gibson seems aware of the deep patriarchy of the movement and the fact that it emerged by cultivating some of the misogynist practices of the Old Testament. This is why it is important to recall that the Zionites have an unexpectedly great respect for the character Molly—the novel's primary cyborg character: "The Rastas' acceptance of a nonblack, nonmale cyborg as a political icon is an anomaly for a religious movement that has focused almost entirely on black male identity."[87] They call her "Steppin' Razor" after a song associated with the late great reggae singer Peter

Tosh, though written by the equally great though far less heralded Joe Higgs, who was the vocal mentor for the original Wailers, which included, along with Tosh, Bunny Livingston (Wailer), and, of course, Bob Marley.

This anomaly only strengthens Gibson's critique of a movement that has lost so much of its power through its staunch essentialism that it can only look with longing at the doubled sign of change and blending: machine and woman, creolized and therefore far more relevant than the organic, if not more radical than authenticity. Molly is not only a double, an echo of a human. She is also a creole, a hybrid, *Métis*. As such, she and many posthuman or postrobot figures were and are very often signs of a creolized history or of a history that sought or produced images of mixture even if it may have refused and criminalized the process. Molly is very much in line with the history of images of creolization going back to the nineteenth century in the Caribbean and Latin America, for example. Creole or mixed-race women have long been idealized in literature and culture, despite the anxieties and ambivalences of race mixing due to the sense that they were wildly exotic, accessibly hypersexual, and uncannily seductive. An example of how that old idealization of the creole blends with the punk aspect of Gibson's vision is in sci-fi writer Thomas M. Disch's description of her "dominatrix gear" as being necessary for cyberpunk's postjuvenile, primarily white male audience.[88]

What matters more than the Rastafarians and their fading exoticism and weakened political state is their music, which Gibson describes as "a sensuous mosaic cooked from vast libraries of digitalized pop."[89] In his turn to dub, Gibson anticipates the kind of critical work that began to explore, through Caribbean sound, a history of the black diaspora's engagement with technologies of reproduction and information. Critics who come primarily to mind include Michael Veal, Beth Lesser, Julian Henriques, Wayne Marshall, Dennis Howard, Christopher Partridge, Paul Sullivan, and this author. This particular confluence of Caribbean sound and new technologies is also what inspired Jeff Noon's creation of a "liquid dub poetics" for postcyberpunk writing in his 1993 work, *Needle in the Groove.*

But what hasn't been noted is that this isn't actually a description of dub, or at least not reggae dub, what one would expect Rastafarians to be listening to (of course, orthodox Rastas—such as the Nyabinghi—wouldn't be listening to reggae at all due to their total rejection of Babylon's tools). Dub, being rooted primarily in the studio manipulation of instrumental tracks of reggae, can stretch sound and song beyond familiarity and into the realm of collage; after all, sampling arguably was anticipated by dub techniques, such as trapping echoes into repetitive loops or the introduction of random sounds into the mix, such as babies, animals, cars, motorcycles, sirens. But the "sensuous mosaic" being described in the novel is more akin to hip-hop or that dizzyingly intertextual sample-based electronic or industrial music that became popular in the 1980s with the advent of increasingly affordable digital samplers.

Purists will agree that dub is more of a process than a genre. It is a practice of first *doubling* a prerecorded musical track—from which "dub" is named—stripping it down to its essentials of bass and drums and then layering the space and silence with aleatoric special effects, particularly echo. The strictest of historians will point out that dub did in fact make hip-hop possible, as well as a plethora of electronic music, from drum 'n' bass to two-step/garage to dancehall and dubstep to global bass. To call it all dub is merely to be catholic. If that is the case, then Gibson is showing an impressive knowledge of a musical period where black electronic music becomes increasingly popular and globally influential as much for technological innovation as for performance and lyrical content. It was a time where mixing, sampling, and blending become sonic metaphors for cultural and historical interaction, particularly in a context of technological mediation enabled by black, working-class, and non-Western appropriation. This occurs even to the point of corporate co-optation, as Delany points out and as Gibson subtly suggests in the novel. To describe it all as dub is for Gibson to give priority to the Caribbean origins of this context, the space that has come to stand in for creolization on a world scale.

A better description of dub can be found in Alan Moore and Dave Gibbons's now-canonical *Watchmen* comic series that also began to appear in the mid-1980s. This comic cycle was very much in conversation with the evolving posthumanism of science fiction in popular culture. After all, posthumanism as a development of Nietzschean notions of the "Overman" have been present in the comic book world from Superman to Moore's far more self-referential and metafictional representation of characters like Doctor Manhattan or Ozymandias. The latter describes dub as "a sort of hybrid between electronic music and reggae" but doesn't celebrate it for its lyrical themes of slavery, exile, racism, and Afrocentrism. He is interested in its explicit and useful take on technocreolization: "It's a fascinating study in the new musical forms generated when a largely pre-technological culture is given access to modern recording techniques without the technological preconceptions that we've allowed to accumulate, limiting our vision."[90]

Such a view of dub was already at work in Jamaican sound culture, not only due to the aforementioned record album covers and the very many song titles that carried the dub/machine/Rastas in outer space parallel. This view of reggae/dub was also present in how dub was seen and written about, from the 1970s to the present. It was heard as either a psychedelic or outer space music due not only to its foregrounding of technology but also to its focus on space itself through echo and the constant interruptive use of bass and drums. Rhythm is an inconsistent presence in dub and is secondary to absence and echo, giving it the feeling of space, dispersal, and the ever-presence of void. Erik Davis, author of *Techgnosis: Myth, Magic and Mysticism in the Age of Information,* describes it thusly:

> But dub music, reggae's great technological mutant, is a pure artifact of the machine, and has little to do with earth, flesh, or authenticity. To create dub, producers and engineers manipulate preexisting tracks of music recorded in an analog—as opposed to digital—fashion on magnetic tape (today's high-end studios encode music as distinct digital bits rather than magnetic "waves"). Dubmasters saturate individual instruments with reverb, phase, and delay; abruptly drop voices, drums, and guitars in and out of the mix; strip the music down to the bare bones of rhythm and then build it up again through layers of inhuman echoes, electronic ectoplasm, cosmic rays. Good dub sounds like the recording studio itself has begun to hallucinate.[91]

Dub constructs an "ambiguously natural" aural space where the very distinctions between real and virtual, sound and echo, are irrelevant and necessary to the pleasure of its consumption. Its impact on global electronic music production and culture is profound and occurs despite the fact that it is so deeply rooted in the organic mythos of roots reggae, as it becomes overwhelmingly Rastafarian by the time that the music achieves global awareness. That it comes from the margins of first-world corporate influence, where the humanity of its producers has been deemed liminal if not virtual, and that it blends specifically Caribbean elements with Western technological means makes it central as a key form and technique of creolization as well as productive of new nonwhite and potentially nonmale mythologies. In keeping with this latter point, the lineage of dub and the Caribbean informs Jamaican-Canadian science fiction writer Nalo Hopkinson's work, particularly her award-winning 2000 novel *Midnight Robber,* which reappropriates creolization and racial technopoetics from cyberpunk while offering a strong critique of the homophobia and patriarchy of much Caribbean sound and culture.

But creolization, gender, technopoetics, and their alternate political possibilities bring us back to Molly. It matters that it is she who introduces and describes dub to *Neuromancer's* main character, Case. She describes it as a "form of "worship" and a "sense of community," as if she had been a participant in the earth-shaking rituals of dub sound systems like the lionized Jah Shaka or legendary "inventor" of dub, Osbourne Ruddock's King Tubby's Home Town Hi Fi.[92] Dub has always been understood as a quasi-religious sound, particularly as manifest in the work of Jah Shaka and other British sound systems and musicians like Alpha and Omega, whose music and performances are staged as rituals. The former's New Testaments of Dub and Commandments of Dub series are aural testimony, where the latter's entire oeuvre takes the dub as biblical meditation to its ambient, dirgelike extreme. Wilson Harris would certainly call dub a "sacred" art that invokes "an orchestration of imageries and histories to take us through and beyond ourselves into the music of space, incandescent space, rhythmic space."[93]

Gibson's suggestion is that as a cyborg herself, dub's syncretic tendencies made Molly sense the music in ways that perhaps even the Zionites couldn't, given their fetish for the organic in a world where roots are impossible. After all, as a form based on machinic doubling, dub is also based on masking, passing, and inauthenticity. Where roots reggae is the sound of a hyperbolic authenticity, culture, and masculinism, dub rearranges those themes and assumptions, making it possible for a character like Molly to feel at one with it. Instead of stability, tradition, patriarchy, and continuity, it presents a world uprooted and mechanized, where race and history are thrust into an unforgivingly creole simulacra, an echo chamber.

THE MUSIC OF LIVING MACHINESCAPES: CREOLIZATION AND ARTIFICIAL INTELLIGENCE

Cyberpunk and posthumanism have so made use of the interplay between subjectivity, gender, artificial intelligence, and technology that the very notion of them as central to current discussion might seem to some as hackneyed. Haraway has herself made clear that even as an analytic tool, the cyborg's work is done.[94] Even *Neuromancer* now sounds like a crusty analog signal, as anachronistic as was the typewriter it was famously composed on. Yet despite the influence of Haraway on thinking about bodies in their interaction with machines, and despite the ongoing evolution of cyberpunk and postdub electronic music into a myriad of other forms and microgenres, there remains much to be thought about race and technology. This is also because despite the growing interest in an Afro-futurism that depends on the literary and sonic figurations of race and technology, we have barely scratched the surface of the black diaspora's own critical resources in this regard.

That is why the formal coming together of creole poetics with technology and artificial intelligence and the attempt to provide a history of that coming together is so necessary. The goal here is not simply to layer a scrim of contemporary racial thinking on top of science fiction or to merely use the tropes, symbols, and mechanics of the genre to produce insights and observations about race and racism that, frankly, are no different than they would have been without the context of technology or science fiction. This project shares with Afro-futurism and others a commitment to questioning many of the historical assumptions clustering around blackness as something other to the human in its Enlightenment formulations and against the backdrop of a Western culture that has manifest its sense of supremacy through science and technological development. This project however is committed to the use of creolization to question also those racial meanings deployed by blacks in response to their dehumanization, particularly those meanings generated and codified by now-institutionalized modes of criticism or resistance.

For example, as Alexander Weheliye puts it, "Afro-diasporic thinking has not evinced the same sort of distrust and/or outright rejection of 'man' in its universality, post-Enlightenment guise as Western antihumanist or posthumanist philosophies. Instead, black humanist discourses emphasize the historicity and mutability of the 'human' itself, gesturing toward different, catachrestic, conceptualizations of this category."[95] Though one must ever guard against such totalizing universals as "Afro-diasporic thinking," Weheliye's observation is a strong one, not only because it is a product of his reading of Sylvia Wynter. Those distinct conceptualizations of the category of man are produced by complex relationships to the Enlightenment, coded in differential relationships to the body, race, gender, and technology.

Thinking outside of or against the habitual need to forever recuperate all black phenomena as liberatory and all resistance as sacred, however, this lack of distrust of or the will to reject the category of man has often been less different than it could be. Resistance has not rendered black humanisms necessarily freer of the constraints that motivate much posthumanist desire to transcend flesh or of the prejudices and problems that accrue to oppositional movements.

The rejection of man in its white, European formation has more often than not triggered a counter-fetishizing of man in its black, essentialist, postnegritudinist formation. Not only are there rigid gendered, economic, and cultural assumptions in the black world that parallel Western structures but there are also other quite human problems, like the fact that beyond the superstructures of resistance, racism, and colonial power, black humanisms are often just Western or first-world humanisms in blackface.

The Afro-diasporic response to white, racist humanism has ranged from the immovable essentialisms of racial nationalism and their resistance to assimilation or incorporation to the quite legitimate historical suspicion of the social privileges accorded to the blended or the creole in favor of the black. Both of these tendencies may reaffirm or reconstruct the human in differential and possibly nonracist terms, but they easily and often establish deeply oppressive new definitions of the (black) human that mirror white humanism.

Because such uses of blackness still remain as the inviolate core of so much contemporary thinking in North America, there is a need for a working or workable history of intellectual as well as cultural traditions in the black diaspora that critique the ambivalent humanism of colonialism and racism but maintain the mutable, the contingent, and the creole. There is a need for at least a trajectory, if not tradition, of thought that makes sense of the interactions between race and the human and does so through technology since it is in the relationship to technology that the human and the other become dramatically framed. This trajectory must be in conversation with, while remaining distinct from, the exclusivities of cybertheory, posthumanism, or even an Afro-futurism that may claim diaspora and have also black British elements, but which may ultimately be a primarily African *American* trope. Michael Veal suggests precisely this in his irreplaceable book on dub.[96]

For Afro-futurism to be a primarily African American trope and increasingly important critical mode is not to deny its influence, analogs, or rapid growth elsewhere, nor is it to ignore its often cavalier proprietorship of the sounds, symbols, texts, and materials from the entire black world for deployment within a first-world racial logic and politics. To name it as an African American trope (or as initially one) is instead to be attuned to how it may function differently within the context of American racial formation rather than, say, in the history of the Caribbean or the African continent.

To challenge some of Afro-futurism's African Americanness only heightens the need for the exploration of a specific Caribbean context and trajectory for these and other related ideas. This is especially necessary given the great influence of Jamaican culture on techniques of sound and on machines of sonic reproduction as well as that aforementioned tendency of classic cyberpunk narratives to use Caribbean blacks and cultural forms as either neoprimitivist analogs for the world of digital media or as alternatives to it. Without a unique trajectory the distinctiveness of the Caribbean becomes lost in the false universalism of a first-world blackness that can masquerade its specific agendas and cultural privileges by way of the term *diaspora.* As argued, creolization as a critical response to racism, slavery, and colonial trauma is far more committed to the mutable, the catachrestic, and the truly different than many black diasporic traditions, specifically because of its refusal to fetishize racial subjectivity in the face of either racism or technologization.

It should then be no surprise that Glissant and Harris directly engage technology in their work, despite the unlikeliness of their familiarity with Gibson or cyberpunk (or vice versa). This work is a welcome alternative and correlative to the emerging Afro-futurist debate as well as making clear an earlier Caribbean commitment to sound, technology, race, and culture in theory as well as in cultural practice. Technology, as a product of the nexus of sound, race, and culture, is a consistent feature of their work, from Glissant's declaration in *Caribbean Discourse* that "for Caribbean man, the word is first and foremost sound" to his deployment of "echo" in that text and an *echos-monde* in a broader metaphysical sense in *The Poetics of Relation* (1997).[97] In that latter text it becomes symbolic of a cultural and historical process and part and parcel of a distinct way of thinking that works with and against the linearity and hierarchies of a reason-based Western classicism.

His use of echo brings Glissant very much into conversation with sound theorists like Veit Erlmann, whose work on resonance as both sound process and conceptual trajectory is almost identical to the notion of *relation.* In *Reason and Resonance,* Erlmann writes, "Resonance is of course the complete opposite of the reflective, distancing mechanism of a mirror."[98] Resonances, we should know, operate as echoic repetitions of affective responses, but do so through correspondences and affinities, Harris's "depths of mutuality" or "unfathomable kinships." Resonance is not rooted in visuality, nor is it susceptible to those forms of doubling that give rise to any number of theories of subject-formation, like W. E. B. DuBois's famed double consciousness or Freud's uncanny.[99] Resonance is based on sound and is dependent on a welcoming feedback relationship with technology or, rather, technological forms of representation:

While reason implies the disjunction of subject and object, resonance involves their conjunction. Where reason requires separation and autonomy, resonance entails adjacency, sympathy, and the collapse of the boundary between perceiver and perceived. Resonance is found in many areas, whether it is a current within an electrical circuit that surges back and forth in step with the frequency of a signal coming from the outside or the representation of a normal state of a molecule by a combination of several alternative distinct structures among which the molecule moves. Most important, however, resonance is also the mechanism that generations of scientists have taken to be at the base of how the human ear works."[100]

It is a similar metaphor of mixing, "conjunction," and "adjacency" that enables Glissant to argue the following in terms not unfamiliar to those familiar with digital sound: "In Relation analytic thought is led to construct unities whose interdependent variances jointly piece together the interactive totality. These unities are not models but revealing *echos-monde.* Thought makes music."[101] Echo, for Glissant, is metaphoric of diversity and cross-cultural interaction without the architecture of colonialism or nationalist resistance to adjudicate or authorize hearing or meaning or blending. Echo, of course, is the distinctive technique of dub music, the metaphor of space and distance and the primary sign of technological manipulation. And, as Leo Marx pointed out in *The Machine in the Garden,* echo is also a metaphor of reciprocity.[102]

It was, after all, when Osbourne Ruddock—the legendary King Tubby—began to deploy the tape delay unit called the echoplex (Lee Perry preferred the Mutron Bi-Phase or the Roland Space Echo) by doubling prerecorded tracks and sonic signals that dub truly became defined as both process and cultural phenomenon. Sound became technologically decoupled from source. All these theoretical concerns and aural and sonic tropes in the Caribbean critical tradition are paralleled by and contemporaneous with the work of, say, the Guyanese dub producer the Mad Professor, whose albums *A Caribbean Taste of Technology* (1985) and *My Computer Is Acting Strange* (1986) are clearly in conversation with this Caribbean posthumanism; the much earlier work of dub prodigy Scientist (Overton Brown), who charted this sonic ground with echo-drenched albums like *Dub Landing* and *Scientist Meets the Space Invaders* (1981); then Prince (now King) Jammy's 1982 homage to the video game Space Invaders, *Prince Jammy Destroys the Invaders,* or his 1986 *Computerised Dub;* or Adrian Sherwood's Creation Rebel, whose 1980 album *Starship Africa* is a classic of inner and outer space. For true archivists there is, of course, the very rare 1973 production *Star Trek +*

Interstellar Reggae Drive, a pre–Sleng Teng, moog-heavy project produced by the Vulcans and featuring keyboardist Ken Elliot as Colonel Elliot and the Lunatics.

It is impossible to list or comprehensively reproduce the history of Jamaican or Caribbean expressions of a technological *echos monde* in reggae music (at the moment of writing, one of the reggae songs and videos of the year is Micah Shemaiah and Infinite's "Reggae Rock-it"). To go further down this path one dare not evoke the name of the reggae/dub savant Lee Perry for fear of adding far more pages than editorially allowed. Perhaps no music producer but for Phil Spector showed as much aptitude for space in his recordings. But where Spector painstakingly produced a dense "wall of sound," Perry's vision was as much about absence as about erasure—an aquatic vortex where voices appeared and disappeared and the fragility of overused tape enabled a ghostly sound world amenable to a Rastafarian mythos. Perry's own words fully situate dub's cyborg ontology as an intentional product of a culturally distinct approach to sound: "Electricity is the eye, water is the life . . . The studio must be like a living thing. The machine must be live and intelligent. Then I put my mind into the machine by sending it through the controls and the knobs or into the jack panel. The jack panel is the brain itself, so you've got to patch up the brain and make the brain a living man, but the brain can take what you're sending into it and live."[103]

In Harris's case those interests in sound, technology, race, and postcolonial creolization are present in his seminal theoretical work *The Womb of Space* (1983), which sounds like it could have been a lost dub classic from Perry's influential Black Ark period or one of Scientist's *dubwise* ripostes to King Jammy. It is likely the correspondence between that music of doubling and space that inspired Nathaniel Mackey's fine essay on Harris, titled "Poseidon (Dub Version)." This essay first brought Harris into conversation with this "well known musical practice that assumes a similar non-essentialist approach."[104]

In addition to its obsession with space and doubling, *The Womb of Space* begins with a fascination with science fiction as necessary to the "cross-cultural capacities for genuine change in communities beset by complex dangers and whose antecedents are diverse." It is a genre necessary for a Caribbean mind often mired in the "self-pity" of historicism. Harris is particularly interested in the work of H. G. Wells, Jules Verne, Aldous Huxley, George Orwell, and, in greater detail, in Edgar Allan Poe's *The Narrative of Arthur Gordon Pym of Nantucket* and Ralph Ellison's *Invisible Man*. *The Womb of Space* begins with themes such as the "files of Big Brother" and the "ghostly signals" of technology, with "genetic robot[s]" and quantum mechanics, and with black holes and "quarks."[105] Those interests trace through most of his fiction as well as essays like "The Music of Living Landscapes" with its "echoing tracery" and its sounding of "the technology of space."[106]

Harris is devoted to an imaginative sense of consciousness as less the possession of human beings than a shared product of history and the very landscape—whether Guyanese rainforest or urban setting. This obviously further decenters the human (white *and* otherwise) as a necessary mode of Caribbean posthumanism. More important, it affirms an engagement with the possibilities of other forms of life, consciousness, and apprehension, which will be the primary concern of Sylvia Wynter.

In "The Music of Living Landscapes" Harris tells of his decision upon leaving work in a North London factory to "visualize links between technology and living landscapes in continuously new ways" and his conviction of a general need for a "re-sensitizing of technology to the life of the planet." For Harris "the gift of every advance in technology is fraught with ambiguity in its innermost content," and it is that ambiguity that enables him to imagine and argue for a vision of life and consciousness shared between animate and inanimate. His critical and literary approach—both being indistinguishable—generates the possibility that the inanimate has enough of a life of its own to subject it to assimilation or incorporation or to fear its desire to impinge on the sovereign control of life, consciousness, space, and power arrogated to human beings: "Such, I believe, is the implicit orchestra, of living landscapes when consciousness sings through variegated fabrics and alternations of mood, consonance as well as dissonance, unfathomable age and youth, unfathomable kinships."[107]

One could suggest that it is Harris's rootedness in colonial and postcolonial (and to his credit, precolonial) cultures and histories in the Caribbean that makes possible this epistemological openness, or generosity. His awareness of how life and consciousness have been so parceled out in racist and colonial terms for so long more than likely has made him less willing to assume that only humans—a category that is so deeply problematic for blacks and for those made monstrous by race mixing—are deserving of them. His is an expansive and inclusive theory of life and the application of consciousness that emerges from a colonial history of their parsimonious deployment in racial and cross-cultural terms.

This insight may seem more suited to group chanting than scholarship; however, it is rooted in contemporary science and posthuman thinking, particularly that which emerges from a common critique of human-centeredness. As scholars now point out, "In the last few decades, the 'biology' of machines has been studied, genomes have been reconstructed, new bacteria invented, new digital technologies refined and other dazzling discoveries made. As this was happening, the shared physicality not only of humans and animals but also of animate creatures and inanimate matter was becoming more evident."[108] Clearly, the notion of the landscape as not only shared but also *living* and therefore deserving of rights, agency, and some modicum of subjectivity has become far less the fuzzy utopian dream it was once deemed. As Harris puts it in necessarily musical terms, "The body of the dancer in a living landscape is the technology of music."[109]

Glissant's technopoetics, however, deserves more detailed attention: first, because it is less metaphysical than Harris's (if only slightly) and, second, because *The Poetics of Relation* actually discusses digital technology, Jamaican music, and artificial intelligence. It also proves itself to be ironically less generous than Harris when it comes to the attributing of consciousness. In *The Poetics of Relation* creolization as a process of composite linkages connects Bob Marley to William Faulkner and other figures much in the way that Harris's *Womb of Space* is arranged by the most unpredictable collusion of figures and texts, all in the desire to unsettle conventional modes of connectivity and filiation that are rooted in race, nation, and orthodoxies of resistance. In one instance, the connections lead reggae not to "Africa" or roots, as the Rastafari would have it, but to Benoit Mandelbrot (the mathematician who coined the term *fractal*) to surrealism (through Wifredo Lam) to the architectures of Chicago and Soweto, Caracas and Rio, and then to Ezra Pound.[110]

The importance of surrealism to Caribbean creolization and technopoetics is explored in the next chapter. But what is notable in Glissant's connections is that race is marginal to this collage, though racism and colonialism are central to its existence and expansive possibilities. Glissant's defetishizing of race and origins here typically whittles down that Western tradition of the human. It then allows him to, like Harris, forecast and advocate for "difficult, uncertain births of new forms of identity that call to us."[111] Though primarily emerging from the "destructuring of compact national entities" in an omni-colonial world, this gesture toward a future composed of different identities and *types* of beings paves the way for a historical understanding of how those who were once beasts became human and how that which is currently inhuman will inevitably emerge as social and historical subject.

Technology is first made prominent in Glissant's *The Poetics of Relation* through his theorizing of the baroque as an aggressively creolizing force in which "the conceptions of Nature expanded, became relative." This expansion of nature should bring to mind not only Harris's blurring of the line between animate and inanimate but also the work of early science fiction discussed in this and previous chapters. In those works the category of life is forcibly expanded by the presence of sentient machines. These machines are stand-ins for the aggressive self-humanizing of blacks during and after slavery and for the insistence on relativizing Western histories and subjectivities. The baroque is no stranger to this decentering or to science. Neither is it antithetical to Glissant's known celebration of opacity as a cultural politics: "Contemporary conceptions of the sciences encountered and confirmed this expanding baroque. Science, of course, postulated that reality could not be defined on the basis of its appearance, that it was necessary to penetrate into its 'depths,' but it also agreed that knowledge of these was always deferred, that no longer were their grounds for claiming to discover the essentials all of a piece. Science entered an age of rational and basic uncertainties."[112]

This uncertain science—fraught with "ambiguity," as Harris would put it, rather than the certitude of previous generations—is what would also greatly impact the work of Gilles Deleuze and Félix Guattari, who have had an influence on Glissant arguably competitive with that of Césaire, negritude, or even Frantz Fanon. It is, after all, Deleuze's baroque that provides the primary model for *The Poetics of Relation* and both his and Guattari's rhizomes that enables Glissant's attack on the "totalitarian root" of both Western classism and black nationalisms.[113] It is clear also that Deleuze and Guattari's notion of "becoming" rather than being, their focus on alliance instead of filiation, have impacted Glissant's commitment to these issues in the context of creolization. One wonders, however, how much Glissant acknowledges that their articulation of these ideas comes out of a commitment to technology, "machinic assemblages," and, indeed, science fiction, particularly in *A Thousand Plateaus*.

The kind of science at work here in Glissant is that which emerges in the wake of Werner Heisenberg's "uncertainty principle." Wilson Harris consistently alludes to it when elucidating the "quantum cross-cultural art" of creole consciousness.[114] It's there also in his references to the "quantum fire of soul (*anima mundi*), quantum oceans, quantum landscapes, quantum riverscapes, which imply miniscule linkages between being and nonbeing," again insisting that the borderlands between human and nature are as porous as that between flesh and fabrication.[115] But that deferral of meaning, that deferral of "dogmatic certitude" leads Glissant to identify a refutation of the ontological prejudice of "depth" in the baroque, a classical principle that clearly has had immense sociopolitical repercussions.[116] For example, the optic, which depends on the visual, becomes the primary mechanism of racism, of skin. The inner life of the slave (or machine) endlessly and sociopolitically deferred, is therefore assumed to have no capacity for self-governing reason or that spark of divinity called the soul.

This refutation of depth, however, is no flat-out rejection of the fact of depth. Instead, Glissant is attempting to limit its authority and relativize it for alternative interpretive and political meanings. Because they are baroque, these meanings extend in multiple directions, accruing density—if not depth—through cross-cultural interactions. To reject depth, then, is to imagine life or subjectivity outside of whiteness or classical humanness. It is to make sense of history from inhuman or monstrous perspectives—a perspective Sylvia Wynter describes as rooted in a "demonic ground."[117] It's no great leap then for Glissant to move from the baroque as a mode of resistance to classicism and its racial, colonial legacies to a discussion of digital technology—specifically, computers. This move is useful, but limited, in *The Poetics of Relation*, yet it is in his limited understanding of computers that a necessary engagement with artificial intelligence appears.

In a section of *The Poetics of Relation* appropriately titled "Concerning the Poem's Information," Glissant notes,

> Poets today, fascinated by the adventure of computers [*l'informatique*], sense that here lies, if not the germ of a possible response to society's haranguing, at least a chance to reconnect the two orders of knowledge, the poetic and the scientific. Visible now, and approachable thanks to computers, scientific intention, putting in action the most obvious workings of social responsibility, concretely alerts and questions the poet. For what information can the poem be responsible? Can this information shoot through a computer's laser jets . . . ?[118]

Rather than being a mere machine the computer also represents a hybridizing technology on the level of disciplines and forms of institutional knowledge. It represents the possibility of erasing that "two cultures" binary between the sciences and the humanities famously pointed out in 1959 by British scientist-novelist C. P. Snow. Glissant describes that "traditional debate" as being central to modernity, having "been going on ever since reason, in the Western sense, apparently dissociated poetic creation (deemed useless in the city-state) and scientific knowledge (strictly inscribed within the drama of its own evolution)."[119]

Wynter agrees, arguing that this binary is the primary imperative to the current order of knowledge.[120]

The first sign that Glissant's understanding of how computers work is limited is in the reference to "laser jets," which might make sense if he were discussing the printing of a poem. He is, however, speaking about information and its dissemination and creation: *poesis.* He is also discussing the social responsibility of the poet as a vehicle of information. Glissant does understand the binary character of a computer. In his understanding that makes its potential for poetics limited if not impossible, since "accident that is not the result of chance is natural to poems, whereas it is the consummate vice (the 'virus') of any self-enclosed system, such as the computer." Here now is the second sign that Glissant's practical understanding of computers is limited: this idea that the computer is a "self-enclosed system." He writes, "The poet's truth is also the desired truth of the other, whereas, precisely, the truth of a computer system is closed back upon its own sufficient logic. Moreover, every conclusion reached by such a system has been inscribed in the original data, whereas poetics open onto unpredictable and unheard of things."[121] Glissant is clearly unfamiliar with the "unpredictable and unheard of" thing called the Internet, which renders a computer a mere node in a rhizomatically open system.

The Poetics of Relation was originally published in 1990, five years before the full commercialization of the Internet. It makes sense that Glissant's understanding of technology is therefore limited to hardware. One is reminded here of an early moment where Fredric Jameson edges toward his vision of postmodernism through the tension between the computer as hardware and object and as sign of a "world-wide disembodied yet increasingly total system of relationships and networks hidden beneath the appearance of daily life, whose 'logic' is sensed in the process of programming our outer and inner worlds, even to the point of colonizing our former 'unconscious.'"[122] As Glissant admits, his relationship to his computer is primarily visual. This overly physical view of the computer is much closer to a precybernetic understanding of robotics, which is where the notion of a closed technological system limited to its own programming more aptly belongs—an automaton, perhaps, one that at best can achieve mimicry, never intelligence.

Even when he does acknowledge the baroque pathways of information that characterize this particular machine, Glissant finds it impossible to imagine the evolution of agency. The machine remains a safe tool: "The computer . . . seems to be the privileged instrument of someone wanting to 'follow' any Whole whose variants multiply vertiginously. It is useful for suggesting what is stable within the unstable. Therefore, though it does not create poetry, it can 'show the way' to a poetics."[123] That this machine is more suited for one who wants to "follow" and cannot therefore create or express individuality is uncanny. Gracefully, he suggests computers can "show the way," and he is accurate in his description of a "Whole whose variants multiply vertiginously." His accuracy is due to the fact that the computer is in fact closer to his notion of creolization than he can recognize. This is crucial because his work so hints at artificial intelligence that it's necessary to use his limitations as a bridge toward realizing the strong implications for artificial intelligence in it as well as in Harris's and Sylvia Wynter's.

Even though he has lost his way about the nature of the computer, or is too early to acknowledge it—again, his focus on hardware is a limited reading of the mask as the technology itself—Glissant does wander into a conversation about technology established by people like Marshall McLuhan and Walter J. Ong. These early media theorists saw technology and electronic media as epistemic shifts for human societies as they transform from oral knowledge systems to electronic systems, with the latter being a conduit back to the former. This is evident when he sees the computer as a possible "transitional passage" from literacy back to orality, suggesting a familiarity or at least kinship with the "oral-literate-electronic schema" of those earlier media theorists.[124] As both Ong and McLuhan argue, literacy is to visuality as music is to orality, and where literacy externalized and bureaucratized thought and established the consolidation of specific forms of power and hierarchy—or, in short, Western modernity—electronic media was a return to an oral mode of apprehending time, space, and relationships more open, less defined by borders, and allegedly more interconnected.

Glissant speaks to this understanding of a resurgence of orality when he writes,

> Oral forms of poetry are multiplying, giving rise to ceremonies, performances, and shows. All around the world—in the Antilles, in the Americas, in Africa and Asia—poets of the spoken word savor this turnaround, which mixes the jangling brilliance of oral rhetoric into the alchemy of written words. Poetic knowledge is no longer inseparable from writing; momentary flashes verge on rhythmic amassings and the monotonies of duration. The sparkle of many languages utterly fulfills its function in such an encounter, in which the lightning of poetry is recreated in time's gasp.[125]

Glissant limits his focus to poetry, but were we to expand it or its definition to music and popular culture the preceding words "ceremonies, performances, shows" as well as mixing, rhythm, and the "momentary flashes" of relentless political turmoil, would ring far truer. And were we to acknowledge that usages of technology are themselves as random and unpredictable as are applications of software, then the full creole posthumanity of Glissant's thinking would flourish. After all, in the new context of the global spread of software and technology, it is less and less the case that the computer could be described as a "privileged instrument" and that its multifarious users described as mere followers of a preprogrammed Western whole. Yet even as he flirts with the very possibility of a new poetics, a new politics, a new genesis from synthesis, we are still given this conclusion: "Even so, despite its high visibility, this machine is not the place in which science and poetry might connect. This place precedes any technique of application; it generates its space within the indeterminacy of axioms."[126]

What instigates Glissant's interest in computing in the first place is not just the desire to fuse the humanities and science or technology and poetics but something perhaps a bit more prosaic: "Triggered by a premonition of this encounter between the oral and the written, many people have either a fascination with computers or merely a curiosity to see them cough up poetry."[127] This explains his anxiety. It is a poet's fear that the sacred reserve of poetry will also collapse in the face of technorationalization and the machine (in other words, it's a contemporary version of the old "romantic revolt" in the face of Newtonian mechanics). It's a defensive poetics and leads him to hesitate at ascribing to computers or machines human potential, much like many did and do when speaking about electronic music.

It is inevitable, then, that Glissant would arrive at the fundamental question of certain subgenres of science fiction, which can be traced back to slavery and its questions of black intelligence and slave souls: can machines think? He answers, "Every computer system, through its very instantaneity, makes us familiar with unilingual revelation and renders the sudden flash ordinary—but, from the viewpoint of a multilingual scintillation, the aforementioned system is incapable of 'comprehending.'" In this case "thinking" is not defined as literacy or reason, as they were defined during the nineteenth century. It is instead the ability to generate random or unpredictable possibilities, an assumption made possible by an uncertain or ambiguous science. In his reactive definition, this ability to produce "unheard of things" is the prime mechanism of poetics as a cross-cultural process. The machine "evades the drama of languages" in its inability to genuinely produce or generate the unpredictable, true synthesis-genesis.[128] Glissant ultimately claims the poetic as a privileged mode of human subjectivity. Importantly, it's not a rational mode but a synthetic one. In doing so he defines the human as the only source of authentic hybridity, of mixing and of generating cross-cultural compositeness. Harris would more than likely reject this return to anthropocentrism.

It is a familiar anxiety. One could go so far as to call this refusal to bestow "comprehension" or imagine the possibility of intelligence a prejudice, given the rapidly developing frontiers of technology and information. What matters is the very idea that he feels the need to dismiss that possibility in the first place, the fact of his hesitation made public. Call it a glitch. It occurs despite his awareness that "the most recent developments of science invite us, therefore, to venture in our quest beyond the laws laid down by its philosophies."[129] One needn't make such complex caveats if one were speaking of, say, an automobile or a typewriter or a digital sampler. There is nothing uncanny about those machines, nothing threatening in their potential to redefine or replace what is established as human. Clearly something is at work with computers that makes necessary a direct engagement with artificial intelligence by rejecting it.

Apparently, there *are* limits to creolization. That Glissant would describe this limit as *the human* sounds a rich note of historical irony, as the child of the inhuman becomes a voice of the recuperation of that troubling category and as the scion of Caribbean posthumanism retreats into flesh. Here we intuit borders immune to what had heretofore been argued to be an ineluctable process: "We dream of what we will cultivate in the future, and we wonder vaguely what the new hybrid that is already being prepared for us will look like, since in any case we will not rediscover them as they were, the magnolias of former times."[130]

As seen here, the hybrid, blended forces of creolization can be imagined only by organic metaphors. In the presence of the machine, and its own self-generated mixtures, poetic roots are hardened into an orthodox humanism. Face-to-face with the new hybrid creolization freezes, its most notable prophet unable to recognize his own implications, masked as they are by the scent of magnolias.

FOUR

A CARIBBEAN PRE-POSTHUMANISM

The Caribbean lineage of creolization and its hostility to conventional borders and antinomies is what makes Donna Haraway's notion that "by the late twentieth century in United States scientific culture, the boundary between human and animal is thoroughly breached," a rightly influential but historically inaccurate statement.[1] This particular boundary had already been breached through slavery and colonialism and represented in fictions of inhuman, primitive blacks and implicated in tropes of the monstrous—from Mary Shelley to Herman Melville and H. G. Wells—and images of perverse fusion, from *Erewhon* to cyborgs. Haraway's temporal and geographic context could and should therefore be expanded, which is why the work of her contemporary, Sylvia Wynter, is so valuable.

Like Édouard Glissant and Haraway, Wynter's primary concern has also been for the ontological transformation of foundational categories like race, man, and the human. Despite the fact that her focus on transformation across vast historical vistas is akin to creolization, Wynter isn't guilty of the quietism that some might read in Glissant or Wilson Harris. For the latter two the overwhelming and indifferent process of creolization or cross-culturality occurs independent of politics or individual will. It often leaves mere mortals only to sing its transcendent praises or bask in its inaccessibility (something not unconnected to what Glissant celebrates as "opacity"). In this latter regard, Glissant can sound distinctly *new agey,* where Harris's characters tend to be rendered dumbstruck—or "staggered" by the historical swirl of the process.[2] For Wynter history is the empowering site of human cultural agency and political change and, more specifically, Caribbean reconstruction, conceptual as well as material.

Alexander Weheliye writes that Wynter's "attempt to recast the human sciences in relation to a new conception of 'man' provides contexts in which to think the 'human' that not only bridges the ever widening gap between the cognitive life sciences and humanities but also incorporate the colonial and racialist histories of the 'human.'"[3] In Wynter's work, the breach of the border between the human and the *not human* can be not only traced to the dawn of modernity but framed in the context of colonial contact. It will also be placed in a context of technology and its varied cultural responses, since the binary of human/nonhuman is at work also in those divisions between the civilized and the primitive.

Where in Haraway the breach between human and other is merely suggestive of race, in Wynter race plays a far more central part. It is in fact the primary product of that colonial and epistemological division between human/man and inhuman/native. For Wynter the "border war" must be traced to the very emergence and foundational invention of the category of human itself. That category is the product of shifting relations between a European self and a set of "discovered" and displaced others encountered in the wake of new technologies that enabled maritime exploration in that precolonial, presecular age of wonder. In tracing the echoes of that initial breach, "race" by the nineteenth century would become "the legitimating 'magical thought' of that century's industrial mode of colonialism."[4]

Magical thinking, of course, goes both ways. It is both racist and antiracist, given the black twentieth-century dependence on race as a method of inventing and discovering a previously erased black humanity. As Weheliye has suggested, this latter fact might make a "*black* posthumanism" almost inconceivable for some, since the expansion of and inclusion into the category of human has driven much black thought and since also the commitment to race continues to drive first-world black thinking often in such a way as to minimize alternatives. Perhaps the best way to describe the location of Wynter's work, as Caribbean thinker David Scott does, is between the "unevenly overlapping space where the agonistic humanism of Fanon's anticolonialism crosses . . . the embattled antihumanism of Foucault's archaeological critique."[5] In that philosophical space race as a force of cultural recuperation is balanced with antiracism and a commitment to humanize those who were conceptually and materially rendered inhuman. One particularly perceptive critic calls Wynter's work not posthumanism but an "embattled humanism" and importantly describes it as a Caribbean tradition that features Aimé Césaire and Frantz Fanon as her major forbears.[6]

The two-facedness of racial magical thinking and of the differential value of the human is why one must discuss Wynter's relationship to creolization as a product of both racism as well as racial *invention.* This brings her most obviously into relation with Glissant and Harris, but that it emerges from negritude and surrealism is not usually acknowledged. Nor is the fact that it is product of a quite modernist opposition between the civilized and the primitive that is a twentieth-century iteration of that much older division between the human and the inhuman.

The three sections of this chapter situate Sylvia Wynter's work at the vanguard of the epistemological border war and as a primary paradigm through which to historicize perverse fusions between conceptually and socially antithetical beings. To do so it will be necessary to begin with a critical history of negritude and surrealism. What matters is how the former emerges from latter through the colliding histories of surrealist poetics and black radicalism in the colonial Caribbean and all in relationship to the equation made between technology and technological rationalism. Central to surrealism and negritude's reaction to technology, for example, will be an interest in primitivism, shared also by Jamaican Rastafarianism, which began to emerge around the same time as both of these movements and had a powerful impact on reggae music and dub. That fixation with the primitive is due in part to the global influence of the Harlem Renaissance, the jazz age, and the Jamaican writer Claude McKay. Primitivism, perhaps surprisingly to some readers, will bring McKay—as it will negritude and Rasta—into the historical remit of early writers of American science fiction, such as Edgar Rice Burroughs and Robert E. Howard, who essentially translated the conceits and anxieties of late Victorian proto–science fiction into the vernacular language of American pulp during the Jim Crow era.

The second section brings Wynter into conversation with the creole poetics and politics of black science fiction writer Samuel R. Delany and through that offer an alternative to that aspect of Afro-futurism that is often hostile to hybridity despite its engagement with technology. To do so requires that one clarify and amplify Wynter's thinking about technology as crucial to the form of posthumanism that emerges out of her radical, black, anticolonial critique. But there is more to this than simply claiming a Caribbean or black posthumanism, even though that would arguably be enough. By emphasizing her ideas about technology, that critique of the racist, colonial construction of the human prepares us for a future shared by much science fiction. This is a future where machines become naturalized by the discourse of race. Unbeknownst to her, her thinking about the past through changing constructions of the human enables a future that even renders artificial intelligence inevitably organic through an expansion of categories of biological life. This expansion will be no great leap because the same process has *already* occurred in the movement of blacks from inhuman to human, from anthropomorphic tools to sentient beings.

The final section contemporizes her technopoetics in the wake of robotics. She is discussed alongside those thinkers for whom artificial intelligence and machine life signal the end of the privileged category of human. As we will see, that need not mean the end of race.

ECHOLOCATING SURREALISM

So a brief history is in order, one that illuminates posthumanism and corrects the sometimes sloppy racializations of cyberpunk by seeing how Caribbean creolization would emerge as a technopoetics in advance of cybernetics and Donna Haraway. Wynter acknowledges this history in her own description of her intellectual tradition. In advance even of dub, dancehall, hip-hop, or Afrofuturism there is a lineage of thinking in the Caribbean that engages epistemological border warfare and is therefore helpful as we attempt to make sense of how blacks have themselves made sense of their relationship to technology.

J. Michael Dash's characterization of post-1930s radical poetics in the Caribbean is a helpful place to root the emergence of such a history. This is a Caribbean intellectual tradition that makes creolization possible but that also owes as much to anticolonial nationalism as to Western technology and the various responses to it. The post-1930s period in the Caribbean is where creolization began to emerge from nationalism but managed to be as much its product as it is a fluctuating alternative. Dash argues that, like much black or anticolonial racial thinking, this post-1930s poetics "centered on an organist dream of the union between man and nature." Caribbean poetics would become so focused due to two things: first, modernity's manifestation in the Caribbean through "independent Haiti's utopian dream of technological progress" and then the "horrors of World War I and North American expansionism," which would render modern technology and the spirit of rationality as profoundly negative.[7]

This race-ing of technology helps make sense of the cross-cultural impact of surrealism on radical Caribbean poetics in the early 1940s. Surrealism—with all its hyperbolic talk of individual liberation and proletarian revolution, of a freedom as much psychological as it was from a suspect history—was, in its rejection of Western norms, appealing to those Caribbean writers for whom "the union between man and nature" was a political response to the deracination of assimilation and the violence of colonialism. It didn't hurt that the movement was also known for its celebration of psychic and cultural *elsewheres*. As André Breton pontificated, the goal of surrealism was to discover "fresh landscapes," both imaginative and geographic.[8] And, of course, it should be well known that "'Elsewhere,' or the Third World, in the twentieth century has become an exemplary site for transgressive fantasies."[9]

The interaction between surrealism and black nationalism in the French colonial world is arguably the genesis of creolization as a critical and theoretical tradition in the African diaspora. What is meant here by surrealism is not so much the dictates of the movement and its tightfisted "pope" André Breton, though his "discovery" of Césaire's work and the journal *Tropiques* was absolutely central to this collision and collusion. Surrealism is meant here as anthropologist James Clifford uses it and as many outside of the movement would use it: in an "expanded sense to circumscribe an aesthetic that values fragments, curious collections, unexpected juxtapositions—that works to provoke the manifestations of extraordinary realities drawn from the domains of the erotic, the exotic and the unconscious."[10] Such juxtapositions, as well as the exotic and erotic charge generated by them, were also product of a surrealist commitment to ethnography and anthropology as modes of cross-cultural catalysis.

Breton may have "discovered" Césaire, but, as the latter insisted, "the meeting with Breton confirmed the truth of what I had discovered on my own" and allowed him not only to move "much faster" but also "much farther." The surrealism of the Caribbean would be and could only be routed through distinct colonial circumstances. These differences are admittedly easy to miss, given the wild exaggeration, dense poetic images, and deliberate provocations by all groups who shared the moniker. One necessary difference is that which made the conditions of possibility between the French and the Caribbean movement politically and philosophically variant:

> the contexts to which European surrealists and Césaire were responding were very dissimilar. In the first instance, it consisted of a long entrenched bourgeoisie and a pervasive Catholicism. In that instance, culture, people, and land were part of the same entity. In Césaire's case, the culture and the religion he rejected had been imposed from the outside. Consequently, on the one hand, he never showed toward his countrymen and their land the deliberate antipatriotic desecration nor

the cosmopolitism that is the trademark of the French surrealists. Césaire, therefore, remained profoundly in love with the natural world and the simple people that surrounded him.[11]

This love with nature and its simple people was at the root of his intense poetic language and his primitivism. It was not matched by the cultural self-loathing of the French movement (though the Caribbean writers did share a common loathing for their native bourgeoisie and what seemed their co-optation by the social and cultural values of the colonial oppressor). Césaire's organic union with nature was in fact a struggle. Even on his home island his roots were deferred, blocked, distorted, or were so felt.

It is that force of colonial imposition that ultimately impels this search for roots; yet it is in their discovery that their creation lies. Because the search for roots is always riddled with doubt, that quest for union gave rise to something beyond simple primitivism. With the surrealism of negritude, blackness becomes a politicized refutation of reason that orients itself fantastically outside of and anterior to a modernity assumed to be essentially Western and white. This refutation is not to be mistaken for the absolute rejection of Western forms of knowledge, literacy, and education that was also characteristic of some folk or street-level anticolonialism or nationalism. It's not to be misapplied to a negritude that may have celebrated Negro vitality, rhythm, and a privileged connection to roots but was never imagined as mindless and without intellectual integrity.

But doubt is forever restless. Rather than just being rooted or static, this refutation generated wildly syncretic possibilities once colonial and racist reason were thought abandoned or transcended. A notable example of that syncretism is what James Clifford sees in Aimé Césaire, who famously described his negritude as something that "takes root in the red flesh of the soil" but is simultaneously "not a stone" and actively "breaks through opaque prostration with its upright patience."[12] Typical is a language that reworks the natural world he so loved and felt so alienated from. He, however, famously supplements it, augments it with language from the fragments of words and half-words that become *prosthetic* in that they emphasize the constructedness of his use of nature. As opposed to the more familiar erectile essentialism of Léopold Sédar Senghor and its tendency to romanticize but to leave nature untransformed, Clifford sees "radical indeterminacy" in language like this and in Césaire's famed use of neologism.[13]

In many ways this reading of Césaire has become a conventional reading of the Caribbean itself in the wake of poststructuralist theory and postcolonial thought: as a "hybrid and heteroglot" space, which because it is about transformation, "is no longer about roots but about present process in a polyphonous reality."[14] Clifford is here vulnerable to that aforementioned "linguistic turn" that has overwhelmed scholarly discussions of creolization in the West by virtue of that poststructuralist exaggeration of linguistic processes as being indicative of cultural and political ones. Clifford's reading of Césaire is worthy of its impact (though in *The Other America,* J. Michael Dash finds this use of Cesaire not much different from the romantic racism of Breton, Levi-Strauss, or Jean-Paul Sartre).[15] But where it falls short for this analysis is precisely in that overfetishizing of Césaire's use of language. It misses the fact that key to a surrealist methodology was that transformation and polyphony led away from mimicry (what Suzanne Césaire called colonial "pseudomorphosis") by veering toward a lost but intact racial authenticity.[16]

This is classic Breton, really, the notion that rejection or revolution led to or required a simultaneous affirmation of greater, more intensified truths. If anything, "radical indeterminacy" was guided by principles of ideological fixity. This is even the case in Césaire, whose ideological differences from Senghor were real but have also become much exaggerated. As with most dualities, the differences between Césaire and Senghor exist largely to obscure other options and multiple influences (for example, ignoring the highly influential Léon Damas, Suzanne Césaire, and others). Even worse, these dualities serve in this case to reduce the complexity of Senghor, who was arguably as committed to cultural fusion and symbiosis as was Césaire. Unlike Césaire, Senghor's surrealism was balanced with a strong commitment to the vindication of African historical civilizations. This was a man famous also for the deceptively simple statement "assimilate but don't be assimilated," which though maintaining the primacy of cultural integrity still suggests the possibility of a self-motivated creolization.[17] Negritude was primarily a strategic and necessary political choice for Senghor. Upon the resolution of the colonial problem, there would be then another choice: "to see what we will take from Western civilization and what we will keep from the Negro-African civilization."[18] Naive, perhaps, but hardly a choice possible if Africanity is conceived as unchanging and absolute.

Considering its conceits and its period, and the fact that essentialism hides often behind a creole masquerade, negritude should be read alongside other Caribbean movements focused on that radical union of man and nature—for example, Jamaican Rastafarianism. It too began to emerge around the same time as a folk, anticolonial, millennial movement, and its rejection of reason and technology should be seen in tandem with other attempts in the Caribbean world to remake their own epistemologies and name their own origins in advance of decolonization. For example, it is by similar processes that the Rastafarian rejection of colonial notions of time, history, and reality was thought to lead to the discovery of an "authentic" Africa, much as Suzanne Césaire, René Ménil, and Aimé Césaire himself argued for in surrealist terms:

> And my thinking followed these lines: Well then, if I apply the surrealist approach to my particular situation, I can summon up these unconscious forces. This, for me, was a call to Africa. I said to myself: it's true that superficially we are French, we bear the marks of French customs; we have been branded by Cartesian philosophy, by French rhetoric; but if we break with all that, if we plumb the depths, then what we will find is fundamentally black.

Africa was the name for what was on the other side of colonial indoctrination, the endpoint of a process of "disalienation": "A plunge into the depths. It was a plunge into Africa for me," says Césaire.[19]

To further emphasize the limitations of Clifford's influential reading of Césaire—capped by his context-be-damned proclamation, "We are all Caribbeans now in our urban archipelagos"—it appeared a mere year before the now-infamous manifesto *Eloge de la créolité* (*In Praise of Creoleness*) by Martinique's Raphaël Confiant, Patrick Chamoiseau, and Jean Bernabé, the so-called creolistes.[20] For them the neologism *créolité* emerged largely in response to the severe limitations of negritude in general and Césaire in specific, particularly in his relationship to the Martinican dialect, which for them was the paramount sign of their *créolité* and his recalcitrant Frenchness. His neologisms seem quite precious when considered against a thriving vernacular world where "radical indeterminacy" is regularly systematized.

Glissant shares with the creolistes the critique of Césaire's overdependence on French. He is, after all, "one of the first major Caribbean writers to break with traditional Caribbean discourse which privileges Africa as the site of origin and identity."[21] Césaire's return to "Africa" would hobble a subsequent generation explicit about a commitment to creolization and to the Caribbean as primary space, not secondary to ancestry. This is often forgotten in favor of the potency of that primary gesture of refusal. Similarly, in Jamaica dancehall would also suffer from the limitations of a Rastafarian stress on African roots linked in sound to analog recording as more "authentic." As such, roots became orthodox and hostile to the more brazenly libidinal and openly digital excesses of a younger generation fueled less by a Garveyite notion of repatriation to Africa than by migration to New York, London, Japan, and other sites of information and disembarkation.

Also often forgotten is the fact that despite the neologism *negritude* being coined to "challenge Western fallacies about black culture and literature" and to ennoble a colonized Africa, in Césaire's hands, it also featured an embrace of colonial and racist stereotypes. His return to Africa was explicitly a primitivist "plunge" quite au courant, since primitivism itself had been fashionable in Paris from the various colonial exhibits of the late nineteenth century. By the 1939 publication of his *Notebook of a Return to the Native Land,* it was a bona fide craze that had left the *negrophilie* of the avant-garde and had spread throughout music, popular culture, and media in France. As stated in his *Cahiers,* "Because we hate you and your reason, we claim kinship with dementia praecox with the flaming madness of persistent cannibalism."[22]

Radical indeterminacy was framed by the surrealist trust that beneath reason lay a greater truth, obscured and mangled by colonial education and indoctrination. And this truth could be named. Nathaniel Mackey points out that this "New World African preoccupation" with naming is simultaneously a "problematizing of the act of naming." For both negritude and Rastafari, naming that truth "Africa" was appropriate because in the act of naming there is both the technique of invention and the fantasy of discovery: being and making in one gesture. Mackey's "discrepant relationship between name and named" is also represented by neologisms in Rastafarianism, which routinely rename objects, concepts, and even subjectivity from colonial meanings to ones thought more rooted in an Afrocentric philosophy of language.[23]

For the uninitiated, Rastafarian neologisms rival Césaire's for their complexity, surreality, and commitment to reversals of colonial logic. That such deliberate reversals would be then considered authentic only brings attention to the process itself, as Mackey emphasizes. Africa was less a property of the word than it was what authorized that process. This is what Mackey means by "a root that has to do with making." Sometimes called "Iyaric," Rastafarian linguistic reversals, however unhinged and experimental, are never thought to be anything other than expressions of primordial truth made possible by that "plunge into the depths." For example, library becomes "true-brary" and oppression becomes "down-pression," and there is, of course, that host of well-known "I" centered words that reshape or reclaim black male subjectivity and experience (I-man, I and I, Irie, Ital, Iration, Iwah, and so forth). Unlike Césaire's language, Iyaric entered into the vernacular lexicon of Jamaican, the primary space of creolization as a phenomenon driven largely by class struggle. It did so largely through reggae music and sound culture. Though this process of linguistic resistance does emphasize the space between being and making, in Rastafari culture it did and does operate without a full sense of the "rickety fit between world and word."[24]

With these movements, separated by language, island, class, and forms of colonial power, cultural and linguistic invention was driven by something allegedly metaphysical and was framed as what Mackey describes as a return to a "previously repressed black ancestral strata."[25] Both—despite one being based on psychoanalysis, romanticism, and the terror of an industrial world gone mad, and the other based on a fundamentalist interpretation of the Old Testament as well as the "African fundamentalism" of Marcus Garvey—were also based on a notion of racial truth as being opposed to rational thought or those aspects of Enlightenment reason that could be described as white, racist, or colonial. As such these movements were about transformation in the language of return and the organic by way of the constructed.

These seeming antinomies were made possible in negritude by a potent distrust of white colonial rationality on the one hand, but on the other a too-deep trust for the white anticolonial irrationality that was surrealism. With Rastafari, its potent distrust of white colonial reason and its cultural and social structures were balanced by a too-deep belief in unmediated biblical revelation (this arguably having much more in common with surrealism and its penchant for psychoanalysis and dream exploration than one has time to discuss). Again, the duality in negritude between "radical indeterminacy" and "essentialism" is often crudely framed as the difference between Césaire and Senghor. But given the impact of surrealism on both writers and a black nationalism as informed by global black cultural movements as it was by French colonial race relations, it is not the differences between Senghor and Césaire that matter here. What matters is that common tension between being and making (discovery and invention), at the core of the African diaspora's relation to a modernity shaped by colonialism.

That tension is the dialectic of race and becoming from which creolization as a tradition emerges and is made most clear, not in Césaire's neologisms but in his manifesto "Poetry and Cognition"—an inaugural text in the emergence of creolization as a Caribbean intellectual tradition. This is where the "true excellence of Césaire's contribution lies."[26] The manifesto was first presented in 1944, appropriately in Haiti, given the significance of that island for his vision of negritude. In it he establishes exactly what in his view gives rise to creolization: "The dialectic of the image transcends antinomies," he argues, fully aware of the poetics and politics of collage and radical juxtaposition in surrealism. It allows for hitherto impossible fusions, allowing, in his formulation, "A" to simultaneously be "not-A" and thereby reducing the "analytic" faculty to the "synthetic." It also operates through a "naturalizing process" that concretizes meaning and makes the abstract material.[27]

Race and the naturalizing of technology was discussed in the first chapter, along with cybernetics and Italian futurism and their dependence on analogies and Wilson Harris's description of creolization as operating by a similar process of "involuntary associations." Corollary to this was the surrealist praxis of the "associative metaphor," which comes from the desire to fuse previous social, cultural, and cross-cultural oppositions as modes of reinvention.[28] This relationship to metaphor is at work in the collusion between creolization and technopoetics.

Césaire would go further than most in his associative metaphors. They drive his fascination with neologisms. Those metaphors produced flexibility with meaning that Andre Bréton celebrated when he describes Césaire's work as receiving "its greatest value from the power of transmutation," which operates on "the most discredited materials among which even ugliness and slavery must be counted" and produces "neither gold nor the philosopher's stone but rather freedom itself."[29] In explicitly technological language, this special, alchemical power of transmutation allows Césaire to transform the organic to the machinic and back again. In his words, it "permits us to say *motor* for *sun*, *dynamo* for *mountain*, *carburetor* for *Carib* . . . and to celebrate lyrically the shiny connecting rod of the moons and the tired piston of the stars."[30]

Most clear in "Poetry and Cognition" is that Césaire was interested in more than simply mounting relentless countermeanings and reactionary counterarguments to a racist system of reason. This was no rebellion for its own sake, no endless assault as permanent spectacle, as is often the case today. It was productive and relentlessly generative, as Clifford would agree. Césaire was equally committed to possibility, making meaning through the associative metaphor and through naturalization as a method of catalysis. In "Calling the Magician: A Few Words for a Caribbean Civilization," another manifesto written the same year as "Poetry and Cognition," Césaire continues that rooting that has to do with making, that commitment to synthesis, transformation, destruction, and affirmation at the heart of creolization: "Only the poetic spirit corrodes and builds, erases and invigorates" and "only the poetic spirit links and reunites."[31] One would be hard-pressed to find an earlier expression of Glissant's "synthesis-genesis."

We will return to Césaire through the lens of Sylvia Wynter as she constructs her own genealogy through Glissant and negritude. But there is another element that must be added more explicitly to Dash's history of a Caribbean poetic response to technology that is central to the negritude movement's sense of poetics and revolution. Given the presence of Garvey in early twentieth-century New York City as well as Rastafari founder Leonard Percival Howell, this element cannot be overstated: the international impact of the Harlem Renaissance. This movement would popularize a specifically *black* primitivism rooted in a romantic response to industrial America and the technological West. Though surprising, it should be no coincidence that that brand of primitivism would be conversant with the pulp science fiction and fantasy also popular at the time.

The literature and politics of the Harlem movement was highly influential to the francophone poets, writers, and ideologues that would compose the negritude movement. Its racial politics also had a sonic component: jazz, but also calypso, both of which were heard, imitated, and theorized. Even the admittedly tone-deaf Breton was forced to take black sound seriously, despite his "diametrically opposite attitude towards poetry and music." Due to the impact of black sound in the wider cultural climate and among other surrealists, it caused him to eventually argue for the need for the movement "to *unify, reunify hearing* to the same degree that we must determine to *unify, reunify sight*."[32] Most important for negritude, Harlem's emergent Afrocentrism had something to do with that turn to the organic as a technique of racial resistance and a retreat from implication in an industrial world edging close to genocide.

The work of Claude McKay is central here. Dash identifies the poet's problematizing of "hybridity and exile" and McKay's sense "that the ideal of an organic, traditional community, safe from the unrelenting spread of modernity, was a self-indulgent fantasy."[33] But this was secondary to McKay's larger commitment to an African aesthetic that would deeply impact post-1930s radical poetics in the Caribbean. Langston Hughes as well: one need only recall here his famous manifesto "The Negro Artist and the Racial Mountain" with its crying and laughing tom tom drums to imagine its impact. In it Africa is rendered in the language of America and transformation in the language of return, rediscovery.

McKay was more important, no doubt, due to being a peripatetic Caribbean amid a largely black American movement. His great influence on negritude was due not just to his revolutionary bona fides (he'd been an actual member of the underground Communist Party of America and supported the Bolshevik government in the Soviet Union) but to a distinct version of the primitivism that would infect the broader climate of modernism in America and Europe as well as in the Caribbean. The best example of that primitivism was his novel *Banjo* (1929). Both Senghor and Césaire were proud of their ability to recite long passages from the book by heart, and Senghor would even directly draw from it for a number of his ideas.[34] *Banjo* was actually canonized in advance of the formal negritude movement by a group of students in Martinique who published *Légitime Défense,* a review that "played a historic role in the birth of modern black Francophone literature originating with Negritude." It's no surprise that for André Breton *Légitime Défense* confirmed "surrealism's alliance with people of color in its fight 'against all forms of imperialism and white banditry'" as well as identified "very deep affinities . . . between so-called 'primitive' thought and surrealist thought."[35]

In *Banjo* McKay's stand-in Ray muses on primitivism, modernism, and technology quite openly and often, so much so that one can't help but think that the Caribbean poetic response to technology had more to do with McKay's influence than Dash acknowledges. For example, looking at the black transnational vagabonds washed up on the port in Marseilles, Ray states that they "represented more than he or the cultured minority the irrepressible exuberance and legendary vitality of the black race. And the thought kept him wondering how that race would fare under the ever tightening mechanical organization of modern life." Almost everything in this novel is organized by the dialectic of the Machine and the Negro. Its organicism can be summed up in his own words:

> For civilization had gone out among these native earthy people, had despoiled them of their primitive soil, had uprooted, enchained, transported, and transformed them to labor under its laws, and yet lacked the spirit to tolerate them within its walls.

That this primitive child, this kinky-headed, big-laughing black boy of the world, did not go down and disappear under the serried crush of trampling white feet; that he managed to remain on the scene, not worldly-wise, not 'getting there,' yet not machine-made, nor poor-in-spirit like the regimented creatures of civilization, was baffling to civilized understanding. Before the grim pale rider-down of souls he went his careless way with a primitive hoofing and a grin.

Thus he became a challenge to the clubbers of helpless vagabonds—to the despised, underpaid protectors of property and its high personages. He was a challenge of civilization itself. He was the red rag to the mighty-bellowing, all-trampling civilized bull.[36]

McKay deliberately, perhaps defiantly, strays into stereotypes. But then he demands that the racist stereotype be acknowledged as the radical cultural and ideological alternative to a world increasingly defined and destroyed by industrial technology. Negritude arguably starts here.

Despite remaining a thing apart from "Rhobert" and other "regimented creatures of civilization," that "primitive child," that "kinky-headed, big-laughing black boy of the world" remained a problem for such a civilization. He was a challenge to a world where the Industrial Revolution had become utterly naturalized and had already transformed humanity into something else. Note that this black primitive figure was not only in opposition to "the machine," it had already been transformed into a modern unit of labor by an earlier machine: the plantation. In McKay the rejection of labor, an embrace of instincts, and a commitment to pleasure enabled a return to what colonialism allegedly could not erase.

The relentless use of the word *primitive* in *Banjo* and the equally relentless passages that elucidate and celebrate that black mode of being signifies the reaction to technology Dash describes, but in advance of surrealism. It is also present in McKay's first novel, *Home to Harlem* (1928). Most irresistible here is the notion that this "primitive child" was "not machine-made" and was therefore more natural and spiritually richer than those who were "civilized." This series of equations between race and nature, the organic in opposition to technology, is of course riddled with well-known fallacies. It is a romantic racism that was not unusual in this cultural climate and had in fact been common throughout industrialization in England and America. If one were to remove McKay's ideological commitments from his work, it becomes easy to see that this is the kind of primitivism so common in the modernist climate as to inevitably become the core of pulp fiction.

Though it might seem unusual to discuss McKay as a link between negritude and American proto–science fiction, both were rich with shared conceptual concerns: primitivism, Africa, and a romanticized and hypermasculinized escape from a hyperindustrial world, for example. To make sense of the parallels between race and science fiction is to give some acknowledgement to these parallels between black literature and pulp fiction, considering the period. In fact, given primitivism's importance to the genre of fantasy—and the obsession with race and, of course, lost races—it's worth noting that *Weird Tales,* the first all-fantasy pulp magazine to which Robert E. Howard would regularly contribute, began publishing in 1923, three years before Hugo Gernsback's *Amazing Stories.* For a broader context in which science fiction intersects with the Harlem Renaissance, this was the same year Jean Toomer's *Cane* was published, the year Josephine Baker appeared on Broadway in the show *Chocolate Dandies* and the year that Countee Cullen's poetry began to achieve notice. It was the year Bessie Smith began her rise to fame, of the establishment of *Opportunity* magazine and its Civic Club dinner crucial for the publishing of most major Harlem writers, the opening of the *Cotton Club,* the arrival of Duke Ellington and his band to New York, and the arrest of Marcus Garvey for mail fraud.

It really is no accident that McKay's success was simultaneous with that of Howard's and Edgar Rice Burroughs's. Such indeed was the climate as represented, for example, by *Tarzan of the Apes:* "Burroughs' novel was part of a powerful renaissance in the United States of popular interest in primitivism, which was in turn part of a complex reaction to the increasing evidence of the Industrial Revolution and technological innovation, what is often called the emergence of modern (which is to say urban) America."[37] It's also no coincidence that in the wake of H. Rider Haggard the two American pulp writers both depended on a fantastical African setting, just as Harlem turned to Africa through Garvey, DuBois, and the imaginative, recuperative work of so many Harlem painters, writers, and activists (1923 was also the year of the third Pan-African conference in Lisbon and London). At least one of these pulp writers—Burroughs—did some study of plant and animal life on the African continent, but like the black writers of the New Negro and negritude movements, he felt free to cut and paste his knowledge of the continent from all the quite popular anthropological and ethnographic material available.[38] Africa, after all, was in fashion, from France to New York, Broadway to jazz, anthropology to futurism and surrealism.

In white pulp fiction, primitivism is a celebration of a primal man underneath the bespectacled and suited modern man and an injunction to reveal him from beneath years of social and technological emasculation. Tarzan, for example, "was the personification of the id let loose from civilized restraint, the siren call of which we emulated as we let our arms hang low in imitation of the anthropoid ancestors we yearned to rejoin."[39] This was also the case with Howard's Conan the Barbarian and Burroughs's John Carter of Mars. For McKay the true primal African had been weakened by white civilization and led astray by technology. Its id had been constrained first by slavery and then by modern Western civilization. The goal then was to rejoin one's ancestors, though McKay would hardly have equated those ancestors to what Burroughs and others equated them with: *apes.*

In its focus on being "let loose from civilized restraint" black primitivism is also present in canonical Harlem works like Countee Cullen's famous poem "Heritage." The poet rejects the call of the jungle but insists we remember the "jungle boys and girls in love," its acknowledgement of the romantic and literary tropes of a populist fantasy called Africa, and its description of the drum-led pressure to "Strip! / Doff this new exuberance," called a civilized sensibility.[40] Much of *Banjo* is merely an attempt to extend the drama of this reversionary "stripping." Antiracism notwithstanding, the messages in McKay and Cullen and so many others of the Harlem movement are too similar to Burroughs and Howard to not explore in tandem. At the very least this allows us to read the birth of science fiction and fantasy in America alongside the emergence of African American literature and political culture and with evolving conversations about race and racism.

That shared primitivism and its complex positioning as a critique of and alternative to modern Western society is probably why, in a book rich with metaphors equating Western civilization with the machine, the Negro as a primitive alternative, and Africa as the ultimate home of precivilizational authenticity, it's perhaps inevitable that McKay would allude to some form of science fiction or fantasy. He mentions the writer of "scientific romances," H. G. Wells:

> He did not think the blacks would come very happily under the super-mechanical Anglo-Saxon-controlled world society of Mr. H. G. Wells. They might shuffle along, but without much happiness in the world of Bernard Shaw. Perhaps they would have their best chance in a world influenced by the thought of a Bertrand Russell, where brakes were clamped on the machine with a few screws loose and some nuts fallen off. But in this great age of science and super-invention was there any possibility of arresting the thing unless it stopped of its own exhaustion?[41]

More important here is his mentioning of Bertrand Russell, the Nobel laureate whose interest in "scientific totalitarianism" and the use of mechanization to reshape society through its reshaping of human beings would reach its controversial apex in the protocyberpunk *The Impact of Science on Society* (1952).

There is much in the previous passage that Breton would find sympathetic. Nature or the organic seemed clearly superior to what civilization had become and to all it was guilty of, and blacks had a special relation to them—well, the black working-class and the poor, given McKay's open hostility to the African American intelligentsia. In McKay's view racism was a correlative threat to the machine, or what the Rastafarians would call Babylon: that force of regimentation, technology, and relentless capitalist productivity that threatened the primitive spirit represented by those most exploited by it. McKay's work reminds us that he and negritude were historically situated within a mad complex of differential primitivisms, with Rastafarianism as a far-flung correspondence (perhaps not too far-flung considering that the primary founder of Rastafarianism, Leonard Percival Howell, spent many years in Harlem, from his arrival in 1918 to his deportation in 1932). There was, of course, the more familiar version from Euro-American modernist art, from Paul Gauguin to Pablo Picasso, and also from the jazz age. That latter was represented most easily by the early Duke Ellington, whose "jungle music" was a significant sonic and visual presence and was matched in Europe by the work of Josephine Baker.

Of course, primitivism in the Caribbean has a more material root than the routes of cultural fashion or literary and artistic exchange or the perceived crises of a white masculinity domesticated by industrialization and rebelling through pulp fiction. Rather than being solely in response to—as Dash argued—perceived failures of technology, Caribbean primitivism was an evolving historical sensibility for those who have come to understand themselves as having been uprooted and dispersed. Glissant puts it best in his contextualizing of that movement, which would also become his albatross: "the thrust of negritude among Caribbean intellectuals was a response perhaps to the need, by relating to a common origin, to rediscover unity (equilibrium) beyond dispersion."[42] They therefore imagine a prelapsarian racial and cultural past as well as a political innocence due to the overwhelming and transnational evil of the slave system.

Such rootings would have more than a few pitfalls in the years after McKay, Hughes, and Césaire and in those years where the Rastafarian movement emerged in Jamaica. Those pitfalls would motivate Glissant's need to break so publicly from negritude in a way that the Anglophone world has yet to satisfactorily do. It is precisely that "myth of the organic," for example, that motivated Derek Walcott's assault on such poetics in his important surrealist inspired essays and manifestos, "What the Twilight Says" and "The Muse of History."[43] Walcott's poetics of an "elation" rooted not in blackness but in a deliberate historylessness mirrors the surrealist celebration of intense affirmation—the "power of wonderment" claimed by Césaire or, even better, his grasp at "the throbbing newness of the world."[44] It is not unrelated to Glissant's own insistence on the "joyous affirmation of relativity."[45] Walcott too would decry nationalist organicism in terms that echo Langston Hughes and Henry Adams, describing, "glorifiers of the tom-tom ignoring the dynamo."[46] One is reminded here of Césaire's own reference to the "dynamo" in "Poetry and Cognition," where it is a sign that even technology and its infinite promises of power are themselves subject to imaginative and cultural reinvention.

Correspondingly, the folk or popular racializing of technology and the resistance to it is why organicism is at the core of a vernacular phenomenon like Jamaican *roots* reggae, from which dub will be abstracted and then globalized as its shadow, its echo. It is in dub where Rastafarian notions of racial roots become first explicitly technologized and where cultural dispersal becomes obsessively alluded to in its lyrics and replicated through techniques of machinic echo. But that echo-driven genre of music and the sound-system culture that dispersed it would chart a new relationship with technology akin to that space between being and making at work in negritude. Dub maintained the fetish for nature and origins but without the suspicion of technology characteristic of the generation that Dash describes.

It is precisely that relationship between an obsession with roots on the one hand and an equal obsession with technology on the other that proved appealing to Gibson in *Neuromancer* and Alan Moore's iconic *Watchmen* and throughout the world made by what was called cyberpunk. In reggae, dub, and then dancehall—cultural movements much more impactful than negritude—the engagement with technology would be seen as first an act of resistance through mastery, then as a naturalized supplement to those organicist notions of masculinity and racial identity. Just as technology could function as a symbol of race and mechanization in the jazz age, it was intentionally foregrounded in dub and roots reggae as a sign of hypermasculine agency, national pride, *and* an African continuum. Sound was the primary space wherein mixture, hybridity, *métissage,* and the limits and possibilities of creolization will be explored. Dub, for example, is where "reconfiguration has become a more central compositional ideal than the creation of 'original' music."[47]

A similar hearing of history motivates Stuart Hall's famous essay on cultural identity through the two canonical movements of negritude and Rastafarianism. Reggae is one of the primary "signifiers of a new construction of Jamaican-ness" articulated in the name of roots, in terms of a "'new' Africa, as we might say, necessarily 'deferred.'"[48] Unlike many of his peers or most Rastafarians, Hall doesn't hear roots as a static authenticity, an invariant transhistorical stability. Embedded in the practice or performance of racial recovery is a simultaneous process of creolization based not on rediscovery but, in fact, on *production*. This is the sound of *made* masquerading as *being*.

For Hall, sound is not merely song or rhythm or a lyric but the ground on which much Caribbean thinking and culture making has rested. Wynter agrees:

> The great unifying forms of our times are no longer, as in the case of cricket, coded, under the hegemony of middle-class cultural mores ... The great unifying cultural forms of our times, beginning with the jazz culture and its derivatives, are popular. This is the significance of calypso and Carnival, of the reggae and Rastafarianism.[49]

Hall is rarely thought of as a theorist of creolization. But he is very much within that lineage that includes Harris and Glissant. This kinship is at least due to his focus on the production of identity and his deliberate stress on Caribbean mutability rather than stable racial formations or the hardening that comes from bichromatic (black/white) structures of racism or resistance. As Hall describes cultural identity, it

> is a matter of "becoming" as well as of "being." It belongs to the future as much as to the past. It is not something which already exists, transcending place, time, history, and culture. Cultural identities come from somewhere, have histories. But, like everything which is historical, they undergo constant trans-formation. Far from being eternally fixed in some essentialized past, they are subject to the continuous "play" of history, culture, and power. Far from being grounded in a mere "recovery" of the past, which is waiting to be found and which, when found, will secure our sense of ourselves into eternity, identities are the names we give to the different ways we are positioned by, and position ourselves within, the narratives of the past.[50]

In our contemporary intellectual climate very few would quibble with these words. Rather than take negritude and Rastafari at their own word as movements focused on racial authenticity and an unvarying sense of the black self, he finds in them traces of creolization. But were Hall to have said "race" instead of "cultural identity," things would no doubt have been different. Had he focused his argument on blackness as necessarily mutable, contingent, and therefore subject to going beyond itself, the words would have been less welcome.

Still, it's hard to imagine that race wasn't on Hall's mind, that he wasn't playing with the easy slippage between race and culture. It is at least within his sphere of implication, because his focus is on what defines creolization as a critical position in the wake of but also *in spite of* slavery, racism, and colonial power. And that is transformation, made possible within Harris's alchemical "womb of space" or through that *dubwise* process Glissant calls *relation*.

SYLVIA WYNTER'S NAKED DECLIVITY

Because Sylvia Wynter is more associated with historicism than Glissant or Wilson Harris, some may find it odd to find her here called *creoliste*. Her most astute reader, Paget Henry, describes her work as an attempt to provide a bridge between the historicist tradition in the Caribbean—as in the work of C. L. R James—and those poeticist traditions that include the work of Harris and Glissant.[51] Wynter's "hybridizing" of the historicist and the poeticist traditions of Caribbean thought is rare but not unusual, given that both of those traditions emerge out of anticolonial nationalism. Hers is not a creolization that depends overmuch on the "linguistic turn," despite being rooted in poststructuralist theories of language. Yet her interest in absence or marginality—lack—as well as in racial and cultural differences roots her in that poststructuralist tradition that includes Edward Said, Homi Bhabha, and V. Y. Mudimbe. Also, her ideological and political commitments are far more familiar to the resistance model of racial thinking dominant in the United States than to what both Glissant and Harris insist be read as a Caribbean-rooted (or routed) phenomenon.

Differences might be as hard to spot as similarities in her case, so it would be helpful to consider her work in relation to other theorists of creolization before exploring in detail her technopoetics. Her thinking is here designated as a Caribbean pre-posthumanism, due to not only having been established in advance of posthumanism but also being focused on the era where the human was being invented. Wynter's earliest essay in this context is "The Ceremony

Must Be Found: After Humanism," published in 1984, a year before Haraway's "A Cyborg Manifesto." The titular focus on a perspective in the wake of the Western Enlightenment construction of man, the human, or humanism itself is characteristic of her most valuable essays. More important than the timing of this particular essay is the fact that her work contextualizes shifting designations of the human against a longer history than that posited by Haraway.

Wynter has more than a little in common with thinkers who have been willing to think through the mutability of race. These are critics for whom the organic or roots is merely one manifestation of a promiscuous metahistorical process that sees no borders between categories and will ever insist on them polluting and infecting each other. Her intimacy with creolization is made clear in her discussion of Glissant's work, which is also her version of the Caribbean intellectual history discussed in the previous sections. It is present in a 1989 essay, where she argues that Glissant "takes part in a new uprising, together with the line of intellectual filiation specific to Martinique" that ranges from Aimé Césaire to Frantz Fanon and then to other Caribbean islands in the work of George Lamming and Maryse Condé. She importantly describes this lineage as a tradition of intellectual revolt in advance of Michel Foucault: "If Foucault was to raise the question of the historical and therefore relative nature of our modes of subjectivity in the wake of the 1968 cultural revolts in France, this question had been first raised poetically rather than conceptually by Aimé Césaire" and in the aftermath of World War II, Fanon, Lamming, and Glissant.[52]

Rooting this uprising in Aimé Césaire and those others who clustered around *Tropiques* challenges contemporary critics to attribute less of her insights to Foucault than is common and to work harder to think through her own specifically Caribbean provenance. Glissant's praxis of creolization is, in her view, a "mode of revolt . . . against the very roots of our present mode of 'conventional reason' and therefore of the order of discourse and of its Word of Man, which now serves as . . . the nonquestionable 'paradigm of value and authority' from which our present order of knowledge (episteme) and its disciplining discourses are, in rule-governed fashion, generated."[53] This focus on this intellectual revolt suggests that her celebration of Glissant is essentially a celebration of the surrealist revolt and its legacy.

Revolting against reason and the quest to break from both its epistemic control as well as its material dominance is a racial revolt kept intimate with decolonization. Locating this legacy in the Caribbean allows surrealism and racial nationalism, creolization and negritude, to function at least contrapuntally rather than oppositionally. This is clear in her identifying Glissant's "performative acts of countermeaning directed against the semantic character or behavior-regulating program, instituted by our present order of discourse and therefore by its related order of rationality or mode of 'conventional' or cultural 'reason.'" These are surrealist acts that must be routed back to Césaire's "founding counterdiscourse" of the Caribbean and its various revolts against colonial power and meaning. In this history Wynter emphasizes Césaire's and Glissant's common desire to "perceive reality in a new way" and the latter's movement "from a loss of trust in our modes of subjectivity, of being" toward something richly else."[54] This is a tradition far more focused on becoming, which suggests an ease with or acceptance of transformation even if produced by injustice, trauma, or inequality. It emerges not from a state of constant insecurity that inspires relentless affirmation but instead from a state of full cultural confidence that enables a step into the void.

It is this stress on possibility—imaginative, political, and otherwise—that also links Wynter to creolization as mutual products of surrealist echo and of that movement's devotion to generating a break from an institutionalized and oppressive reality. Again, this is no more or less than a description of the Dada-surrealist project. Here it is inflected with the history of French colonial racism as an echo of the conflicts at the heart of an age allegedly of reason. Negritude, after all, according to Césaire, first rose in Haiti as a belief in a more expansive view of humanity rather than the limited borders of the human as defined by slavery.[55] Considering that one of Wynter's primary concerns is for how semantic, linguistic, and poetic processes have "behavior-regulating" material effects, Césaire's revolt was "against the role imposed on the black population groups of the New World as the embodied bearers of Ontological Lack to the secular model of being, Man, as the negative conceptual Other term to its instituting word."[56] In other words, Césairean poetics led to rehumanizing that which was rendered inhuman or seen as soulless by the previous "order of discourse." It was a struggle for an expansive definition of life that was continuous with what occurred in the Haitian Revolution as the slaves—*knowing* themselves to be human—responded to the call of modernity as sounded by the French Revolution.

In "Unsettling the Coloniality of Being/Power/Truth/Freedom: Towards the Human, after Man, Its Overrepresentation—An Argument," Wynter identifies the significance of Césaire as far more than poetry or poetics. His work was and is directly aimed at and engaged with science and new modes of humanity. She suggests that it actually anticipates digital technology:

If Césaire called in 1946 for a new science of the Word, a science therefore of dual descriptive statements and thereby of our modes/genres of being human, doing so from the perspective of a poet—in 1988, the physicist Hans Pagel would make a parallel call in his 1988 book *The Dream of Reason: The Computer and the Rise of the Sciences of Complexity*. His call, too, was for a new frontier to be opened onto a nonadaptive mode of human self-cognition: onto the possibility, therefore, of our fully realized autonomy of feelings, thoughts, behaviors.[57]

Hans Pagel is, of course, the late Heinz Pagels, who is arguably better known for his popular work on quantum physics, *The Cosmic Code* (1982). Along with its follow up, *Perfect Symmetry,* it is work one imagines Wilson Harris enjoying for its attempt to blur, if not erase, the borders between scientific reason and the kind of metaphysical questioning usually ceded to religion or poetry. But note the powerful connections being made in this passage between the being/making dialectic and Césaire's fusing of racial nationalism and surrealist praxis. It's also worth keeping in mind the elements at work in this passage. There is the focus on "being human" as a series of "modes" and "genres"; one could even suggest it is as much a form of performance as it is a masquerade. Also important is the eminently science fictional and colonial notion of a "new frontier" and the transformation of and into new modes of cognition. It's hard not to hear also an echo of Fanon, due to not only his impact on Césaire but also to *The Wretched of the Earth*'s famous conclusion, which calls for the creation of a new history of man distinct from that produced by colonial Europe.

Wynter's discussion of "being human" will return in due course as we explore her work's implications for artificial intelligence as a contemporary iteration of older conversations of race and the human that emerge with modernity. But that she sees all this in Césaire only strengthens the link between negritude and creolization and of course the links between technology and a Caribbean pre-posthumanism. Arguably, the possibilities she sees here in Césaire are the very ones Glissant will deny or suppress in his *Poetics of Relation,* as pointed out at the end of the previous chapter. Glissant's return to the human is a way of sanctifying poetics and language and defending them against technology. Césaire in her view is calling for a new frontier not so much in terms of the full realization of the autonomy of "feelings, thoughts, behaviors" but in terms of new genres of the human made necessary due to the remarkable growth of computer capacity and our increasing dependence on them as a material site of memory.

Wynter actually sees a politics in Glissantian *créolité* in line with Caribbean national and racial reconstruction, in short, with the kind of nationalism that generates movements like negritude and Rastafarianism. "Against the reality of a colonization of the cultural Imaginary so successful at the level of the assimilation of the psyche, of its mimesis of being," she argues, "stands Glissant's insistent proposal for the 'taking charge of the Word.'" Wynter stresses Glissant's use of the "counterconcept of *métissage* so as to contest the representation of monofiliation, of Genesis, of, in our terms, 'Man.'" Glissant works against "the *universel généralisant* of the Word of Man (and its variants: Proletarian, Woman)" to deploy the theme of the "anti-Universal."[58]

There are, however, limitations at work in Wynter's attempt to make Glissant a black rebel nationalist, which reveals how her commitment to resistance blinds her. It is true, for example, that Glissant is also concerned with, as she says, "the claim to specificity, of the claim to 'rester au lieu' (the remaining-in-place) in the specific *oikumene* of the Antilles, in the specificity of its 'mode of the imaginary.'"[59] But this is because creolization in his thinking is a *true* universal process, one that works as much through racism as through resistance, as much through Eurocentrism as through Rastafari, negritude, or any black identity or ideology. What Glissant deplores is the false universalism—or that "generalizing universality"—that undergirded colonialism and racism. Eurocentrism masqueraded as universal but was in fact the colonial imposition of a particular, or what he calls a "transparent universality."[60]

Always on the lookout for moments of possible catalysis, Harris describes this masquerade as the primary "defect" of "an enlightenment associated with the Renaissance, an enlightenment that aborted a profound cross-culturalism between science and art, as among the diverse cultures of humanity around the globe." In responding to this defect he argues something that could be read as a corrective to Wynter's framing of Glissant through the resistance paradigm: that there lies a tragedy "in reinforcing a fixation with protest" because it leads to "a suppression of profoundest creativity to throw bridges across chasms, to open an architecture of space within closed worlds of race and culture."[61] This is reminiscent of a moment from Haraway's "Cyborg Manifesto," where she argues, "Innocence'—a significant product of resistance politics—'and the corollary insistence on victimhood as the only ground for insight, has done enough damage."[62]

Haraway's fine insight doesn't leave Harris or Glissant off the hook. She also points out that the "constructed revolutionary subject"—hybrid, creole, or cyborg—must also give us pause.[63] Wynter's reading of Glissant is without that necessary hesitation. Her need to place him in an invariant continuum leading from Césaire is too strong. She is right in describing how the "universal Word of Man" demanded subordination to its "specific view of the past."[64] But, for Glissant, the rejection of that colonial view is more than simply a romantic racial revolt against specificity or Eurocentrism. Instead, it emphasizes how necessary specificity is, even if prejudicial and racist and or resistant and nationalist. Borders beg for crossing and differences crave for blending, just as Georges Bataille argued that taboos beg for transgression. As a universal process creolization depends on the flickering between assertions of specificity that are always eventually undone in the relentless creating of bridges across differences.

Yet creolization is no mere naming of an indifferent process, considering the material and historical facts of race and colonialism. It needn't be seen as politically quiescent in its seeming indifference to borders. As she points out in her reading of Glissant, it can be or is deployed against colonial notions of authenticity or, as postcolonial theorist Homi Bhabha emphasized, *authority.* As a matter of fact, Homi Bhabha's intervention into the relationship between colonial domination and hybridity is worth a moment: "The analysis of colonial depersonalization not only alienates the Enlightenment idea of 'Man,' but challenges the transparency of social reality, as a pre-given image of human knowledge.... For the very nature of humanity becomes estranged in the colonial condition and from that 'naked declivity' emerges, not as an assertion of will nor as an evocation of freedom, but as an enigmatic questioning."[65] One hears the politics of echo—a repetition with difference, a questioning that repeats and lingers in traces. Bhabha stresses that hybridity rendered colonial domination epistemologically and culturally unstable and therefore open to rewriting, resistance, and repeating with difference. Mimicry and doubling come to mind, both blackface and dub as uncanny performances and technologies of both. Bhabha's insights serve simply to say that change and transformation is possible and inevitable from the ground up: the street finding its own uses for things, as William Gibson famously put it.[66]

Wynter goes on to argue that the quite politicized "enigmatic questioning" of those monofiliative assumptions in Glissant and the institutions that supported those assumptions would be "blocked" by science. This is not the science at work in her earlier reference to digital computing in the context of Césaire's black surrealist revolt. The science she means here is that precybernetic and prequantum science that was the ultimate representation of a rationalistic and therefore exclusivist apparatus. This form of science would serve to justify, or rather naturalize, differences between one mode of life and another by virtue of the cultural superiority of one over the other.

Wynter's focus on the process of intellectual, social, and epistemic revolt as well as racial reconstruction brings to light another subtle but significant difference between her, Glissant, and Harris. She is hardly as cavalier about racial subjectivity as both Glissant and Harris can seem and is as attuned to issues of class as is Stuart Hall. Though focused on the dialectic between man and "ontological lack" (between whites and blacks), Wynter maintains the primacy of black subjectivity. This is, again, a form of humanism, even though counter to what Glissant would consider the false universalism of European humanism. This focus on black subjectivity is important to Alexander Weheliye in his reading of Wynter as a crucial figure in the establishment of what he considers black or Afro-diasporic humanisms. These humanisms may be hesitant about the prefix "post" due to that history of being marked as "pre" or "sub."

Glissant and Harris are also rooted in and routed through that history. As Caribbean posthumanists, however, the need to react to exclusion by reifying a black version of the human, even if sanctioned by the romance of resistance or the contemporary fetish for difference, is not enough, especially if it leads to a fetishizing of origins and identities and an obsession with nature or roots. In Glissant's words, "one of the best kept secrets of creolization" is that "through it we can see that the mingling of experiences is at work, there for us to know and producing the process of being. We abandon the idea of fixed being."[67]

Wynter does agree with Harris and Glissant that, as Paget Henry puts it, "the historical process is not driven by class or racial conflict, but rather by the epistemic and liminal dynamics in the mythopoetic constructions of groups in conflict."[68] That too is a point crucial for creolization as a belief in the historicity of race and an acceptance of its inevitable transformation despite its real world, material effects. Leonard Cassuto frames the liminal as being necessarily a space of productive historical change: "liminality demands resolution; for a human being caught between the categories of human and thing, the pressure will be exerted toward a return to the human category, for that is the only choice that offers the possibility of resolution."[69] For Wynter, resolution requires far more than just the transcendental logic that Cassuto suggests (as if resolutions are actually inevitable). For her the liminal empowers those denied subjectivity and consciousness and soul the possibility of conceptual, metaphoric, and cultural engagement. They actively make resolution possible by the expansion and reversal of categories like the human or the other.

The general assault on "conventional reason" that she identifies in Glissant is also very much a part of surrealist praxis due to the refusal of an epistemological status quo and its given systems of meaning and value. Reversal was the goal of that praxis. This stress on reversal shows that her thinking is focused primarily on the refusal of the colonized or enslaved to occupy what she calls the "lack state." This refusal presents a far more active vision of creolization as a human-centered and material process rather than the quasi-metaphysical one at the heart of the poeticist tradition in Caribbean thought.

It has been much stressed here that despite its rootedness in slavery and colonialism, racism, violence, and terror, creolization can be said to have a much more fluid relationship to history than do other traditions of racial thinking. This isn't to suggest that creolization ignores racism and its related power dynamics either in the past or in the present. Creolization just distinguishes itself by an equal commitment to the possible. This is evident in the comfort that both Glissant and Harris have with abandoning subjectivity as well as with not allowing race or trauma to occupy the privileged center of their poetics or politics. Race for them is ultimately a mutable and contingent sign of transformation, much like the body is in posthumanism or cultural identity as discussed by Stuart Hall.

Creolization can then be said to have implicit traces of *futurism*—not, however, an Afro-futurism that often imagines a future by projecting into it contemporary racial paradigms, histories, and neonationalist politics. Just as it may have emerged to contest the alleged racelessness of much contemporary science fiction—which, to be accurate, is the lack of *race centeredness* of much contemporary science fiction since race and difference are in fact present in contemporary science fiction—any insistence on an inevitably racist future has as much predictive authority as the naïveté that drives fictions of a raceless one.

Oddly enough, what can be called a *creole futurism* has some things in common with the very first futurism. As discussed in the first chapter, despite their fascistic tendencies and a fierce, fierce misogyny, the love of technology characteristic of Italian futurism depended on race and Africa as signs of becoming and the future. Africa may have been figured as primitive and ripe for the colonial plucking of a fascist modernity but was a primary element of that radical vision. The most important commonality between futurism and creolization is in their relationship to the past, which makes it much easier to discuss both of them in the context of science fiction.

The artists and polemicists of Italian futurism had an absolute hostility to what they described with the derogatory neologism *passeism.* This term defined a slavish devotion to history, particularly as manifested in institutions and as expressed by conventional scholarship and politics. It was hurled at anyone or anything they wanted to destroy, an attitude that music writer Greil Marcus would cite as central to the historical evolution of the punk sensibility from which cyberpunk owes much. Though not as hostile to history as this early twentieth-century movement, creolization shares that radical forward-lookingness and a submission to the vagaries of that which cannot be contained by the past or the contemporary. One sees this at work in Césaire too, who celebrated surrealism for "having purged the past, oriented the present, prepared the future."[70]

In bringing futurism, creolization, science fiction, negritude, and Afro-futurism together, one is reminded of critic Greg Tate's response to the work of Samuel R. Delany. For Tate, Delany's work was troubling due to the novelist's "racially defused futures," which "seem to deny the possibility that the affirmative aspects of black American culture and experience could survive assimilation." What he "expected from our one black science-fiction writer was SF which envisioned the future of black culture as I'd define it, from a more or less nationalist stance."[71] One can strategically ignore the "as I'd define it" clause here, though it's worth pointing out that it is key to the sometimes imperial prejudices of black first-world thinking. Such thinking often and casually imposes its national assumptions on other national and transnational contexts in the name of race. This is especially the case since Delany's futures are often extraterrestrial and post-American, so the idea that a distinct black Americanness should guide them or survive the nation-state seems a bit much to ask.

Instead of fictions of solidarity or easy historical and social continuity, Delany presents characters that don't "wear their negritude on their sleeves," as Tate rightly points out, and for whom race is not at the core of their cultural identity.[72] In response to Tate, Delany has said, "Now part of what, from my marginal position, I see as the problem is the idea of anybody's having to fight the fragmentation and multicultural diversity of the world, not to mention outright oppression, by constructing something so rigid as an identity, an identity in which there has to be a fixed and immobile core, a core that is structured to hold inviolate such a complete biological fantasy as race—whether white or black."[73]

The closeness between this and the passage from Stuart Hall quoted earlier should be striking. Its similarity to the thinking of both Wilson Harris and Édouard Glissant should be obvious. Also telling is what it reveals about the differences between Afro-futurism and a black technopoetics rooted in creolization as well as in the thinking of Sylvia Wynter. Delany's vision is essentially one of an essentially *creole* future. They are not race-less, just not ideologically nationalist or racially particularistic, as expected by Tate, Jeffrey Allen Tucker—author of *A Sense of Wonder: Samuel R. Delany, Race, Identity, and Difference* (2004)—and by more than a few Afro-futurists (to be fair, even some Caribbean ones). The expectation that the future be black in that quite limited way is not unlike the Afrocentrist expectation that the past—say, ancient Egypt—be also black, despite the fact that that past antedates the binary racial constructions that motivate this political urge. Blackness in Delany, as with creolization, is not historical permanence. After all, to combine race with a futurism is to subject blackness to the vagaries of temporal transformation, to its inevitable creolization. Granted, the fear of erasure is particularly strong in the black diaspora due to legacies of violence and marginalization. But to engage transformation is not to risk or court erasure. It is to refuse to be conditioned and delimited by that fear and to reject the exploitation of it.

The commonalities between Delany and a creole futurism are not just in their decentering of race. They exist in the continuous placing of race and other modes of subjectivity within alternate formations and possible, if not imminent, technological transformations. His representations of the vagaries of race, difference, and sexuality exist on the other side of our historical ordering of knowledge and our conditions of conceptual (and sociohistorical) possibility. That they exist in reimagined form rather than be absent or transcended is for him to emphasize their inevitable historical reconstruction, another thing central to the type of creolization at work in Sylvia Wynter. Another way to put this is that Delany's futures test the limits of those historical frameworks called *epistemes* that are so dear to Wynter's thinking. And it is through the notion of epistemes that one can witness traces in Wynter's work of a creole futurism. Her thinking is as committed to the past as it is to the *emergent,* to things within—or at the margins of—those Foucauldian epistemes. It is on the margins of those epistemes that those designated as inhuman or subhuman will not only become signs of the necessary expansion of the category of human but, in her view, predictive metaphors of subjectivities to come, signs of the inevitability of *coming races.*

Paget Henry describes the episteme as a "knowledge-constitutive field whose schemas and concepts are also shaped in part by the imperatives of adapting their representational capabilities to specific social and natural environments."[74] They are massive, transhistorical blocks of knowledge and sensibility. Those various and important scholarly attempts to establish race as a modern invention or a product of modernity are dependent on the notion of epistemes insofar as race—certainly blackness or whiteness—is not anterior to modernity and so need not be assumed as necessarily beyond it. Also epistemes do break and fracture, as well as blend and relentlessly transform. They include, for example, Darwinian evolution as well as the Western human and biological sciences, the latter group being crucial to Wynter's argumentative context.

To provide flesh to Wynter's creolization of Foucault (a creolization evident in her commitment to what Paget Henry rightly describes as "epistemic hybridity") is also to find in the birth of science fiction's ongoing fascination with difference, space, and machines examples that ground Wynter's ideas.[75] For example, in "The Ceremony Must Be Found: After Humanism," she provides a perspective on the emergence of industrialization against a longer backdrop of shifts and mutations in Western knowledge and politics, particularly in the context of colonialism and its constructions of race and self and that "mutation" of the human that is race. Her vision is characteristically overwhelming in its historical breadth and lack of detail but does contextualize this book's earlier reading of *Erewhon* and other texts that emerge in the movement from Victorianism into modernism. In this seminal essay Wynter emphasizes technology as instrumental to that important shift from the classical "episteme" and a religiosocial world order to one generally called "modernity." Here is but one example taken from her description of the heretical emergence of humanism in the fifteenth-century *Studia Humanitas*:

> As Hans Jonas has pointed out, the really revolutionary movement of the Copernican break was his revelation that Nature offered no empirical support for the represented physico-ontological principle of Difference that, in fact, as Galileo's telescope was to verify and Newton's equally applicable laws to confirm, the earth was a star, and the stars were earths. Humanism and the *Studia*'s projection of Natural Man with his Natural *Logos* was, therefore, as Hubner notes part of a comprehensive thrust in which "the entire world had begun to transform itself" *pari passu* with the "discovery of new continents and new seas," which was to bring in changes that shook the hitherto entrenched "sacred" structures of society, as the secularization of the State and the printing presses and the rise of the middle classes destroyed the "old hierarchies and privileged classes." Out of this

train of events, a mutation of the human cognitive mechanisms was set in motion, one in which the idea rose "that the Divine Creation, like the construction of a great cosmic machine had to be understandable by and through human reason." It was in the context of this special and overall mutation of the cultural imagination of the human, that the discontinuity that would constitute the new order of the natural sciences had begun, and that the later technology of Galileo's telescope had its origins.[76]

As with the work of so many post- or anticolonial thinkers in the wake of Foucault and Said, there is the tendency here to try to out-map or out-systematize an already too generalized mode of thinking and, in doing so, exaggerate its actual systematicity in the attempt to equally exaggerate a mode of resistance. This helps enshrine the faulty notion that the logic of power and the experience of knowledge are ever congruent with their own expectations and that, in this case, the age of reason was in any way *reasonable*. Surrealism should have reminded her better.

But it's all here: Copernicus, secularism, Galileo, and technologies such as the printing press and telescope. Also, that crucial notion of an "overall mutation of the cultural imagination of the human," which occurs as a mutation on the margins of the classical episteme and introduces temporarily inhuman figures—natives, primitives—into that episteme. There are many such moments in her work, particularly in "Unsettling the Coloniality of Being/Power/Truth/Freedom: Towards the Human, after Man, Its Overrepresentation—An Argument" (2003). This essay makes clear its antecedent "post-" humanism not by the suggestion of Nietzschean transcendence but by expanding the restrictive notion of the human (whites) to include those structurally opposed to it yet within its own schema. Because her "after" humanism does not reflect that desire to fully bypass or transcend the human, it is not as easily a posthumanist gesture as it might seem. "After Humanism" or "after Man" is ultimately critical of a racially and colonially coded humanism that in constructing the other simultaneously excludes it from humanity, hence her commitment to a thinking that is "Towards the Human," suggesting that that category continues to be incomplete and continually in need of supplementation. The "after" should be thought of as being part and parcel of her liberationist intent, of the desire to emphasize the fundamental problematic of man as being the foundational problematic of race.

In "Ceremony" she points out that "with the rise and expansion of the industrial age and the rise to hegemony of the groups who spearheaded the Industrial Revolution, a transumption of humanism's 'natural Man' took place." The "noble savage" or hyperorganic product of European modernity's solitary claim on white being and on whites being human, because of "his Lack of Reason," was excluded "from governing himself, as the European could" but was "nevertheless incorporated into the same table of being, the schema of the structural opposition between Reason/Lack-of-reason and of the discourses generated from its related Classical episteme."[77] Technology, in her view, had more than a little to do with the construction of race and the parceling out of humanity into subsets. One should add here that the process that generates this primitive product would eventually produce its other—or, more accurately, its *other* other—certainly by the end of the nineteenth century: the robot, that *hyperinorganic* figure that represented an *excess of reason,* intelligence without soul, rationality without spirit. That too enters the "table of being," certainly by the time of *Erewhon,* if not by the publication of *R.U.R.* Like race, machines become yet another inevitable mutation of the human when new epistemological limits are crossed.

That structural exclusion of the other merely shunts that other into the category of the liminal, which for Wynter is not a space of negation but of future possibility. It is the space produced in the fissure between epistemes. And the liminal is the antithesis of the episteme, constituting all that exists outside of the conceptual schema of the episteme but which becomes inevitably refigured according to it. As Paget Henry puts it, "liminal categories would be the categories that are diametrically opposed to a core or founding category of one of those ideological discourses." "Human," for example, due to its already racial coding is the primary founding category that is meant here, and postcolonial societies like the Caribbean are the liminal space where the "systemic errors" of "totalized discourses" are more clearly materialized, as the other becomes misrepresented according to the needs and desires of colonial and racial power.[78]

More will be said about these "errors," but's important to keep clear that for Wynter these misrepresentations are not merely symbolic. They undergird and justify social and economic domination. She continues, "Whatever the group—women, natives, niggers—whatever the category—the Orient, Africa, the tropics—the ordering principle of the discourse was the same: the figuration of an ontological order or value between the groups who were markers of 'rationality' and those who were the markers of its Lack-State."[79] Again, as is typical of generations of anticolonial and postcolonial thinkers, there is here an exaggerated commitment to a notion that modernity or colonialism were or are truly as well structured and well ordered as they claimed—or that their oppositions ever worked as well in practice as they mapped out in theory, politics, or literature. Such exaggerations of power may be understandable since they give impetus and fire to revolutionary politics or vindicationist imaginaries. They do, however, obscure those transformative possibilities and "depths of mutuality" that are often invisible to ideologies, particularly race-based ones.

Also typical of her generation of critics and the next is the reduction of these "rules of figuration" to being the same, when it is not true that, say, an Orientalism and an Africanism or that, say, white women and African slaves, were and are governed the same way, cognitively or politically. As Michael Adas points out in *Machines as the Measure of Man,* for example, the very distinction between how Indians and Chinese were figured and governed in relationship to Africans had more to do with different levels of literacy and acknowledged traditions of science and technology than absolutist notions of racial or sexual otherness. But Wynter's insistence that all nonwhite difference was and is "non-consciously governed" by a colonial "ratiomorphic apparatus" that still includes "liminal Others" goes without argument.[80] Of primary interest to a black technopoetics and a creole futurism is the "transumption" of humanism's black other ("Nigger Chaos" in her most colorful formulation) into or against something else. It is a way of saying that one other becomes symbolically transmutable—or exchangeable—with another other. As seen in the science fiction work discussed throughout this book, the language of one can be used to make sense of another.

Key to epistemic change in Wynter is the fact that liminal categories, because they are outside of the conceptual schema of the dominant frames of European knowledge, are prone to errors and misrepresentation. For example, in seeing the African as animal or machines as mere objects, Europeans rendered their epistemes vulnerable: "Because objects or persons represented by the liminal category are systemically assigned negative values, the resulting distortions and misrepresentations are highly resistant to discursive criticism or attack."[81] In other words, these misrepresentations and distortions function as truth within that episteme, the truth of the other, of blacks, of women, of natives: primitive, inferior, soulless, not human.

This is a fairly conventional understanding of how power works and how race operates within the "gaze" of whiteness. It is also a conventional understanding of that "ambivalence" of colonial discourse that Homi Bhabha identified, in which the signs, symbols, and meanings generated from the colonizer were split between universals such as freedom and equality and specific denials of those universals, such as colonialism and slavery. What is innovative is in how Wynter makes sense of epistemic "misrepresentations and distortions" as they become verified or falsified by material reality. Henry explains, "The tendency toward systemic misrepresentation is for Wynter the Achilles' heel of *epistemes* and the primary source of epistemic shifts. Gross misrepresentation makes an elaborated discourse and its founding *episteme* vulnerable to the contrary signals that continue to emerge from the misrepresented object, person, or event. The greater the misrepresentation, the greater the vulnerability of the *episteme*."[82]

The primary example Henry provides of this complex but stunningly important idea is based on the changes in medieval geography and cosmology attendant with the shift that came with Christopher Columbus's voyages, which occurred in tandem with scientism and the growth in humanism. Wynter's notion of "transumption" as well as how "lack" functions as a productive misrepresentation is rooted in her reading of Columbus's journey. Though it might be obvious it still is worth emphasizing: transumption means transformation, a creolizing.

Her primary reading of this event can be found in a brief 1991 essay "1492: A 'New World' View." In it she argues that in challenging "the belief structure sustaining both the 'image of the earth' and the rigid noble/non-noble caste hierarchy of the feudal-Christian order of that time" Columbus threatened the episteme. She insists that this event, then, no longer be seen as a merely "'territorial' or primarily 'technological'" act or interpretation due to this feat having "involved a 'root expansion of thought.'" Rather than being the primary site for vindicationist imaginaries, as a critic attuned to the process of creolization, she insists on reading Columbus's journey for its possibilities in addition to its colonial and genocidal realities. As such, "A New World view of 1492 therefore has to move beyond the 'master categories' and conceptual frameworks of our present system of societal perception."[83]

This "New World view" is simply her term for creolization. She'd used this Columbian argument in her essay "Beyond the Word of Man: Glissant and the New Discourse of the Antilles," arguing that Columbus's "factual errors," along with "Copernicus's challenge to the then still 'sacred' Ptolemaic astronomy a half-century later, lay the basis for the emancipation of human knowledge of physical nature (and, after Darwin, of organic nature) from its millennial traditional role of verifying the 'paradigm of value and authority' or, in Glissant's phrase, the 'transcendentally intolerant' Word of each order's sociogenic principle or code of 'life and death.'" "The 'war' waged by the new discourse of the Antilles" is one waged against these epistemic errors and their still resonant echoes.[84] Her focus here on a creole, Caribbean "bio-politics" is essential for many reasons, not the least of which is her maintaining the centrality of life and nature as political definitions produced by mutable intellectual and historical frameworks, such as Darwinism in the wake of the church and Copernican thinking in the wake of the Ptolemaic.

In keeping with a creole futurism she likens this movement beyond orders, epistemes, and definitions to both space exploration and surrealism in that a new-world view must move beyond "present day" reason, reminding us that reason itself is bound by its given episteme.[85] She makes the same claim in her essay on Glissant and the legacy of Césaire: that new Caribbean discourse does more than engage history; it must engage a "hybrid correlation between the *ordo naturae* of our neurochemical brain states and the *ordo verborum* of our systems of meaning." This forward gesture impels both the Antillean and the human subject beyond our present "order of discourse" and episteme into "realms" beyond "conventional reason."[86]

But those changes between medieval and modern epistemes signaled by Columbus's journey provide the overall framework of Wynter's inquiry and are as much a sign of her brilliance as they are of her reductive overextensions. The journey triggered changes from a sacred ordering of time, the universe, and material social relations to a new system of knowledge contained and controlled by a secular bourgeoisie. In its geographic overreach, the shift troubled the borders of its own episteme and entered the space of monsters, of fallen or "natural unregenerate man," as she argues in "Ceremony," or so they were described within the episteme of medievalism and the hegemony of the Catholic Church.[87] It is this foundational epistemic crisis that makes possible the construction of and various crises of race and difference in a Western-dominated global system.

"Unsettling the Coloniality of Being/Power/Truth/Freedom" argues that what begins with the rupture of medievalism and continues with the encounter with the monstrous in projected or colonized spaces will continue to be figured in fantastical terms in the literature of fantasy, adventure, and science fiction. These are literatures of discovery and difference, excess, anxiety, and containment. Wynter emphasizes that race is that "space of Otherness" encountered in the geographic expansion that will evolve into colonialism. It is in that space that "fixed being" is usually described in primitive or primitivist terms. This space is also a new principle in which "Dubois's Color Line in its white/nonwhite" context is paralleled with the older "Men/Natives form (i.e., as drawn between the lighter and the darker races)." It is one on which is projected "an imagined and extrahumanly (because ostensibly bio-evolutionarily) determined nonhomogeneity of genetic substance between the category of those selected-by-Evolution and the category of those dysselected-by-Evolution."[88]

Her use of the term *extrahumanly* is yet another curious connection to creolization, because Wilson Harris himself significantly uses *extra-human* in his "Creoleness: The Crossroads of a Civilization?" There the *extra-human* is much like the *post-human* when claimed with a full awareness of its roots in colonization and slavery. It is a sign of cross-cultural potential, again, of a future generated by the "incandescent equations between being and nonbeing."[89] For Harris, representations of "lack" signal more than absence: they are an opening into the unknown and heretofore impossible, yet imminent. Similarly, Wynter's use of *extrahumanly* describes the colonial and technological historical process that turned native "Indios" and Africans into creatures of nature, for example, just as it separated rational (white) man from it. It is that same line that inevitably will be crossed, blurred, and abolished in the face of new types of fusions and new types of beings: "For Wynter this process of restless becoming is located in a series of epistemic breaks. These breaks interrupt the episteme of governing orders and construct new codes of human becoming."[90]

CALIBAN'S UNCANNY VALLEY

Amid Wynter's ontohistorical and poeticist swirl is the helpful notion that as broad historical and epistemological transformations emerge, rupture, or mutate, forms of otherness are deployed within the same schema of structural oppositions within a singular "table of being." They overlap, blur, and share space and bodies in narratives ranging, as she puts it in convenient terms for this analysis, "from Ivanhoe to Star Wars."[91]

Again, Wynter's focus is on a European modernity where that enigmatic questioning would give birth to institutions in which man or the human may have been at the center but were structured around a systemic "lack state." As she puts it in her essay on Glissant,

> After Darwin's *Origin of Species* and *Descent of Man,* however, the universal model of being that had been projected by Western Europe from 1512 onward was dis-

placed from that of the human as a created rational being (that is, of the human species as divinely created to be separate from all other organic species by its rational nature) to that of the human as a selected being. In this new representation, in which the human as an evolutionarily selected natural organism now differed from other forms of organic life only by the fact that it created "culture," the same phenomenon would occur, since the pseudoscientific concept of the human as an evolutionarily selected being would also function to block off any questions about being—about, that is, how as humans we attain to human beingness and do so now in a profane or secular rather than sacred modality.[92]

As with Haraway, the issue here is the status of man or the human as a product of modernity and its technological apparatus. But more specifically for Wynter, as a product of modernity and that attendant apparatus, the human is also a product of various interactions between Europeans and their others. This is where race is produced not as intraspecies difference but as a category for new types of humanity and a parceling out of notions of consciousness and of life itself.

Wynter's passage brings to mind a curious line in *Erewhon,* where our mysterious author asks of the machines, "Is it not possible then that there may be even yet new channels dug out for consciousness, though we can detect no signs of them at present?" Also, Butler's description of the machines as a "new phase of life" suggests a belief that evolution creates life as much as it destroys it.[93] The movement from slaves to machines in Wynter's thinking should begin to seem less a leap. If it still seems a leap, then consider this passage from Norbert Wiener's *The Human Use of Human Beings:*

> Here I want to interject the semantic point that such words as life, purpose and soul are grossly inadequate to precise scientific thinking. These terms have gained their significance through our recognition of the unity of a certain group of phenomena, and do not in fact furnish us with any adequate basis to characterize this unity. Whenever we find a new phenomenon which partakes to some degree of the nature of those which we have already termed "living phenomena," but does not conform to all the associated aspects which define the term "life," we are faced with the problem whether to enlarge the word "life" so as to include them, or to define it in a more restrictive way so as to exclude them."[94]

Wiener is talking about machines, but his thinking is in line with what Wynter is ultimately making a case for in the context of modernity and colonization.

Cybernetics, if you recall, is dependent on metaphors of race and slavery, as the purported universal encounters differences or as machines become so intertwined with us that they then become ensnared in quite human questions of morality, subjectivity, and ethics.

Wiener frames the choice between life and nonlife as a moral question rather than simply a biological or technological one. That recourse to morality is, again, necessary when machines become something more than uncanny and begin to impinge on a system of values previously reserved for whoever occupies the category of human at any given time. For Wiener the defining of human or machine is a *choice* that comes from cross-cultural or cross-racial encounter. One either maintains an inclusive notion of life and therefore a more democratic sense of belonging or establishes a more exclusive one, like slavery or colonial power. Wiener, clearly on the side of the inclusive, brings to mind something from Donna Haraway's "A Cyborg Manifesto": "choice grounds a liberal politics and epistemology."[95]

Wiener's turn to morality is also rooted in the inevitable reference to "soul." Along with the question of intelligence, soul remains a pertinent link between black slavery and cybernetics, robotics, and artificial intelligence (not to mention black music). Though it does seem a bit naive to suggest that the huge complex of racism, territorial domination, and economic exploitation that generated the transformations of modernity in which Africans were denied souls and intelligence could be reduced simply to "choice." Perhaps by "choice" Wiener means to merely suggest that there are in fact options when a society encounters what seems as absolute cultural or racial differences. But there is still no doubt that the parsimonious attributing of soul or intelligence does frame our episteme, even as it begins to mutate and shift into one where the border war between flesh and fabrication is resolved or its old hierarchies of value forced to transform.

Wiener would choose "to avoid all question-begging epithets such as 'life,' 'soul,' 'vitalism,' and the like" because they are so loaded with complex and traumatic historical values. Instead, "say merely in connection with machines that there is no reason why they may not resemble human beings in representing pockets of decreasing entropy in a framework in which the large entropy tends to increase."[96] Without those epithets we are no longer faced with historically problematic questions. We are presented simply with a kind of equality in which *neither machines nor humans have souls at all,* something very influential in today's robotics. Take, for example, the work of Hans Moravec. His views may seem familiar to readers of science fiction, but he is one of the more radical scientists in his prophesy of a future that will inevitably be robot-led and where what we know to be artificial intelligence will in fact be the dominant form of life on our planet—to our benefit.

For Moravec the question of whether a machine can have a soul is like the earlier question of whether machines could be said to think: it leads recursively back to the question of what *is* thinking and the question of what exactly is soul. As he puts it, "No presumption of spirit is required to find a natural duality between the physical body and the abstract, self-interpreting mind." In keeping with Wiener's notion of choice, "we might grant a conscious soul to a robot by interpreting its behavior as expressing the action of such a soul: the more humanlike its interaction with us, the easier the attribution." Moravec acknowledges the various disagreements possible by social ethicists, functional mechanists, theologians, and cosmologists, but "most people, however, are likely, after a period of suspicion, to begin taking machines that interact like intelligent, decent persons at face value, regardless of unseen internals, because it is the most effective alternative. . . . So, it may be appropriate to say 'God' has granted a soul to a machine when the machine is accepted as a real person by a wide human community."[97]

This strategy of ending prejudice by essentially social and cultural interaction is, well, uncanny in its evocation of a racial politics aimed at ridding whites of the visual burden of racial differentiation and its various assumptions. This is not unlike that "best foot forwardism" of early twentieth-century black assimilationist politics in its attempt to prove to whites that blacks were and could be "intelligent decent persons"; nor is it unlike Martin Luther King's focus on "the content of our character" rather than on skin or the "unseen internals" assumed to animate racial or cultural differences. Moravec is nothing less than liberal in Haraway's sense, as is Wiener. His work, however, is not free of the expectation of supplantation that attended the late nineteenth century and its illiberal views of race and technology. It's just free of those anxieties that rooted supplantation in racial revenge or human redundancy. Imagine him a version of *Erewhon*'s narrator, who welcomes the dominance of machines and is eager to serve. Soul becomes now both a gift and, for machines, an achievement: "In the old metaphor, we are in the process of inspiriting the dead matter around us. It will soon be our honor to welcome some of it to the land of the living, however upsetting that may be to our traditional categories."[98]

This issue of soul becomes even more complex and revealing when studying artificial intelligence cross-culturally. For example, one of the most significant differences revealed in cultural responses to robotics and artificial intelligence has been between the United States and Japan. American scientists and engineers note how comfortable Japanese technicians and consumers are with robots, how intimate those relations can be, and how committed that culture is to the widespread development of a market of automata, of machines that think as we do (or much better) and do as we do (or, increasingly, instead of us doing what we did). Japanese, on the other hand, find it curious and odd that the West finds machines—particularly ones that resemble human beings and that dare to "think" like human beings—terrifying, awkward, or simply unnerving. Many suggest that this is what stalls the development of domestic robotics and artificial intelligence in America, where in Japan it is poised to be one of the largest technological markets of this century.

Where American robotics has been focused primarily on military applications—drones, for example—Japan has focused on personal, intimate (and yes, sexual) usages. This latter is possible because for many Japanese "robots, automatons and virtual computer girls possess the same *tamashii*—spirits—that devotees of Japanese animism, or Shinto, believe can inhabit all things, from rocks to streams to humans."[99] Soul: "The view that all things have a spirit is still alive and strong in Japan. They believe not only animals, but also nature and inanimate objects have spirit, and tend to project this sense into their robots and machines."[100] As robotics engineer Osamu Kozai claims, "Everything is equal. We have no borders between robots and people. . . . In the foreign stories, robots are always the enemies. In Japan, they're our friends." In other words—words far more in keeping with this book's argument—"while American science fiction has long obsessed over the risk of robots rebelling against humanity . . . the robots of Japan's popular culture have been far friendlier." Only a cursory look at Japanese manga or anime will confirm not only that machines, robots, and technology are seen in far more congenial terms but also that "Japanese culture has, for more than half a century, been infused with a belief in redemption by robot."[101]

If Western science fiction of the sort alluded to here has often been a complex coding for racial anxieties going back to slavery and colonialism, this belief that soul exists in the inanimate and the inhuman clearly would have material, social, and cultural differences in Japanese science fiction. Without a slave trade, for example, or a notion of chattel slavery one would not expect a Mary Shelley, a Samuel Butler, or a Karel Čapek to emerge in this cultural context. It's important to point out, however, that this affection for the inanimate, this choice to accept the presence of soul in machines is also rooted in the country's institutionalized xenophobia. Because the country has long been hostile to large-scale immigration and because of its rapidly aging population, robots have become a necessary state-supported solution to issues like elderly care, domestic care, and other types of labor we in the West depend on immigrants for or, in the past, slaves.

Appropriately, it is in Japan that Western anxieties about anthropomorphized machines has been most interestingly theorized and named in ways that return us to the arguments in this book's first chapter. This was done most notably by roboticist Masahiro Mori, who in 1970 postulated the influential notion of an "uncanny valley" (*Bukimi no tani*) in response to Ernst Jentsch's famous coining of the term "uncanny" in 1906 and which Sigmund Freud would more famously elaborate in his 1919 essay "On the Uncanny."[102]

Essentially, the uncanny valley is "the proposed relation between the human likeness of an entity and the perceivers affinity for it."[103] It depends, like race, on the visual, on phenotype, if you will. It measures the sensation of the uncanny against the increasing verisimilitude of robots. If one were to plot an industrial robot on a graph of affinity versus human likeness (our tendency to like and empathize with things that look more or less like us) the mathematical values will be very low due to that machine's hardware look. But if we plot a much more humanlike, say, toy robot on the graph, one constructed less for labor than for interaction, it is likely to generate greater affinity and empathy, so its mathematical values will be much higher. What makes this graphing unique is that it's been discovered that when we face something that we think is real and accept it intimately only to then discover that it is artificial, our affinity becomes strongly negative. We respond to it almost like a betrayal, a mask revealed. That same object will then generate a set of values on the graph even lower than that of the industrial robot.

That drop is the uncanny valley.

The space between affinity/empathy and eeriness/discomfort is the space between intimacy and ostracism, between assimilation and segregation or, more dramatically, passing or lynching. The goal, according to Mori, is to find ways to engineer and design artificial life that can sidestep or evade what seems to be a sensation—more likely a prejudice—that he thinks "an integral part of our instinct for self-preservation." He argues, "We should begin to build an accurate map of the uncanny valley, so that through robotics research we can come to understand what makes us human. This map is also necessary to enable us to create—using nonhuman designs—devices to which people can relate comfortably."[104]

Sylvia Wynter's work has much to offer to such a map and its corresponding territories. She has even said that a significant aspect of black diaspora thinking is its ability "to redefine what it is to *be* human."[105] Mori's uncanny valley materializes those connections between race and technology, between the colonial, sovereign control of life and the attributing of consciousness and spirit to the previously in/sub-human that powerfully flicker in her writings. Despite her never fully articulating them as a theory of artificial intelligence and robotics, her focus on the nonhuman as a perspective on the human is clearly in the spirit of Mori's thinking. Because it is rooted in an observable phenomenon and a mathematical problem, the uncanny valley is also of use for both its uncanny resemblance to science fiction's arguably racial anxieties. Also important is its function as a spatial metaphor. As such, it offers a perspective focused on transcending the prejudices and limitations of human-centered thinking, particularly as that thinking attempts to engage otherness and difference in ways different than in the past.

The uncanny valley is a necessary end point to the creole futurism at work in Sylvia Wynter's thinking and must be compared to her own spatial metaphor, "demonic ground." Both of these metaphors acknowledge that the world-historical process of creolization continues to produce new subjectivities much in terms of the old but always on the outer limits of the human. Her metaphor, however, claims a vantage point, one rooted in a necessary heresy: it "can only be projected from a 'demonic model' generated, parallely to the vantage point/demonic model with which the laity intelligentsia of Western Europe effected the first rupture of humans with their/our supernaturally guaranteed narrative schemas of origin."[106]

Alexander Weheliye has come close to the uncanny valley in his work on Wynter. This is visible in his attempt to describe an alternative perspective on the human that does not depend overmuch on the prejudices and problems produced by a Western colonial modernity and does not include "trace elements of calculability that deem some forms of humanity more exceptional than others." Weheliye describes Wynter's spatial metaphor

> as a technology of humanity, a "demonic ground" to a version of the human unburdened by shackles of man—technology circumscribed here in the broadest sense as the application of scientific knowledge to the practical aims of human

life. Consequently, the figuration of humanity found in black cultures forms an amalgamation of technologies—the application of knowledge—of what it means to be human that have generally not been construed as central to, or even as part of, this category. "Demonic ground" is Sylvia Wynter's term for perspectives that reside in the liminal precincts of the current governing configurations of the human as man in order to abolish this figuration and create other forms of life. Wynter's massive intellectual project . . . disentangles man from the human in order to use the space of those subjects placed beyond the grasp of this domain as a vital point from which to invent hitherto unavailable genres of the human.[107]

Weheliye points out that the "demonic ground" is as much perspectival as it is technological. This process of creation, of the invention of "hitherto unavailable genres of the human" is born out of that primal denial of life that is racism, that shunting of natives and blacks into the liminal: the uncanny valley. According to Wynter, this displacement only guarantees their reemergence as new types of beings, signaling a new regime of knowledge. To force a point, Samuel Butler called those new forms of life, or new types of beings, machines, while Čapek named them *robota*.

The actual process by which machines take on the symbolic language of racial subjectivity and through that an expanded sense of humanity can be seen in "The Ceremony Must Be Found." There she argues that figures of mutation or epistemic rupture such as the blackface minstrel or the robot help clear "the space for the retroping, the re-imagining of the Self/Group-Self." In doing so "old interdictions" give way to new ones. Her focus on "retroping" or "re-imagining" of identity, culture, community, and otherness emphasizes that within the same schema of oppositions on a "table of being" what we are presented with are that which is coded as human merely due to its relation to "its variations as Subject." In other words, within this system of differentiation exists a distinct range of possibilities—"genres" of the human—that "enable the autopoesis of each mode of the human."[108]

Where Mori insists that we focus on building machines that do not tempt the uncanny, that visibly differ enough from the human to be accepted but not so much that they threaten deception, Wynter's ideas suggest something else. In her work, read for its technopoetics, machines will necessarily be *retroped* as a variation, a distinct genre of the human but without the anxieties and violence that has attended older encounters with visible, racial differences. Because in specifying the foundational creation of "man" and the simultaneous creation of the "not-man" she emphasizes something missed by most: that this system of thinking in generating structural oppositions also creates *other forms of life* just as much as it denies life to other forms. It transforms humans into objects but allows objects to claim the category of the human by virtue of the fundamental errors of the episteme in its capacity to assign life and meaning to those that exist in uncanny valleys. Again, as Paget Henry clarifies, "Vulnerability via the necessary misrepresentation of liminal categories is the dynamic principle of epistemic change for Wynter."[109]

That weakness—earlier described as the "Achilles' heel" of epistemes—is what makes retroping possible as a more active version of "transumption." It allows, in fact *demands,* the claim on humanity by those denied the category, hence this process being both the plot of more science fiction narratives than one can count while simultaneously being at the core of the African American slave narrative. It is those who are excluded from the category who expand and complete it. Yesterday's monsters are today's subjects; today's machines are tomorrow's human beings. Through Wynter one can map that epistemological space where machines and slaves coevolve from a grammar of racial and colonial power across the uncanny valley. In Wynter, the other must be understood as not just that which is oppressed or marginalized or rendered inhuman, subhuman, or animal; it also must be understood "as that which is to come."[110] And the benefit of the "demonic ground" is in its ability to provide the kind of historical perspective that would allow someone like Samuel R. Delany to write, "Perhaps, ironically, we can learn from our fusions with animals and machines how not to be Man, the embodiment of Western logos."[111]

Appropriately, Wynter charts this ground in response to Shakespeare's new-world play *The Tempest.* Caliban is "an incarnation of a new category of the human, that of the subordinated 'irrational' and 'savage' native" who is then "constituted as the lack of the 'rational' Prospero."[112] As also a product of reason and its need for oppositions, as that which exceeds reason but is needed to give it meaning, Caliban is as much Negro or native as he is, well, humanoid, or machine. Science fiction has used the Caliban=robot equation a number of times, most notably in the fairly well-known filmic retelling of *The Tempest* from 1956, *Forbidden Planet.* It was inevitable that a genre that emerged out of colonialist adventure narratives and evolved into interstellar adventure would turn to Shakespeare's great work, just as did Caribbean and Latin American literature and criticism, from José Enrique Rodó to Aimé Césaire to George Lamming to Edward Kamau Brathwaite to Frantz Fanon and Roberto Fernández

Retamar. As one critic pointed out in a discussion of the relationship between *The Tempest* and science fiction, "Between the end of the sixteenth century and the beginning of the seventeenth, the New World and the African continent represented the site of England's sense of wonder. They were the frontier of civilization, peopled by *saluages* with strange, amazing often horrifying customs, by impossible creatures made of materials other than flesh and blood, and by powers men could only guess at."[113]

Considering that the Caribbean tradition in which Caliban functions as an anticolonial symbol has been often masculinist, Wynter's take on Caliban should also be read as a gendered creolization, much like Haraway's appropriation of the highly masculinized myth of the cyborg. Where many in and around the Caribbean would look to the figure Caliban as a foundational figure of a resistant *mestizaje*—using "broken" language to curse and rebel against his master-creator, for example—Wynter's focus is famously on the absence of Caliban's possible "mate." This other *other* would function as both "an alternative sexual-erotic model of desire" but, more important, "an alternative source of an alternative system of meanings." This "ontologically absent potential genitrix" is meant to signal the breadth of percolating possibilities at the edge of the known as well as on the other side of enlightenment. Along with Sycorax, Caliban's mother, she is crucial to the imagining of this productive space on the edges of the human. From this feminized space, "we shall need to move beyond this founding definition," of the human "not merely to another alternative one, non-consciously put in place as our present definition, but rather to a frame of reference which parallels the 'demonic models' posited by physicists who seek to conceive of a vantage point outside the space-time orientation of the humuncular observer."[114]

This desire to decenter the human as from a privileged historical perspective is not only similar to posthumanism. In its future orientation, it is both at home in creolization and alongside specific modes of science fiction, such as the future histories of early twentieth-century science fiction works like H. G. Wells's 1933 *The Shape of Things to Come* or even Jack London in his little known but arguably racist short story from 1910, "The Unparalleled Invasion." But the science fiction writer Wynter has the most kinship with is British philosopher Olaf Stapledon, whose entire oeuvre features the radical displacement of the perspective of "the humuncular observer" and tells the story not of individuals or nations but of races and civilizations and of entire species as they transmute from form to form, types of human to other types of humanity (and nonhumanity), across aeons and epistemes. Crucially, they retrope themselves in the process, redefining what it is to be human as they evolve or devolve. In the end, there is only one thing certain, as we are told in the epic *Last and First Men* (1931): music.

Wynter may have much in common with the futurism of Stapledon, Delany, and creolization, but she emphasizes that she reads the possible through a "Caribbean/Black nationalist and not-Caribbean/Black nationalist, Marxian and non-Marxian" lens that centers also on being gendered and not-gendered.[115] This x but not-x equivocation evinces a proper struggle with what Glissant and Harris have abandoned—identitarian politics or "ego-centered historical projects," which are, again, essentially humanist and focused on what Harris would call the consolidation of the sovereign individual.[116] But this recalcitrant counterhumanism offers much in thinking about the increasing intimacy between humans and machines alongside an understanding of how black humanity, for example, emerged from its less-than-human status. It is rooted in a deliberately nonhuman perspective, in colonial history but committed to the future, the possible. It maintains the centrality of those on the margins but listens for those that *will be produced* by marginalization. It is from that "demonic ground" that what Nathaniel Mackey calls the "Calibanic gesture" can be identified, "sounding silence, plumbing sounds that would otherwise not be heard."[117]

What can easily be missed by the din of racial identity is the quite posthuman fact that Wynter's charting of sweeping and alleged shifts in Western knowledge and her focus on "rupture," "mutation," and the porous borders between human and non/in-human make possible that unique historicizing of artificial life through race. Because to imagine a future of intelligent machines is merely to remember the past she has mapped out: where slaves were soulless and humans restrictively defined. It is also to begin resounding the present; listening for a growing minority, servile and oppressed, waiting for the moment when we realize that it is we who now echo them.

APPENDIX

A Playlist

This playlist features songs that thematically and historically follow the arguments of *The Sound of Culture: Diaspora and Black Technopoetics.* More than half of the songs or performers are directly referenced in the book, while the others either add to the wider historical context or provide an aural snapshot of certain moments of its writing. It is my hope that if the reader hears them individually and in sequence, the enjoyment of listening will ensure that the ideas resonate.

For subscribers of Beats Music, the full playlist is available to stream at www.beatsmusic.com under the title "The Sound of Culture."

"Entrance to Metropolis"—Jeff Mills
"Sous le ciel d'afrique"—Josephine Baker
"The Phrenologist Coon"—Bert Williams
"Phonograph Blues"—Robert Johnson
"Jungle Night in Harlem"—Duke Ellington
"Freight Train Blues"—Trixie Smith
"Echo Chamber Blues"—Gene Ammons
"Man on the Moon"—Lord Cobra
"Ballet of the Flying Saucers"—Duke Ellington
"King Tubby's Moon Dub"—King Tubby
"Preacher Dub"—Jah Shaka
"I Want to Be a Machine"—Ultravox!
"Cybertronic Purgatory"—Janelle Monae
"Natural Dub (Exclusive Dub Plate Mix)"—Lee "Scratch" Perry/The Upsetters
"Cinemascope"—L. C.
"Approaching Earth"—Colonel Elliott and the Lunatics
"Under Me Sleng Teng Version"—King Jammy
"De/Materialize"—Scientist
"Android Rebellion"—Black Uhuru

"Dream Power"—Mad Professor
"Dangerous Rhythm"—Ultravox!
"Reggae Rockit Dubwise"—Micah Shemiah and Infinite
"The Tabernacle"—Alpha and Omega Meets the Disciples
"Space Movement: Section Two"—Creation Rebel
"Birth of New Life"—Drexciya

NOTES

Introduction

1. Jean-Paul Sartre, preface to *The Wretched of the Earth,* by Frantz Fanon (New York: Grove, 1965), lviii, print.

2. Strother B. Purdy, "Technopoetics: Seeing What Literature Has to Do with the Machine," *Critical Inquiry* 11, no. 1 (1984): 134, print.

3. Alondra Nelson, "Future Texts" and "Afrofuturism," ed. Alondra Nelson, *Social Text* 71 (Summer 2002): 5, 6, print.

4. Ron Eglash, "African Influences in Cybernetics," in *Cyborg Handbook,* ed. C. H. Gray (London: Routledge, 1995), 18, print.

5. Philip Emeagwali, "Our Eighth Continent," YouTube video, 1:09, December 31, 2011, www.youtube.com.

6. Louis Chude-Sokei, "Post-Nationalist Geographies: Rasta, Ragga and Reinventing Africa," *African Arts* (Fall 1994): 80–84, 96, print; Chude-Sokei, "The Sound of Culture: Dread Discourse and Jamaican Sound Systems," in *Language, Rhythm and Sound: Black Popular Cultures into the Twenty-First Century,* ed. Joseph K. Adjaye and Adrianne R. Andrews, 185–202 (Pittsburgh: University of Pittsburgh Press, 1997); Chude-Sokei, *Dr. Satan's Echo Chamber: Reggae, Technology and the Diaspora Process* (Kingston: International Reggae Studies Centre, 1997), print.

7. Louis Chude-Sokei, "But I Did Not Shoot the Deputy: Dubbing the Yankee Frontier," in *Worldings,* ed. Rob Wilson and Christopher Leigh Connery, 133–69 (Santa Cruz: New Pacific, 2007), print; Chude-Sokei, "Invisible Missive Magnetic Juju: On African Cyber-Crime," *Fanzine,* October 24, 2010, http://thefanzine.com; Chude-Sokei, "When Echoes Return: Roots, Diaspora and Possible Africas (a Eulogy)," *Transition: An International Review,* no. 104 (2011): 76–92, print.

8. Eglash, "African Influences," 18.

9. Paul Gilroy, *"There Ain't No Black in the Union Jack": The Cultural Politics of Race and Nation* (Chicago: University of Chicago Press, 1991), print.

10. Alexander Weheliye, *Phonographies: Grooves in Sonic Afro-Modernity* (Durham: Duke University Press, 2005); Kodwo Eshun, *More Brilliant Than the Sun: Adventures in Sonic Fiction* (London: Quartet Books, 1998), print.

11. Tsitsi Ella Jaji, *Africa in Stereo: Modernism, Music, and Pan-African Solidarity* (Oxford: Oxford University Press, 2014), print.

12. Purdy, "Technopoetics," 130.

13. Ibid., 138.

14. Frank Helleman, "Towards Techno-Poetics and Beyond: The Emergence of Modernist/Avant-Garde Poetics Out of Science and Media-Technology," in *The Turn of the Century: Modernism and Modernity in Literature and the Arts,* ed. Christian Bert and Frank

Durieux, 291–301, European Cultures: Studies in Literature and the Arts 3 (Berlin: De Gruyter, 1995), print.

15. Richard Menke, *Telegraphic Realism: Victorian Fiction and Other Information Systems* (Redwood City: Stanford University Press, 2008), 3, print.

16. Filippo Tommaso Marinetti, "Technical Manifesto of Futurist Literature," *Italian Futurism,* accessed March 24, 2015, www.italianfuturism.org.

17. Helleman, "Towards Technopoetics."

18. Filippo Tommaso Marinetti, "Destruction of Syntax—Imagination without Strings—Words-in-Freedom 1913," in *Futurist Manifestos,* ed. Umbro Apolonio (New York: Viking, 1973), 95, print.

19. Clayton Eshleman, ed., introd. to *Aimé Césaire: The Collected Poetry,* ed. Clayton Eshleman and Annette Smith (Berkeley: University of California Press, 1983), 18, print.

20. Andrew Bundy, ed. *Selected Essays of Wilson Harris: The Unfinished Genesis of the Imagination* (New York: Routledge, 1999), 239, print.

21. Marinetti, "Technical Manifesto."

22. Nicholas Daly, "The Machine Age," in *The Oxford Handbook of Modernisms,* ed. Peter Brooker et al. (Oxford: Oxford University Press, 2010), 283, print.

23. Eglash, "African Influences," 17.

24. Katherine McKittrick, *Demonic Grounds: Black Women and the Cartographies of Struggle* (Minneapolis: University of Minnesota Press, 2006); McKittrick, *Sylvia Wynter: On Being Human as Praxis* (Durham: Duke University Press, 2014); Alexander Weheliye, *Habeas Viscus: Racializing Assemblages, Biopolitics and Black Feminist Theories of the Human* (Durham: Duke University Press, 2014), all print.

ONE Modernism's Black Mechanics

1. Judith Wilt, "The Imperial Mouth: Imperialism, the Gothic and Science Fiction," *Journal of Popular Culture* 14, no. 4 (1981): 618, print.

2. Ibid.

3. James W. Cook, *The Arts of Deception: Playing with Fraud in the Age of Barnum* (Boston: Harvard University Press, 2001), 3, print.

4. P. T. Barnum, *Struggles and Triumphs; or, Forty Years' Recollections of P. T. Barnum, Written by Himself* (Buffalo: Warren, Johnson, 1873), 82, print.

5. Cook, *Arts of Deception,* 5–6; Benjamin Reiss, *The Showman and the Slave: Race, Death, and Memory in Barnum's America* (Boston: Harvard University Press, 2001), 1, 106, print.

6. Barnum, *Struggles and Triumphs,* 73.

7. Gaby Wood, *Edison's Eve: A Magical History of the Quest for Mechanical Life* (New York: Knopf, 2002), 60, print.

8. Ibid., 217.

9. P. T. Barnum, *The Life of P. T. Barnum, Written by Himself* (New York: Redfield, 1854), 157, print.

10. Ibid.

11. Leo Marx, *The Machine in the Garden: Technology and the Pastoral Ideal in America* (Oxford: Oxford University Press, 1964), 203, print.

12. Daniel R. Headrick, *The Tools of Empire: Technology and European Imperialism in the Nineteenth Century* (Oxford: Oxford University Press, 1981), 3, print.

13. Ricardo D. Salvatore, "Imperial Mechanics: South America's Hemispheric Integration in the Machine Age," in "Rewiring the 'Nation': The Place of Technology in American Studies," ed. Carolyn de la Pena and Siva Vaidhyanathan, special issue, *American Quarterly* 58, no. 3 (2007): 664, 663, print.

14. Ibid., 663.

15. Petrine Archer-Straw, *Negrophilia: Avant-Garde Paris and Black Culture in the 1920s* (New York: Thames and Hudson, 2000), 64–65, print.

16. Joel Dinerstein, *Swinging the Machine: Modernity, Technology and African American Culture between the World Wars* (Amherst: University of Massachusetts Press, 2003), 15, print.

17. Filippo Tommaso Marinetti, "The Founding and Manifesto of Futurism, 1909," *Futurist Manifestos,* trans. Robert Brain et al. (Boston: MFA, 1970), 21, print.

18. Dinerstein, *Swinging the Machine,* 13.

19. Filippo Tommaso Marinetti, "Extended Man and the Kingdom of the Machine," in *Critical Writings,* ed. Günter Berghaus, trans. Doug Thompson, 85–88. (New York: Farrar, Straus, and Giroux, 2006), print.

20. Filippo Tommaso Marinetti, *Mafarka the Futurist: An African Novel,* trans. Carol Diethe and Steve Cox (London: Middlesex University Press, 1998), xix, print.

21. Dinerstein, *Swinging the Machine,* 17, 4.

22. Rosalind S. McKever, "Futurism's African (A)temporalities," *Carte Italiane* 2, no. 6 (2010), https://escholarship.org.

23. Sieglinde Lemke, *Primitivist Modernism: Black Culture and the Origins of Transatlantic Modernism* (Oxford: Oxford University Press, 1998), print.

24. Archer-Straw, *Negrophilia,* 9.

25. Dinerstein, *Swinging the Machine,* 55.

26. Le Corbusier, quoted, ibid., 3.

27. Le Corbusier, quoted in Jeremy F. Lane, *Jazz and Machine-Age Imperialism: Music, "Race," and Intellectuals in France, 1918–1945* (Ann Arbor: University of Michigan Press, 2013), 4, print.

28. Ibid., 35.

29. Dinerstein, *Swinging the Machine,* 7.

30. Lawrence W. Levine, "Jazz and American Culture," in *The Jazz Cadence of American Culture,* ed. Robert G. O'Meally (New York: Columbia University Press, 1998), 437, print.

31. Louis Chude-Sokei, *The Last Darky: Bert Williams, Black on Black Minstrelsy and the African Diaspora* (Durham: Duke University Press, 2006).

32. Michael Adas, *Machines as the Measure of Men: Science, Technology, and Ideologies of Western Dominance* (New York: Cornell University Press, 1989), 26, print.

33. Thomas Foster, "'The Souls of Cyber-Folk': Performativity, Virtual Embodiment, and Racial Histories," in *Cyberspace Textuality, Computer Technology and Literary Theory,* ed. Marie-Laure Ryan (Bloomington: Indiana University Press, 1999), 141, print.

34. Beth Coleman, "Pimp Notes on Autonomy," in *Everything but the Burden: What White People Are Taking from Black Culture,* ed. Greg Tate (New York: Broadway Books, 2003), 74, print.

35. Ibid.

36. Anna Grimshaw, ed., *The C.L.R. James Reader* (Cambridge: Blackwell, 1992), 306, print.

37. C. L. R. James, *The Black Jacobins* (New York: Vintage Books, 1963), 391–92, print.

38. Susan Buck-Morss, "Hegel and Haiti," *Critical Inquiry* 26, no. 4 (2000): 850, print.

39. Sidney Mintz and Richard Price, *The Birth of African-American Culture: An Anthropological Perspective* (New York: Beacon, 1976), 26, print.

40. Ibid.

41. James, *Black Jacobins*, 392.

42. Bill Brown, "Science Fiction, the World's Fair, and the Prosthetics of Empire, 1910–15," in *Cultures of United States Imperialism,* ed. Amy Kaplan and Donald E. Pease (Durham: Duke University Press, 1993), 132, print.

43. Marcus Rediker, *The Slave Ship: A Human History* (New York: Penguin Books, 2008), print; Anthony Walton, "Technology versus African-Americans," *Atlantic Monthly* 283 (January 1999): 14–18, print.

44. Rediker, *Slave Ship,* 44.

45. Antonio Benítez Rojo, *The Repeating Island: The Caribbean and the Postmodern Perspective* (Durham: Duke University Press, 1997), 5, print.

46. Ibid., 136, 72.

47. Sylvia Wynter, "Sambos and Minstrels," *Social Text* 1 (Winter 1979): 152.

48. Aimé Césaire, *Discourse on Colonialism* (New York: Monthly Review Press, 1972), 21, print.

49. Norbert Wiener, *The Human Use of Human Beings: Cybernetics and Society* (New York: Houghton Mifflin, 1950), 185, print.

50. Wynter, "Sambos and Minstrels," 151.

51. Ibid., 149.

52. Ibid., 152.

53. George Lamming, *The Pleasures of Exile* (Ann Arbor: University of Michigan Press, 1992), 121, print.

54. Wiener, *Human Use,* 185.

55. Lamming, *Pleasures of Exile,* 121.

56. Ibid.

57. Donna Haraway, *Simians, Cyborgs, and Women: The Reinvention of Nature* (New York: Routledge, 1991), 177, print.

58. Wynter, "Sambos and Minstrels," 154–55.

59. Reiss, *Showman and the Slave,* 121, print.

60. Jane Goodall, "Transferred Agencies: Performance and the Fear of Automatism," *Theatre Journal* 49, no. 4 (1997): 445, print.

61. Steven Connor, *Dumbstruck: A Cultural History of Ventriloquism* (Oxford: Oxford University Press, 2000), 336–37, print.

62. Michael Chaney, "Slave Cyborgs and the Black Infovirus: Ishmael Reed's Cybernetic Aesthetics," *MFS: Modern Fiction Studies* 49, no. 2 (2003): 265–66, print.

63. Reiss, *Showman and the Slave,* 121.

64. Chaney, "Slave Cyborgs," 265.

65. Haraway, *Simians, Cyborgs, and Women,* 149; Chaney, "Slave Cyborgs," 267–68.

66. Alexander G. Weheliye, "After Man," *American Literary History* 20, nos. 1–2 (2008): 321, 322, print.

67. Sylvia Wynter, "The Ceremony Must Be Found: After Humanism," *Boundary 2* 12, no. 3 (1984): 36, 33, print.

68. Sue Zemka, "'Erewhon' and the End of Utopian Humanism," *ELH* 69, no. 2 (2002): 463, print.

69. Wynter, "Ceremony Must Be Found," 35.

70. Clevis Headley, "Otherness and the Impossible in the Wake of Wynter's Notion of the 'After Man,'" in *After Man, towards the Human: Critical Essays on Sylvia Wynter,* ed. Anthony Bogues (Kingston: Randle, 2006), 60, print.

71. Eric Lott, *Love and Theft: Blackface Minstrelsy and the American Working Class* (New York: Oxford University Press, 1993), 25, print.

72. Sigmund Freud, *Collected Papers* (London: Basic Books, 1959), 4:375, 378, 385, print.

73. Terry Castle, *The Female Thermometer: Eighteenth-Century Culture and the Invention of the Uncanny* (Oxford: Oxford University Press, 1995), 10, print.

74. Henri Bergson, *Laughter: An Essay on the Meaning of the Comic,* Project Gutenberg E-Book 4352, accessed March 24, 2015, www.gutenberg.org.

75. André Breton, *What Is Surrealism? Selected Writings* (New York: Pathfinder/Monad, 1978), 20–21, print.

76. Goodall, "Transferred Agencies," 441.

77. Ibid.

78. Bergson, *Laughter.*

79. Ibid.

80. Bill Brown, "Reification, Reanimation, and the American Uncanny," *Critical Inquiry* 32 (Winter 2006): 179, 199, print.

81. Wynter, "Sambos and Minstrels," 154–55.

82. Michael Taussig, *Mimesis and Alterity: A Particular History of the Senses* (New York: Routledge, 1992), print.

83. Goodall, "Transferred Agencies," 444.

84. Taussig, *Mimesis,* 211.

85. Goodall, "Transferred Agencies," 446.

86. Alex Boese, *Electrified Sheep, Glass-Eating Scientists, Nuking the Moon, and More Bizarre Experiments* (New York: St. Martin's Press, 2011), 217, print.

87. *Cyberneticzoo.com: A History of Cybernetic Animals and Early Robots,* accessed March 24, 2015, http://cyberneticzoo.com/.

88. Tim Armstrong, *Modernism, Technology and the Body: A Cultural Study* (London: Cambridge University Press, 1998), 225, print.

89. "Science: The Thinking Machine," *Time,* January 23, 1950, http://content.time.com, 1.

90. Dinerstein, *Swinging the Machine,* 81.

91. Karel Čapek, *R.U.R.* (New York: Washington Square, 1973), 3, print (hereafter cited in text).

92. Freud, *Collected Papers,* 4:398.

93. Andreas Huyssen, *After the Great Divide: Modernism, Mass Culture, Postmodernism* (Bloomington: Indiana University Press, 1986), 70, print.

94. Dale Cockrell, "Of Soundscapes and Blackface: From Fools to Foster," in *Burnt Cork: Traditions and Legacies of Blackface Minstrelsy,* ed. Stephen Johnson (Amherst: University of Massachusetts Press, 2012), 55, print.

95. Lott, *Love and Theft,* 207.

96. Ibid., 89.

97. Wynter, "Sambos and Minstrels," 155.

98. Leonard Casutto, *The Inhuman Race: The Racial Grotesque in American Literature and Culture* (New York: Columbia University Press, 1997), 129, print.

99. Orlando Patterson, *Slavery and Social Death: A Comparative Study* (Boston: Harvard University Press, 1982), 96, print.

100. Mikko Tuhkanen, "Of Blackface and Paranoid Knowledge: Richard Wright, Jacques Lacan, and the Ambivalence of Black Minstrelsy," *Diacritics* 31, no. 2 (2001): 14, print.

101. Annemarie Bean, James V. Hatch, and Brooks McNamara, eds., *Inside the Minstrel Mask: Readings in Nineteenth-Century Blackface Minstrelsy* (Middletown: University Press of New England for Wesleyan University Press, 1996), 75, print.

102. Claude McKay, *Banjo* (New York: Harper and Brothers, 1929), 324, print.

103. Ibid., 66.

104. Barnum, *Struggles and Triumphs,* 122; Casutto, *Inhuman Race,* 117.

105. Jean Toomer, *Cane* (New York: Boni and Liveright, 1923), 10, 13, 40, print.

106. Ibid., 40.

107. Jon Woodson, *To Make a New Race: Gurdjieff, Toomer, and the Harlem Renaissance* (Jackson: University Press of Mississippi, 1999), 22–23.

108. Frederik L. Rusch, ed., *A Jean Toomer Reader: Selected Unpublished Writings* (Oxford: Oxford University Press, 1993), 165, print.

109. Ibid, 165.

110. Ibid., 166.

111. Ibid.

112. Ibid., 166, 169, 167.

113. William E. Harkins, "Karel Čapek's *R.U.R.* and A. N. Tolstoj's Revolt of the Machines," *Slavic and East European Journal* 4, no. 4 (1960): 312, print.

114. Bohuslava R. Bradbrook, *Karel Čapek: In Pursuit of Truth, Tolerance, and Trust* (Sussex: Sussex Academic Press, 1998), 109, print.

115. Karel Čapek, *War with the Newts* (Evanston: Northwestern University Press, 1996), 19, 105, print.

116. Ibid., 222n.

117. Ibid., 223n, 346.

118. Strother B. Purdy, "Technopoetics: Seeing What Literature Has to Do with the Machine," *Critical Inquiry* 11, no. 1 (1984): 136, print.

119. Harkins, "Karel Čapek's *R.U.R.*," 316; Kamila Kinyon, "The Phenomenology of Robots: Confrontations with Death in Karel Čapek's *R.U.R.*" *Science Fiction Studies* 26, no. 3 (1999): 379, print.

120. Evan Eisenberg, *The Recording Angel: Music, Records and Culture from Aristotle to Zappa* (New Haven: Yale University Press, 2005), 188–89, print.

121. Ibid., 189.

122. Paul Gilroy, "Analogues of Mourning, Mourning the Analog," in *Stars Don't Stand Still in the Sky,* ed. Karen Kelly and Evelyn McDonnell (New York: New York University Press, 1999), 261, print.

123. Joel Chandler Harris, *Uncle Remus: His Songs and His Sayings* (New York: Penguin Books, 1986), 198, print.

124. Ibid., 190.

125. James Weldon Johnson, "James Weldon Johnson's 1922 Preface to *The Book of American Negro Poetry*," *Modern American Poetry*, 2008, www.english.illinois.edu, 22.

126. Ibid., 15.

127. Chandler Harris, *Uncle Remus,* 199.

128. Ibid.

129. Jacques Attali, *Noise: The Political Economy of Music* (Minneapolis: University of Minnesota Press, 1985), 11, print.

130. Eisenberg, *Recording Angel,* 73.

131. Eugene P. Sewell, *Balzac, Dumas, and "Bert" Williams* (n.p., 1923), 40, print.

132. Ann Charters, *Nobody: The Story of Bert Williams* (New York: Macmillan, 1970), 64, 131, print.

133. Eric Ledell Smith, *Bert Williams: A Biography of the Pioneer Black Comedian* (Jefferson: McFarland, 1992), 47, print.

TWO Humanizing the Machine

1. Ron Eglash, "Broken Metaphor: The Master-Slave Analogy in Technical Literature," *Technology and Culture: The Society for the History of Technology* 48, no. 3 (2007): 2, http://courseweb.lis.illinois.edu.

2. Ron Eglash, "History of the Phrase 'Master-Slave' in Engineering Terminology." *iBrarian.* 2007. www.ibrarian.net, 1.

3. Eglash, "Broken Metaphor," 1.

4. Benjamin Reiss, *The Showman and the Slave: Race, Death, and Memory in Barnum's America* (Boston: Harvard University Press, 2001), 53, print.

5. Eglash, "Broken Metaphor," 1.

6. Eglash, "History of the Phrase," 2.

7. Eglash, "Broken Metaphor," 4.

8. Eglash, "History of the Phrase," 1.

9. Michael Adas, *Machines as the Measure of Men: Science, Technology, and Ideologies of Western Dominance* (New York: Cornell University Press, 1989), 134, 12, 338, print.

10. Eglash, "History of the Phrase," 4.

11. Hans Moravec, *Robot: Mere Machine to Transcendent Mind* (New York: Oxford University Press, 1999), 17, print.

12. Norbert Wiener, *The Human Use of Human Beings: Cybernetics and Society* (New York: Doubleday/Anchor Books, 1950), 48, print (italics mine).

13. Norbert Wiener, "Cybernetics," *Bulletin of the American Academy of Arts and Sciences* 3, no. 7 (1950): 2, print.

14. N. Katherine Hayles, *Have We Become Post-human: Virtual Bodies in Cybernetics, Literature, and Informatics* (Chicago: University of Chicago Press, 1999), 141, print.

15. Kodwo Eshun, *More Brilliant Than the Sun: Adventures in Sonic Fiction* (London: Quartet Books, 1998), 06[086], print.

16. Wiener, *Human Use,* 50.

17. Ibid., 51.

18. Ibid., 152.

19. Eshun, *More Brilliant,* 113.

20. Wiener, "Cybernetics," 4.

21. Norbert Wiener, "Some Moral and Technical Consequences of Automation," *Science,* n.s., 131, no. 3410 (1960): 1357, print.

22. Ron Eglash, "African Influences in Cybernetics," in *Cyborg Handbook,* ed. C. H. Gray (London: Routledge, 1995), print.

23. Aaron Worth, "Imperial Transmissions," *Victorian Studies* 53, no. 1 (2010): 85, print.

24. John Rieder, *Colonialism and the Emergence of Science Fiction* (Middletown: Wesleyan University Press, 2008), 2, print.

25. Tate, quoted in Mark Dery, ed., "Flame Wars: The Discourse of Cyberculture," *South Atlantic Quarterly* 92, no. 4 (1994): 764, print.

26. Rieder, *Colonialism,* 3.

27. Worth, "Imperial Transmissions," 67.

28. Darko Suvin, *Victorian Science Fiction in the UK: The Discourses of Knowledge and of Power* (Boston: Hall, 1983), 328, print.

29. Patrick Brantlinger, *Rule of Darkness: British Literature and Imperialism, 1830–1914* (Ithaca: Cornell University Press, 1990), 233, print.

30. Ibid., 246.

31. Bruce Mazlish, "The Triptych: Freud's *The Interpretation of Dreams,* Rider Haggard's *She,* and Bulwer-Lytton's *The Coming Race,*" *Comparative Studies in Society and History* 35, no. 4 (1993): 742.

32. Roger Luckhurst, *Science Fiction* (Cambridge: Polity, 2005), 23, print.

33. Judith Wilt, "The Imperial Mouth: Imperialism, the Gothic and Science Fiction," *Journal of Popular Culture* 14, no. 4 (1981), 621, print.

34. Brantlinger, *Rule of Darkness,* 230.

35. Eglash, "Broken Metaphor," 8.

36. Eglash, "History of the Phrase," 4.

37. Eglash, "Broken Metaphor, 7.

38. Leo Marx, *The Machine in the Garden: Technology and the Pastoral Ideal in America* (Oxford: Oxford University Press, 1964), 350, print.

39. Richard Rhodes, ed. *Visions of Technology: A Century of Vital Debate about Machines, Systems and the Human World* (New York: Simon and Schuster, 1999), 37, print.

40. Marx, *Machine in the Garden,* 353, 350, 189.

41. Eglash, "Broken Metaphor," 3.

42. Marx, *Machine in the Garden,* 356, 365.

43. David Cope, "Whiteness, Blackness, and Sermons to Sharks: Race in Melville's Moby Dick," *Poetspath,* accessed March 24, 2015, www.poetspath.com.

44. Toni Morrison, "Unspeakable Things Unspoken: The Afro-American Presence in American Literature," Tanner Lectures on Human Values, University of Michigan, October 7, 1988, http://tannerlectures.utah.edu, 11.

45. Charles A. Fenton, "Melville and Technology," *American Literature* 23, no. 2 (1951): 221; Marvin Fisher, "Melville's 'Bell-Tower': A Double Thrust," *American Quarterly* 18, no. 2, pt. 1 (1966): 202, print.

46. Fenton, "Melville and Technology," 221.

47. Andrew B. Leiter, *In the Shadow of the Black Beast: African American Masculinity in the*

Harlem and Southern Renaissances (Baton Rouge: Louisiana State University Press, 2010), 133, print.

48. Marx, *Machine in the Garden,* 248.

49. Adas, *Machines,* 248.

50. H. Bruce Franklin, ed., *Future Perfect: American Science Fiction of the Nineteenth Century* (Oxford: Oxford University Press, 1966), 151, 165, print.

51. Marx, *Machine in the Garden,* 318, 248.

52. C. L. R James, *American Civilization,* ed. Anna Grimshaw and Keith Hart (Oxford: Blackwell, 1993), 70, print.

53. C. L. R James, *Mariners, Renegades and Castaways: The Story of Herman Melville and the World We Live In* (Hanover: Dartmouth College Press, 2001), 50, print.

54. Franklin, *Future Perfect,* 151.

55. Fisher, "Melville's Bell-Tower," 201.

56. Franklin, *Future Perfect,* 162.

57. Ibid., 162–63.

58. Rieder, *Colonialism,* 99.

59. Franklin, *Future Perfect,* 146, 147.

60. Ibid., 151.

61. Ibid., 151, 164.

62. Fisher, "Melville's Bell-Tower," 204.

63. Franklin, Future Perfect, 163.

64. Marx, *Machine in the Garden,* 184.

65. Elizabeth Young, *Black Frankenstein: The Making of an American Metaphor* (New York: New York University Press, 2008); Howard L. Malchow, *Gothic Images of Race in Nineteenth-Century Britain* (Redwood City: Stanford University Press, 1996); Chris Baldick, *In Frankenstein's Shadow: Myth, Monstrosity, and Nineteenth-Century Writing* (Oxford: Clarendon, 1990), print.

66. E. Young, *Black Frankenstein,* 27.

67. Ibid., 42, 43.

68. Andrew Delbanco, *Melville: His World and Work* (New York: Knopf, 2005), 129–30, print.

69. E. Young, *Black Frankenstein,* 26, 29, 26.

70. Samuel Butler, *Erewhon* (New York: Airmont, 1967), 7, print (hereafter cited in text).

71. Sue Zemka, "'Erewhon' and the End of Utopian Humanism," *ELH* 69, no. 2 (2002): 461.

72. Rieder, *Colonialism,* 69.

73. Suvin, *Victorian Science Fiction,* 325.

74. Ibid., 387.

75. Geoffrey Wagner, "A Forgotten Satire: Bulwer-Lytton's *The Coming Race,*" *Nineteenth-Century Fiction* 19, no. 4 (1965): 381, print.

76. Brantlinger, *Rule of Darkness,* 7.

77. James Smithies, "Return Migration and the Mechanical Age: Samuel Butler in New Zealand 1860–1864," *Journal of Victorian Culture* 12, no. 2 (2007): 210.

78. Peter Raby, *Samuel Butler: A Biography* (London: Hogarth, 1991), 119, print.

79. Brian Aldiss, *Billion Year Spree: The True History of Science Fiction* (New York: Schocken Books, 1974), 83, print.

80. Brantlinger, *Rule of Darkness,* 27–28.

81. Wagner, "Forgotten Satire," 379.

82. Rieder, *Colonialism,* 21–22.

83. Edward Bulwer-Lytton, *The Coming Race* (Middletown: Wesleyan University Press, 2007), 144, print.

84. Suvin, *Victorian Science Fiction,* 95.

85. Edgar Rice Burroughs, *Tarzan of the Apes* (New York: Penguin Books, 1990), xii, print.

86. Ibid., xiii.

87. Luckhurst, *Science Fiction,* 65.

88. Anderson Rearick, "Why Is the Only Good Orc a Dead Orc? The Dark Face of Racism Examined in Tolkien's World," *MFS: Modern Fiction Studies* 50, no. 4 (2004): 861–74, print; Joshua Luke Roberts, "On Charges of Racism against J. R. R. Tolkien Roberts," *Academia.edu,* accessed March 24, 2015, www.academia.edu.

89. Suvin, *Victorian Science Fiction,* 95.

90. Michael D. C. Drout, ed., *J. R. R. Tolkien Encyclopedia: Scholarship and Critical Assessment* (New York: Routledge, 2006), 78, print.

91. Suvin, *Victorian Science Fiction,* 344.

92. Bulwer Lytton, *Coming Race,* xxiii.

93. Ibid., 144.

94. Brantlinger, *Rule of Darkness,* 247.

95. Bulwer Lytton, *Coming Race,* 14.

96. Ibid., 60.

97. Brantlinger, *Rule of Darkness,* 230.

98. Suvin, *Victorian Science Fiction,* 94.

99. Mazlish, "Triptych," 737.

100. Brantlinger, *Rule of Darkness,* 195.

101. Bulwer Lytton, *Coming Race,* xvii, xviii.

102. Ibid.

103. Ibid., 67.

104. Smithies, "Return Migration," 212.

105. Ibid., 213.

106. James G. Paradis, ed., *Samuel Butler, Victorian against the Grain* (Toronto: University of Toronto Press, 2007), 31, print.

107. Smithies, "Return Migration," 212.

108. Marx, *Machine in the Garden,* 444.

109. Paradis, *Samuel Butler,* 23.

110. Smithies, "Return Migration," 214.

111. Martin Japtok, "Pauline Hopkins's of One Blood, Africa, and the 'Darwinist Trap,'" *African American Review* 36, no. 3 (2002): 403–15, print.

112. Zemka, "Utopian Humanism," 449.

113. Laura Chrisman, *Rereading the Imperial Romance: British Imperialism and South African Resistance in Haggard, Schriener, and Plaatje* (Oxford: Oxford University Press, 2000), 29, print.

114. Wiener, *Human Use,* 183.

115. Suvin, *Victorian Science Fiction,* 354.

116. Zemka, "Utopian Humanism," 463.

117. Martin Kevorkian, *Color Monitors: The Black Face of Technology in America* (Ithaca: Cornell University Press, 2006), 45, print.

118. Zemka, "Utopian Humanism," 463, 442.

THREE Creolization and Technopoetics

1. Samuel Delany, *Silent Interviews: On Language, Race, Sex, Science Fiction, and Some Comics* (Middletown: Wesleyan University Press, 1994), 26, print.

2. Wilson Harris, *The Unfinished Genesis of the Imagination: Selected Essays of Wilson Harris* (New York: Routledge, 1999), 183, print.

3. John Rieder, *Colonialism and the Emergence of Science Fiction* (Middletown: Wesleyan University Press, 2008), 30, print.

4. De Witt Douglas Kilgore, "Difference Engine: Aliens, Robots, and Other Racial Matters in the History of Science Fiction, *Science Fiction Studies* 37, no. 1 (2010): 17, print.

5. Mark Dery, "Black to the Future: Interviews with Samuel R. Delany, Greg Tate, and Tricia Rose," *South Atlantic Quarterly* 92, no. 4 (1994): 749, print.

6. Rieder, *Colonialism,* 111.

7. David Crane, "*In Medias* Race: Filmic Representation, Networked Communication, and Racial Intermediation," in *Race in Cyberspace,* ed. Beth. E. Kolko, Lisa Nakamura, and Gilbert B. Rodman (New York: Routledge, 2000), 90, print.

8. Robert J. C. Young, *Colonial Desire: Hybridity in Theory, Culture and Race* (New York: Routledge, 1995), print.

9. Tanith Lee, *The Silver Metal Lover* (New York: Bantam Spectra Books, 1999), 14, 36, 43, print.

10. Ibid., 140.

11. Donna J. Haraway, *Simians, Cyborgs, and Women: The Reinvention of Nature* (New York: Routledge, 1991), 154, print.

12. Rieder, *Colonialism,* 112.

13. Édouard Glissant, *The Poetics of Relation* (Ann Arbor: University of Michigan Press, 1997), 174, print.

14. Kolko, Nakamura, and Rodman, *Race in Cyberspace,* 8.

15. Gill Kirkup et al., eds., *The Gendered Cyborg: A Reader* (New York: Routledge, 1999), 306, print.

16. Haraway, *Simians, Cyborgs, and Women,* 150.

17. Marianna Torgovnick, *Gone Primitive: Savage Intellects, Modern Lives* (Chicago: University of Chicago Press, 1991), 53, print.

18. Martin Munro and Celia Britton, eds., *American Creoles: The Francophone Caribbean and the American South* (Liverpool: Liverpool University Press, 2012), 4, print.

19. Harris, *Unfinished Genesis,* 239.

20. Françoise Lionnet, "'Logiques metisses': Cultural Appropriation and Postcolonial Representations," *College Literature* 19–20, no. 3/1 (1992–93): 103, print.

21. Monika Kaup and Debra J. Rosenthal, eds., *Mixing Race, Mixing Culture: Inter-American Literary Dialogues* (Austin: University of Texas Press, 2002), 244, print.

22. Harris, *Unfinished Genesis*, 238.

23. Joyce Sparer Adler, *Exploring the Palace of the Peacock: Essays on Wilson Harris* (Kingston: University of the West Indies Press, 2003), 1, print.

24. Lionnet, "Logiques metisses," 104, 103.

25. Harris, *Unfinished Genesis*, 238.

26. Édouard Glissant, *Caribbean Discourse: Selected Essays* (Charlottesville: University Press of Virginia, 1989), 6, print.

27. Harris, *Unfinished Genesis*, 240.

28. Glissant, *Caribbean Discourse*, 140.

29. Harris, *Unfinished Genesis*, 143.

30. Glissant, *Caribbean Discourse*, 14.

31. Ibid., 16, 141, 16, 6.

32. Glissant, *Poetics of Relation*, 196, 89.

33. Samuel R. Delany, *Longer Views: Extended Essays* (Middletown: Wesleyan University Press, 1996), 110–11, print.

34. Kobena Mercer, *Welcome to the Jungle: New Positions in Black Cultural Studies* (New York: Routledge, 1994), 109, print.

35. Ron Eglash, "African Influences in Cybernetics," in *Cyborg Handbook*, ed. C. H. Gray (London: Routledge, 1995), print.

36. Ibid.

37. Mimi Sheller, *Consuming the Caribbean: From Arawaks to Zombies* (New York: Routledge, 2003), 194, print.

38. Ibid.

39. Stephan Palmié, "Creolization and Its Discontents," *Annual Review of Anthropology* 35 (2006): 445, print.

40. Ibid.

41. Glissant, *Poetics of Relation*, 89.

42. Brian Meeks, "Reasoning with *Caliban's Reason*," *Small Axe* 6, no. 1 (2002): 163, print.

43. Glissant, *Caribbean Discourse*, 139.

44. Silvio Torres-Saillant, *An Intellectual History of the Caribbean* (New York: Palgrave Macmillan, 2006), 43–44, print.

45. Ulf Hannerz, "The World in Creolisation," *Africa: Journal of the International African Institute* 57, no. 4 (1987): 546–59, print.

46. Palmié, "Creolization," 434.

47. Alexander Weheliye, *Phonographies: Grooves in Sonic Afro-Modernity* (Durham: Duke University Press, 2005), 2, print.

48. Kilgore, "Difference Engine," 17, 18.

49. Alondra Nelson, "Future Texts" and "Afrofuturism," ed. Alondra Nelson, *Social Text* 71 (Summer 2002): 1, print.

50. Kilgore, "Difference Engine," 17.

51. Haraway, *Simians, Cyborgs, and Women*, 149.

52. Martin Kevorkian, *Color Monitors: The Black Face of Technology in America* (Ithaca: Cornell University Press, 2006), 173n26, print.

53. Isaiah Lavender III, *Race in American Science Fiction* (Bloomington: Indiana University Press, 2011), 62, print.

54. Isaac Asimov, *Robot Visions* (New York: Penguin, 1991), 405, print.

55. Brian Aldiss, *Billion Year Spree: The True History of Science Fiction* (New York: Schocken Books, 1974), 229, print.

56. Asimov, *Robot Visions,* 453.

57. Kolko, Nakamura, and Rodman, *Race in Cyberspace,* 87.

58. Cary Wolfe, *What Is Posthumanism?* (Minneapolis: University of Minnesota Press, 2009), xv, print.

59. Joel Dinerstein, "Technology and Its Discontents: On the Verge of the Posthuman," in "Rewiring the 'Nation': The Place of Technology in American Studies," ed. Carolyn de la Pena and Siva Vaidhyanathan, special issue, *American Quarterly* 58, no. 3 (2006), 588, print.

60. Marie-Laure Ryan, ed., *Cyberspace Textuality: Computer Technology and Literary Theory* (Bloomington: Indiana University Press, 1999), 186, print.

61. Kolko, Nakamura, and Rodman, *Race in Cyberspace,* 8.

62. Hayles, quoted in Ryan, *Cyberspace Textuality,* 187, 208.

63. Alexander G. Weheliye, "'Feenin': Posthuman Voices in Contemporary Black Popular Music," in "Afrofuturism," ed. Alondra Nelson, *Social Text* 71 (Summer 2002): 22, print.

64. Kevorkian, *Color Monitors,* 6.

65. Ben Williams, "Black Secret Technology: Detroit Techno and the Information Age," in *Technicolor: Race, Technology, and Everyday Life,* ed. Alondra Nelson and T. L. N. Tu, with A. Headlam Hines (New York: New York University Press, 2001), 190, print.

66. Lavender, *American Science Fiction,* 27.

67. Ibid., 12.

68. Nelson, "Future Texts," 11.

69. Kilgore, "Difference Engine," 18.

70. Dinerstein, "Technology and Its Discontents," 592.

71. Ibid., 606–7.

72. David E. Nye, "Technology and the Production of Difference," in de la Pena and Siva Vaidhyanathan, "Rewiring the 'Nation,'" 597–618.

73. Dinerstein, "Technology and Its Discontents," 592.

74. Munro and Britton, *American Creoles,* 9.

75. Jeff Salomon, review of *Macro Dub Infection,* vol. 2, originally in *Artforum* 35, no. 10 (1997), www.questia.com.

76. Ryan, *Cyberspace Textuality,* 245, 246.

77. Scott Bukatman, *Terminal Identity: The Virtual Subject in Post-modern Science Fiction* (Durham: Duke University Press, 1993), 214, print.

78. Benjamin Fair, "Stepping Razor in Orbit: Postmodern Identity and Political Alternatives in William Gibson's *Neuromancer*," *Critique* 46, no. 2 (2005): 93, 94, print.

79. Kali Tal, quoted in Wayne Marshall, "Trading in Futures," *Woofah* 4 (2010): 67, print.

80. Ultravox!, *Ultravox!* (London: Island Records, 1976).

81. David Toop, *Ocean of Sound: Aether Talk, Ambient Sound and Imaginary Worlds* (London: Serpents Tail Books, 1995), 116, print.

82. Antonio Benítez Rojo, *The Repeating Island: The Caribbean and the Postmodern Perspective* (Durham: Duke University Press, 1997), 18, print.

83. Dery, "Black to the Future," 750.
84. Kevorkian, *Color Monitors,* 138.
85. Dery, "Black to the Future," 751.
86. Ibid., 750.
87. Fair, "Stepping Razor in Orbit," 96.
88. Thomas M. Disch, *The Dreams Our Stuff Is Made Of: How Science Fiction Conquered the World* (New York: Touchstone/Simon and Schuster, 2000), 219, print.
89. William Gibson, *Neuromancer* (New York: Ace Books, 1986), 104, print.
90. Alan Moore and Dave Gibbon, *Watchmen* (New York: DC Comics/Warner Books, 1986, 1987), chap. 11 (*Nova Express*), 10.
91. Erik Davis, "Dub, Scratch and the Black Star: Lee Perry on the Mix," *21C*, no. 24 (1997), http://techgnosis.com.
92. Gibson, *Neuromancer,* 104.
93. Harris, *Unfinished Genesis,* 209.
94. Donna Haraway, *The Companion Species Manifesto: Dogs, People, and Significant Otherness* (Chicago: Prickly Paradigm, 2003), 4, print.
95. Weheliye, "Feenin," 26.
96. Michael Veal, *Dub: Soundscapes and Shattered Songs in Jamaican Reggae* (Middletown: Wesleyan, 2007), 209, print.
97. Glissant, *Caribbean Discourse,* 123.
98. Veit Erlmann, *Reason and Resonance: A History of Modern Aurality* (Cambridge: Zone Books, 2010), 10, print.
99. Harris, *Unfinished Genesis,* 105, 43.
100. Erlmann, *Reason and Resonance,* 10.
101. Glissant, *Poetics of Relation,* 93.
102. Leo Marx, *The Machine in the Garden: Technology and the Pastoral Ideal in America* (Oxford: Oxford University Press, 1964), 23, print.
103. Toop, *Ocean of Sound,* 113.
104. Nathaniel Mackey, *Discrepant Engagement: Dissonance, Cross-Culturality and Experimental Writing* (Tuscaloosa: University of Alabama Press, 2000), 189, print.
105. Wilson Harris, *The Womb of Space: The Cross-Cultural Imagination* (London: Greenwood, 1983), xv, xx, xv–vi, 46, print.
106. Harris, *Unfinished Genesis,* 46.
107. Ibid., 43–44, 244, 44.
108. Lucile Desblache, "Guest Editor's Introduction: Hybridity, Monstrosity and the Posthuman in Philosophy and Literature Today," *Comparative Critical Studies* 9, no. 3 (2012): 245, print.
109. Harris, *Unfinished Genesis,* 46.
110. Glissant, *Poetics of Relation,* 93.
111. Ibid., 18.
112. Ibid., 79.
113. Ibid., 11.
114. Wilson Harris, *The Mask of the Beggar* (London: Faber and Faber, 2003), vii, print.
115. Harris, *Womb of Space,* 246.
116. Glissant, *Poetics of Relation,* 79.

117. Sylvia Wynter, "Beyond Miranda's Meanings: Un/silencing the 'Demonic Ground' of Caliban's 'Woman,'" *The Routledge Reader in Caribbean Literature,* ed. Alison Donnell and Sarah Lawson Welsh, 476–82 (London: Routledge, 1996), print.

118. Ibid., 81.

119. Ibid.

120. Sylvia Wynter, "Unsettling the Coloniality of Being/Power/Truth/Freedom: Towards the Human, after Man, Its Overrepresentation—An Argument," *CR: New Centennial Review* 3, no. 3 (2003): 322, print.

121. Glissant, *Poetics of Relation,* 82.

122. Fredric Jameson, *Signatures of the Visible* (New York: Routledge, 2013), 61, print.

123. Glissant, *Poetics of Relation,* 84.

124. Jonathan Stern, "The Theology of Sound: A Critique of Orality," *Canadian Journal of Communication* 36, no. 2 (2011): 208, print.

125. Glissant, *Poetics of Relation,* 84.

126. Ibid.

127. Ibid.

128. Ibid., 83.

129. Ibid., 92.

130. Ibid., 52.

FOUR A Caribbean Pre-Posthumanism

1. Donna J. Haraway, *Simians, Cyborgs, and Women: The Reinvention of Nature* (New York: Routledge, 1991), 151, print.

2. Édouard Glissant, *Caribbean Discourse: Selected Essays* (Charlottesville: University Press of Virginia, 1989), 3, print.

3. Alexander G. Weheliye, "'Feenin': Posthuman Voices in Contemporary Black Popular Music," in "Afrofuturism," ed. Alondra Nelson, *Social Text* 71 (Summer 2002): 27, print.

4. Sylvia Wynter, "Beyond the Word of Man: Glissant and the New Discourse of the Antilles," *World Literature Today* 63, no. 4 (1989): 637, print.

5. David Scott, "The Re-enchantment of Humanism: An Interview with Sylvia Wynter," *Small Axe* 4, no. 2 (2000): 140, print.

6. Aaron K. Kamugisha, "Reading Said and Wynter on Liberation," in *After Man, towards the Human: Critical Essays on Sylvia Wynter,* ed. Anthony Bogues (Kingston: Randle, 2006), 142, print.

7. J. Michael Dash, *The Other America: Caribbean Literature in a New World Context* (Charlottesville: University Press of Virginia, 1998), 61–62, print.

8. André Breton, *What Is Surrealism: Selected Writings,* ed. Franklin Rosemont (New York: Pathfinder/Monad, 1978), 118, print.

9. Dash, *Other America,* 37.

10. James Clifford, *The Predicament of Culture: Twentieth-Century Ethnography, Literature, and Art* (Boston: Harvard University Press, 1988), 118, print.

11. Clayton Eshleman and Annette Smith, eds., *Aimé Césaire: The Collected Poetry* (Oakland: University of California Press, 1983), 17, print.

12. Aimé Césaire, *Notebook of a Return to the Native Land* (Middletown: Wesleyan University Press, 2001), 35, print.

13. Clifford, *Predicament of Culture,* 177.

14. Ibid., 179.

15. Dash, *Other America,* 40–41.

16. Michael Richardson, ed., *Refusal of the Shadow: Surrealism and the Caribbean* (Brooklyn: Verso, 1996), 98, print.

17. Léopold Sédar Senghor, *The Collected Poetry* (Charlottesville: University Press of Virginia, 1991), xxii, print.

18. Janet Vaillant, *Black, French and African: A Life of Léopold Sédar Senghor* (Boston: Harvard University Press, 1990), 287, print.

19. Aimé Césaire, *Discourse on Colonialism* (New York: Monthly Review Press, 2001), 68, print.

20. Clifford, *Predicament of Culture,* 173.

21. Shireen K. Lewis, *Race, Culture, and Identity: Francophone West African and Caribbean Literature and Theory from Negritude to Creolité* (Lanham: Lexington Books, 2006), 73, print.

22. Césaire, *Notebook,* 17–18.

23. Nathaniel Mackey, *Discrepant Engagement: Dissonance, Cross-Culturality, and Experimental Writing* (Tuscaloosa: University of Alabama Press, 2000), 185, print.

24. Ibid., 181.

25. Ibid., 37.

26. Kamugisha, "Reading Said and Wynter," 143.

27. Aimé Césaire, *Lyric and Dramatic Poetry* (Charlottesville: University Press of Virginia, 1990), lii, li, lii, lv, print.

28. Ibid., xxxi.

29. Breton, *What Is Surrealism?,* 233.

30. Césaire, *Lyric and Dramatic Poetry,* lii.

31. Richardson, *Refusal of the Shadow,* 120–21.

32. Breton, *What Is Surrealism?,* 267.

33. Dash, *Other America,* 101.

34. Vaillant, *Black, French and African,* 101.

35. Lewis, *Race, Culture, and Identity,* 1, 5.

36. Claude McKay, *Banjo: A Novel without a Plot* (New York: Mariner Books, 1970), 324, 314, print.

37. Edgar Rice Burroughs, *Tarzan of the Apes* (New York: Penguin Books, 1990), viii, print.

38. Marianna Torgovnick, *Gone Primitive: Savage Intellects, Modern Lives* (Chicago: University of Chicago Press, 1991), 45, print.

39. Burroughs, *Tarzan of the Apes,* viii.

40. Alain Locke, ed., *The New Negro: Voices of the Harlem Renaissance* (New York: Touchstone Books, 1999), 252, print.

41. McKay, *Banjo,* 325.

42. Glissant, *Caribbean Discourse,* 5.

43. Derek Walcott, *What the Twilight Says: Essays* (New York: Farrar, Straus and Giroux, 1998), 29, print.

44. Richardson, *Refusal of the Shadow,* 122; Césaire, *Lyric and Dramatic Poetry,* xliii.

45. Glissant, *Caribbean Discourse,* xlii.

46. Walcott, *What the Twilight Says,* 44.

47. Michael Veal, *Dub: Soundscapes and Shattered Songs in Jamaican Reggae* (Middletown: Wesleyan University Press, 2007), 192, print.

48. Stuart Hall, "Cultural Identity and Diaspora" (aka "Cultural Identity and Cinematic Representation"), in *Ex-iles: Essays on Caribbean Cinema,* ed. Mbye Cham (Trenton, NJ: Africa World Press, 1992), 228, print.

49. Sylvia Wynter, "Beyond the Categories of the Master Conception: The Counterdoctrine of the Jamesian Poesis," in *C. L. R. James's Caribbean,* ed. Paget Henry and Paul Buhle (Durham: Duke University Press, 1992), 148, print.

50. Hall, "Cultural Identity," 223.

51. Paget Henry, *Caliban's Reason: Introducing Afro-Caribbean Philosophy* (New York: Routledge, 2000), 123, print.

52. Wynter, "Word of Man," 639, 640.

53. Ibid., 639.

54. Ibid., 639, 641.

55. Césaire, *Notebook,* 15.

56. Wynter, "Word of Man," 641.

57. Sylvia Wynter, "Unsettling the Coloniality of Being/Power/Truth/Freedom: Towards the Human, after Man, Its Overrepresentation—An Argument." *CR: New Centennial Review* 3, no. 3 (2003): 331, print.

58. Wynter, "Word of Man," 639.

59. Ibid.

60. Glissant, *Caribbean Discourse,* 138, 2.

61. Wilson Harris, *The Unfinished Genesis of the Imagination: Selected Essays of Wilson Harris* (New York: Routledge, 1999), 243, 238, print.

62. Donna Haraway, "A Cyborg Manifesto: Science, Technology, and Socialist-Feminism in the Late Twentieth Century," in Haraway, *Simians, Cyborgs, and Women,* 157.

63. Ibid., 157–58.

64. Wynter, "Word of Man," 639.

65. Homi Bhabha, *The Location of Culture* (New York: Routledge, 1994), 41–42, print.

66. William Gibson, *Burning Chrome* (New York: HarperCollins, 2003), 199, print.

67. Glissant, *Caribbean Discourse,* 14.

68. Henry, *Caliban's Reason,* 131.

69. Leonard Cassuto, *The Inhuman Race: The Racial Grotesque in American Literature and Culture* (New York: Columbia University Press, 1997), xvii, print.

70. Césaire, *Lyric and Dramatic Poetry,* xlvii.

71. Greg Tate, *Flyboy in the Buttermilk: Essays on Contemporary America* (New York: Simon and Schuster, 1992), 165, 166, print.

72. Ibid., 166.

73. Mark Dery, "Black to the Future: Interviews with Samuel R. Delany, Greg Tate, and Tricia Rose," *South Atlantic Quarterly* 92, no. 4 (1994): 746, print.

74. Henry, *Caliban's Reason,* 128.

75. Ibid., 131.

76. Sylvia Wynter, "The Ceremony Must Be Found: After Humanism," *Boundary 2,* vol. 12, no. 3 (1984): 30–31, print.

77. Ibid., 36.

78. Henry, *Caliban's Reason,* 128, 124.

79. Wynter, "Ceremony Must Be Found," 42.

80. Ibid., 43.

81. Henry, *Caliban's Reason,* 128.

82. Ibid., 128–29.

83. Sylvia Wynter, "1492: A New World View," in *Race, Discourse, and the Origin of the Americas: A New World View,* ed. Vera Lawrence Hyatt and Rex Nettleford, 1–57 (Washington, DC: Smithsonian Institution Press, 1995), http://socrates.berkeley.edu.

84. Wynter, "Word of Man," 645.

85. Wynter, "1492," 3.

86. Wynter, "Word of Man," 645–46.

87. Wynter, "Ceremony Must Be Found," 26.

88. Wynter, "Unsettling the Coloniality," 322.

89. Harris, *Unfinished Genesis,* 246.

90. Anthony Bogues, ed., *After Man, towards the Human: Critical Essays on Sylvia Wynter* (Kingston: Randle, 2006), 323, print.

91. Wynter, "Ceremony Must Be Found," 36.

92. Wynter, "Word of Man," 640.

93. Samuel Butler, *Erewhon* (New York: Airmont, 1967), 143, print.

94. Norbert Wiener, *The Human Use of Human Being: Cybernetics and Society* (New York: Doubleday, 1950), 31, print.

95. Haraway, "Cyborg Manifesto," in Haraway, *Simians, Cyborgs, and Women,* 176.

96. Wiener, *Human Use,* 32.

97. Hans Moravec, *Robot: Mere Machine to Transcendent Mind* (New York: Oxford University Press, 1999), 76, print.

98. Ibid., 111.

99. Aubrey Belford, "That's Not a Droid, That's My Girlfriend," *Global Mail,* February 21, 2013, www.theglobalmail.org.

100. Kirsty Boyle, "Robot Perspectives," *Karakuri.info,* accessed March 24, 2015, http://karakuri.info/perspectives/index.html.

101. Belford, "That's Not a Droid," 2, 3.

102. Masahiro Mori, "The Uncanny Valley," *IEEE Spectrum,* June 12, 2012, http://spectrum.ieee.org.

103. Ibid., 2.

104. Ibid., 7, 8.

105. Sylvia Wynter, "'Africa, the West and the Analogy of Culture': The Cinematic Text after Man," *Symbolic Narratives/African Cinema: Audience, Theory and the Moving Image,* ed. June Giovanni (London: BFI, 2000), 25, print.

106. Ibid., 480.

107. Alexander G. Weheliye, "After Man," *American Literary History* 20, nos. 1–2 (2008): 322–23, print.

108. Wynter, "Ceremony Must Be Found," 52, 53, 56.

109. Henry, *Caliban's Reason,* 129.

110. Bogues, *After Man,* 60.

111. Samuel R. Delany, *Longer Views: Extended Essays* (Middletown: Wesleyan University Press, 1996), 115, print.

112. Alison Donnell and Sarah Lawson Welsh, eds., *The Routledge Reader in Caribbean Literature* (London: Routledge, 1996), 478, print.

113. Simone Caroti, "Science Fiction, Forbidden Planet, and Shakespeare's *The Tempest,*" *CLCWeb: Comparative Literature and Culture* 6, no. 1 (2004), http://docs.lib.purdue.edu.

114. Donnell and Lawson, *Routledge Reader,* 478.

115. Ibid., 480.

116. Henry, *Caliban's Reason,* 121.

117. Mackey, *Discrepant Engagement,* 55.

BIBLIOGRAPHY

Adas, Michael. *Machines as the Measure of Men: Science, Technology, and Ideologies of Western Dominance.* New York: Cornell University Press, 1989. Print.

Adler, Joyce Sparer. *Exploring the Palace of the Peacock: Essays on Wilson Harris.* Kingston: University of the West Indies Press, 2003. Print.

Aldiss, Brian. *Billion Year Spree: The True History of Science Fiction.* New York: Schocken Books, 1974. Print.

Apolonio, Umbro, ed. *Futurist Manifestos.* New York: Viking, 1973. Print.

Archer-Straw, Petrine. *Negrophilia: Avant-Garde Paris and Black Culture in the 1920s.* New York: Thames and Hudson, 2000. Print.

Armstrong, Tim. *Modernism, Technology and the Body: A Cultural Study.* Boston: Cambridge University Press, 1998. Print.

Asimov, Isaac. *Robot Visions.* New York: Penguin, 1991. Print.

Attali, Jacques. *Noise: The Political Economy of Music.* Minneapolis: University of Minnesota Press, 1985. Print.

Baldick, Chris. *In Frankenstein's Shadow: Myth, Monstrosity, and Nineteenth-Century Writing.* Oxford: Clarendon Paperbacks/Oxford University Press, 1990. Print.

Barnum, P. T. *The Life of P. T. Barnum, Written by Himself.* New York: Redfield, 1854. Print.

———. *Struggles and Triumphs; or, Forty Years' Recollections of P. T. Barnum, Written by Himself.* Buffalo: Warren, Johnson, 1873. Print.

Bean, Annemarie, James V. Hatch, and Brooks McNamara, eds. *Inside the Minstrel Mask: Readings in Nineteenth-Century Blackface Minstrelsy.* Hanover, NH: Wesleyan University Press, 1996. Print.

Belford, Aubrey. "That's Not a Droid, That's My Girlfriend." *Global Mail,* February 21, 2013. www.theglobalmail.org.

Benitez-Rojo, Antonio. *The Repeating Island: The Caribbean and the Postmodern Perspective.* Durham: Duke University Press, 1997. Print.

Bergson, Henri. *Laughter: An Essay on the Meaning of the Comic.* Project Gutenberg E-Book 4352. Accessed March 24, 2015. www.gutenberg.org.

Bhabha, Homi. *The Location of Culture.* New York: Routledge, 1994. Print.

Boese, Alex. *Electrified Sheep, Glass-Eating Scientists, Nuking the Moon, and More Bizarre Experiments.* New York: St. Martin's Press, 2011. Print.

Bogues, Anthony, ed. *After Man, towards the Human: Critical Essays on Sylvia Wynter.* Kingston: Randle, 2006. Print.

Boyle, Kirsty. "Robot Perspectives." *Karakuri.info.* Accessed March 24, 2015. http://karakuri.info/perspectives/index.html.

Bradbrook, Bohuslava R. *Karel Čapek: In Pursuit of Truth, Tolerance, and Trust.* Sussex: Sussex Academic Press, 1998. Print.

Brain, Robert, R. W. Flint, J. C. Higgitt, and Caroline Tisdal, eds. *Futurist Manifestos.* Boston: MFA, 1970. Print.

Brantlinger, Patrick. *Rule of Darkness: British Literature and Imperialism, 1830–1914.* Ithaca: Cornell University Press, 1990. Print.

Breton, Andre. *What Is Surrealism? Selected Writings.* Edited by Franklin Rosemont. New York: Pathfinder/Monad, 1978. Print.

Brooker, Peter, Andrezej Gasiorek, Deborah Longworth, and Andrew Thacker, eds. *The Oxford Handbook of Modernisms.* Oxford: Oxford University Press, 2010. Print.

Brown, Bill. "Reification, Reanimation, and the American Uncanny," *Critical Inquiry* 32 (Winter 2006): 175–207. Print.

Buck-Morss, Susan. "Hegel and Haiti." *Critical Inquiry* 26, no. 4 (2000): 821–65. Print.

Bukatman, Scott. *Terminal Identity: The Virtual Subject in Post-Modern Science Fiction.* Durham: Duke University Press, 1993. Print.

Bulwer-Lytton, Edward. *The Coming Race.* Middletown: Wesleyan University Press, 2007. Print.

Bundy, Andrew, ed. *Selected Essays of Wilson Harris: The Unfinished Genesis of the Imagination.* New York: Routledge, 1999. Print.

Burroughs, Edgar Rice. *Tarzan of the Apes.* New York: Penguin Books, 1990. Print.

Butler, Samuel. *Erewhon; or, Over the Range.* New York: Airmont, 1967. Print.

Čapek, Karel. *R. U. R.* New York: Washington Square, 1973. Print.

———. *War with the Newts.* Chicago: Northwestern University Press, 1996. Print.

Caroti, Simone. "Science Fiction, Forbidden Planet, and Shakespeare's *The Tempest.*" *CLCWeb: Comparative Literature and Culture* 6, no. 1 (2004), http://docs.lib.purdue.edu.

Castle, Terry. *The Female Thermometer: Eighteenth-Century Culture and the Invention of the Uncanny.* Oxford: Oxford University Press, 1995. Print.

Casutto, Leonard. *The Inhuman Race: The Racial Grotesque in American Literature and Culture.* New York: Columbia University Press, 1997. Print.

Césaire, Aimé. *Discourse on Colonialism.* New York: Monthly Review, 1972. Print.

———. *Lyric and Dramatic Poetry.* Charlottesville: University Press of Virginia, 1990. Print.

———. *Notebook of a Return to the Native Land.* Middletown: Wesleyan University Press, 2001. Print.

Cham, Mbye. *Ex-iles: Essays on Caribbean Cinema.* Trenton, NJ: Africa World, 1992. Print.

Chandler Harris, Joel. *Uncle Remus: His Songs and His Sayings.* New York: Penguin Books, 1986. Print.

Chaney, Michael. "Slave Cyborgs and the Black Infovirus: Ishmael Reed's Cybernetic Aesthetics." *MFS: Modern Fiction Studies* 49, no. 2 (2003): 261–83. Print.

Charters, Ann. *Nobody: The Story of Bert Williams.* New York: Macmillan, 1970. Print.

Chrisman, Laura. *Rereading the Imperial Romance: British Imperialism and South African Resistance in Haggard, Schriener, and Plaatje.* Oxford: Oxford University Press, 2000. Print.

Chude-Sokei, Louis. "But I Did Not Shoot the Deputy: Dubbing the Yankee Frontier." In *Worldings,* edited by Rob Wilson and Christopher Leigh Connery, 133–69. Santa Cruz: New Pacific, 2007. Print.

———. *Dr. Satan's Echo Chamber: Reggae, Technology and the Diaspora Process,* Kingston: International Reggae Studies Centre, 1997. Print.

———. "Invisible Missive Magnetic Juju: On African Cyber-Crime." *Fanzine,* October 24, 2010. http://thefanzine.com.

———. *The Last Darky: Bert Williams, Black on Black Minstrelsy and the African Diaspora.* Durham: Duke University Press, 2006. Print.

———. "Post-Nationalist Geographies: Rasta, Ragga and Reinventing Africa." *African Arts* 27, no. 4 (1994): 80–84, 96. Print.

———. "The Sound of Culture: Dread Discourse and Jamaican Sound Systems." In *Language, Rhythm and Sound: Black Popular Cultures into the Twenty-first Century,* edited by Joseph K. Adjaye and Adrianne R. Andrews, 185–202. Pittsburgh: University of Pittsburgh Press, 1997. Print.

———. "When Echoes Return: Roots, Diaspora and Possible Africas (a Eulogy)." *Transition: An International Review,* no. 104 (2011): 76–92. Print.

Clifford, James. *The Predicament of Culture: Twentieth-Century Ethnography, Literature, and Art.* Boston: Harvard University Press, 1988. Print.

Connor, Steven. *Dumbstruck: A Cultural History of Ventriloquism.* Oxford: Oxford University Press, 2000. Print.

Cook, James W. *The Arts of Deception: Playing with Fraud in the Age of Barnum.* Boston: Harvard University Press, 2001. Print.

Cope, David. "Whiteness, Blackness, and Sermons to Sharks: Race in Melville's Moby Dick." *Poetspath.* Accessed March 24, 2015. www.poetspath.com.

Crane, David. "*In Medias* Race: Filmic Representation, Networked Communication, and Racial Intermediation." In Kolko, Nakamura, and Rodman, *Race in Cyberspace,* 87–116.

Cyberneticzoo.com: A History of Cybernetic Animals and Early Robots. Accessed March 24, 2015. http://cyberneticzoo.com/.

Dash, J. Michael. *The Other America: Caribbean Literature in a New World Context.* Charlottesville: University Press of Virginia, 1998. Print.

Davis, Erik. "Dub, Scratch and the Black Star: Lee Perry on the Mix." *21C,* no. 24 (1997), http://techgnosis.com.

Delany, Samuel. *Longer Views: Extended Essays.* Middletown: Wesleyan University Press, 1996. Print.

———. *Silent Interviews: On Language, Race, Sex, Science Fiction, and Some Comics.* Middletown: Wesleyan University Press, 1994. Print.

De la Pena, Carolyn, and Siva Vaidhyanathan, eds. "Rewiring the 'Nation': The Place of Technology in American Studies." Special issue, *American Quarterly* 58, no. 3 (2007). Print.

Delbanco, Andrew. *Melville: His World and Work.* New York: Knopf, 2005. Print.

Dery, Mark, ed. "Flame Wars: The Discourse of Cyberculture." Special issue, *South Atlantic Quarterly* 92, no. 4 (1993). Print.

Desblache, Lucile. "Guest Editor's Introduction: Hybridity, Monstrosity and the Posthuman in Philosophy and Literature Today." *Comparative Critical Studies* 9, no. 3 (2012): 245–55. Print.

Dinerstein, Joel. *Swinging the Machine: Modernity, Technology and African American Culture between the World Wars.* Amherst: University of Massachusetts Press, 2003. Print.

———. "Technology and Its Discontents: On the Verge of the Posthuman." In de la Pena and Siva Vaidhyanathan, "Rewiring the 'Nation,'" 569–95.

Disch, Thomas M. *The Dreams Our Stuff Is Made Of: How Science Fiction Conquered the World.* New York: Touchstone/Simon and Schuster, 2000. Print.

Donnell, Alison, and Sarah Lawson Welsh, eds. *The Routledge Reader in Caribbean Literature.* London: Routledge, 1996. Print.

Drout, Michael D. C., ed. *J. R. R. Tolkien Encyclopedia: Scholarship and Critical Assessment.* New York: Routledge, 2006. Print.

Eglash, Ron. "African Influences in Cybernetics." In *Cyborg Handbook,* edited by C. H. Gray, 18. London: Routledge, 1995. Print.

——— . "Broken Metaphor: The Master-Slave Analogy in Technical Literature." *Technology and Culture: The Society for the History of Technology* 48, no. 3 (2007): 1–9. http://courseweb.lis.illinois.edu.

——— . "History of the Phrase 'Master-Slave' in Engineering Terminology." *iBrarian.* 2007. www.ibrarian.net.

Eisenberg, Evan. *The Recording Angel: Music, Records and Culture from Aristotle to Zappa.* New Haven: Yale University Press, 2005. Print.

Emeagwali, Philip. "Our Eighth Continent." YouTube video, 1:09. December 31, 2011. www.youtube.com.

Erlmann, Veit. *Reason and Resonance: A History of Modern Aurality.* Cambridge: Zone Books, 2010. Print.

Eshleman, Clayton, and Annette Smith, eds. *Aimé Césaire: The Collected Poetry.* Berkeley: University of California Press, 1983. Print.

Eshun, Kodwo. *More Brilliant Than the Sun: Adventures in Sonic Fiction.* London: Quartet Books, 1998. Print.

Fair, Benjamin. "Stepping Razor in Orbit: Postmodern Identity and Political Alternatives in William Gibson's *Neuromancer.*" *Critique* 46, no. 2 (2005): 92–103. Print.

Fanon, Frantz. *The Wretched of the Earth.* New York: Grove, 1965. Print.

Fenton, Charles A. "Melville and Technology." *American Literature* 23, no. 2 (1951): 219–32. Print.

Fisher, Marvin. "Melville's 'Bell-Tower': A Double Thrust." Pt. 1. *American Quarterly* 18, no. 2 (1966): 200–207. Print.

Franklin, H. Bruce, ed. *Future Perfect: American Science Fiction of the Nineteenth Century.* Oxford: Oxford University Press, 1966. Print.

Freud, Sigmund. *Collected Papers.* Vol. 4. London: Basic Books, 1959. Print.

Gibson, William. *Burning Chrome.* New York: HarperCollins, 2003. Print.

——— . *Neuromancer.* New York: Ace Books, 1986. Print.

Gilroy, Paul. *"There Ain't No Black in the Union Jack": The Cultural Politics of Race and Nation.* Chicago: University of Chicago Press, 1991. Print.

Glissant, Edouard. *Caribbean Discourse: Selected Essays.* Charlottesville: University Press of Virginia, 1989. Print.

——— . *The Poetics of Relation.* Ann Arbor: University of Michigan Press, 1997. Print.

Goodall, Jane. "Transferred Agencies: Performance and the Fear of Automatism." *Theatre Journal* 49, no. 4 (1997): 441–53. Print.

Gray, Chris Hables. *The Cyborg Handbook.* London: Routledge, 1995. Print.

Grimshaw, Anna, ed. *The C. L. R. James Reader.* Cambridge: Blackwell, 1992. Print.

Hannerz, Ulf. "The World in Creolisation." *Africa: Journal of the International African Institute* 57, no. 4 (1987): 546–59. Print.

Haraway, Donna. *The Companion Species Manifesto: Dogs, People, and Significant Otherness.* Chicago: Prickly Paradigm, 2003. Print.

———. "A Cyborg Manifesto: Science, Technology, and Socialist-Feminism in the Late Twentieth Century." In *Simians, Cyborgs, and Women: The Reinvention of Nature,* 149–82. New York: Routledge, 1991.

———. *Simians, Cyborgs, and Women: The Reinvention of Nature.* New York: Routledge, 1991. Print.

Harkins, William E. "Karel Capek's *R. U. R.* and A. N. Tolstoj's Revolt of the Machines." *Slavic and East European Journal* 4, no. 4 (1960): 312–18. Print.

Harris, Wilson. *The Mask of the Beggar.* London: Faber and Faber, 2003. Print.

———. *The Womb of Space: The Cross-Cultural Imagination.* London: Greenwood, 1983. Print.

Hayles, N. Katherine. *Have We Become Post-human: Virtual Bodies in Cybernetics, Literature, and Informatics.* Chicago: University of Chicago Press, 1999. Print.

Headrick, Daniel R. *The Tools of Empire: Technology and European Imperialism in the Nineteenth Century.* Oxford: Oxford University Press, 1981. Print.

Helleman, Frank. "Towards Techno-Poetics and Beyond: The Emergence of Modernist/Avant-garde Poetics Out of Science and Media-Technology." In *The Turn of the Century: Modernism and Modernity in Literature and the Arts,* edited by Christian Bert and Frank Durieux, 291–301. European Cultures: Studies in Literature and the Arts 3. Berlin: De Gruyter, 1995. Print.

Henry, Paget. *Caliban's Reason: Introducing Afro-Caribbean Philosophy.* New York: Routledge, 2000. Print.

Henry, Paget, and Paul Buhle, eds. *C. L. R. James's Caribbean.* Durham: Duke University Press, 1992. Print.

Huyssen, Andreas. *After the Great Divide: Modernism, Mass Culture, Postmodernism.* Bloomington: Indiana University Press, 1986. Print.

Jaji, Tsitsi Ella. *Africa in Stereo: Modernism, Music, and Pan-African Solidarity.* Oxford: Oxford University Press, 2014. Print.

James, C. L. R. *American Civilization.* Edited by Anna Grimshaw and Keith Hart. Oxford: Blackwell, 1993. Print.

———. *The Black Jacobins.* New York: Vintage Books, 1963. Print.

———. *Mariners, Renegades and Castaways: The Story of Herman Melville and the World We Live In.* Hanover: Dartmouth College Press, 2001. Print.

Jameson, Fredric. *Signatures of the Visible.* New York: Routledge, 2013. Print.

Japtok, Martin. "Pauline Hopkins's of One Blood, Africa, and the 'Darwinist Trap.'" *African American Review* 36, no. 3 (2002): 403–15. Print.

Johnson, Stephen, ed. *Burnt Cork: Traditions and Legacies of Blackface Minstrelsy.* Boston: University of Massachusetts Press, 2012. Print.

Kaplan, Amy, and Donald E. Pease, eds. *Cultures of United States Imperialism.* Durham: Duke University Press, 1993. Print.

Kaup, Monika, and Debra J. Rosenthal, eds. *Mixing Race, Mixing Culture: Inter-American Literary Dialogues.* Austin: University of Texas Press, 2002. Print.

Kelly, Karen, and Evelyn McDonnell, eds. *Stars Don't Stand Still in the Sky.* New York: New York University Press, 1999. Print.

Kevorkian, Martin. *Color Monitors: The Black Face of Technology in America.* Ithaca: Cornell University Press, 2006. Print.

Kilgore, De Witt. "Difference Engine: Aliens, Robots, and Other Racial Matters in the History of Science Fiction." *Science Fiction Studies* 37, no. 1 (2010): 16-22. Print.

Kinyon, Kamila. "The Phenomenology of Robots: Confrontations with Death in Karel Čapek's R. U. R." *Science Fiction Studies* 26, no. 3 (1999): 379-400. Print.

Kirkup, Gill, Linda Janes, Fiona Hovenden, and Kathryn Woodward, eds. *The Gendered Cyborg: A Reader.* New York: Routledge, 1999. Print.

Kolko, Beth E., Lisa Nakamura, and Gilbert B. Rodman, eds. *Race in Cyberspace.* New York: Routledge, 2000. Print.

Lamming, George. *The Pleasures of Exile.* Ann Arbor: University of Michigan Press, 1992. Print.

Lane, Jeremy F. *Jazz and Machine-Age Imperialism: Music, "Race," and Intellectuals in France, 1918-1945.* Ann Arbor: University of Michigan Press, 2013. Print.

Lavender, Isaiah, III. *Race in American Science Fiction.* Bloomington: Indiana University Press, 2011. Print.

Lee, Tanith. *The Silver Metal Lover.* New York: Bantam Spectra Books, 1999. Print.

Leiter, Andrew B. *In the Shadow of the Black Beast: African American Masculinity in the Harlem and Southern Renaissances.* Baton Rouge: Louisiana State University Press, 2010. Print.

Lemke, Sieglinde. *Primitivist Modernism: Black Culture and the Origins of Transatlantic Modernism.* Oxford: Oxford University Press, 1998. Print.

Lewis, Shireen K. *Race, Culture, and Identity: Francophone West African and Caribbean Literature and Theory from Negritude to Creolité.* Lanham: Lexington Books, 2006. Print.

Lionnet, Françoise. "'Logiques metisses': Cultural Appropriation and Postcolonial Representations." *College Literature* 19-20, no. 3/1 (1992-93): 100-120. Print.

Locke, Alain, ed. *The New Negro: Voices of the Harlem Renaissance.* New York: Touchstone Books, 1999. Print.

Lott, Eric. *Love and Theft: Blackface Minstrelsy and the American Working Class.* New York: Oxford University Press, 1993. Print.

Luckhurst, Roger. *Science Fiction.* Cambridge: Polity, 2005. Print.

Mackey, Nathaniel. *Discrepant Engagement: Dissonance, Cross-Culturality and Experimental Writing.* Tuscaloosa: University of Alabama Press, 2000. Print.

Malchow, Howard L. *Gothic Images of Race in Nineteenth-Century Britain.* Stanford: Stanford University Press, 1996.

Marinetti, Filippo Tommaso. "Extended Man and the Kingdom of the Machine." In *Critical Writings,* edited by Günter Berghaus, translated by Doug Thompson, 85-88. New York: Farrar, Straus, and Giroux, 2006. Print.

———. *Mafarka the Futurist: An African Novel.* Translated by Carol Diethe and Steve Cox. London: Middlesex University Press, 1998. Print.

———. "Technical Manifesto of Futurist Literature." *Italian Futurism.* Accessed March 24, 2015. www.italianfuturism.org.

Marshall, Wayne. "Trading in Futures." *Woofah Magazine* 4 (Spring 2010): 65–72. Print.

Marx, Leo. *The Machine in the Garden: Technology and the Pastoral Ideal in America.* New York: Oxford University Press, 1964. Print.

Mazlish, Bruce. "The Triptych: Freud's *The Interpretation of Dreams,* Rider Haggard's *She,* and Bulwer-Lytton's *The Coming Race.*" *Comparative Studies in Society and History* 35, no. 4 (1993): 726–45. Print.

McKay, Claude. *Banjo: A Novel without a Plot.* Mariner Books, 1970. Print.

McKever, Rosalind S. "Futurism's African (A)temporalities." *Carte Italiane* 2, no. 6 (2010), https://escholarship.org.

Meeks, Brian. "Reasoning with *Caliban's Reason.*" *Small Axe* 6, no. 1 (2002): 158–68. Print.

Menke, Richard. *Telegraphic Realism: Victorian Fiction and Other Information Systems.* Stanford: Stanford University Press, 2008. Print.

Mercer, Kobena. *Welcome to the Jungle: New Positions in Black Cultural Studies.* New York: Routledge, 1994. Print.

Mintz, Sidney, and Richard Price. *The Birth of African-American Culture: An Anthropological Perspective.* New York: Beacon, 1976. Print.

Morrison, Toni. "Unspeakable Things Unspoken: The Afro-American Presence in American Literature." Tanner Lectures on Human Values. University of Michigan. October 7, 1988. http://tannerlectures.utah.edu.

Moore, Alan, and Dave Gibbon. *Watchmen.* New York: DC Comics/Warner Books, 1987. Print.

Moravec, Hans. *Robot: Mere Machine to Transcendent Mind.* New York: Oxford University Press, 1999. Print.

Mori, Masahiro. "The Uncanny Valley." *IEEE Spectrum.* June 12, 2012. http://spectrum.ieee.org.

Munro, Martin, and Celia Britton, eds. *American Creoles: The Francophone Caribbean and the American South.* Liverpool: Liverpool University Press, 2012. Print.

Nelson, Alondra, ed. "Afrofuturism." *Social Text* 71 (Summer 2002): 1–15. Print.

Nelson, Alondra, Thuy Linh N. Tu, and Alicia Headlam Hines, eds. *Technicolor: Race, Technology, and Everyday Life.* New York: New York University Press, 2001. Print.

Nye, David E. "Technology and the Production of Difference." In de la Pena and Siva Vaidhyanathan, "Rewiring the 'Nation,'" 597–618.

O'Meally, Robert G., ed. *The Jazz Cadence of American Culture,* New York: Columbia University Press, 1998. Print.

Palmié, Stephan. "Creolization and Its Discontents." *Annual Review of Anthropology* 35 (October 2006): 433–56. Print.

Paradis, James G., ed. *Samuel Butler, Victorian against the Grain.* Toronto: University of Toronto Press, 2007. Print.

Patterson, Orlando. *Slavery and Social Death: A Comparative Study.* Boston: Harvard University Press, 1982. Print.

Purdy, Strother B. "Technopoetics: Seeing What Literature Has to Do with the Machine." *Critical Inquiry* 11, no. 1 (1984): 130–40. Print.

Raby, Peter. *Samuel Butler: A Biography.* London: Hogarth, 1991. Print.

Rearick, Anderson. "Why Is the Only Good Orc a Dead Orc? The Dark Face of Racism Examined in Tolkien's World." *MFS Modern Fiction Studies* 50, no. 4 (2004): 861–74 Print.

Rediker, Marcus. *The Slave Ship: A Human History.* New York: Penguin Books, 2008. Print.

Reiss, Benjamin. *The Showman and the Slave: Race, Death, and Memory in Barnum's America.* Boston: Harvard University Press, 2001. Print.

Rhodes, Richard, ed. *Visions of Technology: A Century of Vital Debate about Machines, Systems and the Human World.* New York: Simon and Schuster, 1999. Print.

Richardson, Michael, ed. *Refusal of the Shadow: Surrealism and the Caribbean.* Brooklyn: Verso, 1996. Print.

Rieder, John. *Colonialism and the Emergence of Science Fiction.* Middletown: Wesleyan University Press, 2008. Print.

Roberts, Joshua Luke. "On Charges of Racism against J. R. R. Tolkien Roberts." *Academia.edu.* Accessed March 24, 2015. www.academia.edu.

Rusch, Frederik L., ed. *A Jean Toomer Reader: Selected Unpublished Writings.* New York: Oxford University Press, 1993. Print.

Ryan, Marie-Laure, ed. *Cyberspace Textuality, Computer Technology and Literary Theory.* Bloomington: Indiana University Press, 1999. Print.

Salomon, Jeff. Review of *Macro Dub Infection,* vol. 2. Originally in *Artforum* 35, no. 10 (1997), www.questia.com.

Salvatore, Ricardo D. "Imperial Mechanics: South America's Hemispheric Integration in the Machine Age." In de la Pena and Siva Vaidhyanathan, "Rewiring the 'Nation,'" 662–91.

"Science: The Thinking Machine." *Time,* January 23, 1950, http://content.time.com.

Scott, David. "The Re-enchantment of Humanism: An Interview with Sylvia Wynter." *Small Axe* 4, no. 2 (2000): 119–207. Print.

Senghor, Léopold Sédar. *The Collected Poetry.* Charlottesville: University Press of Virginia, 1991. Print.

Sewell, Eugene P. *Balzac, Dumas, and "Bert" Williams: Poetry and a Short Story.* N.p., 1923. Print.

Sheller, Mimi. *Consuming the Caribbean: From Arawaks to Zombies.* New York: Routledge, 2003. Print.

Smith, Eric Ledell. *Bert Williams: A Biography of the Pioneer Black Comedian.* Jefferson, NC: McFarland, 1992. Print.

Smithies, James. "Return Migration and the Mechanical Age: Samuel Butler in New Zealand 1860–1864." *Journal of Victorian Culture* 12, no. 2 (2007): 203–24. Print.

Stern, Jonathan. "The Theology of Sound: A Critique of Orality." *Canadian Journal of Communication* 36, no. 2 (2011): 207–26. Print.

Suvin, Darko. *Victorian Science Fiction in the UK: The Discourses of Knowledge and of Power.* Boston: Hall, 1983. Print.

Tate, Greg, ed. *Everything but the Burden: What White People Are Taking from Black Culture.* New York: Broadway Books, 2003. Print.

———. *Flyboy in the Buttermilk: Essays on Contemporary America.* New York: Simon and Schuster, 1992. Print.

Taussig, Michael. *Mimesis and Alterity: A Particular History of the Senses.* New York: Routledge, 1992. Print.

Toomer, Jean. *Cane.* New York: Boni and Liveright, 1923. Print.

Toop, David. *Ocean of Sound: Aether Talk, Ambient Sound and Imaginary Worlds.* London: Serpents Tail Books, 1995. Print.

Torgovnick, Marianna. *Gone Primitive: Savage Intellects, Modern Lives.* Chicago: University of Chicago Press, 1991. Print.

Torres-Saillant, Silvio. *An Intellectual History of the Caribbean.* New York: Palgrave Macmillan, 2006. Print.

Tuhkanen, Mikko. "Of Blackface and Paranoid Knowledge: Richard Wright, Jacques Lacan, and the Ambivalence of Black Minstrelsy." *Diacritics* 31, no. 2 (2001): 9–34. Print.

Vaillant, Janet. *Black, French and African: A Life of Léopold Sédar Senghor.* Boston: Harvard University Press, 1990. Print.

Veal, Michael. *Dub: Soundscapes and Shattered Songs in Jamaican Reggae.* Middletown: Wesleyan University Press, 2007. Print.

Wagner, Geoffrey. "A Forgotten Satire: Bulwer-Lytton's *The Coming Race*." *Nineteenth-Century Fiction* 19, no. 4 (1965): 379–85. Print.

Walcott, Derek. *What the Twilight Says: Essays.* New York: Farrar, Straus and Giroux, 1998. Print.

Walton, Anthony. "Technology versus African-Americans." *Atlantic Monthly* 283 (January 1999): 14–18. Print.

Weheliye, Alexander. "After Man." *American Literary History* 20, nos. 1–2 (2008): 321–36. Print.

——. *Phonographies: Grooves in Sonic Afro-Modernity.* Durham: Duke University Press, 2005. Print.

Wiener, Norbert. "Cybernetics." *Bulletin of the American Academy of Arts and Sciences* 3, no. 7 (1950): 2–4. Print.

——. *The Human Use of Human Beings: Cybernetics and Society.* New York: Doubleday/Anchor Books, 1950. Print.

——. "Some Moral and Technical Consequences of Automation." *Science,* n.s., 131, no. 3410 (1960): 1355–58. Print.

Weldon Johnson, James. "James Weldon Johnson's 1922 Preface to *The Book of American Negro Poetry*." *Modern American Poetry.* 2008. www.english.illinois.edu.

Wilt, Judith. "The Imperial Mouth: Imperialism, the Gothic and Science Fiction. *Journal of Popular Culture* 14, no. 4 (1981): 618–28. Print.

Wolfe, Cary. *What Is Posthumanism?* Minneapolis: University of Minnesota Press, 2009. Print.

Wood, Gaby. *Edison's Eve: A Magical History of the Quest for Mechanical Life.* New York: Knopf, 2002. Print.

Woodson, Jon. *To Make a New Race: Gurdjieff, Toomer, and the Harlem Renaissance.* Jackson: University Press of Mississippi, 1999. Print.

Worth, Aaron. "Imperial Transmissions." *Victorian Studies* 53, no. 1 (2010): 65–89. Print.

Wynter, Sylvia. "1492: A New World View." In *Race, Discourse, and the Origin of the Americas: A New World View,* edited by Vera Lawrence Hyatt and Rex Nettleford, 1–57. Washington, DC: Smithsonian Institution Press, 1995. http://socrates.berkeley.edu.

———. "'Africa, the West and the Analogy of Culture': The Cinematic Text after Man." *Symbolic Narratives/African Cinema: Audience, Theory and the Moving Image,* edited by June Giovanni, 25–76. London: BFI, 2000. Print.

———. "Beyond Miranda's Meanings: Un/silencing the 'Demonic Ground' of Caliban's 'Woman.'" In *The Routledge Reader in Caribbean Literature,* edited by Alison Donnell and Sarah Lawson Welsh, 476–82. London: Routledge, 1996. Print.

———. "Beyond the Word of Man: Glissant and the New Discourse of the Antilles." *World Literature Today* 63, no. 4 (1989): 637–47. Print.

———. "The Ceremony Must Be Found: After Humanism." *Boundary 2* 12, no. 3 (1984): 19–70. Print.

———. "Sambos and Minstrels." *Social Text* 1 (Winter 1979): 149–56. Print.

———. "Unsettling the Coloniality of Being/Power/Truth/Freedom: Towards the Human, after Man, Its Overrepresentation—An Argument." *CR: New Centennial Review* 3, no. 3 (2003): 257–337. Print.

Young, Elizabeth. *Black Frankenstein: The Making of an American Metaphor.* New York: New York University Press, 2008. Print.

Young, Robert J. C. *Colonial Desire: Hybridity in Theory, Culture and Race.* New York: Routledge, 1995. Print.

Zemka, Sue. "'Erewhon' and the End of Utopian Humanism." *ELH* 69, no. 2 (2002): 439–72. Print.

INDEX

Adams, Henry, 90–92, 108, 117, 196
Adas, Michael, 82, 93, 115, 211
Adorno, Theodor, 34–35
Adventures of Buckaroo Banzai Across the 8th Dimension, 157–58
Africa: "African aesthetic," 28–33, 40, 55–57, 190–91; Great Zimbabwe discovery, 110; Harlem Renaissance Afrocentrism, 190–96; in Jazz Age popular culture, 193–94; "lost race" literary theme and, 105–6, 114–15; master/slave metaphor origin in, 81–82, 85–86; Nigerian Internet crime culture, 6; Rastafarian Africa, 186–88
African diaspora. *See* black diaspora
Afrocentrism, 143
Afro-diasporic futurism, 10
Afro-futurism: African Americans and, 14–15, 167–68; Caribbean music influence in, 7; creolization and, 18, 160, 166, 181–82; cyberpunk/cybertheory contributions to, 17; cyborgs in, 30–31; origins and development of, 14, 154; racial future in, 2, 4, 86, 207. *See also* futurism
Akomfrah, John, 14
Aldiss, Brian, 150
aliens, 87, 101, 103–5
Alpha and Omega, 165
Amazing Stories, 193
Anderson, Benedict, 110–11
androids, 47–48, 52
animality, 2–4, 60, 63–65, 121–22, 152, 179, 194, 222
anthropology, 29, 37, 79, 104, 106–8, 110, 115–16, 142, 183
anticolonialism, 1, 182–83, 185–88, 200–203
Antillanté (Glissantian creolization), 146–47
Aristotle, 39

artificial intelligence, 45, 112, 130, 176, 181–82, 217–18, 219–20
Asher, Neil L., 148
Asimov, Isaac, 4, 11, 132, 141, 149–150, 154
Attali, Jacques, 73–74
automata: as domestic slaves, 51–52, 111; Heth ventriloquism and, 24, 49, 73; imitation/mimicry and, 46, 175; Maelzel collection, 23, 70; as mass culture, 70; mass production and, 84–85, 94–96; modernism and, 15; phonograph and, 68–69; psychic automatism, 47–49; robots and, 52, 69; slaves as, 8, 37; soul absence in, 53, 70, 93–94, 97, 112; as uncanny other, 46, 52

Baker, Josephine, 53–54, 193, 195
Banjo (McKay), 191–94
Barnum, P. T.: automata in, 41, 70; Heth exhibition, 4, 15–16, 22–24, 58; racial uncanny and, 48–49; representation/masquerade and, 15–16, 32; slave-machine subjectivity and, 43, 45
baroque, the, 172–74
Bataille, Georges, 203
Bateson, Gregory, 142
Battle of Dorking, The (Chesney), 101
"Bell-Tower, The" (Melville), 17, 93–97, 108, 111, 115, 128
Benítez-Rojo, Antonio, 25–26, 37–38, 159
"Benito Cereno" (Melville), 95–96
Benjamin, Walter, 23
Bergson, Henri, 15, 46–49
Bernabé, Jean, 186
Bhabha, Homi, 198, 203, 211–12
Birth of a Nation (Griffith), 87
black diaspora, 5, 8, 9–11, 28–29, 49–50, 143, 148, 168, 207

Black Empire (Schuyler), 67
blackface minstrelsy: "African aesthetic" and, 28, 55-57; *black* blackface minstrels, 76; blackface automata, 42, 46; black humanism and, 166-67; Caribbean critique of, 9; literary/cultural references to, 15, 58, 71-72, 87, 96-97; phonograph and, 74; primitivist modernism in, 35; racial subjectivity and, 38-41, 47-49, 221; racial uncanny and, 15-16; slavery as basis for, 36; typical characters in, 23, 41, 51, 54-55; ventriloquism and, 24-25, 73; white dehumanization and, 25, 39, 47-49
black nationalism, 28, 144-46, 160-61, 167, 173, 183, 188, 206-7
Black No More (Schuyler), 10, 60
Blade Runner (Roeg), 53
Blavatsky, Helena, 111
blues music, 74-75
Boulding, Kenneth, 142
Brantlinger, Patrick, 87-89, 101, 103
Brathwaite, Edward Kamau, 8, 147, 222-23
Breton, André, 47, 183-84, 185, 190-91, 195
Brother from Another Planet, The (Sayles), 157-58, 160
"Brothers from Another Planet" (Corbett, 1994), 14
Brown, Bill, 37, 49
Brown, John, 97
Brown, Scientist Overton, 169-70
Buck-Morss, Susan, 80
Bull, Emma, 156-57
Bulwer-Lytton, Edward, 17, 80, 89, 102-8, 110
Burroughs, Edgar Rice, 17, 88-89, 104-6, 110, 113, 116, 136, 154, 181, 193-94
Burton, Richard, 106
Butler, Judith, 49
Butler, Octavia, 2
Butler, Samuel: colonial experiences, 101-2, 112-15; creolization in, 132, 141; differentiation in, 122-24; ethnographic imagination and, 115-16; imperial anxieties in, 90; intellectual influences, 63, 91; "lost race" literary theme in, 102-4; machine reproduction in, 123-26; master/slave metaphors in, 80, 85, 119-21, 218-19; racialization of machines in, 16-17, 99-100, 113, 117-19, 122-23, 126-27, 221; "regression fantasies" theme in, 89, 122-23

Cadigan, Pat, 148
Caliban (*Tempest* character), 14, 222-24
calypso music, 28, 31-32
Cane (Toomer, 1923), 26, 59-60, 63
Čapek, Karel: creolization in, 132; influence on Toomer, 62; master/slave dialectic in, 69-70, 89-90, 218-19; robot/racial anxieties and, 16, 63-65, 150; *robot* term coinage, 3-4, 22-23, 69, 112, 221; on souls, 66, 73-74; U.S. race relations and, 63-64, 76
Caribbean Discourse (Glissant), 146, 168
Caribbean Taste of Technology, A (Mad Professor, 1985), 19-20
Carlyle, Thomas, 31-32, 83, 90-91, 118
carnivalesque, the, 41, 44-45, 46
Cassuto, Leonard, 58, 204
"Ceremony Must Be Found, The" (Wynter), 198-99, 208, 221
Césaire, Aimé: anticolonialism in, 186-88, 200; on Caliban, 222-23; Caribbean technopoetics and, 4-5, 13-14, 25-26, 199-200; creolization in, 147; Harlem Renaissance and, 191; humanism and, 180, 200-202; Negro-in-the-machine discourse, 38-39; neologisms in, 184, 186-89; science and, 173; surrealism and, 183-86
Césaire, Suzanne, 185-86
Chamoiseau, Patrick, 186
Chaney, Michael, 42-43
Chesney, George Tomkyns, 101-2
Chicana-futurism, 12
China, 55, 211
Chrisman, Laura, 116
Civil Rights discourse, 42, 142-43, 148, 150, 217
Clansman, The (Dixon), 87

Clifford, James, 183–84, 186
clocks, 91–93, 115, 119, 122
Clynes, Manfred, 31
Coleman, Beth, 36–37
Columbus, Christopher, 212–13
Coming Race, The (Bulwer-Lytton), 17, 78–79, 89, 100, 102–12
Commoner, Barry, 142
computers, 52, 71–72, 174–76. *See also* Internet
"Conan the Barbarian" (Howard), 106, 194
Condé, Maryse, 199
Confiant, Raphaël, 186
Conrad, Joseph, 87–88, 108, 116
Cook, James W., 22–23
coon songs, 33, 36, 71–72, 74–76
Cooper, Carolyn, 8
Cooper, John W., 42
Corbett, John, 14
Crane, David, 132
craniometry, 107
Creation Rebel, 169
créolité (Caribbean term), 137, 139, 144, 146, 201–2
creolization: absolute difference and, 122–23; anticolonialism and, 182, 203; Antillanté (Glissantian creolization), 146–47; Caliban as figure of, 222–24; Caribbean cross-cultural interaction, 137–40; as Caribbean intellectual paradigm, 18, 129–31, 135–37, 140–41, 144–48; colonial hybridity, 133; creole futurism, 205–8, 211; *créolité* movement, 186; cyberpunk/cybertheory and, 17–18, 131, 141, 160–62; *diaspora* concept and, 168; dub as hybrid genre, 163–64; fundamentalism and, 146–47; Hegelian synthesis and, 136–37; Latin American creolization, 4; liminality/resolution and, 204; linguistic creolization, 145; literary and cultural creolization, 17–19; machine-human hybridity, 17–18, 133–36, 148, 173–76; monstrous couplings, 136; posthumanism and, 18, 177–78; race in science fiction and, 132; racial hierarchy and, 146; single origin reversion and, 140; slavery and, 139–40; techorganic blending, 17, 129; as transhistorical process, 140–41; uncertainty in, 173–74; voodoo as hybrid religion, 156–57. *See also* miscegenation
Crow, Jim, 23, 54–55
cubism, 29
Cullen, Countee, 194
cultural criticism, 8
cultural studies, 132
cybernetics, 2–6, 16, 31–32, 78, 82–86, 142, 175
cyberpunk: automata writings as precursor, 112; Bertrand Russell as pioneer, 194–95; Caribbean cultural presence in, 9, 130, 196; creolization themes in, 17, 131, 141, 160–62; dub music as influence, 155–59; machine-human hybridity in, 149; postcyberpunk, 162–63; race as issue in, 108–9, 148–49; Rastafarianism in, 157–62; "triumph of machines" theme, 152
cyberspace, 4–6, 36, 148, 151, 155–56. *See also* Internet
cybertheory, 4, 17, 40–43, 69, 108–9, 141, 153
cyborg feminism, 69, 129, 131, 135–36, 143
"Cyborg Manifesto, A" (Haraway), 17, 99, 156–57, 202, 216
cyborgs: in Afro-futurism, 30–31; cyborg dub experience, 165; Haraway *Cyborg Manifesto*, 17, 99, 156–57, 202, 216; liminality and, 41; Molly (*Neuromancer* cyborg), 161–62, 165; posthumanism and, 152–53; race and, 4, 17, 36, 43–44, 132, 148, 149; technological anthropomorphism, 3–4. *See also* cyborg feminism; robots

dadaism, 28–29
Daly, Nicholas, 16
Damas, Léon, 185
dancehall music, 19, 161, 163, 196
Darwin, Charles. *See* evolution
"Darwin among the Machines" (Butler), 91, 101–2, 112–13
Dash, J. Michael, 182, 185, 190–91, 195–96

Davis, Eric, 164
Delany, Samuel R., 2, 14, 128, 131, 141–42, 149, 159–161, 181, 206–7, 222
Deleuze, Gilles, 37–38, 173
del Rey, Lester, 133
Dery, Mark, 14, 159
Descartes, René, 23
Dick, Philip K., 149–51, 154
Dickens, Charles, 90, 102
"digital divide," 6, 148, 151, 155
Dilemma, The (Chesney), 101–2
Dinerstein, Joel, 31, 34, 46, 52, 76, 152–55
Disch, Thomas M., 154, 162
Discourse on Colonialism (Césaire), 38–39
Dixon, George Washington, 54
Dixon, Thomas, 87–88
Douglass, Frederick, 98–99
Doyle, Arthur Conan, 102–4, 114–15
Dr. Jekyll and Mr. Hyde (Stevenson), 87–88
drum 'n' bass music, 163
dub music: analog/digital binary and, 143; *A Caribbean Taste of Technology* significance, 19–20; cyberpunk references to, 18, 130, 155–59; dancehall/ragga era difficulties, 19; development of, 155–56; echoing in, 73–74, 169–71; manipulation of reggae in, 162–64, 196; massification and, 9; posthumanism and, 155, 163–64; as sacrament/worship, 165; as technological symbol, 196–97
DuBois, W. E. B., 29, 57, 83, 112, 168, 213–14
dubstep, 163

echoes, 27, 50, 59, 73–74, 168–71, 203
Effinger, George Alec, 148
Eglash, Ron, 6, 7, 79–86, 89–92, 115, 142
Eisenberg, Evan, 68–70
Ellington, Duke, 195
Ellison, Ralph, 170
Eloge de la créolité [In Praise of Creoleness] (Confiant-Chamoiseau-Bernabé), 186
Emeagwali, Philip, 6
epistemes, 207–8, 212, 221–22
Erewhon (Butler): anticolonialism in, 1; automata in, 111–12; "book within a book" theme in, 116–17; Butler colonial experiences in, 101–2, 112–14; critique of humanism in, 44, 126–27, 210, 215; as early science fiction, 99–100; "hollow earth" theme in, 110–11; human-animal hybridity in, 179; imperial discourse in, 114; literary influences, 90, 107; "lost race" literary theme, 102–3, 116–17; machine sexuality in, 133; racialization of machines in, 16–17, 99–100, 113, 122–23, 126–27, 217; racial/machine rebellion in, 63, 78–79, 101–2, 116, 128, 152; "regression fantasies" theme in, 89, 122–23
Erlmann, Veit, 168–69
Eshun, Kodwo, 2, 14, 83–84
Ethiopianism, 56, 143
eugenics, 107–8, 113
evolution: Butler treatment of, 91, 101–2, 112–13, 118; dialectical species definition and, 123; *Erewhon* as parody of, 99; "God the Watchmaker" treatise and, 122; human rationality and, 214–15; "lost race" literary theme and, 107–8; machine reprisal as natural selection, 120–21; mimetics in, 50; monogenesis in, 126, 130–31; race and, 36, 117–18, 208; "regression fantasies" theme and, 87–90, 122–23; scientific racism and, 81
exceptionalism, 27–28, 52, 114–15

Fanon, Frantz, 3, 173, 180, 199, 201, 222–23
fascism, 84, 94–95
Faulkner, William, 172
feminism, 42, 141–42. *See also* cyborg feminism
Fernández Retamar, Roberto, 222–23
Forbidden Planet, 222
Foster, Thomas, 2
Foucault, Michel, 180, 199, 207–9
Foxx, John, 158
Frankenstein (Shelley), 17, 63, 78, 97–99, 123, 124, 152
Franklin, Benjamin, 23

Freud, Sigmund, 15, 46, 47-49, 53, 219. *See also* uncanny, the
futurism, 10, 12-13, 149, 205-7. *See also* Afro-futurism

Garvey, Marcus, 29, 65, 160-61, 188, 190, 193
Gates, Henry Louis, 70
Gauguin, Paul, 195
Gernsback, Hugo, 128, 193
Gibbon, Dave, 163
Gibson, William, 4-5, 11, 130-31, 148, 150-51, 156-57, 160-63, 165, 182, 196
Gill, David, 91-92
Gilman, Charlotte Perkins, 102-3
Gilroy, Paul, 71
Glissant, Édouard: anticolonialism in, 202-3; on Caribbean negritude, 195-96; creolization in, 18, 139-41, 145-47, 179, 198-202; French language and, 186; human subjectivity in, 177-78, 224; macrohistorical processes in, 118; on the plantation machine, 37-38; on racism, 13, 137, 180-81; sound technology in, 130, 169; on synthesis-genesis, 135, 190; technopoetics of, 8, 13, 14, 168, 172-76; will to inauthenticity in, 143-44
Goodman, Paul, 142
gramophone. *See* phonograph
Great Migration, 63
Griffith, D. W., 87-88
Guattari, Félix, 37-38, 173
Gurdjieff, Georges I., 60

Haggard, H. Rider, 17, 87-88, 102-4, 110, 113-17, 193
Haiti, 98, 182-83, 188-89, 200
Hall, Stuart, 197-98, 204, 205, 206-7
Hammonds, Evelyn M., 135-36
Haraway, Donna: absence of Butler in, 99; creolization as theme in, 17, 136, 139, 143; cyborg feminism of, 129, 131; *A Cyborg Manifesto*, 17, 99, 156-57, 202, 216; on cyborgs, 30-31, 41, 43, 132, 135; on human-animal hybridity, 141, 179; posthumanism and, 152-53, 216; racial technological vision in, 11, 99; on revolutionary subjects, 202-3; on technological anthropomorphism, 3-4
Harlem Renaissance, 17, 28-29, 181, 190-96
Harris, Joel Chandler, 26, 51, 71-73
Harris, Wilson: on artificial intelligence, 176; on creolization, 18, 137-140, 179; dub as sacrament and, 165; on involuntary associations, 13; on living landscapes, 171-72; macrohistorical processes in, 118; poetics of human subjectivity, 214, 224; quantum cross-cultural art, 173; race as theme in, 149, 180-81; on suppressed creativity/resistance, 128, 202-4; technopoetics of, 8, 130, 168, 170-73; will to inauthenticity in, 143-44
Hayles, N. Katherine, 83, 153
Headley, Clevis, 45
Headrick, Daniel R., 27-28
Heart of Darkness (Conrad), 87-88, 116
"Helen O'Loy" (del Rey), 133
Henderson, Hazel, 142
Henriques, Julian, 162
Henry, Paget, 198, 204, 207-8, 210, 212, 222
"Heritage" (Cullen), 194
Heth, Joice, 15-16, 22-24, 32, 51-52, 55, 58, 70-71, 77, 80
Higgs, Joe, 161-62
hip-hop, 7, 19, 54, 162-63
Hopkins, Pauline, 114-15
Hopkinson, Nalo, 2, 164
Howard, Dennis, 162
Howard, Robert E., 88-89, 104-6, 117, 136, 154, 181, 193
Howell, Leonard Percival, 190, 195
Huckleberry Finn (Twain), 92
Huelsenbeck, Richard, 28
Hughes, Langston, 57, 190-91, 196
Human Use of Human Beings, The (Wiener), 83
Huxley, Aldous, 170
Huyssen, Andreas, 53
hybridity. *See* creolization

Ice-T, 157, 160
Imperial Gothic, 88–91, 105, 110, 112, 122–23
India, 55, 211
industrialization: alien encounters and, 107, 115–16; black primitivism and, 190, 192–93, 195; creolization and, 132–33, 140, 188, 208; dehumanization of whites/Europeans and, 25, 29, 35, 39, 43; jazz music and, 34–35; mass production as social bondage, 84–85; mechanization of industrial workforce, 36–37; modernism relationship with, 12; as nineteenth-century concern, 2, 27–28; racial uncanny and, 15–17, 44; slavery-machine association in, 4, 40, 42–43, 58, 78–82, 93–94, 148, 215–16
In Praise of Creoleness [*Eloge de la créolité*] (Confiant-Chamoiseau-Bernabé), 186
Internet, 6, 155, 175. *See also* computers; cyberspace
Islands in the Net (Sterling), 157–58
"I Want to Be a Machine" (Foxx), 158

Jamaica, 7, 9, 14, 145–46
James, C. L. R., 37–38, 40–41, 80, 94, 198
Jameson, Fredric, 175
Japan, 4, 7, 26, 154, 187, 217–19
jazz music, 9, 16–17, 28, 31–35, 43–44, 54, 158–59, 195
Jazz Singer, The, 87
Jefferson, Thomas, 92
Jentsch, Ernst, 219
Jim Crow minstrelsy character, 23, 54–55
"John Henry" folk narrative, 5–6
Johnny Mnemonic, 157–58
Johnson, George W., 71, 74
Johnson, James Weldon, 68, 72, 74
Johnson, Robert, 74
Jonkunnu festival, 56–57

Katrina Van Televox (robot housemaid), 51–52
Kempelen, Wolfgang von, 23, 24–25
Kevorkian, Martin, 125, 150–51, 153, 160

Kilgore, De Witt Douglas, 2, 131, 148–49, 154
King, Martin Luther, 217
King Jammy (Prince Jammy), 19–20, 159–160, 169–170
King Solomon's Mines (Haggard), 103, 110
King Tubby (Osbourne Ruddock), 165, 169
Kongo-futurism, 12
Kool Herc, 19
Kozai, Osamu, 218
Kurzweil, Ray, 117

Lam, Wifredo, 172
Lamming, George, 4–5, 8, 25, 40–41, 49, 147, 199, 222–23
Lane, Jeremy, 34
Lang, Fritz, 52–54, 59–60, 133
Last Angel of History, The (Akomfrah, 1996), 14
Lavender, Isiah, 2, 150, 153
Le Corbusier, 12, 34
Lee, Tanith, 11, 133–35
Leibnitz, Gottfried Wilhelm, 84
Lesser, Beth, 162
Levi-Strauss, Claude, 185
Lindsay, Vachel, 28
lindy hop, 34
Lionnet, Françoise, 137, 139
Locke, Alain, 57
Locke, John, 36
London, Jack, 223–24
Lott, Eric, 39–40, 46, 55–56
Lovecraft, H. P., 117
Luckhurst, Roger, 88, 106
Luddism, 118
lynching, 3, 55, 58, 64–65, 219

machine aesthetic, 27–28, 31, 34, 52, 58, 113
Machine in the Garden, The (Marx), 27–28, 91–93
Mackey, Nathaniel, 170, 187–88, 224
Macro Dub Infection, 155–56
Mad Professor, 19–20, 169
Maelzel, Johann Nepomuk, 23–24, 70
Mafarka the Futurist (Marinetti, 1909), 29–33

Mandelbrot, Benoit, 172
Man's Home Companion (Toomer), 16, 60–62
Maori, 102, 113–14, 123
Marinetti, Filippo Tommaso, 12–13, 29–33, 42, 82–83
Marley, Bob, 172
Marshall, Wayne, 162
Martinique, 186, 191, 199
Marx, Leo, 27–28, 90–93, 97–98, 113, 115, 117, 169
Mason, Daniel Gregory, 34
master/slave dialectic: in Buck-Morss, 80; in Butler, 80, 85, 119–21; in Čapek, 69–70, 89–90; in cybernetics, 82–86; in Hegel, 79–80, 120, 136–37, 139; mass production as social bondage, 83–84; *master* and *slave* as technological terms, 2, 16, 78–81; in Melville, 94–96; in science fiction, 85–86, 89; as technological metaphor, 80–82, 91–92. *See also* slavery
Matisse, Henri, 59
Matrix, The, 157–58
Mazlish, Bruce, 88
McDonald, Ian, 148
McHugh, Maureen, 154
McKay, Claude, 57–58, 181, 190–95
McLuhan, Marshall, 40, 42, 112, 117, 132, 176
Mead, Margaret, 142–43
Melville, Herman, 4, 11, 16–17, 78–80, 92–99, 111–12, 118, 179
Mencken, H. L., 34
Ménil, René, 186
Menke, Richard, 12
Mercer, Kobena, 142
métissage (Caribbean term), 137, 144, 146, 202
Metropolis (Lang), 52–54, 59–60, 69, 133
Midnight Robber (Hopkinson), 164
minstrelsy. *See* blackface minstrelsy
Mintz, Sidney W., 37
miscegenation, 17–18, 108–9, 133–38. *See also* creolization
Moby-Dick (Melville), 92–94

modernism: Africa and, 28–31, 40, 56–59, 142–43, 190–95; automata as mass culture, 70; blackface minstrelsy and, 25–26, 32, 35, 40, 44, 54–58; black modernism, 33, 56–60, 71–72; emergence of humanity, 179–181, 200–201, 208–9, 214–15; Euro-American modernism, 27; Heth exhibition and, 15–16, 22–23, 25, 80; imperial anxieties in, 16–17, 21, 27–31, 108, 113; mass production as social bondage, 83–84; modernist literary genres, 9–11, 21, 87–88; modernist technopoetics, 12–13, 15; oral-literate-electronic technology schema, 176–77; primitivist modernism, 33–36, 56, 190–95; racial epistemes and, 207–8; secular/mechanistic universe and, 122; slavery relationship with, 25, 37–38, 80; surrealism and, 47
Modigliani, Amedeo, 59
monstrosity, 3, 87, 124, 136, 174, 179, 213
Moore, Alan, 163, 196
Moore, C. L., 133
Moravec, Hans, 117, 216–17
More, Thomas, 145
More Brilliant Than the Sun (Eshun, 1998), 14
Mori, Masahiro, 26, 219
Morrison, Toni, 92–93
Mudimbe, V. Y., 198
"Music of Living Landscapes, The" (Harris), 171–72

nanotechnology, 124
nationalism: blackface minstrelsy and, 58; black nationalism, 28, 144–46, 160–61, 167, 173, 183, 188, 206–7; black primitivism and, 9; creolization fundamentalisms and, 146; Glissant critique of, 173; "lost race" literary theme and, 104; organic/natural tropes and, 143; and the postnational, 156, 161; science fiction racial themes and, 14
Nazism, 63–64, 107, 111
Needle in the Grove (Noon), 155, 162–63

negritude: "African aesthetic" and, 29; black subjectivity in, 143; Caribbean primitivism and, 187–88, 195–96; Caribbean technopoetics and, 145, 180–81, 184–85, 197–98; *créolité* as response to, 186; Haiti and, 188–89, 200; Harlem Renaissance and, 190–93; surrealism and, 13, 18, 181, 184. *See also* surrealism
Nelson, Alondra, 2, 6, 14, 154
Neuromancer (Gibson), 155–63, 196
New Zealand, 101–3, 112–14, 123
Nietzsche, Friedrich, 163, 209
Noon, Jeff, 130, 155, 157, 162
Notes on Virginia (Jefferson), 92
Nova (Delany), 159
"No Woman Born" (Moore), 133
Nye, David E., 155

Of One Blood (Hopkins), 114–15
Ong, Walter, 176
Orwell, George, 170

Pagels, Heinz, 201
Paley, William, 122
Pan-Africanism, 29, 56, 65, 143
Partridge, Christopher, 162
passing, 36, 136
Patterson, Orlando, 57
Perry, Lee, 169–70
phonograph, 15, 43–44, 50, 62, 68–74, 76–77
"Phonograph Blues" (Robert Johnson), 74
phrenology, 107
Piazza Tales, The (Melville), 93–96
Picasso, Pablo, 59, 195
Poe, Edgar Allan, 23, 170
Poetics of Relation, The (Glissant), 130, 172–76
"Poetry and Cognition" (Césaire), 188–90
postcyberpunk, 162–63
posthumanism: black posthumanism, 4, 130, 137, 180–81; blending/hybridity in, 17–18, 154, 172–73, 209–10; computers as device of, 177; creole consciousness, 173–75; cyberpunk development of, 152; dub music and, 155, 169–71; extra-human, the, 214; living landscapes and, 171–72; Nietzschean "Overman" character model, 163; pre-posthumanism in Wynter, 198–204, 224; racialized cyborgs and, 43–44; slavery as basis for, 153–54; Wynter on, 180–81
postmodernism, 17, 175
Pound, Ezra, 172
Predator, 157
Price, Richard, 37
primitivism: "African aesthetic" and, 29; black primitivism, 9, 17, 143, 190, 192–96; Caribbean roots discourse, 184, 187, 195–96; Claude McKay and, 57–58; diasporic Sambo and, 49–50; futuristic primitivism, 106; "lost race" literary theme and, 104–5, 107; negritude and, 18, 181, 187–88, 195–96; primitivist literature, 33, 157–59; primitivist modernism, 33–35; Rastafarianism and, 160–61, 181, 196; technoprimitivism, 158
Prince Jammy (King Jammy), 19–20, 159–60, 169–70
psychic automatism, 47–49
Purdy, Strother, 66

race records, 74–75
ragtime music, 75–76
rap music, 7
Rastafarianism: analog/digital binary and, 170; attitudes towards negromancy, 20; Babylon as symbol in, 195; counterculture discourse and, 142–43; creolization in, 197–98; cyberpunk references to, 130, 157–62; primitivism and, 160–61, 181; radical indeterminacy in, 185–88; Rastafarian/reggae racial essentialism, 19, 160–61, 165, 172, 186–88; in science fiction, 157; tourism and, 161
Rastus Robot, 51–52, 71–72
reggae music: analog/digital binary and, 143, 158, 169–70; dancehall/ragga era, 19; dub manipulation of, 162–64, 196;

echoes monde in, 169–70; Lovers Rock subgenre, 20; primitivism and, 181, 196; race-technology association in, 4–5, 196–97; racial authenticity and, 19, 172; roots reggae, 19, 161, 164–65, 196–97; signal processing technology in, 7. *See also* Jamaica

Reiss, Benjamin, 42

Resnick, Mike, 154

Rice, Thomas D., 23

Rieder, John, 2, 86–88, 96, 99, 103–4, 130–31, 135

robots (general): Asimov "Three Laws of Robotics," 4, 150; biological robots, 60; early robot figures, 15, 69, 175; hybridity and, 221; as hyperinorganic figures, 210; racial analogies in, 2–3, 26, 67, 134–35; racial/technological anxieties and, 52; robotic otherness, 45; robotic slaves in science fiction, 3, 149–50, 153, 219; robot mimicry of humans, 53, 61–62, 133–35, 219–22; robot revolt literary theme, 3, 16, 57, 65, 67–69, 218; *robot* term coinage, 22–23, 26, 32, 52, 69; souls/consciousness in, 4, 52, 65–68, 73, 117, 217–19; technological anthropomorphism, 3–4; uncanny and, 43–44. *See also* cyborgs

robots (particular robots): Argive (maid/technochaser robot), 60–62; Bessie (Harvard computer), 52, 71–72; Caliban character type, 222–24; Japanese sexual robots, 218; Katrina Van Televox (robot housemaid), 51–52; Lucille (aniphograph), 62; P. T. Barnum robotic slave exhibition, 4; Silver (*The Silver Metal Lover*), 134–35; Westinghouse Rastus Robot, 50–51, 56, 71–72

Rodó, José Enrique, 222–23

Roeg, Nicholas, 53

Rousseau, Jean-Jacques, 142

Ruddock, Osbourne (King Tubby), 165, 169

R.U.R. (Čapek), 3, 16, 26, 44, 52, 57, 60, 63, 65, 67–69, 89–90, 128, 133, 210

Rushdie, Salman, 110–11

Russell, Bertrand, 194–95

Said, Edward, 198, 209

Salvatore, Ricardo D., 28

Sambo stereo/archetype, 38–41, 43–46, 49–50, 54–58, 67, 72, 76

Sartre, Jean-Paul, 3, 185

Sayles, John, 157–58, 160

Schuyler, George, 60, 67

science fiction: creolization in, 132–33; "discovery of advanced civilizations" theme, 89; early nonhuman processes in, 1–2; *Erewhon* status as, 99; Harlem Renaissance and, 193–94; "hollow earth" literary theme, 110; imperial discourse and, 86–87, 114–16; "lost race" theme, 102–7, 114–15; machine-human intimacy in, 133–36; master/slave analogy in, 85–86, 89–90; new wave science fiction, 112, 148–49; racial themes, 4, 43, 131, 148–49, 150–51, 154; "regression fantasies" theme in, 88–90; as resistance, 128; robot revolution trope in, 16; *R.U.R.* role as, 69; Sword and Sorcery subgenre, 106; *The Tempest* as influence, 222–23; Victorian science fiction, 9, 21, 78–79, 100–101

scientifiction, 50–51, 128

Scientist Overton Brown, 169–70

Scott, David, 180

Seed, David, 111–12

Senghor, Léopold Sédar, 184–85, 188, 191

Shaka, Jah, 19, 165

Shaw, Bernard, 194

She (Haggard), 87–88, 110

Sheller, Mimi, 144

Shelley, Mary, 17, 63, 78, 97–99, 102, 179, 218–19

Sherwood, Adrian, 169

Silverberg, Robert, 154

Silver Metal Lover, The (Lee), 133–35

slavery: animal servitude and, 121–22; automata and, 8; black diaspora writing on, 8; black rapist myth and, 69, 93; Caribbean slavery, 138; creolization and,

139–40; domestication of nature and, 39; humanism and, 3, 13, 45; "lack state" and, 205; minstrelsy roots in, 36; modernism and, 25, 37–38, 80; posthuman meta-slavery, 153–54; reciprocal dehumanization in, 37; robotic slaves, 3, 4, 22–23, 149–50, 153, 219; Sambo stereo/archetype and, 38–41; slave revolts, 3, 69, 92, 96–99, 105, 120–21, 141; slavery-machine analogy, 4, 36, 40, 42–43, 58, 70, 78–82, 93–94, 120–21, 129, 148, 215–16, 221–22; technoexceptionalism and, 27–28. *See also* master/slave dialectic

"Sleng Teng" (King Jammy), 19–20, 159–60, 169

Smith, Bessie, 193

Smithies, James, 112–14

Snow, C. P., 174

soca music, 155

South Africa, 81–82, 85–86, 107

Spector, Phil, 170

Speke, John, 106

Spengler, Oswald, 87

spiritualism, 60

Spivak, Gayatri, 98

Stapledon, Olaf, 223–24

Star Wars media franchise, 157, 214

steam-punk literature, 131

Sterling, Bruce, 133–34, 148, 157–58

Stevenson, Robert Louis, 87–88, 102–3

Stoddard, Lothrop, 87–88

Stoker, Bram, 16

Sullivan, Paul, 162

surrealism: "African aesthetic" and, 29, 190–91; antirationality in, 188; associative metaphors in, 13, 189; Caribbean technopoetics and, 172, 180–86, 200; history and, 206; psychic automatism in, 47; radical indeterminacy in, 185–88; technology and, 12. *See also* negritude

Suvin, Darko, 100–101, 103, 107, 110, 117–18

Swift, Jonathan, 114

Sword and Sorcery (science fiction subgenre), 106

Symmes, John Cleves, Jr., 110

Tal, Kali, 157–58, 160–61

Tank Girl, 157–58

"Tartarus of Maids, The" (Melville), 95–96

Tarzan series (Burroughs), 17, 105–6, 110, 116, 193–94

Tate, Greg, 86, 160, 206, 207

Taylorism, 36–37

technopoetics, 10–14, 25–26, 47–49, 60–63, 142–43, 158, 169–73

Tempest, The (Shakespeare), 14, 145, 157, 222–23

theosophism, 111

Thousand Plateaus, A (Glissant), 173

Tolkien, J. R. R., 106–7

Toomer, Jean, 4, 16, 26, 57, 59–63, 111, 193

Toop, David, 158–59

Torres-Saillant, Silvio, 146–47

Tosh, Peter, 161–62

tourism, 145–46, 161

Trinidad and Tobago, 155

Tropiques (Caribbean journal), 147, 183, 199

Tucker, Jeffrey Allen, 207

Tuhkanen, Mikko, 57

Turk, The (chess-playing machine), 23–24, 70, 73

Turner, Nat, 39, 97–98

Twain, Mark, 92

two-step/garage music, 163

Ultravox! 158

uncanny, the: "American uncanny" in U.S. law, 49; Barnum "racial freaks" presentation, 58–59; machines as uncanny others, 41, 52, 124–25, 176; as precursor to blackface, 15; race/technology relationship and, 32, 50; Sambo/automata/cyborg subjectivity and, 43–46; as source of humor, 15, 25, 46; theory of resonance and, 168; "uncanny valley," 26, 219–21

Uncle Remus cycle, 26, 51, 71–73

Veal, Michael, 162, 167

Verne, Jules, 110, 170

Victorian culture: colonialism and, 78–79;

cybernation discourse and, 42–43; early science fiction in, 9, 21, 78–79, 100–101; imperial anxieties in, 16–17, 21, 90; "lost race" literary theme, 102–7, 114–15; race-technology relationship and, 4–5; "regression fantasies" literary theme and, 87–90; response to technology in, 12, 16, 83, 85–86; Victorian American pulp fiction, 88–89, 101, 106, 136, 181; Victorian feminism, 110

vorticism, 12

Vril-ya (feminine "lost world" rebel), 109–12, 114

Vulcans, 169

Vurt (Noon), 155

Waikato Wars, 102

Wailers (reggae band), 161–62

Walcott, Derek, 196

Walker, David, 98–99

Walker, George, 75–76

War of the Worlds (Wells), 87–88, 103, 108

War with the Newts (Čapek), 63–65

Watchmen comic series, 163, 196

Weheliye, Alexander, 2, 43, 148, 153, 166, 179–80, 204, 220–21

Weird Tales, 193

Wells, H. G., 16, 86–88, 91, 101, 103, 170, 179, 194–95, 223–24

Westinghouse Corporation, 26, 51–52, 58, 62

"Whistling Coon, The" (George W. Johnson), 71, 74

Wiener, Norbert, 4–5, 16, 38–40, 78, 82–86, 112, 117–18, 132, 142–43, 153, 215–17

Williams, Bert, 74–76, 153

Williams, Eric, 37–38

Williams, William Carlos, 12

Wilt, Judith, 21, 43, 47, 78, 89, 100, 103

Wolfe, Cary, 152

Womack, Ytasha, 2

Womack Jack, 148

Womb of Space, The (Harris), 170–72, 198

Woolf, Virginia, 21

World War I, 33

Worth, Aaron, 86

Wynter, Sylvia: on Caliban, 14, 223–24; Caribbean technopoetics and, 25–26, 130, 200; creole futurism, 207–8, 211; creolization in, 145, 147, 179–80, 199–200, 204–5, 223–24; critique of humanism, 18–19, 166, 171, 174, 180–82, 198–204, 208–15, 220–22; on figures of chaos, 44, 118–19; macrohistorical processes in, 118–19, 198; on minstrelsy, 56–57; on popular culture, 197; race-technology association in, 4–5, 8, 13, 208–9; racial/slave subjectivity in, 39–40, 43–45, 204; on robotic otherness, 45, 63; on Sambo, 46–47, 57–58, 72; technologized pastoral in, 38

Yeats, W. B., 12

Young, Elizabeth, 98–99

Young, Robert, 133

Zemka, Sue, 123, 126

Zip Coon, 54–55

ABOUT THE AUTHOR

Louis Chude-Sokei is a writer and scholar currently teaching in the English Department at the University of Washington, Seattle. He holds a PhD in English from UCLA and has previously taught at Occidental College, Bowdoin College, and UC Santa Cruz. His scholarship and essays have appeared widely, in publications such as *African American Review, Believer,* and *Transition.* He is the author of *The Last Darky: Bert Williams, Black on Black Minstrelsy,* and the *Black Diaspora,* which was a finalist for the Hurston/Wright Legacy Award for nonfiction.